CREATING
COLETTE

□□□□

CREATING
COLETTE

□□□□

VOLUME ONE

FROM INGENUE
TO LIBERTINE
1 8 7 3 ⁄ 1 9 1 3

□□□□

CLAUDE FRANCIS &
FERNANDE GONTIER

STEERFORTH PRESS
SOUTH ROYALTON, VERMONT

For information about permission to reproduce selections
from this book, write to: Steerforth Press L.C.,
P.O. Box 70, South Royalton, Vermont 05068.

First published in France under the title *Colette* by Librairie Académique Perrin.

Library of Congress Cataloging-in-Publication Data
Francis, Claude.
Creating Colette / Claude Francis & Fernande Gontier.
p.   cm.
Includes bibliographical references and index.
Contents: v. 1. From Ingénue to libertine, 1873–1913.
ISBN 1–883642–91–4 (alk. paper)
1. Colette, 1873–1954. 2. Authors, French—20th century—Biography.
I. Gontier, Fernande.   II. Title.
PQ8605.028Z66475   1998
848'.91209—dc21
[B]   98–25211
                                                              CIP

The text of this book was composed by Steerforth Press
using a digital version of Bembo.

Manufactured in the United States of America

SECOND PRINTING

CONTENTS

PROLOGUE

$\mathcal{T}$HEY HAVE OF ME an old stereotype image," complained Colette at the end of her life. A genius at self-promotion,
Colette had become the mythical figure she and a collective act of faith
had created.

Until World War II, the literary and social circles of Paris had applauded Colette's refulgent personality. A writer who mocked clichés
on all subjects, she blazed a trail of scandals and never recognized sexuality, matrimony, or motherhood in their traditional apparel. Colette's
first transformation occurred during World War II, when the Vichy
government presented military defeat as retribution for sins and held
the corruption of urban high society responsible. Colette went from
high-society corrupt darling to rustic madonna, and in spite of her
own assertions that her grandfather was "a quadroon," she downplayed
her African ancestry and became pure Burgundian. The stereotype of
Colette as a country girl was in place.

After the war, de Gaulle stressed the grandeur of France, while André
Malraux, minister of culture, stressed that the greatness of France was
best reflected in the greatness of her writers. Colette became an icon.

She embodied all the French values: deep country roots, love in its sensuous splendor, a taste for naughtiness, a discriminating knowledge of wines and gourmet cuisine. She shared the national worship of *le mot juste* and *le beau language,* and no one wanted to dwell on her black ancestry.

Most of the misconceptions about Colette arose and endured because her family background was never investigated; yet it is impossible to understand Colette — her sensualist philosophy, her music-hall career, her nude dances, her uninhibited sexual behavior, her denunciation of militant feminism, her lack of interest in politics, the daring of her novels, the philosophy of her essay "Le Pur et L'Impur" — without an understanding of the ultraradical cultural background of her maternal family.

Colette asserted that her mother was the primary influence in her life, so to understand Colette we studied Sido. The daughter of a wealthy black entrepreneur, Sido had a boundless admiration for her father. Colette herself never disclaimed her Caribbean origins. At thirty-one she wrote to the poet Francis Jammes, "You are not aware that my ascendants came from sun drenched islands, from far away, just like your own, however mine must have been much darker . . . That is the point, I have a black drop in my bloodstream, does it repulse you?"[1]

When their correspondence was published in 1945 the last line was deleted. It is not the only time Colette mentions her black ancestors. "As I mellow, the most impetuous atavisms surge; . . . at the slightest thrust I find myself rolling toward a sea which brought at the beginning of the century colored with colonial blood, with kinky hair and iridescent nails touched with purple like seashells, the cocoa harvesters, my mother's forebears."[2] When she went on the stage she introduced herself as "Colette Willy . . . with a true Burgundian accent, but beyond that — not too far — one finds very dark ancestors."[3] Her American friend and lover, Natalie Barney, ungraciously mentioned Colette's quadroon complexion. But Colette never needed to disclaim her Caribbean origins: her biographers did it for her. The last one thought it was a literary conceit, while others asserted that "there was nothing exotic in the Landoy's family tree."[4]

We saw no reason to distrust Colette, and started our own investigation. We found evidence of her ancestors, Huguenots who had fled persecution, in Martinique as early as the seventeenth century. At the end of the eighteenth century, Colette's great-grandfather, a mulatto, settled in

Northern France as a trader. His son married a well-to-do girl from Versailles and settled first in Paris, then in Belgium, where Colette's mother, Sido, grew up with her two elder brothers (both prominent journalists, writers, and publishers). Their lifelong friend was Victor Considérant, the most active proponent of the philosophy of nineteenth-century utopian socialist Charles Fourier. Sido grew up in a hotbed of radicalism, surrounded by artists, musicians, and intellectuals. She was an atheist and a Fourierist. The cliché of Sido as a country housewife tending her garden does not stand up to a scrutiny of archives, notary files, and transcripts of hearings.

Sido, who extolled free love, expounded for her daughter an ethic as radical today as it was in Saint-Sauveur over a century ago, an ethic based on total freedom of the individual and the abolition of marriage. Marriage was only acceptable as a means of reaching greater wealth, for wealth promoted the fulfillment of all human potentials. She left no taboos unmentioned, not even incest and followed "a law written by herself for herself." Colette wrote that Sido "reshaped for us the whole image of human feelings."

At twenty-two Sido accepted an arranged marriage to a very wealthy gentleman from Saint-Sauveur, a mentally retarded alcoholic twice her age. This marriage made her part of the gentry and she lived accordingly. She spent lavishly, never missing a season in Paris or Brussels, and had many love affairs. One of her lovers was Captain Colette, a disabled veteran who had been appointed tax collector in Saint-Sauveur. As soon as her first husband died, Sido married Captain Colette.

Captain Colette was a flamboyant southerner with political and literary ambitions. He wrote poetry and, when his political career floundered, numerous scientific and scholarly articles. An alumnus of the prestigious military academy Saint-Cyr, he had many friends in the government.

A popular myth is that Colette herself married an old man who corrupted and exploited her. As revealed in her letters, it was Sido who ardently wanted Colette to marry Henry Gauthier-Villars, the thirty-three-year-old scion of a family of publishers. He was an avant-garde aesthete who launched literary reviews before becoming an influential music critic, one of the top journalists of his generation, and the darling of Tout-Paris. (Tout-Paris was the sum of the one thousand people who never missed first-nights, the five hundred who were invited to the opening of a new exhibit, the five hundred first readers of a new book, and the one hundred invited to an important dinner party. Tout-Paris recognized its own. Some were accepted by consensus, others did not belong for reasons unexpressed and fathomless to outsiders. Why some were "in" and others "out" remains a mystery. Colette, Proust, and Valéry were "in," Gide never was.)

Sido saw a chance to ensnare Henry Gauthier-Villars when his mistress died and he was left with an illegitimate child. He married Colette without enthusiasm, but their fascination with each other grew to become a passion. A dark side to their relationship was the "mysterious illness" that almost killed Colette during the first year of her marriage: Gauthier-Villars had syphilis and transmitted it to his wife. Doctor Jullien, the leading specialist in venereal diseases, treated her with his experimental procedure: weekly steaming baths which gradually raised her temperature to 104°F. To alleviate her pain, she took ether. Colette never admitted that she had syphilis.

From the day Colette married the famous boulevardier she became part of Tout-Paris, and the media never stopped tracking her. At twenty-one she was adopted by leading Parisian hostesses and the intellectual avant-garde, particularly the musical avant-garde. Colette became a Parisian hostess. In her unorthodox salon Fauré, Vincent d'Indy, Gabriel de Toulouse-Latrec, Pierre Louys, Marcel Schwob, Jean Lorrain, Forain, the celebrated Countess Grefhulle, and foreign journalists mixed with the famous courtesans Liane de Pougy, la Belle Otero: the connocenti and the naughty. Colette signed as a music critic in *La Cocarde* while writing her daring first pseudobiographical *Claudine à l'Ecole* which was rejected by several publishers. Six years later the novel was released, signed "Willy" (one of the many pseudonyms adopted by her husband). Colette had refused to sign it for personal reasons — her brother had just married into an aristocratic family — but soon the word was out that she was the author of this novel and its sequels. After the scandalous success of the *Claudine*s, Colette and Willy were both megastars.

From the start Colette and Willy had an open marriage that fitted Fourier's philosophy allowing bisexuality, homosexuality, and multiple involvement around a pivotal love. Colette had affairs of every kind, not only during her marriage to Willy (hence the myth of Willy as corruptor), but — albeit less flamboyantly — throughout her two other marriages. Their marriage survived their philandering but reached the breaking point when the dashing American socialite Georgie Raoul-Duval seduced them both. After six years of separation and reconciliation, they divorced in 1910. During those stormy times, Colette and Willy began a unique literary dialogue, putting themselves in their respective novels and articles, dissecting their lives in public. Their output of revenge novels continued even after their divorce and culminated with Colette's *Mes Apprentessages* in 1936.

In order to finance her free and luxurious life, Colette went on stage and appeared in pantomimes, plays, and nude dances. She competed with courtesans such as la Belle Otéro — whom she described as her mentor — and music-hall stars like Polaire. Her career on stage was launched with enormous publicity and a series of fabricated scandals. Never an "aspiring" actress, she always had top billing and earned top wages. Famous as a nude dancer, she endorsed Fourier's "museum orgies,"(nude appearances by beautiful people solely for aesthetic pleasure) and always defended nudity on stage. She declined, in public, to live within her means, behave modestly, or renounce her radical reconsideration of society's ethics. "I want to do what I want. I want to play in pantomimes and comedies. I want to dance naked if the leotard bothers me and spoils my figure. I want to retire to a desert island if that is my pleasure or enjoy the company of ladies who use their beauty to make a living. I want to write chaste books celebrating landscapes, sorrow, pride, and the innocence of charming animals who are scared of humans."

Colette was kept lavishly by men as well as by women — the most famous of them being the Emperor's niece, the marquise de Morny — but she never stopped writing. Recognition of her literary genius exempted her from the proper behavior expected of women and she was called *un homme de lettres*, enjoying the special status of a Casanova. There seemed to be a breaking point between the Modern Age and the still predominant Victorian era: a devil-may-care hedonism reigned, and the rich flaunted middle class morals and old conventions.

The editor in chief of *Le Matin* and dashing womanizer Baron Henry de Jouvenel fell madly in love with Colette. At forty she opted for a title and a taste of respectability — three months pregnant, she bade farewell to the stage and married. As baronne de Jouvenel, Colette concentrated her energies on journalism and became a reporter-at-large for *Le Matin* as well as its drama critic and literary editor. As in her Willy days, her salon was frequented by cosmopolitan Paris, and for fourteen years she moved in the circles where French politics and European diplomacy were forged. She had many lovers, among them the film star Musidora (the original vamp) and her own adolescent stepson, Bertrand de Jouvenel.

In 1925 she divorced Jouvenel, severed her relationship with her stepson, sold her Parisian *hôtel particulier* and estate in Brittany, and settled down with Maurice Goudeket, a dealer in gems who was fifteen years her junior. Colette married Goudeket in 1935, when he lost his fortune in the aftermath of the Great Depression. A common myth grossly demeans Goudeket, presenting him as a gigolo. But Colette's letters show that she deeply loved and esteemed this scholarly young man, who was the first to understand her philosophy. He prompted her to abandon her journalistic career and to write her major essays "La Naissance du Jour," and "Le Pur et l'Impur" as well as several novels illustrating her Fourierist outlook on love. Colette died on August 3, 1954, and even her death brought her a dramatic apotheosis: she was the first French woman writer to be given a state funeral.

We exhaustively researched and reexamined every aspect of Colette's tumultuous life and complex, ambiguous works. As the real Colette emerged from the collected myths, she became for us an even greater writer, one of the most original thinkers of her time. She related to the twentieth century in its total complexity. With the publication of the *Claudine* novels in the 1900s she spearheaded the expression of contemporary attitudes. She frequented every notable circle where *modernité* was brewing — *Le Mercure de France,* the *d'Harcourt* group, *Le Chat Noir,* and *La Revue Blanche* — but she stepped beyond current literary trends. The frankness of her literature differed from the morbid eroticism of the symbolists/decadents and the didactic eroticism of Rachilde. Like Proust, her contemporary, she swept through the psychological liberation of homosexuality and bisexuality. But she did so more daringly than Proust, who treated homosexuality in his works but denied his actual sexual preference, even fighting a duel to counter innuendoes. Colette not only wrote but openly lived according to her beliefs.

Novelist, journalist, playwright, dancer, actress, film producer, scriptwriter, amateur painter, and admirable musician, Colette, for eighty-one years, six months, and six days, feasted on life.

I

COLETTE'S FAMILY

"Should I go back today, to Martinique?"
L'Etoile Vesper

$\mathcal{A}$DÈLE EUGÉNIE Sidonie Landois, Colette's mother, was born on August 31, 1835. That year Hallcy's comet crossed the skies. "If in the month of October 1835, I kept my nurse awake, she may have contemplated the comet . . . and since I was born with the sin of curiosity, maybe I have seen it too,"[1] wrote Sido to Colette. Adèle was nicknamed Sido by her brothers, and this was the name her daughter made famous. (Although she signed official papers "Adèle Landoy," for the sake of clarity we will refer to her as "Sido.")

Less than two months after Sido's birth her mother died. Her father was devastated. For a long time he could not get over his grief, and was never able to love Sido. She remained a cause for pain and bitter remembrance. "As for me, I never was anything but sorrow for my father because my birth had cost my mother her life and I reminded him too vividly of that painful moment."[2]

Henri Marie Landois, Colette's grandfather, was born in Charleville on September 23, 1792. He was the son of Robert Landois, a wealthy mulatto from Martinique who had settled in 1787 in Charleville, a smuggling center of colonial goods between France and the Netherlands (see appendix: Regarding Colette's Black Ancestry). He was an *épicier*, a member of the powerful Spicer's Guild which had the exclusive rights to the trade in citrus, coffee, and chocolate. Robert married Marie Mathis, the daughter of a boatman who owned barges on the River Meuse. Henri was "a mulatto with pale eyes, ugly but well built. . . and seductive."[3] This is how Sido described him. She loved to evoke his impeccable taste, his grand manners, his dashing figure as a man of the world. She extolled his way of life. At twenty he had to join the army — Napoleon's war machine was in constant need of soldiers. Thanks to his connections, Henri enlisted in the elite Second Regiment of Light Horse Lancers, created by Napoleon two years earlier. The emperor, who decked out his army in the most spectacular uniforms, gave the new regiment an even more splendid garb. They must have looked formidable when they rode into battle, each with a nine-foot-three-inch lance, saber and pistol, and carbine secured to the saddle. They became the favorite regiment of the French, who sang lancers' songs and danced lancers' quadrilles. They dazzled women.

While the Lancers were stationed in Versailles, Henri seduced Sophie Châtenay, twenty-three, the daughter of the administrator of the Versailles clock factory. Their encounter was not entirely accidental, for Sophie's Delahaut uncles lived in Charleville; one was a prosecutor and captain in the National Guard, the other a draper. Henri's dark complexion must have added an exotic touch to the prestige of the dashing cavalier. Colette thought that Sophie Céleste Châtenay, all peaches and cream, must have been irresistible to this Othello: "No doubt her husband, who was *colored*, had been seduced by the clear complexion of this Parisian from Boulevard Bonne Nouvelle."[4] (Colette was mistaken. Her grandmother was born in Versailles and later lived at 3 Cité d'Orléans, Boulevard St. Denis, in Paris.)

Fair Sophie became pregnant; Henri Landois had no choice but to marry. He requested a leave, which was granted, and on April 29, 1815, Sophie and Henri's marriage was celebrated in Versailles. A few days later, on May 7, they signed a *contrat de mariage* and both spouses made a reciprocal donation of all their possessions. Monsieur and Madame Châtenay jointly gave the sum of four thousand gold francs to their daughter as an advance on her future inheritance. It was a substantial dowry. Using all the intricacies of the recently adopted French civil law known as the *code Napoléon*, the Châtenays took great care to protect their daughter's inheritance. It was specified that if Henri should survive, he would have only the usufruct of the estate. Should Sophie be the survivor, however, she would enjoy complete ownership of the estate.

No sooner was the wedding party over than Henri was called to his regiment under the command of the ill-inspired Marshal Grouchy, whose misreading of the situation in the darkest hour of the empire allowed the Prussians to join forces with Wellington and crush Napoleon at Waterloo. Over forty thousand French were killed, but Grouchy managed to slip away and bring his men back to Paris without any casualties.

It was a time of uncertainty for the soldiers. Napoleon was now in exile in St. Helena. In Paris the king was quick to disband what was left of Napoleon's army and encourage all citizens to rebuild the economy. Henri joined his father Robert[5] in the spice business in Charleville. The guilds had been abolished but the democratization of the profession was slow. The *épicerie* business, having nothing to limit or hinder its expansion, entered a tremendous boom period. Henri prospered, and on November 26, 1815, Sophie gave birth to a son, Henri-Célestin, who died twenty days later. On October 17, 1816, she had a second son, Henri-Eugène-Célestin. The Landois then moved to a new house at 112 Rue du Petit-Bois. Two years later Paul-Emile was born (he died three and a half years later). In 1821 a fourth son, Jules-Hippolyte, lived only one day. But on July 31, 1823, a fifth son was born — Jules-Paulin, known as Paul. By now Henri Landois was referred to as *sieur* in official documents, a sign of his wealth and influence, but business ventures kept him away from home. When Paul-Emile died, a Mr. Delahaut signed the death certificate. Henri was also not there in December 1825 to sign the legal separation of goods that his wife and in-laws had introduced in the district court of Versailles. He was ordered to refund the four thousand francs of his wife's dowry, and Sophie was released from any debts cosigned with her husband.[6] This legal procedure was a way of sheltering her fortune. Henri was nowhere to be found; the judgment was served on him four years later on December 22, 1829. He had probably been trading in the West Indies along with his elder son Henri-Eugène (Sido's brother), who was to write in *L'Illustration,* "I was taken at an early age from my native land. My adventurous boyhood was spent on many shores."[7] In Eugène's prolific output as a novelist and journalist there are hints of the traumatic experience of a nine-year-old separated from a mother he adored.

Henri and Eugène returned triumphant. As the financial situation was once more flourishing, Henri commissioned the renowned miniaturist Foulard to paint a portrait of Sophie. Colette inherited it, and it can be seen today at the Musée Colette in Saint-Sauveur. On this fragile ivory medallion Sophie looks the epitome of a romantic lady in her fashionable dress with its plunging neckline, large puffed sleeves, and tiny waist caught in a tight belt with a large buckle. Two pendant earrings, almost six inches long, bespeak her wealth. Her fair hair, done up in a high bun with curls over the ears, was dressed in the fashion of the day. She had large blue eyes, a smiling, rosebud mouth, and a clear rosy complexion. At thirty-eight, Sophie looked young, pampered, and happy.

A daguerreotype of Henri Landois shows a fashionable man, his hair brushed up in short curls as if ruffled by a breeze, a romantic hairdo favored by poets and politicians. Henri's coat is beautifully tailored and his large tie slips into an elegantly pleated vest with careless grace. His eyes have a piercing, thoughtful gaze, his full lips are set in a haughty smile. The image is that of a clever, concentrated man, not handsome in a classical way, but interesting and attractive because of the awesome determination behind his features.

Like his grandfather, Henri established his business at 35 Rue des Drapiers in Le Havre, an important harbor west of Paris, and traded mainly in coffee, cocoa, cotton, rum, and dye woods. Henri was now a *négociant*, a word coined under King Louis-Philippe for the entrepreneurs who dealt in wholesale trade. In 1834 he expanded his business under the name of *Henri Père et Fils* at 4 Cité d'Orléans, Boulevard St. Denis in Paris. That same year in Le Havre, on the twenty-third of May, the Landois had a sixth child, Irma Céleste Désirée, named to reflect their joy in their first daughter. Shortly after her birth the Landois moved to their Parisian residence at 3 Cité d'Orléans. It was located above the mezzanine on what was known as *l'étage noble* — the noble floor.

The Landois had expensive tastes and the means to satisfy them. Their furniture was insured for the enormous sum of ten thousand gold francs. At the time of the empire imported exotic woods, particularly mahogany, had replaced the indigenous fruit-tree woods and were outrageously expensive. All the Landois' furniture was made from mahogany. Henri collected paperweights, as did Colette, who made it a fad in the thirties. He had one topped with a bronze poodle, another with a bronze horse, and a third with a bronze centaur; two were covered with

Moroccan leather; three were of precious marble. He liked elegant writing instruments: his letter opener had a mother-of-pearl handle and on his desk was a portable writing table of gilt china with painted scenes and matching pens. Later Colette would brag of having the first fountain pen in Paris. The Landois were musicians and one of them played the guitar; they would also pass down their love of music to Colette. On the mantelpiece a clock priced at one hundred and twenty gold francs, a masterpiece of Sophie's father's manufacture inlaid with Brazilian purple woods, supported a group of figures in gilt copper protected by a glass dome; Colette saw it in her mother's drawing room. The Landois had a cabriolet, a two-wheeled horse-drawn vehicle with a hood, prudently insured for ten years. An insurance for fifty thousand gold francs covered the merchandise stocked at 4 Cité d'Orléans and the wines in the cellars rented from Monsieur Soupault at 5 Grande Villette and 50 Rue de Flandres.

In the hall several fencing masks, two pairs of fencing gloves, and twenty-five swords were on display. This taste for weapons was inherited by Colette, who always carried a folding knife and a small revolver in her purse. White leather gear and a cartridge pouch from the National Guard give us a clue to Henri's social standing and political leaning. The National Guard was a militia organized at the outbreak of the French Revolution on the eve of the storming of the Bastille, with Lafayette as its commander in chief. The National Guard was bourgeois, had liberal ideas, and favored a representative government. It supported the constitutional monarchy and the rights and liberties included in the new constitution. When Charles x, swayed by ultraconservative ministers, curtailed those rights, the National Guard greeted the king with shouts of "Long live the constitution! Down with the ministers! Down with the Jesuits!" This anticlerical and liberal attitude was immediately punished and the guard dissolved. Liberals went underground and became extremely active in the secret societies that sprouted up in defense of liberty: the Society of the Friends of the People, the Knights of Freedom, the Society for Human Rights, and the Carbonari. Conservative King Charles x was replaced by his liberal cousin, Louis-Philippe. The National Guard was reorganized, and once more this middle-class armed militia supported the constitutional monarchy until it became too conservative for its liking. Under Louis-Philippe only men who paid real-estate taxes and could afford the costly uniform could enlist.

That wealthy, liberal, bourgeois brigade counted among its ranks Marcel Proust's maternal great-grandfather, Nathé Weil, as well as Colette's grandfather.

On December 4, 1835, after Sido's birth and Sophie's death, Henri Landois named as his general and special agent Philippe Dupuis, giving him full power of attorney to administer and manage Henri's personal estate as well as that of his four children. This notarized act mentions in detail an impressive number of goods, real estate, notes, loans, and mortgages on buildings. Henri Landois specified that his general agent was to receive all rents from tenants and farmers, do all necessary repairs, accept or reject all bids, pay all bills, receive all sums due, acquire or sell real estate at the best price, obtain and give all titles, buy and sell bonds and shares, select brokers, check and sign all books, and settle the estate of Sophie Landois.

Henri Landois left Paris with Henri-Eugène, Paul, and Irma and her nurse, and traveled to Belgium. It was a precipitous departure. Eugène was in trouble. Like many young romantics, he had joined one of the secret societies that were agitating against the government. The Society of the Friends of the People, a group led by François Raspail, advocated a vast program of political and social reforms ranging from total freedom of expression to a complete overthrow of the scientific establishment. Raspail was an avant-garde scientist. Politically he was a staunch liberal, a *carbonaro* who fought on the barricades during the Revolution of 1830. The citizen-king, Louis-Philippe tried to lure him to his side and appointed him head curator of all the collections of the museum, also awarding him the Legion of Honor. Raspail refused all gestures of appeasement and remained with the most radical wing of the Republicans. He lectured in political clubs and wrote blazing articles blasting the citizen-king.

A hero to the young, Raspail gave them an outlet for their frustrations in the columns of his paper, *Le Réformateur*. Young Eugène Landois contributed to these, as well as to *Le Figaro,* then a satirical political newspaper. But the government finally found a way to muzzle Raspail. In July of 1835, during a celebration of the Revolution, the anarchist Fieschi exploded a complicated piece of machinery aimed at the king and his family. The royal family was spared but nineteen people died, and the police crackdown was harsh. *Le Réformateur* was fined one hundred and twelve thousand gold francs and had to fold. By the end of the year there was an exodus of liberals to the safe haven of Belgium. Among them were the Landois.[8]

Little Sido was left in the care of Philippe Dupuis. She had a wet nurse from Puisaye, a poor, backward region that shared with Brittany and the Morvan the dubious honor of being wet-nurse purveyors to the bourgeois urban class. Her *nounou* took Sido to Les Matignons, a hamlet near Mézilles, where her husband was a blacksmith. The 1837 census indicates that Adèle (Sido) Landois, two years old, was still living with the Guilles. (Usually children were out to nurse for two to three years. Many died, and those who survived returned home with rustic manners and spoke the barbarous patois. Only during the Third Republic (1870–1940) was it made a requirement for every French citizen to speak French; previously the local patois were spoken, except among the educated classes.) Some of Colette's scholars have said that Sido remained in Mézilles until she was thirteen. This seems very unlikely, since Sido wrote an elegant French, played the piano, and was well read.

In Paris Philippe Dupuis was faced with the arduous task of sorting out the Landois estate. He called for the family council, an institution recently created for the protection of the interests of minors. The council was composed of seven members, three from the mother's side, three from the father's, and was presided over by the local justice of the peace. Henri was represented by Philippe Dupuis, proprietor, Laurent Jousserandot, glass and crystal manufacturer, and a Landois who lived on Rue des Fossés Saint-Jacques.

On March 28, the justice of the peace started reporting the inventory at numbers 3 and 4 Cité d'Orléans. This report was continued on April 2, 7, and 9, resumed on June 4 and 6, and finalized on June 14, 1836. It covers twenty pages, in the small handwriting of the clerk. Everything was meticulously reported, including the wines: Château Margaux, Saint-Emilion, Beaune, Frontignan, Sauterne, Château-Lafitte, Madère, champagne, l'Hermitage, Médoc, and Saint-Estèphe. Sido was from a family of connoisseurs and had an inborn respect for fine wines. She told Colette that during the Prussian invasion of France one of the first things she did was to bury all her vintage bottles in her garden to save them from the enemy.

The inventory gives us a hint of the Landois standard of living and of their precipitous departure. All the clothes had been removed from the drawers except for two baby bibs; there were eight empty jewelry boxes, two pairs of copper earrings, and an empty guitar case. Henri had left behind all his personal papers, including his military discharge, for he was traveling under an assumed name. When the clerk started to audit the 1835 ledgers of the company Henri Père et Fils and Philippe Dupuis declared that all the doctors and funeral expenses had been paid for in full, he felt compelled to add that "the bad state of affairs of Mr. Landois had necessitated his departure to a foreign land some five months ago, and because of that the ledgers have not been kept regularly, not a single account has been checked and cannot be because of lack of exact documents."[9] Since Sophie's estate was protected against any creditor's claims, the children inherited it. Sido had an income and was not a penniless orphan, as she was later described by Colette.

In Brussels Henri Landois was again in the wholesale cocoa business. Somewhere along the way he started to manufacture chocolate, a trade for which Belgium is famous. In the newly created Belgian kingdom tariffs were not regulated, and soon the import of chocolate and tobacco made some traders very rich. Once again the Landois were riding the crest. They now spelled their name with a "y," although the old spelling appears in official papers. Possibly to hide from creditors, Henri now called himself Eugène.[10]

The Landoys lived in the Marolles district of Brussels "in a pretty white house three stories high." Eugène (the son) was homesick. "Away from civilization, sick and lonely, I sit on the marble windowsill and search in the distance for the wooded hills of the Ardennes where I spent such a happy and peaceful childhood."[11]

Less than two years after Sophie's death, Henri, now forty-five, married Thérèse Leroux, the thirty-nine-year-old widow of a chocolate-factory owner, and took over the management of his wife's business.

Life around Henri was never peaceful; he was a restless man. At some point he had little Sido brought back from La Puisaye to give her an education. When she was eight, her father — "all the women were falling for him" — brought home a newborn baby girl and her nurse. He told Sido, "Bring her up, she is your sister."[12] Sido knew that Henri liked long, aristocratic fingers; having noticed that the baby's hands had plump, tiny ones, she decided to mold them to her father's liking. She longed to be loved and thought that if she could reshape her sister's fingers, her father would be pleased with her. A doctor was called in to find out what caused the swelling of the baby's hands, but Sido did not volunteer a clue.

She herself had beautiful hands, which she always displayed artistically in her photographs. Later she taught Colette to do the same.

Sido grew up with Eugène, Paul, Irma, her newborn sister, and a pet monkey named Jean. As in Paris, the Landoys' house was filled with expensive furniture and paintings, most notably a painting by Salvatore Rosa, a seventeenth-century Italian painter famous for his military scenes and fantastic landscapes. Sido acquired her father's expensive taste for clothes, furniture, and food. Later, in her letters to Colette, she kept asking for exotic foods, chocolate, teas from Rebattet and Hediard, fresh citrus shipped from the French Riviera. At seventy she maintained that she had never been able to drink out of a glass not made of crystal or a cup not of bone china.

Sido's liberal ideas and the education she gave her children (which shocked so many people later in Saint-Sauveur) came from her brothers. In Brussels Eugène had quickly become a noted political commentator for *L'Emancipation,* a liberal, highly political newspaper that supported the struggle for an independent Belgian state and for the freedom of the press. Eugène was still in touch with the Carbonari. He continued to collaborate with *Le Figaro* in Paris and its director, Alphonse Karr. Karr's other journal *Les Guêpes* (The Wasps) was relentlessly attacking the political, literary, and artistic establishments. Eugène admired Karr so much that he took "A Wasp in Exile" as one of his pseudonyms, and the Landoy home became a refuge for "any French-speaking Wasp" who "had to flee from an angry master."[13]

Well-established as a political journalist at *L'Emancipation,* Eugène started a successful publishing press at 67 Rue Longue. He cleverly exploited two new markets: the expanding railroad and the health spas. His *Guide to Belgium* (1840) ran to at least forty-two printings and *The Indispensable Traveler's Guide to Belgian Railways* (1844) was a must for the many visitors and immigrants from all over Europe who flocked to Belgian cities. They could find practical tips and useful articles peppered with cartoons and jokes in *Le Moniteur des Chemins de Fer, Journal des Touristes et des Flâneurs,* which was sold in the railroad stations. But the liberal was never far from the businessman. As soon as it was released in Paris, Eugène published Raspail's *The Family Doctor* (1843) and *The Health Directory.* These books by the radical French scientist had a lasting impact on Sido, who adopted his revolutionary precepts on hygiene. Raspail startled the medical establishment by stating that most

diseases were triggered by air pollution and bad assimilation of food, tobacco, alcohol, or any toxic substance, including any medicine with side
effects; he also noted psychological traumas as a cause of bad health. A
strong advocate of healthy living and preventative medicine, he tried to
spread notions of hygiene and moderation among the poor by operating
free clinics.

In the spring of 1848 winds of change were sweeping through Europe.
In Paris, Republicans were marching in solidarity with Poland, which was
occupied by the Russians. Liberals were rallying around Arago, Lamartine,
Cabet, and Raspail, who was jailed for participating in the march for the
liberation of Poland. Eugène Landoy, thirty-two, and Sido, thirteen, were
in Paris. Whether Sido came with her brother or was staying with her
tutor on Boulevard Bonne Nouvelle is not clear. But in the midst of the
growing unrest, she was sent to the safety of Mézilles, where she stayed for
a while. She appears on the Mézilles census of 1848. Her visit started the
rumor, still in circulation in Saint-Sauveur, that Sido was brought to the
village by Freemasons. At thirteen Sido had a strong, independent personality. "I adore storms and have always loved them. When I was still in
Mézilles, every time I saw a storm brewing, I would run to the highest
mountain, my hair in the wind."[14] Sido was a guest at the Château du
Fort, a country manor owned by Monsieur and Madame de Vathaire, who
had two daughters about her age. She remained friends with the sisters,
who moved a few years later to a newly built manor, Le Château des
Gouttes in the township of Saint-Sauveur.

Back in Brussels Eugène Landoy, wasting no time, published a *History
of the French Revolution of 1848*, which was released the same year. In
melodramatic prose, Eugène declared: "The government of the people
by the people is the law of God, the only divine right. The governments
of an ambitious oligarchy, of an aristocratic nobility, of an insolent and
self-centered bourgeoisie, of a dictator who assumes a monstrous power,
all those forms of government which drained the people for the sole
benefit of a hateful and immoral power or for the satisfaction of a few
private interests have been imposed upon mankind so it would better
appreciate the value of freedom and happiness." Following a romantic
view of history, Eugène contended that God was leading humanity step
by step through an ascending spiral, and that on its way up humanity
would shed all forms of tyranny. For Landoy the 1848 uprising tolled the
bells of "all the oligarchies, of all the monarchies on the surface of the

earth." Among the participants in this historic moment was a young cadet just expelled from Saint-Cyr — France's most prestigious military academy — Jules Colette. When he later embarked on a political career, he bragged about those days, and his flamboyant style impressed his daughter Colette.

The French Republic was short-lived. Napoleon III crushed all dreams of liberty. This dampened Eugène's faith in a divine ascending spiral, and his style lost its heroic tone; he cultivated thereafter a gentle and elegant irony. After forty years of success, he would say that his only defense had been a velvet shield. In 1851 he became editor in chief of *L'Emancipation* and reviewed theatrical and musical events for the weekly *Journal de Gand* in a very popular column that he signed "Bertram." He wrote sporadically for the French magazine *L'Illustration,* for *La Revue des Deux Mondes,* and for *L'Annuaire des Deux Mondes,* using several pseudonyms: "Marc Lebreuil," "A Wasp in Exile," and "Bertram," which became his most famous and lasting one. An amateur painter, for several years he published a series of books titled *Salons,* which he signed "A Wasp in Exile." Many painters came to the Landoy home. Among the regulars were the Stevens brothers. Joseph, the elder, was a painter of animals and Alfred, a society painter famous for his portraits, was one of the best of the realists along with Millet and Courbet. Sido recalled a trip to Ostende with Alfred Stevens and Eugène. On the beach they saw a pretty English girl — "slender, blond, delicate . . . with a Great Dane at her feet. It was a scene for a good painter. Alfred Stevens wanted to make a sketch of the group but it was difficult to ask the young lady to agree to it."[15]

Paul Landoy also started working as a journalist for *L'Indépendance Belge, Le Constitutionnel de Mons,* and *Le Télégraphe de Bruxelles.* But after twenty years as editor in chief, he became head of the Fine Arts Administration, then director of the Kursaal, a fashionable Ostende casino.

Back from Mézilles, Sido found the Landoys living in a hotbed of radicalism. Every day new exiles poured into Belgium to escape the imperial police, since Belgium remained a haven for free expression. Until World War I anything from the political to the sleazy that was censured in France was printed in Belgium, which had a booming publishing business. At the dawn of the twentieth century this small kingdom boasted five hundred dailies and six hundred weeklies. After 1848 the banished members of the French Assemblée Législative flocked to Belgium. Some of the most radical thinkers of the century visited the Landoy household: Schoelcher, the Lincoln of the West Indies, a representative of Martinique and Guadeloupe who fought to abolish slavery; Edgar Quinet, who fought for the separation of church and state; Ledru-Rollin; and Etienne Arago. But the theorist who would most profoundly affect Sido was the lifelong friend of the Landoys and standard bearer of Fourierism, Victor Considérant, probably the most brilliant mind of the group.

Victor Considérant, more than any other social thinker, shaped Sido's personality and through her, Colette's, who constantly referred to her mother as "the leading character in my whole life."[16] Sido's influence went beyond the education of her daughter — she provided Colette with a philosophy, an ethic rooted in Charles Fourier's philosophy of voluptuousness. In *The Break of Day, Sido,* and *The Pure and the Impure,* Colette, then over fifty, reflected on her mother's principles and asserted that her mother's philosophy was her own.

Love was at the center of Fourier's society. "Passions," he said, "are the mistresses of the world."[17] Around this concept he constructed a social system based on mutual attraction and an economic one devised to promote health, luxury, and peace. Social harmony, he believed, sprang from universal passional affinity. He claimed that sexual repression was at the root of all the evils of civilization. In his utopian society, *harmony*, the passions — labeled vices in our Western civilization, or deadly sins in Christianity — would be put to use sagaciously. Instead of smothering them, Fourier would increase their intensity and through gratification reach the social harmony that constraints destroy. Before Freud he denounced the ravages caused by sexual inhibitions and the pathological or even criminal forms displayed by repressed passions when they boil over. Fourier, however, was against anarchy; he did not want to let raw passions run loose but proposed instead to channel them from antisocial to social behavior.

Fourier's code of social harmony was based on a sexual revolution of such audacity that he overstepped the most daring sexologists of the twentieth century. Compared to his radicalism, Freud's, Wilhelm Reich's, or Kinsey's theories seem shy. His primary concern as a psychologist was to analyze all the sexual drives and integrate them into a new social order. The most important vehicles of social integration were Les Séries Passionnelles, passional groups that acted as melting pots. Individuals would associate and regroup themselves according to their driving passions.

His new world order was based on the premise that human beings were not created equal, that there were natural diversities in character and intelligence. An individual's place in society was not determined by gender or race but by individual differences. Fourier did not believe in an egalitarian system; personal value determined the place of the individual. "Inequality, so much maligned by the philosophers, is not displeasing to man. Only if he lacks what is necessary does he begin to detest his superiors and the rules of society."[18] Fourier attacked the liberal conception of freedom as empty and formalistic and argued that there was a cruel irony in the concept of "the sovereignty of the people" if the individual was "a living automaton" locked up in psychological slavery. In his enormous body of work Fourier asserted that he had found a way to ensure humanity's emotional equilibrium, without which there could be no freedom. Every passion being part of an immense orchestra, each one should be finetuned to reach perfect harmony. Homosexuality, called *unisexuality* (a term Colette uses in *The Pure and the Impure*), any type of polygamy for man and woman, abolition of marriage, and unfettered sexual drive should all be encouraged, since nature desires variety in its pleasures. However, the exception was as useful as the rule as long as it neither vexed nor harmed anyone and created multiple social bonds. Fourier thought that it would take three centuries to transform our civilization into *harmony*, his ideal social order. Sido lapped up these theories. She used to say, "evil and good can be equally resplendent and fruitful."[19] She wrote to Colette in 1909, "I have always been a little crazy but not so much as you think. This is the fact: I came into this world three hundred years too soon and this world does not understand me."[20] Fourier's utopian ideas are the undercurrent on which Colette's ethic rides; they are the essence and philosophy of *The Pure and the Impure*, her essay on love.

Like Fourier, Considérant believed in the fundamental harmony between mankind, the environment, and the cosmos, but he recommended practical deviations from pure Fourierism, arguing that society was far from ready to accept and implement Fourier's code of social harmony. He championed the concept of total female emancipation. He was the only senator in the Parliament who fought to include a provision in the constitution guaranteeing women's political and legal equality. His wife Julie, who came from an aristocratic family, was a staunch disciple of

Fourier, and his mother-in-law, a famous beauty and woman of letters, dedicated her salon exclusively to the study of Fourier.

Sido lived in a Belgium buzzing with ideas. Considérant's friend Alexandre Dumas, who was not trying to escape the imperial police but his own creditors, polarized the socialites while Victor Hugo polarized the intelligentsia. The banished poet immediately adopted the life of an outlaw. Though none of his property had been confiscated and his royalties were still pouring in, he took a room in the frugal Hôtel de la Porte Verte, 31 Rue de la Violette, a run-down place from which he wrote: "I lead the life of a monk."[21]

Hugo was followed by another giant, Raspail. When his wife died in March of 1853, over one hundred thousand people attended her funeral. The message was not lost on Napoleon III, who commuted Raspail's jail sentence to exile in April. Raspail, who had once proclaimed "God and country," now declared that freethinkers should be born without priests, marry without priests, and die without priests. This credo was to have a lasting effect on Sido, now eighteen. She became an atheist and took every opportunity to attack religion. Only once did she ally herself with her parish priest, "to protest against the municipality which denies the right to march to the Catholic band. I found that unfair."[22] She was a freethinker and remained such. At sixty-one she wrote to Colette: "Mme Hardy . . . she is a doctor's widow from here; well, we are getting along very well, I, an atheist and she, very religious. The dear woman has decided to convert me. She absolutely wants me to read the two fat books written by Father Bommard! Can you see me reading that?"[23]

In January of 1854 Henri Landoy died in the city hospital in Lyons, France. His death certificate states that he was "an ex-merchant from Brussels" and is signed by two clerks, which indicates that no family member was present. He probably died in the plague epidemic that killed thousands of people in Marseilles and Lyons.

Soon after his father's death, Eugène married into an aristocratic French family, the Cuvelier de Trye. Caroline was a wealthy heiress, daughter of the now forgotten but once immensely successful playwright Cuvelier de Trye, who staged grandiose historical shows famous for their battle scenes on horseback. Caroline was an accomplished hostess, fluent in several languages, well read, and a talented musician — the charmed circle that gathered in her salon found her an admirable interpreter of Chopin. She was a beauty with raven black hair and sea green eyes.

Colette, who saw her several times, described her as Tante Coeur (Aunt Heart) in *Claudine at School (Claudine à l'Ecole)*: "Like the Empress Eugénie, she had an aristocratic nose, the heavy bandeaux with a touch of gray, a slightly condescending smile and arched eyebrows *à l'espagnole*."[24] The first time she visited her, she was intimidated by Caroline's extremely polished and elegant French. But what impressed her even more was the contrast between her aunt's Victorian looks and the art nouveau decor in which she lived. She found her uncle handsome and imposing with his flowing white mane. Eugène was a womanizer and marriage did not change his ways. Sido admired Caroline's sophisticated and cool approach to her husband's numerous affairs. "My sister-in-law paid off her husband's mistress or mistresses. My brother was rather handsome and always in love, but so what?"[25] He had at least one known illegitimate daughter with a Mrs. Deleau, whom Colette later met in Brussels.

Sido was happy in that sophisticated, liberal milieu. "Nothing supplanted in my mother's heart the beautiful Belgian cities, the warmth of their refined and gentle life, epicurean and enamored of the things of the mind."[26]

He Was Ugly . . . More or Less Retarded But He Was Rich

In 1856 Sido was twenty-one, fair, slender, and strong — "not very pretty but charming . . . with a wide mouth but a delicate chin, a free young girl accustomed to living uninhibited among men, her brothers and their friends, the youthful Bohemia of French and Belgian painters, musicians, artists."[27] Her eyes were gray, the "color of rain," "fluttering" when she tried to conceal her willful, lusty, and defiant nature. "In her eyes could be seen a sort of smiling frenzy, a universal contempt, a boiling scorn."[28] At moments, her true nature would surge out into wild facial expressions; then she appeared "free of obligations, of charity, of humanity,"[29] but people seldom realized it, so caught up were they by her sensuous charm.

She could boast of her graceful hands and small feet. She walked gracefully with her toes turned out, barely putting any weight on her heels. Her voice "was a shaded soprano . . . a shimmering voice, full of nuance, vascillating at the slightest emotion."[30] A daguerreotype of Sido taken when she was eighteen shows a slim girl in a stamped velvet dress with a large lace collar and flowing lace cuffs. She wears a richly bejeweled bracelet.

Since she always felt that her father had rejected her she needed to attract attention and quickly learned how to become the center of interest. She had "an intolerant way of discussing, of refuting an argument,"[31] which she practiced in Caroline's salon. Sido had inherited one fourth of her mother's estate and had independent means, but this was not considered a large dowry. News came from Mézilles that the Bourgoin family was searching for a bride for their forty-two-year-old bachelor cousin. They invited Sido to spend some time with them. As was the custom in those days, Sido would stay several months with her hosts and ample occasions would be provided for her to meet with her proposed husband, the wealthy landowner Claude Jules Robineau-Duclos. "A well-mannered man, most of the time. Of his forgotten patrician ancestry, he kept the haughtiness, the politeness, the brutality and a taste for domination.[32]

Sido found herself a pawn in a family plot: Jules Robineau-Duclos's only sister, six years his junior, had tried to have him declared legally incompetent, a scheme strongly opposed by some of Jules's first cousins, who felt it was an insult to the family name. For centuries the Robineaus had been glassblowers; glassmakers belonged to the nobility as long as they carried on their trade. The creation of the Manufacture Royale de Saint-Gobain put them out of business, but the Robineaus were still regarded as gentry in La Puisaye.

Jules Robineau-Duclos, born in February of 1814, grew up, according to one of his neighbors, "like a wild beast"[33] — to which he bore a striking resemblance, having grown a double row of teeth. When he turned sixteen, he agreed to have fourteen teeth pulled out all on the same day, an operation either performed by the local barber or by some traveling so-called surgeon, with iron pliers, a bottle of spirits, and sheer strength. This feat of dentistry left a strong impression on the folks of Saint-Sauveur, who talked about it long after the fact. Jules "was frightfully ugly."[34] Frequent intermarriages between cousins had bred a streak of melancholy, if not outright madness, in the family. His uncle and mother were both committed to an asylum.

Jules was educated near Paris in the College of Fontenay-aux-Roses. He was fifteen when his mother was placed in the asylum, where she died seven years later. That same year his father divided the estate between his two children, emancipated his daughter (who was still a minor), appointed a Monsieur Givry as their tutor, and died. The tutor promptly married his son to the heiress.

At twenty-two, Jules inherited farms, fields, wooded lands, cattle, and a vineyard that produced fifty-six hundred liters of wine and brandy, worth about five hundred thousand gold francs. Dressed in boots for most of the day, he would ride through his woods and fields, watching the crops and checking the charcoal made in his forests and the sale of his lumber. What the land lacked in productivity was offset by its large acreage.

Jules Robineau was a traumatized introvert afraid of the dark, who could not bear to be left alone at night. One of his servants, Marie Miton, a miller's daughter, became his mistress. In 1843 she bore him a son, who was registered as Antonin Miton. His birth certificate bore the words "father unknown." Marie lived well in the master's house; all the other servants addressed her as "Mademoiselle Marie," and for twenty years she managed everything. Marie's relationship with Jules was a stormy one. Lucien, a stable boy, remembered that around midnight, Marie Miton came to the stable in her nightgown, woke him up, and ordered him to carry her son to her sister's house. "I came back to Robineau-Duclos's home, I went back to sleep in the stable next to the donkeys. . . ." Robineau-Duclos walked in. He asked Lucien to follow him into the kitchen, put two bottles of white wine and one bottle of brandy on the table and told him, "my little donkey, we are going to drink that, then go to bed." "I drank with him, then followed him to his bedroom and slept in his bed, not to offend him, because when he sleeps alone, he gets very frightened. He was angry, I was scared, I did not sleep much but daybreak came soon enough."[35]

Jules drank so much that he started to experience periods of delusion and was treated for behavioral disorders. He was afraid of being poisoned and refused to take any medicine. When forced to do so, he became violent and threatened to shoot anyone around. After he tried to kill his game-keeper, his servants hid his hunting guns. In 1855 he had another fit of madness. He wanted to shoot two of his maids in order to use their corpses as bait for crawfish. The two girls barricaded themselves in the barn. They heard one shot. Jules shot at the door, then went away singing, "Pick up your guns, citizens, let's march with young girls at our side, a bottle in our hand," to the tune of *La Marseillaise*. He went to the police station, where he complained that all the women had fled and that his house was now full of soldiers from the African regiments. At this point his sister, Louise Givry and her husband tried to have him declared legally incompetent. A judge investigated the case. Friends and relatives split into two camps, the Givrys' supporters against those who saw Givry himself as an adventurer who, having married the heiress, was now after her brother's fortune.

For three days twenty-eight witnesses testified. Escorted by his cousins, Doctors Carreau, Robineau-Desvoidy, and Lachassagne, and Victor Gandrille, who kept him sober, Jules appeared in court. The judge noted that his slouching attitude and tired looks made him look much older than his forty-two years. He spoke haltingly and his intelligence "seemed very slow." Doctor Rocheux, appointed by the judge, called him "an over-grown child" and said that his weird behavior came from excessive drinking. Jules's cousins counterattacked. "They say that Robineau-Duclos is insane, that is false. He is simply surrounded by wicked people." The most wicked of them all, they felt, was his brother-in-law Givry, who was always meddling in his affairs. The mere sight of Givry could send Jules into raving fits of anger.

On the Givrys' side was the eighteenth witness, Lucien Breuille, a la-borer, age thirty-two, who had worked for Jules for six years. He said that once when a cow had broken a leg, Jules Robineau-Duclos came to the injured animal with a whip to beat it, then stabbed it with his knife. Jules had had to be dragged away. During that period Jules used to seize a meat skewer and brandish it, screaming, "This is my *bâton*, I am a field mar-shal." He would hang his cap on the doorknob of the dining room and a rag on the doorknob of the drawing room and say that they were sen-tries. He instructed Breuille to let no one in until the sentries were re-lieved of their duty. Jules's eccentric behavior could take a political turn. At the dawn of the Second Empire, when Napoleon III and Queen Victoria declared war on Russia, Jules ordered an enormous lunch to be prepared by Mr. Bord, the caterer, to host the Russians, "who were coming." This lunch ordered for the enemies by one of its prominent citizens scandalized Saint-Sauveur.

Several young servants, one barely thirteen, testified that he chased them around or asked them to scratch his legs. They said that Jules went several months without changing his shirts and underwear. Their testimonies were rejected as "mere gossip" by the twenty-first witness, a schoolmate of Jules and the mayor of Saint-Sauveur, who had been directed by the prefect to monitor the situation. In his weekly visits, he said, he had found Jules, sometimes drunk, and sometimes busy with the management of his farms. He had never noticed that Jules should change his linen, and he did not see him as very odd. In his opinion, Jules Robineau-Duclos's farms were very well managed. At these dismal proceedings, the long array of witnesses produced by Givry were servants, field hands, and stable boys. The star witnesses in favor of Jules were the mayor of Saint-Sauveur and a retired lawyer. The judge found no reason to deprive Jules of his rights and place his fortune in the care of his brother-in-law.

The scandal started by the Givrys smeared everyone in the Robineau clan and resentment knitted the cousins together. The Bourgoins, the Lachassagnes, the Gandrilles, and the Bourgneufs decided that the only way to protect Jules was to get him married, but finding him a wife was not simple. In the French bourgeoisie, few marriages were love matches, and little stood in the way of a marriage except madness and consumption, but after the scandal a local bride was not to be found; the Robineau clan looked elsewhere. The Bourgoins's candidate was Sido. She was willful and well educated; she could manage Jules; and more importantly, she would owe her fortune to the Robineau family — through her they could control Jules. One of the cousins, Doctor Lachassagne, traveled to Brussels to discuss the terms of this marriage with Eugène Landoy. Sido, he felt, would protect Jules from a conniving mistress, an unscrupulous sister, and a greedy brother-in-law. The offer was tempting; at almost twenty two, Sido's chances for a wealthy match were dwindling. She came to Mézilles. When sober, Jules was a gentle, well-mannered man, and he was enchanted by Sido's charm.

They all went back to Brussels, Jules escorted by his cousin, Doctor Thomas Lachassagne, who monitored him every step of the way. On January 7, 1857, they signed a contract in the office of the attorney Jacques Langendries, stating that both fiancés being French, they would be married according to the French code under the joint estate provision. But they added three clauses. Neither one of them would be responsible for any debts made before the marriage. Sido's debts would be paid by her or by her brothers, an indication that Sido was outspending her income. In case of death, the surviving spouse would receive a sum of ten thousand francs in money or furniture before the estate could be divided between their heirs. The last item stated that as proof of their mutual affection, the future spouses would give all the proceeds of their joint estates to the survivor. (This third clause would be at the root of a feud between Sido's children.) The two-page contract was signed by Jules Robineau-Duclos, Adèle Landoy (Sido), Eugène and Caroline Landoy, and Doctor Thomas and Hortense Lachassagne. There was little doubt in their minds that Jules would be the first one to die; if he did not produce an heir, the estate would remain in the Robineau family, but as long as she lived, Sido would receive all its proceeds. This marriage gave Sido the means to maintain the standard of living to which she had grown accustomed and enjoy the luxury she so craved.

In 1922 in *My Mother's House* (*La Maison de Claudine*), Colette wrote her own version of her mother's first marriage. She nicknamed Robineau-Duclos "the Savage" — a term of endearment Sido liked to use for her children. While visiting his farms on horseback, he saw the fair Sido, who met his glance "without batting an eyelid and without a smile," and dreamed of her. Sido became a maiden of eighteen impressed by a man who had "the pale complexion of a refined vampire," a black beard, and a horse as "red as a heart cherry." He begged relatives and friends to plead his case with Sido's brothers. Sido, playing with her blond curls, could only "accept her luck and thank God,"[36] for the man was wealthy. Colette's tale reads like a richly embroidered legend from a medieval ballad. She had turned Robineau-Duclos, "the slouching alcoholic," into a romantic hero.

On January 15, 1857, Sido's actual marriage took place in Schaerbeek, a fashionable suburb of Brussels where the Eugène Landoys were now living with their infant son, Eugène II. It was the end of January when Sido and Jules, escorted by Doctor Lachassagne and his wife, undertook the trip back to Saint-Sauveur. It was a long journey through the lugubrious mining towns of Belgium and northern France. They changed trains in Paris, then went on to Auxerre. From Auxerre, a horse-driven carriage took them to Saint-Sauveur, sleepy in the winter cold.

Marriage Brings No Happiness . . . Except If One Acquires a Great Fortune

Saint-Sauveur-en-Puisaye is a relic of centuries of turbulence in an impoverished region. "It is a village, not even a very pretty one," wrote Colette in *Claudine at School*. Built on the east side of a hill surrounded by marshlands and vast forest in a region known as "the poor Burgundy," it has every reason to envy the "rich Burgundy" with its unsurpassable vineyards and immense production of famous wines such as Beaujolais, Beaune, and Chablis.

Saint-Sauveur was a point of assembly for the scarce and scattered people inhabiting those marshy lands, an outpost of the duchy of Burgundy and heavily fortified against the kings of France. Nothing grand, it was above all a military fortress surrounded by three walls. Outside lay the town with its church. From their hilltop, the seigneurs of Saint-Sauveur controlled passage through the valley of the Loing to the greater valley of the Yonne, which merges with the Seine around Fontainebleau. Vandalized, sacked, restored, and ruined again, the medieval structure all but vanished when the villagers plundered its stones for their own use. When the duke of Burgundy sealed an alliance with the king of France, Charles VII, he lost all interest in this outpost, which meagerly survived.

Today there are no formidable ruins at the top of the hill but an architecturally ill-defined building overlooking the clustered roofs of the village. Begun in 1600, it took a whole century to build, which accounts for the diversity of its styles. Thrusting out of the commons, the ruins of a twelfth-century round tower called "the Saracen tower . . . low, girdled with ivy, with its top crumbling little by little every day"[37] rises above the poplars. It must have been part of a defensive system built to warn of the approach of the Saracens, the dreaded Moslem armies. Like most defensive systems, this medieval Maginot line was in place long after the threat of Saracen invasion had passed.

There is no castle here worthy of the name, and no steeple, either. In the twelfth century, during the great surge of religious enthusiasm that covered France with cathedrals, monasteries, and churches, the town of Saint-Sauveur built a new church on the site of the primitive Gallic-Roman one. They labored for three centuries. Built on a ferruginous vein, the church had the dubious quality of attracting lightning. Repeatedly struck by thunderbolts, it was repeatedly repaired. In the midnineteenth century the town turned Republican, stopped its fight against the wrath of the elements, and left the church without a steeple. "The people of Puisaye are doomed by their climate which saps their energies,"[38] stated Doctor Robineau-Desvoidy, who wrote local history.

According to the census of 1881, Saint-Sauveur had eleven hundred inhabitants, but even that figure may have been exaggerated by officials, who wanted a railroad station built in their district. There were only two paved streets, one going up the steep hill to the so-called château, another branching out from the small, uneven marketplace on the flatter part of the hillside where the city walls used to be. The other three or four streets were lined with stones on each side to allow the wheels of the carts to ride on level ground, but their centers were only packed soil. "Thank Heaven! The streets are not paved. The showers tumble in small torrents . . ."[39] wrote Colette, who as a child liked to hop from stone to stone when sent on an errand. There were no trees. The streets, winding and narrow, were lined with low stone houses, each with one window and one door. Only the few bourgeois dwellings had two stories with rows of windows on the street. This deprivation of air and light was due to the Impôt sur les Portes et Fenêtres, a tax assessed by the internal revenue service according to a home's number of doors and windows. To avoid paying, the French limited their number of windows and concealed all doors nonessential to passage by wallpapering them to blend them with the walls.

Jules Robineau's house, on the steep, narrow Rue de l'Hospice, was a two-story structure blackened by age, sitting in a row of uneven, smaller dwellings. On the façade eleven windows flaunted the wealth of its owner. A double wooden gate, large enough for wagon and horses, had a little door cut out in one of the big ones, so that one could enter the barnyard without having to open the gate. This served as the servants' entrance. Situated in the heart of the village, the house testified to the ancient roots of the Robineau family. The new middle class was building on the town's outskirts, large square houses surrounded by gardens with winding graveled paths protected by ten-foot walls.

When Sido arrived, she climbed the small, uneven stone landing, eight steps on one side, six on the other. On the railing she noticed the initials of Robineau-Duclos wrought in iron. The heavy door opened. Five servants, two women and two men supervised by Marie Miton, were waiting. Sido stepped into the white and gilded drawing room. The three large main rooms, with their twelve-foot-high ceilings and stone floors and a parlor, opened onto a little terrace to the south. At the end of the hall were the servants' quarters. Then came the surprise: The second floor of the large house was deserted, abandoned — the humid rooms had saltpetre rot on the walls. Since 1829, when Jules's mother was committed to the asylum, no one had taken care of the house except Marie Miton. The second floor had reverted to traditional country use: a storage place for chestnuts, apples, and nuts. Around the yard on the south side of the house there were several low buildings — the stables, the coach house, a dairy with two cows, the henhouse, the wash house. The garden grew wild; lower on the slope there was an orchard.

Sido took charge immediately. She reorganized every room and had the kitchen whitewashed and restocked. She taught the cooks Belgian recipes; venison appeared in style, raisin cakes were *flambés* with liquor made from local berries. The deep cupboards were a treasure trove of antique crystal, the legacy of the Robineaus' ancestral trade. Sido, graceful in her silk dresses, placed dishes and flatware stamped with the Robineau coat of arms (a goat standing on its hind legs) on lace tablecloths. She watched the old servants spin hemp from her fields and weave rough linen for the kitchen and the domestics' beds. "Milkmaids churned milk, made butter, pressed cheese."[40] Servants were hardly a luxury; even workers could afford a maid. But their number was a status symbol. With four live-in servants, a headmaid, a seamstress, and helpers who were hired to do the washing, ironing, and spring-cleaning, Sido's standard of living was upper middle class.

But her honeymoon was short. Two months after her marriage, Jules started to drink heavily again. One day he suddenly lunged at her to hit her, as he had done to Marie Miton. Sido grabbed everything that was on the mantelpiece — crystal vases, statues, and a heavy metal lampholder with sharp points and angles — and threw them in Jules's face; the lampholder struck him in the cheek. A large scar remained as proof of Sido's self-defense; Jules did not try to beat her again.

He was now spending more time with Marie than with Sido. The family intervened once more, and on August 3, 1857, Marie married Jean Cèbe, fourteen years her junior. Jean declared Antonin Miton to be his own son, a son he would have fathered when he was barely fourteen. The family settled Marie, her husband, and her son Antonin in a little house that shared a common wall with Sido's garden. Saint-Sauveur had ethics of its own. Proprieties were kept and Marie was next door to help when Jules got out of hand. She was the only one able to calm him down. Marie and Cèbe lived in the house until they died. They had no children besides Antonin. Jean Cèbe was an ardent Republican. When the fourteenth of

July became a national holiday celebrated in every French village, he strolled the streets followed by his white dog, its head painted blue, its hind legs and tail a glorious red. The tricolor dog became part of Saint-Sauveur's folklore.

Jules was becoming more and more saturnine, riding in the woods for hours, hunting or simply watching the seasons go by. Even when he was unable to manage his properties efficiently, the rhythm of the yearly chores and the relationship between master and farmers remained unaltered. There was an entrenched loyalty to a family farmers had served for generations. The rents were paid in kind at fixed dates — after the harvest, after the gathering of grapes. Country life was collective, extremely sociable, and highly structured. Sido, a brilliant conversationalist and atheist whose favorite pastime was chess, who read Parisian and Belgian newspapers, who, when obliged for social reasons to go to church, replaced her prayer book with the plays of Corneille, made the plain people of Saint-Sauveur uneasy.

In the fall there were daily hunting parties. The local gentry hunted boars and wolves, ending the hunts with banquets during which wonderful tales were told. Sido loved them and passed that love on to Colette. She told her of the fox who took grass in his mouth so as not to drown while he let himself slowly sink into a pond to get rid of his fleas, and of the famished wolf who one summer followed Sido and her husband for five hours as they rode in their carriage. She learned the signs of the changing seasons and how to foretell the weather. In 1908 she wrote to Colette that she felt qualified to judge whether or not Rudyard Kipling had really seen all the animals he described so well, for she had spent "some ten years of her life among hunters."[41] She had the enthusiasm of a city girl for the things of nature and never ceased to marvel at the beauty of the outdoors.

But she craved culture, refinement, ideas, a life she could only find in Paris or Brussels. There she indulged in concerts, plays, and exhibitions. "In one week, she would see the newly exhumed mummy, the new wing of the museum, the new department store, hear music from Burma." Sido had "her soul focused on Paris. Parisian theaters, fashion, Parisian events were neither indifferent nor alien to her."[42] She had for them "an aggressive passion." She often traveled to Paris, where she had many friends. She bought silk dresses, furs, "very expensive gloves," shopped at the most chic grocers and spice stores, and spent money lavishly.

Sido was no Emma Bovary; she was witty, outspoken, well read. She created a stir wherever she went, she charmed, she mesmerized. She never did or said anything quite the way she was supposed to. In a letter to Colette she wrote that the mere idea of a daily schedule made her yawn. Her fleeting gray eyes were quick to see, quick to catch a change in someone's expression. She would notice the unnoticed, say what no one dared to say. She could not be intimidated or forced to change her mind. Her friends admired her eagerness for all new things; but she was sometimes harshly criticized, said "to be scatterbrained, to be disorderly," to be unable to run a home decently, to be "a disastrous housewife," "to spend madly." Even with an income of "ten times twelve thousand she could not afford the careless life she was leading."[43] She found a convenient source of money in a young lawyer, Adrien Jarry, the brother of her best friend and confidant, Adrienne Jarry. He lent Sido over eighty thousand gold francs and he was also her lover.

Even in Saint-Sauveur, Sido led an active social life. Invitations came from the Château des Baronets, one mile south of Saint-Sauveur, which belonged to Monsieur de la Cour, former ambassador to Turkey and commander of the Legion of Honor; from the Château de Ratilly in Treigny, only a few miles away, property of the Viviens, who remained lifelong friends of Sido; from the Château des Gouttes, home of Octavie Vathaire, Sido's childhood playmate; from the Château des Jarrets. A Parisian banker and local politician, Mr. Fremy, owned the Château de l'Orme du Pont and the Château des Bennes. But the real castle was the thirteenth-century Château of Saint-Fargeau. Enlarged and modernized through the centuries, it was a place that bred opposition; it had belonged to Anne Marie Louise d'Orléans, better known as La Grande Mademoiselle, who rebelled against King Louis XIV and ordered her troops to fire on her royal cousin from the battlements of the Bastille. The last duke of Saint-Fargeau voted for the death of Louis XVI and was murdered by the king's bodyguard the day after Louis was guillotined. The revolutionaries made him a "freedom martyr." Then the manager of his château, Monsieur Lacour, claimed it as his own. Sido must have felt at ease within those rebellious walls. She was a frequent guest at Saint-Fargeau, as is attested in local correspondence.

Jules's first cousin, Victor Gandrille, was a millionaire bachelor who owned the Château de Saint-Sauveur. He spent part of the year in his residence in Paris and part in Saint-Sauveur, where he seduced many young girls and numerous wives and made lasting enemies. When this Don Juan tried to be elected mayor, he was defeated "because he had enraged so many fathers and husbands."[44]

The eccentric millionaire bachelor[45] was very fond of Sido and always took her side when her interests were at stake. He had been one of the plotters who had arranged her marriage to Jules. He may have become her lover, but there was so much jealousy and scandal surrounding Sido that it could have been gossip. According to the imperial prosecutor, she had several lovers, one of them being "a very wealthy taxpayer."[46]

Three and a half years after her wedding Sido had a daughter — the long-awaited heir to Jules's estate. She was named Juliette Héloise Emilie: Juliette for her father, Héloise for Jean-Jacques Rousseau's famous heroine, whose fate women had mourned for half a century. Juliette was dark, with thick, jet black hair, large black eyes, and features that re-minded Sido of her ancestors from the tropical islands.

Captain Colette: "Born to Seduce and to Fight . . .
He Was a Poet and a Man of the World"

The year of Juliette's birth, an unexpected character appeared in the midst of all these interrelated families. Jules-Joseph Colette was a war hero straight from the victorious armies of Napoleon III, who had lost his left leg at the battle of Melegnano. Captain Colette swept Sido into a passionate love affair. It happens, she would muse later, that some people fling themselves into your life, upset your existence, thwart your plans — "This is what your father did to my life."[47]

What were the plans thwarted by Captain Colette? In 1860 Sido's only concern was to keep her husband out of her life. She found it con-venient to let Jules indulge in a twenty-four-hour-a-day drunken haze. "Do you know," wrote Jean-Paul Sartre to Simone de Beauvoir in 1939, "that Sido, Colette's famous mother, had simply poisoned her husband to marry Mr. Colette, a local gay blade?" Sartre was visiting the Emerys, cousins of Jules Robineau-Duclos, who told him what had been whis-pered for years. "Jules liked to drink but had been forbidden to do so because he had a cirrhosis of the liver. Mr. Colette appeared and from that day on, Sido's husband found flasks of brandy or cognac, bottles of burgundy, glasses of absinthe everywhere."[48]

Sido became pregnant and bore a son on January 27, 1863. No one doubted that the father was Captain Colette, but legally he was Jules's son. He was named Edme Jules Achille Robineau-Duclos; Edme after Marshal Edme de Mac-Mahon, a man deeply admired by Captain Colette, who spent years writing his biography. Jules was the name of both the legitimate and illegitimate fathers. Achille was the name of the greatest warrior of *The Iliad*. Robineau was no warrior, but Captain Colette was.

Captain Jules Colette was a southerner, born in 1829 in Mourillon near Toulon, on the Mediterranean coast. He came from a navy family — his grandfather, Jacques Colette, had died as a prisoner of war on the reddened deck of a British ship. His father, a captain in the navy, spent seven years as an administrator in Guiana, the French penal colony in South America. He lived in Cayenne with his wife, Thérèse, and his two children, Jules and Magdaleine.

Jules Colette did not follow the family tradition. He chose the army and in 1847 was admitted to the prestigious military academy of Saint-Cyr, which had a total enrollment of three hundred and fifty men. The competitive entrance examination was extremely difficult. The studies lasted two years and the core curriculum comprised mathematics, physics, chemistry, drawing, topography, history, geography, military administration, and artillery. To complete their education, the cadets had to take two languages — German and English — literature, fencing, dancing, and horseback riding. They rose at 4:30 A.M. and went to bed at 8:15 P.M. Discipline was strict. At the end of two years they graduated with the rank of second lieutenant. They wore the distinctive uniform of Saint-Cyr: red trousers, long blue coats, red epaulettes, and tall caps with a white plume.

Saint-Cyriens were known for their pranks, so cruel and rough that some first-year students preferred to leave the school rather than be subjected to their seniors' ruthless tricks. The cadets' meeting place in Paris was Le Café Hollandais in the red-light district of the Palais Royal; they prohibited entrance to anyone they disliked, hissing, barking, grunting, or singing obscene songs. The special train that took them back to Saint-Cyr was the nightmare of the Northern Railroad Company. They repeatedly tore down the partitions of the carriages and threw them out the windows. "United we stand" was their alleged reason for vandalism. No one dared board *le train des Saints-Cyriens*.

The Saint-Cyriens were divided into small fraternities named after their native provinces. Some had political affiliations. Their rivalries — political or not — were so fierce that even a stare could start a duel. Cadet Colette had joined the fraternity of Charles Bourbaki, a future general, who became his military mentor. Bourbaki belonged to the Society of the Carbonari, a network of secret associations throughout France and Italy. Jules Colette joined the Carbonari, who were experiencing their hour of glory. Louis Napoleon Bonaparte had been a Carbonaro and kept very strong ties with the organization. As a young prince exiled to Italy, he fought with the revolutionaries who attempted to oust the pope from Rome and the Austrians from Italy. He had caught the romantic imagination of many young middle-class liberals, who found the bourgeois King Louis-Phillipe lacking in luster. His friends were actively recruiting in the military academies.

Jules Colette, a strapping fellow with fair hair, a beautiful baritone voice, and all the ebullience of his native south, was one of the most restive young men in his class. In 1847 he was expelled and reduced to the rank of private in a regiment of enlisted men, a supreme dishonor in the elitist academy. It was the specific punishment for fighting a duel in which one of the cadets was killed. At Saint-Cyr duels were strictly prohibited.

The duel between Jules Colette and his opponent may have been motivated by political infighting. It certainly took raw courage. Duels at Saint-Cyr were traditionally fought by bayonet, but after the death of several cadets the school administration ordered all bayonets removed from the muskets. This did not stop the cadets. They devised a weapon: a broomstick split into two at one end, to which they fastened a pair of compasses. They fought at night in the dark, in the attic, on a landing, behind a door — anyplace they hoped not to be discovered. Their fights were noiseless, vicious, merciless. They knew that if the thin blade penetrated the chest, the wound would be fatal, not being large enough for the blood to gush out; the wounded cadet hemorrhaged internally and died within days.

To be expelled from such an elitist corps, to see his dreams shattered, was a traumatic experience for Jules Colette. He tried to prepare for the entrance exam to L'Ecole Polytechnique, another highly selective French school. He published an article on spheric trigonometry in the school journal, *Les Nouvelles Annales de Mathématiques*. He changed the spelling of his name to J. Collete. The year was 1848, and a third French revolution was about to topple the last king. Nineteen-year-old Jules joined the victorious mob. Later, when he went into politics, he liked to recall those days in a rousing prose. "This Republican of long standing, this inveterate democrat is the one who stood at L'Hôtel de Ville side by side with Lamartine, Arago, Ledru-Rollin . . . ."[49] Jules Colette knew how to interpret history to his own advantage.

His father intervened and the youthful revolutionary was transferred to the Third Regiment of Marine Infantry, which was to leave for French Guiana, a tough assignment and a way to be forgotten while friends appealed his case. One year later Jules was back at Saint-Cyr. He graduated in 1850 and ranked 138th out of 150. Second Lieutenant Colette threw himself into his military career with the same bravado he had put into fighting his duel. He looked like "a Cossack" with his snub nose, small catlike eyes, clear and terrible under the bushy eyebrows, "those gray-blue eyes which no one has ever been able to read."[50] Like "a Cossack" he loved war. After seventeen months spent with the Thirty-eighth Regiment of Infantry, he asked to be transferred to the newly created First Regiment of Zouaves in Algeria, whose commanding officer was his mentor, Colonel Bourbaki. Named after a North African Berber tribe, the Zouaves were noted for their strict discipline, fighting ability, and exotic oriental costumes. They wore wide red trousers, blue tunics with pleated skirts, large leather belts, and red caps. They favored fierce moustaches.

By 1848 Algeria had been virtually conquered and declared a French territory. From all over Europe, young aristocrats and rich bourgeois sons were enlisting in the French army, lured by propaganda of action and glory. However, they found themselves protecting the construction of the first railroad and defending the new colonists — mainly unemployed Parisians with government grants — against guerilla warfare from wandering tribes. Some were disillusioned: "Wherever the French turned up in Africa, the trees disappeared, the wells dried up, the inhabitants fled, and all that remained was the desert."[51]

When not pacifying rebel Kabyls, the Zouaves took part in colorful parades to impress the local population. Life in officers' clubs was easygoing and boisterous, but that was soon to change. In 1854 France, England, and Turkey declared war on Russia. Jules Colette's First Zouave Regiment embarked for the battlefields of Crimea from Toulon, where the Army of the Orient had been regrouped. (He loved to tell his children about his military feats. In a moving short story, "The Zouave," Colette described him as a jolly fellow who laughed away all the hardships of a short but murderous war.) An epidemic of cholera had broken out in the south of France and the disease spread with the troops. A whole regiment of Turkish mercenaries, the Bashi-Bouzouks, were found in a village, lying dead in the streets. In Constantinople three hundred men died in a single night. The Zouaves retreated to the shore. On their way, soldiers shoveling earth to dig graves would collapse and be buried with the others. When they reached the sea, some, burning with fever, rushed to the water and drowned in their bulky uniforms, never reaching the ship *Calypso*. Soldiers died from typhus and cholera in such numbers that their plight touched Florence Nightingale, who, with British efficiency, organized a group of volunteer nurses and sailed to Constantinople.

(Jules Colette's tale of the epidemic became a cruel "Gallic farce." "I convinced Guillemin, that nut, that he was turning green and had no more than two hours to live! He believed it, he was there seated in the snow, holding his belly, wriggling. . . . I would not have traded my place for an invitation to the Tuileries."[52])

At Alma Jules led the victorious assault against a telegraphic tower held by the Russians, was knocked down by a bullet, and got some bruises on his chest. He was promoted to first lieutenant by the French and awarded the Crimean Medal by the British.

The Zouaves were ordered to assault Fort Malakoff. They rushed forward with such determination that thirty minutes later the flag of the First Regiment of Zouaves floated over the fort. The following day Sebastopol, in rubble, was evacuated by the Russians. Jules was promoted to captain and given his third stripe. To celebrate their victory, the Parisians built a new bridge, Le Pont de l'Alma, with a gigantic statue of a Zouave; ever since, they have measured the flood level of the Seine by how much of the Zouave stands above the waters.

Captain Colette went back to North Africa to pacify the Kabyls, who had refused to surrender, and won the Africa Medal. Then his regiment was sent to Italy, since Napoleon III, the former Carbonaro, was still haunted by his youthful dream of freeing Italy from the Austrians. Should he succeed, he could claim as his prize the provinces of Savoy and Nice on the French Riviera. The French did dislodge the Austrians from Milan, but while cheering crowds were dancing in the streets there, General Canrobert, whose idle armies had not shared in the victory, decided to deal a final blow to the retreating Austrians. A thousand soldiers died on the flat road to Melegnano, easy targets for the Austrians. Many were wounded; Captain Colette had his left leg crushed at the thigh. Two Zouaves carried him to safety.

"Where do you want us to put you?"

"In the middle of the battlefield under the flag."[53]

Colette gave a more histrionic version. "One day he was wounded, left abandoned alone in a ditch, one of his men came back to look for him, put him on his back and carried him away under fire. As he walked, the soldier heard above his head the laughter of the wounded man, who was pulling the private's hair by the handful, saying: 'Four days in the stockade for Private Fournes! First: wears his hair too long, second: lacks respect for his Captain.'"

The following day an endless flow of carriages and coaches rolled through the gates of Milan to Melegnano, fifteen miles away. As a gesture of thanks to their liberators, the ladies of Milan went in search of the wounded and brought them into their homes. Nothing was spared for their well-being and romance flourished. "Ah! my friend! Those Milanese women! What memories! It was the most beautiful year of my life,"[54] reminisced Captain Colette. But on June 9, he had his left leg amputated. Napoleon III, on a visit to the wounded, stopped at the bedside of the twenty-nine-year-old captain whose military future had been blown away:

"I would like to do something for you."

"Give me a crutch, Sire," was the terse answer.

He received the Cross of the Legion of Honor and a sinecure as tax collector in the small town of Saint-Sauveur — a modest "crutch."

He was a charmer, and the best society of the Puisaye opened its door, eager to greet a hero acquainted with Field Marshal Mac-Mahon. Had not the emperor himself pinned the Legion of Honor on his chest? Barely a year after his arrival in Saint-Sauveur, the strapping new tax collector had fathered an illegitimate child with the attractive Madame Robineau-Duclos. That same year on May 17, Captain Colette was notified that he was suspended and was to be replaced by Monsieur Pichon, probably for political reasons. Political opposition to Napoleon III had never stopped. The masses of industrial workers were increasingly attracted to the socialist theories of Proudhon, Marx, and Bakunin. In the 1863 election, opposition candidates had polled about two million votes, mainly in big cities, and were pressing for a return to full parliamentary rule. Colette, a former Carbonaro, had made his Republican views widely known and was paying for it, but he had powerful friends. The minister of finance himself wrote to the prefect of the department that a number of people had approached him on the captain's behalf. On June 13, the minister rescinded the suspension order. But a year later Colette was refused a two-week paid leave of absence to go to his sister's funeral in Toulon. His supervisor wrote in his annual evaluation that Monsieur Colette lacked zeal and enthusiasm. He recovered overdue taxes lazily and late, and many proofs of negligence had been noted in his administration. In spite of this, the head tax collector wrote in his report to the minister that the Saint-Sauveur office was well managed. Captain Colette learned his lesson; in 1874 he supported a Bonapartist candidate against a Republican.

On January 30, 1865, after eight years of marriage, Jules Robineau-Duclos died. He had not called his servant that day and was found lying on his bed; he had died the previous night.

All day long farmers, neighbors, and family flocked to the wake. They sat, chatted, drank, and ate. It was a unique opportunity to satisfy their curiosity, to enter the white and gilt parlor, to glance at the luxuries surrounding Sido, and to see how she expressed her grief, if at all. Jules Robineau-Duclos was buried the following day, since it was customary in rural France to bury the dead within twenty-four hours. Men on one side and women on the other followed the horse-drawn, richly decorated hearse, stamped with Robineau-Duclos initials. For Sido it was the end of an era, one she would come to look back on with nostalgia — it had meant wealth, freedom to do as she pleased, and a well-defined, privileged social status.

Captain Colette was elated; he told Sido that he would put a bullet in her head if she did not marry him. Losing all sense of propriety, they openly flaunted their relationship. Colette took over the management of Robineau's estate. In order to clear the way for his marriage, he sent the girl he had seduced and her child to Paris and started to staff the family council which was to administer Juliette's and Achille's inheritance with "people blindly devoted to Mrs. Robineau-Duclos." Victor Gandrille, Sido's unfailing protector, made several trips to persuade Givry to accept in the council a friend of Sido, Monsieur Vivien, the owner of the Château de Ratigny. Another was convinced to give his power of attorney to a newly established lawyer in Saint-Sauveur, Monsieur de Fourolle, Captain

Colette's lawyer and — according to the local judge — very eager to count wealthy Sido among his clients.

Captain Colette was trying to oust Adrien Jarry, the lawyer representing the estate, who not only had been Sido's lover and "bragged about it," but held eighty thousand gold francs in notes secured by the estate. Furthermore, Jarry represented Marie Cèbe, née Miton, who had produced a will in the handwriting of Jules Robineau-Duclos giving her furniture, linens, two hundred and seventy-five bushels of wheat, and ten thousand gold francs. In his will Jules Robineau-Duclos had also imposed on his legitimate heirs the obligation of paying an insurance premium on Antonin's life, with his mother as beneficiary.

Sido attacked the will's validity and filed a lawsuit. At this point the local judge, Judge Crançon, legal chairman of the family council representing the financial interests of the two Robineau-Duclos children and official guardian of public morals, wrote a long report to the imperial justice stating "the people of Saint-Sauveur who are used to witness many immoral behaviors are scandalized by so much lewdness, by such disregard for common decency."

Sido's every move was causing a scandal. A few weeks after her husband's death she had gone to Brussels to seek advice from her brothers, leaving Juliette and Achille in the care of Captain Colette, who was supervising "the many workers" he had hired to entirely remodel Sido's house. Except for Victor Gandrille, most of her in-laws were now shunning her. The scandal reached its peak when Captain Colette taught Achille to stand to attention and shout, "I am Colette the second." "Of the two children," wrote Judge Crançon, "Mr. Colette treats the eldest who is a little girl rather harshly while he shows a lot of concern for the little boy whom he considers as his own." Judge Crançon chastised the Givrys, who could not wait to put their hands on Robineau-Duclos's estate; he chastized the Robineau clan, who had used their wealth and influence in a power game whose pawn was "a stuttering half-wit, ugly beyond description"; and he questioned Captain Colette's motives.

To the judge's surprise even the captain's mother, who came to witness the impending wedding babbled about her son. "If we believe Madame Colette, her son is a spendthrift who has ruined his family. She sacrificed for him the interest of her daughter who has just died leaving several children and no estate." The judge felt that Captain Colette's income of six thousand francs did not match the one hundred and twenty thousand francs of Madame Robineau-Duclos. In his mind, Captain Colette's duty was to support his deceased sister's children and his own illegitimate child, discreetly hidden in Paris.

As for Sido, the judge declared: "Madame Robineau is a woman without order, no sense of husbandry, incapable of running a house. She has five servants, three women and two men, which is a lot for an income of a twelve times ten thousand francs." By the end of November, the family council was called to determine if it was in the best interest of the children to maintain "the widow Robineau-Duclos" as one of the trustees of her children's estate. "This is a serious question since forests comprise more than half of their fortune. An unskilled manager or one who is a pleasure-seeker can depress their value either by making premature cuttings or by logging the reserve."[55] The question was as much about Sido herself as about Captain Colette's managerial skills and personal morals. But this attempt to exclude Sido failed and Judge Crançon's foresight proved true. The Colettes plunged into the good life with renewed gusto. The friendly family council never questioned the captain's management of the estate.

On December 20, 1865, Sido and Captain Colette were married in the city hall of Saint-Sauveur at eight in the evening. They immediately traveled to Belgium for a religious ceremony, followed by a reception in the elegant home of Eugène and Caroline Landoy.

On October 22, 1866, their first legitimate son, Léopold Jean Colette, was born in Saint-Sauveur. Sido's longing for Belgium was so great that she named her son after Léopold, king of Belgium.

II

"What a queen of the world I was at age twelve."
LE MIROIR

SIDONIE-GABRIELLE COLETTE was born at 10 P.M. on
January 28, 1873. Sido was thirty-eight, Captain Colette forty-four,
Juliette thirteen, Achille ten, and Léo seven.

After three days and two nights of labor, "my mother expelled me
from her womb, but since I arrived all blue and silent, nobody took care
of me . . ." Everybody's attention was turned to Sido, and the servants,
after several sleepless nights, were all exhausted. According to Colette, it
was "my own self-determination and sheer will which started my life."[1]

Her birth certificate states that "Jules Colette, tax collector, has presented an infant of female sex, born in his house." A Napoleonic law required that the sex of each newborn child be verified within three days at
city hall so that France would not be cheated out of future soldiers. Many
people who wanted their sons to work on the farm had them registered as
girls to avoid the draft.

Born in a well-to-do family, Gabri was not taken to city hall on a cold
winter day; Victor Gandrille, the ever-present friend, signed the birth certificate. The other witness, Colonel Desandré (soon to become General
Desandré), was Captain Colette's personal friend; three weeks earlier, the

captain had been Desandré's witness at his marriage to the heiress of the Château des Janets. General Desandré and his wife, Eugénie, were Gabrielle's godparents, but since they were unable to come to her baptism on April 11, 1874, Achille and Juliette acted as their substitutes.

Gabri had two wet nurses. Early in January Madame Jollet from the Thureau farm had given birth to her fourth child, Yvonne, who as "Claire" is the beloved foster-sister "with beautiful, tender eyes and a romantic soul"[2] in *Claudine at School*. All through their lives, Gabri and Yvonne wrote to each other. Their last letter is dated February, 1954; both died that year.

Gabri's second nurse was Emilie Fleury, nicknamed Mélie. She appears under that name in *Claudine at School* and its four sequels. She had given birth a month earlier to an illegitimate child; she was herself illegitimate and had been adopted by her mother's husband, Monsieur Fleury, a Saint-Sauveur carpenter. Sido took her in, creating an uproar in Saint-Sauveur. To her friend Madame de Saint-Aubin, she explained: "It is not such an offense to help an unrepentant and beautiful girl with a fruitful belly."[3] Mélie stayed for four years as a nurse, married the gardener, left for a while, and then came back as a cook.

Sido insisted that she came from a very distinguished family and instilled in her children the belief that they were different from the common people of Saint-Sauveur. They ate exotic fruits, such as oranges and bananas, that most children in the village had never seen. At Christmas they did not have the traditional black pudding or turkey with chestnuts, but a dainty cake decorated with different kinds of raisins from Smyrna, Corinth, and Malaga and stuffed with candied melon, citron, and oranges. For Sido gastronomy bordered on philosophy. It was the first precept of a Fourierist education, which started by careful training of the senses at an early age. Next to love, the most powerful passion was *gourmandise*. Children should be taught to recognize and develop their tastes for particular dishes, flavors, and dressings. *Gourmandise* went beyond the discriminatory delight of satisfying one's hunger — it was gratification of all five senses. The aroma of the food should please the olfactory sense; its texture, the sense of touch; its color and display should appeal to the eye. Even the ear participated in the pleasure of the gourmet, as the food crackled on the grill, and the wine or water tinkled into crystal glasses. Colette described herself using her senses expertly as a child to enhance her pleasure. To better enjoy the Christmas cake, she called up her memory of Christmas past: "Didn't I summon to the help of my taste buds the immutable color of the carpet and the lampshades, the whining of the easterly wind under the door, the smell of a beautiful new volume and the grain of its slightly gummy cover?"[4] In a Fourierist perspective, Colette stressed the perfect orchestration of her fine-tuned senses; she enjoyed the recreation of the moment, well aware that such sensual delight — "the joy of the five senses!" — would be branded as pagan.

Gabri was not yet three when Captain Colette filled her silver goblet with "muscatel from Frontignan . . . At the age when I started to learn my letters, I learned to spell drop by drop vintage red Bordeaux, dazzling Château Yquem. Then it would be the turn of Champagne. . . . Daintily I drained the best of my father's cellar goblet by goblet."[5] She was the only one of the Colettes to love wines. Captain Colette did not drink, Sido drank a glass of wine on special occasions only, and Léo preferred heavy syrups.

Sido's children, like "little *harmonians*," were encouraged to expect even the simplest food to be prepared to their exact specifications; they were never coerced into eating anything they did not choose. As an afternoon snack Gabri demanded a drumstick, a thick layer of beans cooked in wine, and a piece of hard cheese. On Sundays, when the French traditionally gathered for festive fare, Captain Colette favored salads and vegetables, Léo ate sweet buns laden with jam and sipped thick hot chocolate, and Gabri wanted anything with lots of garlic. She never lost her taste for the pungent bulb and would later brag of eating forty cloves for lunch.

Variety and lightness were the hallmarks of Fourierist cuisine, emphasizing the consumption of natural foods, particularly vegetables and fruits, some fowl, and fat-free meat at a time when French gastronomy was becoming an institution. These were the days of the great gourmets Antonin Carême and Brillat-Savarin, whom Fourier called an ignoramus for not knowing that gastronomy was not only an art, but a science and branch of hygiene.

Fourier pioneered health foods as dietary remedies and recommended jams, fine liquors, and other delicacies as preventative medicines. He called these "attractive medicines," since pleasure was a healer. Colette recounted that when she was barely five and running a very high fever, she refused to take milk, fruit, or broth and cured herself by demanding

Camembert over the doctor's objections. In *The Evening Star* (L'Etoile Vesper) she credits hot pepper for the instant cure of a severe attack of fever during a trip to Tunisia. There is not a book by Colette without a paragraph in praise of food and its power as an expression of love, bond maker, source of happiness, and healer in time of crisis. As Colette grew older, she believed even more strongly in "gastrosophy" and changed friends' and lovers' eating habits, taking credit for their improved health.

Elegance was also extremely important. Sido went to Paris to buy gowns, hats, and "very expensive gloves." She was proud of her sartorial chic, the trademark of the Landoys. Even in her old age, she wore the latest fashion. When she tended her garden, she put on a large hat of very fine reddish straw with a ribbon of brown silk. She educated Gabri in the subtle art of being chic.

A friend of the family, a painter from Lyons known for his etchings, made a pastel of eighteen-month-old Gabri with her hand on an open book and a ribbon "à la Vigée-Lebrun" in her hair. This was the first of many paintings and sculptures of Colette by some of the most fashionable artists of the time. When she was five, Sido took her to Auxerre to have a picture taken, and she posed so gracefully that the photographer called to his wife, "Come, come and see the little jewel we have here!" [6] In her pictures she never smiled, and had a sad, dreamy look on her face, but — imitating Sido — she always delicately displayed her hands.

What most strongly set the Colettes apart was the way they traveled, going to Toulon, Lyons, Paris, and Brussels. The French traveled little in those days; there was no railroad station in Saint-Sauveur until the 1880s. Most villagers had never even seen a train, and most women had never been further than the county seat, Saint-Fargeau, four miles away. A trip to Auxerre, where Sido went every three months, was an expedition few could afford. To take the train cost money, and people preferred to walk or ride on the exceptionally well-kept French roads. Every male of eighteen to sixty had to work three days a year on the roads or pay his way out.

The Colettes spent lavishly on their travels. In 1878 Gabri, five and a half, was thought old enough to go to Paris to see the Exposition Universelle. It was the showcase of the Third Republic, proclaimed three years earlier. Its main attractions were the installed gaslights flooding the residence of the French president, the hippodrome, and the newly finished Place de la Concorde. Every Republican lit up his windows with colored lanterns; the Bonapartist windows remained dark. On Republican holidays Captain Colette never failed to make "paper lanterns decorated with emblems that he hung in the trees,"[7] but the political significance was lost on Gabri, who found her father "childish."

Captain Colette was ebullient now that Marshal Mac-Mahon was president. Many of his friends were in the government and he was determined to launch his own political career. His political advisor and close friend was Paul Bert, a liberal senator soon to be appointed minister of education. He shared with Captain Colette a deep admiration for Victor Considérant, who was back in Paris after his failed attempt to establish a Fourierist society in Texas. Julie and Victor had settled at 48 Rue du Cardinal Lemoine on the Left Bank. They struggled to make a living, Julie as a painter, Victor as the foreign corespondent for *L'Echo du Parlement Belge*. He refused several offers to run for the National Assembly, and each year flew a large American flag on the fourth of July as the symbol of a national system protecting individual freedoms. Liberals came to him for guidance and inspiration. Captain Colette, who saw in politics "a way to amount to something,"[8] took part in the new socialist effervescence. After making contacts in Paris, the Colettes went to Brussels to visit the Landoys.

Gabri loved her uncle's house at 25 Rue Botanique. She enjoyed the warmth of this typically Belgian home, where comfort was as important as beauty and refinement. In the middle of the drawing room stood Aunt Caroline's concert grand piano. The armchairs, large and deep, the sturdy cabinet, the heavy tables of exotic wood, waxed and polished until they reflected the copper pitchers and the paintings on the walls, enchanted Gabri. When she furnished her first apartment, she chose Dutch furniture.

The Landoys' home had kept some of the exotic Caribbean touch — Jean the monkey, who had been the family pet when Sido was a girl, had been replaced by green and gray parrots. On cushions and sofa there were also imposing Persian cats. "All the Landoys felt a mysterious adoration for that sacred animal. . . . Their relationship with the animal kingdom was their common trademark: a true Landoy loved animals, large or small, great or humble."[9] A daguerreotype showed Eugène Landoy the elder with a parakeet on his shoulder.

Gabri was a silent, well-behaved child. Sido had no patience with "the indecent tears of childhood." She was happy that Minet Chéri, her "darling kitten," her "golden jewel," her "radiant sunshine" already knew so many things and could discuss them so cleverly. Gabri liked to sit on a little stool at her mother's feet, her head leaning against her knee, and listen. She noticed that in Brussels, Sido was different; she argued, laughed, and sparkled in Aunt Caroline's salon among the artists and journalists. As Gabri grew up, she noticed more and more that Sido was first and foremost a Landoy. She constantly praised her brothers, maintaining a correspondence with them and her Belgian friends. She subscribed to her brothers' newspapers, read their books, adopted their philosophy, and expected her children to do the same. Eugène had launched *L'Office de Publicité,* a newspaper entirely financed by advertising. This was a new concept, and he made a fortune. Always an idealist and philanthropist, he initiated a campaign to create shelters for the children of poor working mothers and homeless children, tapping his large readership. Donations came pouring in. He presided over this charitable organization until his death.

Soon after their trip to Brussels, their old friend Julie Considérant died. Years later Sido still remembered the drama that ensued — overnight, Julie's body became so swollen it could not fit in the ebony coffin with solid silver handles that Considérant had bought at great cost. He gave the magnificent casket to Julie's best friend, Caroline Landoy, as a memorial of his beloved wife. Caro shuddered at the gift and passed it on to her chambermaid. Sido was furious at her sister-in-law: "Why didn't she give it to me? I love luxury...."[10]

I Never Had Friends of My Kind

In the fall of 1879 Sido and the captain saw an opportunity to demonstrate their liberal, Republican, and anticlerical feelings — they decided to enroll Gabri in the newly opened lay school. It has been assumed that Gabri was sent to this lay school, which plays such a central role in her works, because of the Colettes' dwindling wealth. The fact is that their financial difficulties started five years later, after Juliette's marriage.

It was obvious that Gabri was not like the other students. In the first photograph taken in the schoolyard she is dressed in a fancy oversized Eton collar, cuffs of Belgian lace, a velvet vest, and a pleated silk skirt over bloomers hemmed with lace. Her schoolmates, daughters of local shopkeepers, noncommissioned officers, and farmers smelled so awfully, according to Colette, "that after three hours of studies, the odors were enough to knock you out."[11] Wealthy people sent their children to private boarding schools in Auxerre or in Paris, but students fared no better there. Her two brothers, who were attending college in Auxerre, came back for the vacations angry, thin, and pale "with fleabites in summer and frostbite in winter." Juliette came back home from her private school "looking poor and mean."[12]

In Saint-Sauveur the rival school was Catholic. Students were divided along political and religious lines; when they met, they made faces at each other, hissed, or even fought. Traditionally, the clergy had been in charge of parochial schools, but the Republic found their instruction lacking. The church was pictured as keeping the masses in the dark to have a hold on them. After the collapse of the Second Empire, the partisans of the Third Republic had vociferously opposed the Catholic church, which was supported by the monarchists and Bonapartists, and broke its monopoly on elementary education. They pointed to the high degree of illiteracy — seventeen percent of the draftees could neither read nor write, and twenty-five percent of the brides could not sign their name and marked their marriage certificates with a cross. The village schools became a hotbed of lay Republicanism, although the new Republic taught its children to read in *The Little Book of Sacred History* for lack of elementary primers. "That year we learned to read in the New Testament, the old Mlle. Fanny banging her ruler on her desk, punctuating the sacred syllables that we chanted: 'In! those! days! Je!-sus! said! to! his! dis!-cip!-les! . . .'"[13]

The Saint-Sauveur school had thirty-eight students, two teachers, and two classrooms. It was located on Monsieur Paultre's estate, which had just been bought by city hall. The main building housed the girls, the stables the boys. The Republic had a different program of instruction for each gender.

Gabri felt important. "I never had any friends of my kind."[14] She was the token Republican pupil from a wealthy family and was given preferential treatment. She became the standard-bearer for the school, the one who gave the bunch of flowers to the mayor, the one who recited poems on special occasions, poems usually written by Captain Colette. She was also the smartest and was called upon to answer the dreaded questions of the inspector general of schools on his visits. She loved going to school. Here was the theater where she could play out her fantasies, where she could upstage everybody. Summer vacations made her "languid with the desire to go back to school. September! September!"[15]

Gabri was a precocious child; at twenty-one months she knew her letters (no wonder Stephane Baron had chosen to paint her as a toddler with her hand on a book). Captain Colette had a large library, which Gabri was free to explore. Everyone in the house was a voracious reader, so no one was surprised that she could read. Instead, they were surprised that it took her so long "to adopt interesting books."[16] At six she was given Balzac to read. She called him "my cradle, my forest, my travels." In an interview in 1949 she acknowledged that "I was born in Balzac. . . . I dwelled in Balzac."[17] Sido owned a tiepin that had belonged to Honoré de Balzac. "Once in a while," wrote Colette, "I would ask my mother to allow me to see Balzac's tiepin . . . a reddish pearl of sard girdled by a gold snake."[18] It was no coincidence that Balzac was part of Colette's education. A contemporary of Fourier's, he called him "one of the great innovators, like Jesus" for having "broken with all the past" and for having envisioned a new society ruled by passions.

Sido, whose favorite reading was Saint-Simon's *Memoirs* in eighteen volumes, asked Colette: "Why don't you read Saint-Simon?" and was astonished that Gabri, at eight, did not yet share her fascination with the intrigues of the court of Louis XIV. She allowed her to read anything she wanted. "You should wait a year or two . . . well! Sort it out yourself, darling Kitten. You are intelligent enough not to talk about what you will understand too much. After all, maybe there are no bad books." And Sido gave her one by one the complete works of Zola, which Captain Colette did not want Gabri to read, for the sole reason that "Zola bored him."[19]

Gabri's favorite stories were travelers' tales that told how to wrestle with alligators under water "chest to chest" or how to catch a snake asleep on the roof of a straw hut, twirl it around, and smash its brains on a stone. In her seventies, Colette, paralyzed by arthritis, still enjoyed the tales told by some traveler of the nineteenth century: "With him I hunt the lion, I save a hummingbird caught in the pincers of two oversized and ferocious ants and I delicately conquer on some gigantic branch between a starving python and a nest of wasps the extravagant *oncidieae* of Galeotti. . . ."[20] Her little playmates, who had never seen anything but the sloping streets of Saint-Sauveur and the misty ponds in the woods, listened open-mouthed to the tall tales of Gabri. Like Captain Colette, she was a born storyteller.

At eight, when she went to the circus, she decided she wanted to be a horsewoman galloping in the wind. She despised a frightened circus girl of barely five, whom she heard whimpering: "Enough, enough." She admired an acrobat of her own age who danced and performed somersaults on a horse. She promised herself that she would do everything others could do, only better, and knew at the age of eight that reward and anguish go together, that the best performance is the most dangerous, "that the point of honor is to put a life on the line."[21]

A Fourierist Education

The teachings of the lay school were not radical enough for Sido, who was determined to instill her own philosophy into her children's minds. She chipped away at everything Gabri learned at school. "She reshaped for us the whole image of human feelings."[22] She would illustrate her views by pointing to animals or plants to explain human behavior. Her first rule was "look but do not interfere,"[23] which Gabri found difficult — her curiosity was not intellectual like her mother's, but sensual. In *The Break of Day,* Colette contrasted her own need to touch, smell, and interfere with things and animals to her mother's noninterventionist attitude. Sido let the wisteria destroy the garden wall because that was the way plants were. Following the Fourierist precept that children should be led to appreciate the perfection of flowers and be entrusted with the protection of plants and animals, Sido scolded Gabri for digging up a chrysalis: "You are nothing but an eight-year-old little murderer."[24] She observed her children the way she observed nature, trying not to hamper their development. Traditional concepts like motherhood, fatherhood, and marriage were reexamined in a Fourierist perspective. The day Gabri talked about "the sacred love between mother and daughter,"[25] Sido immediately brushed it off, "a fleeting anger in her gray eyes." The "sacred love" did nothing but poison human relationship and turn mothers and daughters into liars and enemies. Once Gabri saw a kitten beating its mother and was appalled. Sido seized the occasion to show the true meaning of motherhood, her face lighting up "with that unscrutable and aggressive merriment" that so often puzzled Gabri.

"The times have come. What can we do? It is written."

"Written where?"

"Everywhere."

Gabri asked with some anguish if it was written that she would some day beat Sido. The answer was surprising. "No, I won't be young enough for that," said her mother, anticipating her old age and the dampening of her own emotions, "but you will leave me." This was the natural law, beyond which any notion of "sacred love" became a perversion, a passion turned awry. Colette illustrated this in "About Mothers and Children" (*Des Mères et des Enfants*), the story of Madame Thomazeau, who fell ill because her daughter got married. Sido called her "a harpy, a bad mother, an old hag, a dangerous lunatic, a faker, a criminal and that is only part of it." The emotional pressure she inflicted on her daughter was as unnatural and evil as witchcraft. According to Fourier, some of the worst aspects of civilization stemmed from *familism* — family passions imposed by the patriarchs as the affective norms on the rest of society. The insidious alliance of family passions with the institution of marriage repressed the autonomy of the individual. Not that family passions did not exist but, as illustrated by Sido's analysis of motherhood, they should never run beyond their natural course. If they did, they became subversive and turned a person into "a dangerous lunatic." Motherhood did not entail "an inalterable, rigid love dubbed sacred."

Gabri also learned that there was a place assigned to fathers and that it was not with young children. She cried when Sido pushed aside their hunting dog, a good-natured father who sat watchfully next to a basket full of his own puppies. "Poor Moffino," whimpered Gabri, "where do you want him to go?" Sido answered that a father's place was at the café, playing cards with a friend or flirting with a pretty seamstress. She mocked all the traditional values or beliefs that formed the core of village life. For instance, large families were much admired; every year the largest one received an award from the French president himself. Sido told Gabri that in large families the children seemed to be accumulated in a hurry and looked somewhat unfinished. When Gabri pointed out to her that the nine Pluvier children were all beautiful, her mother's curt answer was, "Beautiful, yes, a nightmare of beautiful children." France was implementing a natalist policy that went against Sido's beliefs. Women "were not meant to have such litters."[26] She spoke of a family of twenty-two as a plague, "an invasion."

A prolific father was nothing but "an old goat." Here Sido echoed Fourier, who despised "the carnal man" who recklessly produces children, "absolving himself, since it is God who sends them." But it is no excuse to ignore that God has endowed mankind with reason, intelligence, foresight, and prudence. "Man reduces himself to the level of an insect when he creates heaps of children who will be reduced to devouring one another because of their sheer numbers."[27] Fourier warned that it is vain to increase the means of productivity if mankind "is condemned to proliferate." Overpopulation brought about wars, plunders, and the ravage of the environment, "a plague" indeed. The "sensible man" wanted to have just a few children, in order to give them the wealth without which there was no happiness.

Fourier believed that strenuous exercise delayed the onset of puberty. Gymnastics and athletics were his chosen means of birth control in the harmonian society. "Integral gymnastics" for girls as well as boys was an innovation, and Sido had a complete gymnasium installed in her garden. Colette never stopped practicing the rings, the parallel bars, and the trapeze; this uncommon training made it easy for her to turn dancer and mime. She could unveil a firm, muscular well-shaped body, quite different from the curvaceously soft, fleshy, feminine figures shown on the stage before 1914.

Sido saw her family as a gathering of superior individuals free to pursue their own interests. Convinced that she had produced only geniuses, she would applaud any of their idiosyncrasies, anything that made them different from one another and "the common people."

Gabri was perturbed by her mother's lofty approach to their education; she could not understand why she never came to meet her after school as other mothers did. Gabri would ask her schoolmates: "Does your mother come to fetch you at four ?" "Yes, she does." "But mine, my 'mom' never came to fetch me."[28]

Colette was seventy-six when she wrote those lines, still feeling the traumatic experience of a little girl left to walk home by herself.

Sido "shook off, tore away from me with an imperious hand"[29] all commonplace ideas. At school Gabri heard about Christmas, the wooden shoes in the fireplace, the mysterious coming of presents, and enthusiastically recounted these tales to Sido. To relax Gabri and find out if she really believed such stories, Sido gave her daughter a full measure of *vin sucré,* wine with a lump of sugar in a "tiny silver goblet." Gabri babbled away about Juliette, who saw a comet drop into the fireplace, Fifine, who saw a moon shine in her wooden shoes and a wreath of flowers descending through the chimney, and Mathilde's mother, who saw a star above the woodshed. Sido listened without a smile and asked seriously: "You believe this? Darling kitten, do you believe this? If you do . . . "[30]

Sido was upset by this intrusion of religion and folklore in her child's consciousness; it was damaging the equilibrium of a natural education. On the other hand, Gabri wanted so badly to have a Christmas present! On Christmas night Gabri saw her mother step into her room, the ancient porter's lodge, with two parcels. She placed them on the wooden shoes Gabri had left near the fireplace. Half asleep, as in a dream, Gabri watched her mother go to the window, gaze into the night, bite her fingertip as she always did when she was perplexed, turn on her heels, pick up the gifts, and stealthily leave the room. As usual, Gabri found her presents on her breakfast plate on New Year's Day. Once her grandmother sent her a Christmas tree in a large wooden box. From every branch, carefully wrapped in glossy silvery paper, dangled hand-painted plaster figurines. It might not have been a work of art, but five-year-old Gabri was delighted. But Sido made caustic remarks about her mother-in-law's lack of taste, which spoiled Gabri's pleasure. Sentimentalism was no virtue for Sido, who believed adults should instill a sense of beauty in children. She loved Walter Crane; around 1880 she bought Gabri a series of tales illustrated by him. Another Christmas Gabri tried once more to entice her mother into buying some glistening glass decorations — like the ones she had seen "in a manor" — only to meet with the same firm determination. "How strange that we are still fetishists,"[31] commented Sido.

In March of 1880 Captain Colette went into politics with his eye on the prize, a seat in the senate. For some time he had wanted to break away from his bureaucratic career. He had been promoted to second-class tax collector, which was as high as he could go in Saint-Sauveur. And he had come into money of his own. His mother, "my unkind grandmother" as Colette defined her, had died in 1877, and he had inherited a large house in Toulon and a small estate overlooking the Mediterranean Sea. It was his chance "to amount to something." On the pretext of a case of dyspepsia, he retired.

That year Paul Bert was president of the commission in charge of supervising the 1880 laws on education, which made it mandatory for boys and girls to attend school till the age of twelve. The most daring reform was the creation of lycées for girls, which met with formidable resistance. Even enlightened Republican families refused to send their daughters to study mathematics, sciences, and biology, which were considered exclusively masculine matters.

The Colettes were often Paul Bert's guests. Bert "lived in Auxerre in a large house with a garden." His wife was English and raised their four daughters "the English way," an education that seemed to make them weatherproof. "All year round they had short sleeves and bare legs," causing Gabri to envy a freedom she did not have. Her admiration for English education never wavered. Her stepson was sent to a boarding school outside London and her daughter was brought up by an English nanny, then sent to an English boarding school — and she never wore socks in the winter. Forty years before it became a Parisian fashion, Madame Bert wore short, bobbed hair. "I was absolutely enthralled by Mme Bert."[32]

Gabri went campaigning with her father, who ran as the education candidate. He had been impressed at the Exposition Universelle by Caroline Kleinhan's method of teaching geography through topography. The students were taught to draw a survey of their school and to pass on gradually to maps of their county, their province, France, Europe, and the world. Captain Colette took a microscope, a projector, slides, and maps to illustrate his speech. Gabri handled the projector. She loved being on the stage and felt like a magician's partner. She was the model of what a good lay education could do for women and was presented proudly by her father.

Captain Colette was an idealist and a man of his time. He had noble delusions about what politics should be: "By educating the people, I will win them over."[33] He thought he would garner votes by proposing a curriculum that included natural history, physics, elementary chemistry, and, of course, topography. Driven by Antoine, their coachman, Gabri and her father went from country school to country school handing out educational material. Sometimes Captain Colette lectured against alcoholism until his audience wept with anguish at his description of the tragic future of the drunken man and his unfortunate family. Light applause welcomed the end of the educational lectures. Village mayors congratulated the captain, who, in his grand style, invited everyone to the local tavern for a drink. It was fall, and the weather was cold. Although the captain drank only soda water, hot wine with cinnamon was always warming on the embers of the stove, and Gabri never refused when the tavern keeper politely suggested that the young lady take a drop of hot wine. The young lady held up her goblet firmly and ordered: "To the brim!" She drank like a trooper, then knocked the empty glass on the table. She knew how to push her glass towards the kettle and say heartily, "It does a lot of good on its way down."[34] She acted like the men around the table and knew how to win an audience. They laughed loudly and gave the captain friendly slaps on the shoulder; the electoral campaign became jolly and noisy. Gabri, fast asleep, was carried back to the buggy, and Antoine drove them home. When Sido discovered that her daughter was tipsy, she put an end to her campaigning. Gabri, who loved to be the center of attention and enjoyed being on stage, was angry at Sido. She felt she had let her father down, that with her help he could have won. She always pictured her father as giving in to his wife's demands.

When the results for the election to the Yonne general council were in, Doctor Pierre Merlou, who had campaigned for a railroad station in Saint-Sauveur, came in first with 842 votes. Captain Colette came in second with 549 votes. He could not accept that Merlou, who had opened his practice in Saint-Sauveur less than a year earlier, could beat him, and contended that the elections had been rigged. In time Merlou would become mayor of Saint-Sauveur, deputy, minister, and ambassador to Peru, a political career Captain Colette had dreamed of for himself.

The captain turned his energy to local politics. On January 9, 1881, he was elected alderman of Saint-Sauveur. At once he stood alone by refusing to sign the decree nominating Monsieur Habert, a tailor, mayor of Saint-Sauveur for a second term. In her novels Colette vilified everyone who had prevented Captain Colette from succeeding in a political career. In *Claudine at School,* she pilloried Doctor Merlou, picturing him as a womanizer who got the principal pregnant and fondled the students. In "Propagande" Captain Colette is depicted as a victim of his "childish trust" in Doctor Merlou. "It is Monsieur Pierre Merlou, later minister for a day, who ousted my father from the council and prevented him from being a candidate for the senate." In "Progéniture," an article published in *Le Figaro* in 1924, she accused Doctor Merlou of being an abortionist and a murderer. "A lady who came to Puisaye . . . for three months left, having entrusted her child in care of a doctor. The child died within a week. The doctor died much later, having added to his M.D. degree the ephemeral title of Minister of Finances." Colette loved her father and she could not reconcile his failures with the idealized image she had of him. "Born to please and to fight, with a talent for telling anecdotes and for impromptu remarks, I thought later that he should have succeeded and charmed the senate the way he charmed a woman."[35]

Gabri was Captain Colette's favorite child. Very reserved with his children, he never kissed her but played and talked with her. He built a tiny dwelling, complete with glazed windows and ornate doors, for her beetles. The world was simple and orderly with the captain, while there were always tensions in the air with Sido, "secretly whimsical and who adhered to no rule."[36] Gabri, overpowered by her mother, took solace in Captain Colette, who made her feel she was his equal, "his peer."

The Lore of a Village

Gabri was eight when her nurse Mélie came back as a cook. With Mélie, "devoted dog, blond and fair slave," Gabri indulged in "childish behavior."[37] The house was split into two distinct worlds, her parents' quarters, where she was the precocious child who read Parisian and Belgian newspapers and played the piano, and the kitchen, which put her in touch with the culture of the Puisaye.

Mélie's mother was a peddler who went from village to village around Saint-Sauveur selling her goods on market days. Her brother was an itinerant musician who played at weddings and fairs. Mélie knew the local customs and gossip. She had a sunny disposition. Before starting to cook she liked to play "a little tune" on her red violin for herself. She had a vast repertoire of old songs with a preference for "saucy, even obscene ones,"[38] which abound in French folklore. Gabri listened and memorized most of them. She remembered later that when she was a little girl, "her chin barely reaching the table," she would idle her time away in the kitchen with the servants, "trotting about like an inquisitive mouse." She spoke very little, but listened. "In the dark kitchen the reels were spinning, rattling with a rapid sinister sound, the oval balls of gray linen thread rolled one by one in the wooden box, which held the stand of the reel and my nurse sang with that high-pitched, sad voice, the voice of the spinner, which no girl from Saint-Sauveur possesses any more. In another corner, maids were cracking nuts for the oil press; I trotted around like a rat, curious and silent, and the uneasy feeling brought on by the late hours, the shadows cast by the light of the candles, the forgotten legends sung by the women: 'Cain dipped his hands in every fountain' . . . added an enchanting terror to my delight."[39]

Watching Mélie, Gabri learned the cardinal rules of country cooking. Meals were prepared on a tiled stand with four square holes filled with charcoal. Braised dishes were cooked in a saucepan under a concave lid filled with embers. Baked dishes were sent to the baker, who put them in the oven after the bread had been removed. The roasting was done on a spit in the kitchen fireplace.

Love and terror were the stuff of Mélie's tales. Wolves still roamed the woods of Puisaye; in cold winters they could sometimes be spotted around the farms. Fire was the most immediate threat. The fear of fire was such that in Saint-Sauveur it was forbidden to light a pipe or to smoke in any season in the streets, in a barn, in a stable, or in front of a house. These regulations were not always enforced; for instance, carrying embers in pots was forbidden, but during the winter children were allowed to take a foot warmer filled with charcoal to school. Colette remembered that "massive emanations of carbon monoxide rose from those *braseros*. Children fell asleep, somewhat suffocated . . . sometimes a small child who wanted to sit on her foot warmer to warm herself screamed because she had burnt her little behind."[40]

The ban on fire was lifted in September when hemp, the main crop around Saint-Sauveur, was harvested, left to dry, and then crushed. It was done in the streets around bonfires fed with the hemp stalks. Fall was Gabri's favorite season. She walked through the woods to gather wild pears, berries, mushrooms, "chestnuts, filberts, apples, choke-berries, beech-nuts." In the fall farmers delivered their share of crops, wine, and nut oil to the Colettes. "I drank nut oil straight from the bottle."[41] She took the oil-cake to school as a snack. Above all she liked chestnuts, which she boiled, peeled, mashed in a handkerchief, molded into a round cake, and powdered with sugar.

Mélie, with her tales, songs, and earthy ways, initiated Gabri to the many facets of village life. It was with Mélie and Yvonne, her *soeur de lait,* that Gabri took part in Saint-Sauveur's life: marriages, first communions, and local celebrations. On the Feast of St. John they ate "the cookies of St. John" for eight days. On Palm Sunday they ate a cake made with fresh cheese, cream, butter, and eggs. On Rogation days in the spring, after strewing the streets with flowers, the villagers marched in procession along the winding roads and through the fields, preceded by the church banners and the portrait of the patron saint, to exorcise the mice and to ask God to bless the crops.

The crops were protected by a *garde-champêtre* or game warden, who wore a large blue blouse, wide belt, and *képi;* his main duty was to watch the harvest and ring the bells to warn of incoming storms, a practice that led to the belief that bells had the power to chase away storms. He was also in charge of the curfew. Drinking was forbidden on Sundays and holidays after ten at night. The warden made the rounds of the taverns, beating on his drum. In fact, the *garde-champêtre* and his drum were part of every event. On New Year's Day he marched through the streets at the crack of dawn; it was the signal for everyone to jump out of bed. Gabri waited for that day "in a state of expectation, close to tears."[42] Then the excitement started. First came the baker, who delivered a hundred pounds of bread to the Colettes; throughout the morning Gabri and her brothers gave a loaf of bread and a penny to the needy, to poor children, to tramps who trotted from house to house. The farmers came in their Sunday best to pay their respects with a present — a rabbit or some winter fowl — and were treated to a glass of good wine and a piece of cake. In the morning chill the streets of Saint-Sauveur were bursting with life. Many, having copiously toasted the new year, were tottering along to the uncertain beat of the town drummer.

What attracted Gabri to the kitchen was the casual way Mélie treated everything in nature. Sex was a part of life she thought should be encouraged; in spring she put out plates full of meat to attract tom-cats to her tabby and "obligingly watched their lovemaking."[43] Love stories made her cry, and she knew everything about people's affairs, as life in a nineteenth-century village was lived collectively. Married couples often shared bedrooms with children and servants. For centuries privacy had been unknown; it was just starting to appear in the lives of the more affluent.

Mélie told Gabri that before getting married she should try out all her suitors. "Try them out beforehand so it is an honest deal and no one is deceived." Virginity had little value for her. "Before, after, if you think that they don't enjoy it all the same!"[44] Even so, in Mélie's paradoxical thinking, marriage was the supreme feast, and Gabri shared her taste for those gargantuan celebrations. When she was thirteen, the chambermaid married the gardener and asked Gabri to be her maid of honor. The Colettes were invited but declined. Gabri, fearful that Sido would not allow her to go, had prepared a speech expounding why it was safe for her to go. Sido did not like Gabri's friends, deplored Gabri's "bad manners," and concluded, looking at her "with ironic contempt," "Say no more. Just say 'I adore the servants' weddings.' "[45] Liberal Sido had a background of elitist values. In Burgundy a wedding lasted three full days, three days that Gabri did not want to miss. The first day a procession with fifes and drums and flying ribbons summoned the bride's maids from their homes. The following day they all went to city hall, where the official marriage took place, and then to church. On their way back the bride and groom, strewing sweetmeats right and left, were showered with a golden rain of corn from the windows. This was "the sowing of the newlyweds," a blessing on the marriage and an invocation to Ceres, the goddess of plenty, a ceremony that had survived since Roman times.

The feast began with *la trempée,* a toast to the newlyweds. While relatives and friends in procession gave the bride the kiss of *la trempée,* the guests clanked their glasses, drank, and ritually clanked them again. Gabri loved the enormous banquet served in the barn — the endless parade of heavy dishes rich with thick sauce, the lumps of sugar dipped in a bowl of red wine to stir the appetite between the rabbit stew, the roast with garlic, or the egg dish cooked in red wine. The feast lasted the whole afternoon, interrupted by extraordinary challenges. One was dared to drink an entire pail of white wine, another to eat a whole leg of mutton to the acclaim of the guests. After the meal, the dance started and lasted well into the night. (Gabri found in that gargantuan ambiance a pleasure that neither Sido nor Captain Colette shared. Both were very spartan in their tastes and preferred salads, roasts, and fruits to Burgundian cuisine.)

On the third day a group of boys carrying bottles of wine and a spray of laurel decked with ribbons climbed on top of the bride's roof and tied the laurels to the highest chimney. They sprinkled the laurel with sparkling wine, threw sugar plums to the children in the street below, and toasted everything.

She Banished All Human Religions

As Gabri grew up, she felt more and more torn between Sido's ways and Saint-Sauveur's customs. The rift was significant in matters of religion; Sido was an atheist. "It is a fact that I do not know my Paternoster,"[46] she said. Her children were baptized, but she did not accept the dogma, the Catholic ritual, or the Catholic holidays. Neither did Captain Colette; a nonbeliever, he saw no reason to give in to social behavior or traditions. Sido knew from her upbringing that although radical ideas could be debated in private, in intellectual circles with your peers, one should be discreet enough not to confront the domestics, the neighbors, the common people. Gabri would take after her father and placidly shock public opinion, while Sido, torn between her beliefs and social etiquette, ended up doing things she violently opposed and shocking her community all the same.

On Sundays Sido took her two daughters to mass, where social status was affirmed. At the entrance of the church straw-caned chairs were stacked high; for a few pennies a sexton would carry them to the parishioner's location of choice. The poor remained standing, while the wealthiest had their reserved pew marked with an engraved copper plate. "We sat in our family pew," wrote Colette. However, it was not engraved with her name, but bore the name Robineau-Duclos, patronym of her two elder siblings.

Captain Colette never attended; the few men who did stood near the door and talked quietly. The priest, Father Millot, started by saying a de profundis for the dead, whose families paid five francs a year for this service. Every Sunday he repeated the names, at seventy Colette could still repeat the list of the dead she had heard when she was a child. The priest's sermons were simplistic and lasted at least a half an hour. He ended by announcing oncoming sales, city hall meetings, balls, christenings, and marriages. Sido could not stand this protracted speech and asked Father Millot to cut his sermons down to ten minutes; when he would not grant her wish, she took her watch out ostentatiously and swung it like a pendulum.

Many times Gabri caught that merry disregard for everyone in her mother's mischievous gray eyes. But Sido's arrogance was tempered by her generosity with money. With an exiled Polish doctor who had come to Saint-Sauveur after the 1870 war, she took care of needy children, lambasting the fathers who sired so many offspring and reaffirming her credo of free love in commending and protecting unwed mothers.

Children want to conform to their peers; Gabri was left free to explore Catholicism. She wanted to be like the other girls who, in May, a month devoted to the Virgin Mary, took flowers to church for the priest's blessing. One day she came home with a bouquet of "blessed flowers." Sido laughed, her light, crystal-clear laughter ironic. She asked Gabri if she truly believed that flowers needed the intervention of a priest to be blessed — were they not already and naturally blessed?

When she was eleven Gabri asked her mother to let her prepare for her first communion. She wanted to wear the long white dress and lace bonnet of the *communiante*. She loved the exchange of pious images and rosaries; the novelty of it all thrilled her. She would later give an explanation of the lure of religion more in line with her aesthetics: "The day a little girl leaned against my shoulder, a shoulder just like mine, and a fair braid slithered along one of my braids and curled up on my open book ... I was conquered."[47]

Sido did not say "no" to Gabri's newfound religious zeal. Sido never said "no," but pelted her daughter "with nasty remarks." She could not help getting angry every time she saw Gabri's catechism book, in which she found no redeeming feature. She objected to the questions "What is God? What is this? What is that? All those question marks." The book was pervaded with "a mania of Inquest and Inquisition."[48]

The Captain enjoyed pushing Sido to face her own contradictions; if she did not like the catechism, why didn't she take the book away from Gabri? For him it was very simple. Not for Sido. Colette painted her torn between her own beliefs and her professed desire not to impose them on her children. In pure Fourierist style, she wanted them to fulfill their inclinations. Since "one always drops the way one leans," Sido saw fit not to interfere with her children's personalities. "Oh, the freedom of Sido's children,"[49] mused Colette.

Sido fostered free will and free inquiry, two principles her Huguenot ancestors would have approved. Nothing threatened them more than the confession of the Roman Catholic church, and Sido found the idea unhealthy: "Confession tends to develop in a child a taste for verbosity, for self-pity." She believed it was more "self-gratification than humility" and thought her children should be taught "never to confess or admit to anything, to hold their tongues, to learn to punish themselves in the secret of their hearts."[50] So Gabri learned to hold back.

Savages, Savages . . . What to Do with Such Savages?

Gabri did not see much of her brothers, as they left their boarding school only for Christmas and summer holidays. When she was nine Achille, the eldest, entered the medical school in Paris. Gabri's rapport with Achille may have been a source of emotional turmoil; she never felt threatened by Léo but competed with Achille for her mother's affection. It was a vain contest, for Sido never lost the dazzled adoration she lavished on her handsome son, "the one without rival,"[51] the one she called *Beauté*. He was six foot six and slender, with green-gray eyes and brown curls, defiantly independent and somewhat of a misanthrope, a trait that increased with age. Whenever an unexpected visitor called, Achille would stealthily leap out of the nearest window with the elegance of a dancer. At their sister Juliette's wedding he vanished from the ballroom as soon as the violin struck up. Finding the house closed, he broke a windowpane and went to bed. "Imagine," said Sido to Colette, "he wanted to be alone, away from those sweaty people . . . Such a good child!"[52]

In *Looking Backwards (Journal à Rebours)* Colette described Sido's love for Achille as her passion, a passion that lasted until she died. For him she had "a lover's cajoleries." Sick in bed, for him alone she coifed her hair and put on a Spanish lace wrap. When she was not with him she followed him in her mind. She recognized the sound of his car. In *The Break of Day* Colette recalled her mother brooding dramatically during the adolescence of her elder son, "the very handsome one, the seductor . . . In those days, I felt that she was wild . . . vulgar, growing ugly, always on the lookout. How well I recall her, wasting away, her cheeks flushed with the red of jealousy and fury."[53] This drew Colette to conclude that the mother-son relationship was incestuous, if not in fact, at least in its display. A passionate woman, Sido never let her favorite son stray from her emotionally. She "knew that she was forever without a rival in her son's heart,"[54] as he was in hers.

Achille liked to push intellectual debates to the limit, a type of challenge the family enjoyed. During one of his visits Domino, a six-month-old black-and-white puppy, was killed by the wheel of the carriage. Achille picked it up. Why not eat Domino, since they ate "cute little rabbits, lambs, and baby goats?" He put it to steep in a marinade he prepared himself. Domino marinated for three days while the family discussed it and found good reasons why they were not "wanton fools, camouflaged bloodthirsty people." Sido agreed to "all the darings of her beautiful son." Léo expanded on his brother's idea; Captain Colette concluded that during the war in Crimea they would not have flinched. Gabri refused to see the marinating puppy: "No! No! I will only see him cooked." On Sunday their cook Adèle, looking sad, served the roasted puppy. When Achille picked it up with the serving fork, the roast slipped and splashed back into the sauce. Gabri screamed. "So, what is wrong with you?" asked Sido. "God, that child is so stupid," commented Achille. He called her "faint-hearted. A victim of such prejudices."[55] Gabri fled to the garden, followed by Sido and Léo. When the aroma of coffee signaled the end of the meal, the three of them reentered the dining room. Captain Colette and Achille were engaged in a lofty conversation, and the roast had vanished. The hunting dog was licking his chops; Sido took one look at him and chased him out into the garden

The second son, Léo, was a born musician — he could replay on the piano whatever symphony or song he had heard only once. Thrilled by the sound of any band of traveling musicians, he would often follow them. When he was six he walked four miles in the footsteps of a beggar playing the clarinet while his parents were frantically searching the woods and wells. He came back and could not understand why they were blaming him, since he played all of the clarinet player's tunes on the piano for them. Gabri and Achille could also play any tune by ear and adapt any symphony to the piano. Léo's talent was outstanding, but nothing could force him to work. The "lazzarone," as Sido called him, did escape music, never finished his studies in pharmacy, and never married. He remained secretive and unpredictable. Sido kept on losing him and searching for him, as he could be anywhere anytime: in the box of a grandfather clock, perched somewhere near the ceiling, or hanging on to a column. He could disappear in a cellar, since he was never frightened of darkness or solitude. Whenever he had a chance he disassembled watches and put them back together again. He visited all the nearby cemeteries and described the most elaborate mausoleums and tombs to Gabri. "At thirteen, he scarcely seemed to differentiate between the living and the dead. While my games evoked before my eyes imaginary persons, transparent and visible, whom I greeted, my brother, inventing his imaginary dead, treated them with the utmost friendliness and adorned them to the best of his ability."[56] At fourteen he pictured himself as a mortician, and Gabri, at seven, was his dutiful assistant. "Get ready tomorrow at ten, there will be a funeral." The meeting place was the large attic filled with baskets, discarded furniture, china, piles of newspapers, old frocks, and all sorts of luggage, including the servants' trunks — those long, narrow boxes with their lids slightly curved and covered with goatskins. There Léo cut out cardboard in the shape of tombstones of different models and sizes. He carefully drew epitaphs celebrating the virtues of the deceased. With great precision Léo painted the dates of birth and death and the names, usually extravagantly ridiculous, such as "Astoniphronque" or "Egremimy." He would list the names of the children of the pseudodeceased and the highlights of their lives. Echoing Sido's scornful description of husbands, he explained to Gabri that whatever a husband did during his lifetime, he had to be eulogized at his funeral as a perfect father and spouse. Gabri grasped that fiction was more powerful than reality.

When the attic overflowed, the cardboard tombstones spilled over into a secret part of the garden hidden by a hedge. One day Sido discovered them and gasped in horror. She ran off, came back with a rake, and destroyed the whole fake burial ground. "This is vampirism, sacrilege, I don't even know what it is,"[57] she said, predicting that her son would end up in an asylum. Colette saw him as wandering through a mental realm unchanged since childhood. He had the fancy of "a six-year-old." He chose to subsist on a diet of candies, syrups, and sweet cakes. Colette, in *Julie de Carneilhan,* gave Léo's peculiarities to the character she named Léon.

The brothers never quarreled. They nicknamed Gabri "the Cossack's daughter" and excluded her from their games because she still "ate candle drippings."[58] She had strange cravings, eating the cakes of white sealing wax her father tried to hide in vain until he replaced them with multicolored ones without the same appeal. "The Cossack's daughter" resented being treated as a child and she tried to emulate everything Achille did. A competitive urge drove her to outwit him. She developed an amazing quickness at mastering information.

Her brothers loved music and put together a small orchestra with the musicians of Saint-Sauveur; they transcribed and performed the success of the day, Gounod's opera, *Faust*. At home, they played *à quatre mains* Beethoven, Stradella, Saint-Saens, Bizet, and Toselli. Music was sacred; they never allowed Gabri to sink into mediocrity. Under their watchful eyes she became an accomplished musician. She would later say that music was her first calling.

Achille "loved plants more than human beings and animals more than plants."[59] With Léo in tow he had been collecting butterflies for years, and their magnificent collection was carefully catalogued. Achille also started to catalog plants around Saint-Sauveur. Later Colette graded herself as "above average" in the knowledge of butterflies: she could name all those found in France and most of the North African species. The whole family immersed itself in botany and entomology. Captain Colette provided the Latin names and showed Gabri the plants in illustrated books, but puzzled her by his inability to recognize them in the wild. Sido kept on hand the complete works of the entomologist Fabre; she would observe without interference a caterpillar devouring her favorite plants or a spider that descended at night to drink chocolate from the cup on her nightstand and slowly ascended back to the ceiling. Like many of their generation, the Colettes' faith in science was absolute. Darwin, Berthelot, Renan, Claude Bernard, Ribot, and Pasteur reshaped the scientific landscape. Simplifying their theories, the freethinking Republicans believed that the human mind could resolve any scientific or human problems by *la méthode expérimentale*. Magnifier in hand, the intellectual elite analyzed, categorized, examined, dissected, and drew conclusions.

Achille felt compelled to become a doctor, following in the footsteps of a close relative, Jean-Baptiste Robineau-Desvoidy, the millionaire doctor, scientist, and entomologist who had engineered Sido's first marriage. He was a curious character, whose legend so impressed Gabri that she turned him into Claudine's father in her *Claudine* tetralogy.

Dr. Robineau-Desvoidy spent his life studying insects around Saint-Sauveur and Paris reaching enough international recognition to be given a full half-page in the British *Bibliographia Zoologica*. A friend of Raspail's and Geoffroy Saint-Hilaire's, Desvoidy was part of that group of scientists whose findings rocked the scientific world and whose political associations made them suspect. The Academy of Science refused to publish his works on the discovery of the olfactory organs of shellfish; he defiantly published the findings at his own expense, accompanied by a preface attacking the scientific establishment. That was not his first brush with the authorities. The previous year, already clad in his academic robes and about to receive his doctorate, he was abruptly stopped on the steps of the tribune and told that his dissertation was rejected, its printing stopped by the royal attorney general. He rewrote his dissertation, paid all the additional expenses, received his doctoral degree, and returned to Saint-Sauveur an angry man. There he practiced medicine, but devoted his pent-up energy to studying plants, insects, and local archeology. While his scientific works earned him recognition, he antagonized everybody in Saint-Sauveur. In 1838 he published a locally funded statistical essay on Saint-Sauveur that startled his sponsors: the people of Saint-Sauveur were described as "wilted," lacking the energy to better their lives because of the climate's humidity. Desvoidy told his readers that over the past thirty-five years, "one hundred and nine bastards were born in Saint-Sauveur alone," which sent the whole town into a rage. Asked to delete the most offensive paragraphs, Desvoidy refused and had his book published in Brussels by Amédée Gratiot at 11 Rue de la Monnaie. He turned it into a radical pamphlet attacking the public health policy of the préfet, "who should limit himself to the elegant hygiene of his manicured nails." Like Raspail, Desvoidy fought for daily hygiene, with baths for all, a concept opposed by the Catholic church on the grounds of modesty. The feud between the church and Desvoidy was additionally fueled by his archeological discoveries; he asserted that Christianity had willfully destroyed the Celtic civilization in France and he rewrote the history of the Auxerrois region. Where the church had seen the tombs of four saints, he saw Celtic landmarks pointing to the four cardinal points and was later proven right. He became an advocate of the Celtic language and druidic revival.

In the 1850s an underground druidic movement was in full swing in England and France. The United Order of the Ancient Druids adopted Masonic rites and tried to resurrect druidic customs such as the culling of the mistletoe by a young priestess in a white robe. There was more to it than a reenactment of ancient ceremonies: druidic culture considered men and women to be equals. In contrast with Roman and Christian law, in Gaul women did not fall in *mariti manu,* under their husband's rule; they owned property, took part in the political, diplomatic, and religious life of the city, and divorced at will, since marriage had no sacred connotation. Colette described her heroine, "the true Claudine, exalted and wild like a young druidess"[60] as free and independent, another pagan roaming the woods where centuries earlier the Celtic druidesses had honored the deities of their pantheon.

Desvoidy was a precursor of the movement that flourished two decades later when writers and historians, looking back to the provinces' culture, tried to revive the Celtic, Catalan, and Provençal idioms the Republic was trying to eradicate. Colette peppered her novels with local idiom, as did Daudet. Proust embarked in quest of things past. Frédéric Mistral received the Nobel Prize for Literature in 1904 for works written in Provençal. Colette extolled her province and described with entomological precision the inhabitants of Saint-Sauveur, as well as its fauna and flora. In her first novel Colette modeled Claudine's father after Robineau: He gives all his care to slugs and snails and keeps a precise diary filled with data such as "the *Limax flavus* devours 0.24 grammes of food in one day, while the *Belix ventricosa* only consumes 0.19 grammes" — observations straight out of Desvoidy's works.

Achille was Doctor Desvoidy's spiritual heir. He taught Gabri the entomologist's cardinal rule: "Observe over and over again what you have already observed a hundred times." "Look" was also Sido's favorite word: "Look at the hairy caterpillar . . . look at the first bean sprout . . . look at the wasp, how it cuts a bit of raw meat with its mandibles like nippers . . . look at the color of the sunset, it forecasts strong winds and a storm . . . look quickly at the black iris bud which is opening up."[61] This was at the epicenter of Colette's literary credo, echoing Desvoidy's "art is only born in the study of nature." His last words were for the flies he had studied all his life: "Flies who have always been my greatest delight, I am your liege. . . . Write my name on your diaphanous wings, carry it into the mystery of the skies."[62]

To live in a French village was to skirt a multitude of beliefs. Elements of witchcraft, magic, and sorcery were taken for granted. Some families had sinister reputations due to the secrecy of their rituals. Many families owned *The Book,* a collection of remedies and their accompanying rituals. This book was secretly handed down from generation to generation. *The Book* was "written on notebooks or on cheap blotting paper, cut at the folds and stitched with a red cotton thread."[63] It provided some innocuous advice: don't leave the windows open, the bats will come in and pick out your eyes; to get a healthy growth of hair, don't cut it when the moon is descending; don't stand in the ray of the full moon for fear of becoming mad. It also had some stranger remedies — powders made from animals or plants gathered during the full moon, rituals to get rid of one's enemy, or at least to vent one's frustration.

Gabri was fascinated by all aspects of the supernatural and wanted to know all about the herbs and their powers, while Sido did not believe in the curative power of herbs and never used them. She told Gabri that every woman who gathered them was "a death threat."[64] But Gabri would follow La Varenne, an old woman who wore, tied by a thread around her belly, a large apricot pit that had been in her family for generations, passed down from mother to daughter. La Varenne told her which berries were safe to eat and taught her the herbs that cured and those that could kill a dog. She showed her the snake plant, under which snakes burrow. She taught her to sort out herbs that are diuretic, purgative, or aphrodisiac; every time they found one, La Varenne made lewd comments. Plants, even more than animals, are present in all Colette's works. She amazed her friends, for she could name all the plants in the woods and fields and knew their properties. She also remained intrigued by the occult. All her life she went to clairvoyants and attended seances in which mediums communicated with the dead. She read the cards and deciphered her friends' destinies in the palms of their hands. She used a pendulum to sense vibrations and boasted of her ability to communicate with animals and children. When everything else had failed, she could stop the cries of a baby or the barking of a dog just by looking at them. She believed in extrasensory perception.

In *The Pure and the Impure,* she confessed to engaging in a duel of spells with a woman of whom she was jealous and whom she wanted to see dead. According to Colette, her rival was a stronger sorceress than herself, and unusual things started to happen. Colette fell into an open trench in the Place du Trocadéro, then caught bronchitis. Then she lost the last chapters of the manuscript of *Mitsou* in the métro and had to rewrite it, as she had kept no copy. A cabdriver snatched one hundred francs from her and left her standing in the rain. A mysterious epidemic killed her three angora kittens. She then counterattacked with her own spells. Finally she struck up a friendship with her rival sorceress. In "Rain Moon" (La Lune de Pluie) she tells the strange story of a woman who moved into the apartment Colette had lived in after separating from her first husband. The woman had cast spells on her husband "for seven moons" until he died. Colette remembered how, in the same bedroom, she, too, had cast a spell on her husband, using the old ritual of "summoning a person." "You say a name, nothing but a name, a hundred times, a thousand times . . . without eating or drinking as long as you can, you repeat the name, nothing but the name."[65]

Her freethinking parents would have been surprised to know that Gabri, "a captor of sources" as she called herself, would practice *les voies extra-humaines,* (the extrahuman ways). But at a very young age Gabri had developed the fine art of deceit: "to feign without faltering, with a silence, with a smile, to become someone different, this is the feat which leaves far behind the little chattering lies."[66]

As a child, when Gabri felt estranged, alone, or psychologically split, she gave herself an imaginary twin she called Marie, a name she would later use as a pseudonym. Marie had long, braided hair, wore a blue cotton dress, a checkered blue-and-white pinafore, and yellow, buttoned boots. At night Gabri slept on the edge of the bed to make room for Marie; Sido wondered why her daughter slept so uncomfortably. Whenever Sido leaned over her, Gabri hoped her mother would not notice her "clandestine twin — the little girl with flat hair she could love."[67] Gabri dreaded that her mother would prefer her imaginary self. From her early days she remembered "that powerful and sensuous genius in us, which creates and nurtures the visions of childhood, then mysteriously vanishes . . ."[68] She remembered her walks alone in the woods, calling into existence charmed creatures — sylphs, fauns, the spirits haunting the trees. "I lived in a paradise inhabited by my gods, my talking animals, my nymphs, and my satyrs." These were her companions. "I remember that one day as I fell asleep on the bank of a noisy little river (I loved to sleep in the open), the language of the waters changed, translating into human speech as I slipped from consciousness to dream."[69] Of these years she remembered, too, the routine of her days, an antidote to her mother's seemingly erratic but extremely demanding education. Sido was a mother "who liked no rules, loved the unforeseen, disliked anything repetitive and shrugged off impatiently rules and regulations."[70]

Gabri was growing up free, shedding clichés and prejudices in sleepy Saint-Sauveur. "You can't imagine what queen of the world I was when I was twelve! Sturdy, with a rough voice, two tight braids of hair which lashed around me like whips, with tanned, scratched, scarred hands, a square boyish forehead, which I now hide down to my eyebrows. . . . How I miss myself!"[71]

That year her world started to crumble. "My twelfth year saw the onset of bad luck, departures, separations. . . ."[72]

My Mysterious Half Sister

Juliette Robineau-Duclos was thirteen years older than Gabri, "a stranger to us, a stranger to everybody, willingly isolated in the bosom of her family."[73] When Gabri was five Juliette, who had finished her schooling at Mademoiselle Ravaire's institute in Auxerre, came home. For ten years she had worn a strict uniform: black woolen dress, black coat, black hat with a violet ribbon in winter; black skirt, white blouse, and straw hat in summer. Sido had had her daughter raised in a boarding school with the most progressive curriculum available for girls. Mademoiselle Ravaire was proud of "an instruction based on religion and simple tastes" and put "a particular emphasis on needlework . . . believing that a woman who knows how to occupy herself strengthens her heart on the paths of her duty."[74] She charged four hundred and fifty francs a year, music and drawing lessons not included. Juliette was educated like the wealthy heiress she was; what was unusual was that Sido had enrolled her in a program meant for young women who would teach in grammar schools or open private institutions. It was an extremely rigid curriculum, and the state exam was difficult. Only girls who had to earn a living and had a good chance of success were coached for it. Obviously, Sido had plans for Juliette. In 1877 Juliette took her Brevet exam and failed; only fifteen out of thirty-nine passed that year. Juliette came home.

Captain Colette showed no interest in her and no efforts were made to get her married. She was not pretty, "my half sister with Mongolian eyes," "my sister with long hair," wrote Colette. She was graceful and small, with strange, large, slightly slanting black eyes under thick, silky eyebrows, a well-formed mouth with full lips, and incredibly long, luxuriant, curly black hair — which, when undone, "covered her to the feet like a tent." Braided into heavy tresses, Juliette's hair should have been a matter of pride, but instead became an object of ridicule. Sido talked of it "as of an incurable disease" and held her daughter responsible for all her aches and pains. "I am spent. . . . My left leg is aching. I have just finished combing Juliette's hair."[75] Gabri, reflecting her family's feelings, never liked her sister. In *Fair Seasons (Belles Saisons),* she writes of Juliette: "Crouched under the weight of her four braids intertwined into a makeshift diadem, she was pitiful and made everybody laugh; any hat perched on top of that edifice became almost ridiculous."[76]

Juliette felt that she did not measure up to her mother's expectations and stayed in her room. It was a pretty one with pearl gray wallpaper, enlivened by sprays of blue cornflowers. Estranged in her own home, Juliette took refuge in the world of books; she read in bed most of the night and started reading as soon as she opened her eyes, barely eating, looking dazed. Sido tried to take away her lamp and hide the candles, but Juliette read in the moonlight. Gradually she felt so isolated that she locked herself in her room, reading Stendhal, Dumas, Hugo, Dickens, Voltaire, de Musset, modern novels, English novels, adventure stories, historical novels, love stories, newspapers, and magazines. Any printed matter that came into the house ended up on her unfinished embroidery, on a chair in the garden, among the cushions of the drawing-room chairs, on her bed. She clipped and stitched together the novels serialized in *La Revue des Deux Mondes,* in *La Revue Bleue,* in *Le Journal des Dames et des Demoiselles.* She memorized poetry, "she read with a hard look on her face." When spoken to, she answered as if "between us there were miles of space and silence."[77]

Juliette's growing neurosis emerged plainly when she caught typhoid fever. She became delirious and kept repeating, "I don't know anybody here . . . I don't know anybody." In her delirium she conversed with Catulle Mendès, a decadent poet, friend of Baudelaire, and imitator of Edgar Allen Poe. Sido watched "horrified by that stranger who, in her delirium, addressed herself only to unfamiliar people."[78]

Later Sido would try to change Gabri's mind about her sister. "Juliette is not stupid, particularly when she is with me. She is very intelligent and very knowledgeable."[79] But by then Gabri, her father, and her brothers had cast Juliette away forever. After six years of passionate reading, Juliette became engaged to Charles Roché, a twenty-nine-year-old doctor who had just opened his practice on the Rue de la Roche in Saint-Sauveur. This marriage upset Sido, who made her views widely known. She called it "an accident," "a desperate move." When asked whom Juliette was mar-

rying, her curt answer was: "O Lord! the first running dog."[80] Achille and
Léo avoided "the bloke who smells of vermouth,"[81] and Captain Colette
was hostile. Achille declared he would not wear white tie and tails, would
not be part of the procession in the church, and would not sit at the
formal dinner. Léo sided with his brother. When Sido remonstrated that
he was to escort the maid of honor, Léo retorted that his sister had no
business marrying, as she always kept to herself and "did not need us to
get wed."[82] The brothers found a way out: they had the Aucher piano
moved to the church and played "like angels" throughout the ceremony.

Juliette and Doctor Charles Roché were married on April 14, 1884.
A photograph shows the diminutive Juliette leaning against her tall,
slender, bearded husband, while Gabri reclines against her father, who
looks disheveled. Among the numerous guests are two very elegant
Landoys in tophats and a general. Farmers and servants are included in
the picture. It was a beautiful wedding.

In May Captain Colette was again frantically campaigning to be mayor
of Saint-Sauveur "or at least to unseat poor Habert."[83] He was determined to win, paying people "to advertise him."[84] To ingratiate himself
with his in-laws, Doctor Roché got involved, but to no avail; the captain was never to be mayor of Saint-Sauveur. He was now heavily in
debt, and the fortunes of the Colettes took a turn for the worst. A ter-
rific rift opened up, which widened until the deaths of all those concerned. It was a tale of greed and jealousy right out of Balzac. Doctor
Roché, not satisfied with Juliette's dowry, asked for a detailed account
of Captain Colette's management of the Robineau estate. Before
Juliette's marriage, the captain thought he had skillfully apportioned the
inheritances of his two stepchildren; he, Sido, Juliette, and Achille had
signed an agreement settling the guardianship account of the estate
valued at four hundred thousand gold francs. Achille and Juliette each
received a quarter of the estate and the other half went to Sido, a
quarter in sole ownership, and the income of the remaining quarter.
The settlement favored Sido who, according to her marriage contract,
was entitled only to the income of the estate and no ownership whatsoever. To pay for his mounting debts, Captain Colette had sold his
Mediterranean estate three years earlier. The situation became even
more entangled when the captain's "unforgivable prodigality"[85] forced

him to borrow one hundred and twenty thousand gold francs from the Crédit Foncier to pay Juliette's dowry. The loan was guaranteed by the large estate of La Massue and the woods of Champigneulles; Juliette and Achille cosigned the loan and La Massue was mortgaged, further reducing the two heirs' income.

No sooner had Juliette and her husband settled in their home across the garden facing the Colettes' house than Doctor Roché, feeling that his wife had been deprived of her rightful share, consulted several lawyers, who all agreed that the earlier March 8 settlement had not been legal. The most unpleasant gossip started to rock Saint-Sauveur. In July one of Sido's good friends wrote to another: "Your poor neighbors, the Colettes, are deep in a dreadful mess. Their son-in-law wants to reexamine the accounts given by Captain Colette and if one is to believe the gossip one hears, there are very startling facts. Today, all the Roché family and a lawyer have a meeting in order to audit the books, it is awful! And you should hear what people say."[86] Juliette avoided the Colettes and refused to talk to them.

Without exception the Robineau relatives sided with Juliette, who signed a petition asking for a revised settlement of the Jules Robineau-Duclos estate. The captain and Sido fought back, refusing to reconsider. The Rochés were ready to file a lawsuit. Saint-Sauveur took sides and gave the divided families no rest. It was the Montagues and the Capulets all over, except that Juliette, married to her tall, dark Romeo, felt battered on all sides — her husband and his family on one side, her mother and stepfather on the other. Juliette was a passionate woman and had given her husband the love for which the Colettes had no use. Now she wanted love in return for her total devotion, but her husband was only concerned with her estate. Torn between husband and mother, two months after her marriage Juliette tried to commit suicide; she swallowed some pills, but survived. When the news reached the Colettes, the captain sent the messenger back to Doctor Roché, threatening to kill him if he did not save Juliette, whom — on that occasion he called "my daughter." Saint-Sauveur was in an uproar. "We had become the talk of the town."[87] Gabri felt that they were hunted by gossipmongers who were feeding on their grief: "A village has no pity."[88]

After Juliette's attempted suicide, everyone agreed that a settlement had to be reached. On September 4, the parties met in the office of Monsieur Coudron, the lawyer. They reached an agreement after much discussion:

Juliette, Achille, and Sido each received a third of the estate in sole owner-ship. The heavily mortgaged La Massue was left to Sido and the captain, who were to pay an indemnity of forty thousand gold francs to Juliette. Achille waived his right to the indemnity and even pledged to be respon-sible for the payment of his mother's share. This generous move aroused the town gossips. "It is said that in order to convince Achille that he had to be disinterested in these matters, he was told that he was a Robineau-Duclos in name only."[89]

It was said, too, that before the first settlement Captain Colette had cut all the tall timber on Juliette's share of the woods, so in the new set-tlement the age of the trees had to be stated. Sido's income was now one-third of what she had enjoyed; but she was not poor. Her share was over one hundred thousand gold francs.

Gabri felt that the whole town had turned against them. Old stories resurfaced, and she came to realize that her own social status was very uncertain. She had lived like "a hermit crab" in a shell that was not hers: the house, the lands, the carriage, the family pew at church — everything bore the Robineau-Duclos seal. Sido refused more and more to go out. She liked to reminisce about the past, "the dead ones she had loved."[90] She talked about her father, about "Eugène, Paul, Irma...."[91] She evoked her life with her first husband, leaving Gabri with the impression of by-gone halcyon days.

In 1885 Juliette gave birth to a daughter, Yvonne. The Colettes were not even notified.

Gabri won first prize in a reading contest; the contestants had to read a page of prose and another of poetry, and were graded on their pronunci-ation and diction. She was awarded a diploma and a book bound in red leather and embossed in gold. In June she took le Certificat d'Etudes, an examination that ended elementary studies and, for most French people, schooling. At twelve she was among the youngest graduates, some being as old as seventeen. The diploma declared that she had completed a cur-riculum consisting of moral and religious instruction, reading, writing, the grammatical elements of French, arithmetic, the metric system, the history and geography of France, and the English language. The Saint-Sauveur school offered nothing more, but Gabri, like Juliette, was to pursue her studies and was enrolled in a boarding school. The feeling of being locked-up was a traumatic experience for Gabri, who fell ill; after a second attempt to matriculate at the boarding school, she either fell sick or escaped, and stayed thereafter in Saint-Sauveur. Captain Colette had a talent for teaching, and Gabri probably took private lessons at school with her father supplementing the curriculum.

The Colettes thought of moving, but that meant paying off their debts, so they decided to stay until Achille graduated from medical school. In October 1885 Captain Colette sold La Massue to repay the loan and Juliette's share of the settlement. However, this did not solve the financial problem. Creditors were growing impatient. Yet their way of life did not change much; they trimmed their staff and traveled a little less.

What changed most was the atmosphere. The Colette children's distrust of people was such that they could not understand why their father kept on going to play a game of *écarté* at Le Canari, owned by Trouillard, the violinist innkeeper, or attending political banquets, sitting on local committees, and giving lectures at the Yonne Society of Historical and Natural Sciences. They felt betrayed, attacked at the very roots of their social and intellectual prestige. Gabri never forgave the people of Saint-Sauveur (whom she would paint in vitriolic terms), but she remained attached to the village, woods, and ponds, where she found refuge.

Whenever Sido wanted to discuss their problems, the captain brushed them off. To cheer up his family, this "urban man" would organize picnics "away from the doorbell, from the merchants anxious to be paid, away from cunning people."[92] Cunning like Laroche from their farm Les Lamberts, who refused to pay his rent and was lending them money through an accomplice at the outrageous rate of seven percent, when the current rate was less than three percent.

Gabri's favorite refuge was her father's study. It was a soldier's study — neat, orderly, and well stocked with reams of all sorts of paper: watermarked paper, cream laid paper, ruled paper. There was sealing wax in all colors, amber cakes of solid glue, liquid glue, a small burner to melt the wax, and "gold powder to sprinkle over fresh ink to dry the written words."[93] This study satisfied Gabri's craving for security and stability. She made a niche for herself in the mahogany bookcase which reached to the ceiling and spread from wall to wall. She had only to pull out two doors to have a cubicle of her own. Her father nicknamed her *Bel Gazou,* "Pretty Warbler." She had long conversations with him. He "had a special talent for the intricacies of spelling. When I was seven or eight I had discussions with him on that subject and I loved to find him at fault."[94] Captain Colette trusted his daughter's literary judgment. In his rich baritone he would recite his latest poem, marking the rhythm. "I listened carefully. It would be a beautiful oration, an ode, easy verse glorified by rhythm, rhymes thundering like a mountain storm. To him I owe the emotion which brings tears to my eyes at a concert or at a ballet. . . . He haunted me when I started to write."[95]

At eighty, Colette would write "a line of poetry does not have to be good to remain in the deepest of our memory."[96] She said that as an adolescent she never indulged in the outpouring of emotions on a sheet of paper. Writing was always a matter of style, which meant discipline and self-control.

Having failed in politics, Captain Colette put his energy into writing. A few years earlier, after the Franco-Prussian war, he had published "To The Army, To The French People, To The Assembly," an essay in which he proposed measures for the defense of the country. His utopian dreams thwarted, he now set himself to become what he saw as the epitome of a learned man, "the historian-geographer." He wrote scores of book reviews for *Le Bulletin de la Réunion des Officiers* and the elegant *Revue du Cercle Militaire.* He sent articles to scientific reviews on the different uses of algebra, geometry, and spheric trigonometry. In the *Revue de Géographie* he compared old geographical treatises with new ones. In the *Bulletin of the Topographical Society of France* he wrote about the Rossignol compass (1887) and the new invention for surveyors, the alidade compass of Colonel Peigné. He wrote numerous biographical sketches of French topographers who had mapped France and Africa, and for his study of the history of the Society of Topography he received a silver medal from the Sorbonne. He was a member of the Yonne Society of the Historical and Natural Sciences, the Society of Topography, and the Society of Geography and was a member of L'Alliance Française. He went to their meetings, giving lectures on his favorite topics. A true scholar, he also taught Gabri astronomy. At sunset when the evening stars appeared over the woods, he would exclaim, "Vesper!" and launch into a poem by de Musset while he set up his telescope to watch the constellations. Gabri learned that vesper, the evening star, was also known as Venus, the goddess of love — and in the morning Lucifer, the fallen angel, the seducer of mankind. Colette used "the star with three names"[97] as a metaphor of her life in *The Evening Star,* the book she thought was to be her last.

She Reshaped for Us the Whole Chart of Human Feelings

Sido took great care to reshape the concept of love for her daughter. She warned against the misconceptions she would find in the novels she was reading: "You and your brothers, did you ever hear me harping on love as people do in books?"[98] and methodically tutored her in a grammar of passions rooted in Fourier's ideology.

Thanks to Sido's "bold candor and the life of the animals,"[99] Gabri learned early about sexuality, but for years felt a repulsion for the things of the flesh. She looked the other way when the cat was giving birth. Watching Achille's dog La Toutouque, a benign beast who loved music, kittens, chicks, and toddlers, turn into a ferocious fighter, she became aware that "sexuality can change into an evil force the sweetest creature."[100] At her maid's wedding she sneaked into the newlyweds' bedroom, but felt sick when she imagined their wedding night. Once she stumbled across one of the maids kissing the gardener and felt "disgusted." Upset by a realistic description of childbirth written by Zola, who spoke of "torn flesh, feces, defiled blood,"[101] Gabri fainted.

She also witnessed the ambiguous feelings between the captain and Sido and her father's rage when Sido flirted with younger men. Whenever Gabri pronounced the word "marriage," Sido waged war. She called her marriage to Captain Colette "a blunder."[102] "At the beginning, he liked to dazzle her until the day when, overwhelmed by his love, he lost even the desire to impress her."[103] In her letters to Colette she later deplored the fact that she could not "throw off the yoke." "It is not divorce I blame," said Sido, "it is marriage."[104] This reflects Fourier's statement: "Domestic policy founded on fidelity enters not at all in God's design. If he gave young women an appetite for dissipation and pleasure, it is obvious that he did not intend them either for marriage or household life, which requires a taste for retirement. Matrimony oppresses women; the repressed woman has to defy existing moral standards in order to gain the slightest gratification."[105]

Gabri soon noticed that her parents slept in separate beds "far apart."[106] Later they slept in separate bedrooms. Sido, who extolled free love, disapproved of open displays of affection. Her advice to her daughter about marriage was clear: "Do as I say, don't do as I did."[107] She talked of "the deep peace of a gynoecium"[108] and dreamed of a woman's world where children would not belong to their mothers but be indiscriminately suckled and raised by any group of women. Sido expounded for her daughter an ethic as radical today as it was in Saint-Sauveur over a century ago, an ethic based on total freedom of the individual and the abolition of marriage. "It seems to me that anything is better than marriage,"[109] she told Colette. Marriage was "a bureaucracy" and like any other bureaucracy should either serve a useful purpose or not exist. Sido condoned marriage only as a means of reaching greater wealth. The redeeming factor in that case was that wealth promoted the fulfillment of all human potentials.

No taboo was left untouched, even incest. In a toned-down short story, "Le Sieur Binard," a widowed farmer lives with his four apparently happy daughters, who lovingly take care of their home and the offspring of their incestuous relationship. Sido is pictured blaming the "impure widower"[110] but marveling at the beauty of the fifteen-year-old nursing her baby and also ruminating on the practices of the ancient patriarchs. Although Colette did not dwell on the mores of the ancient patriarchs, she described incestuous matings in the world of animals as occasional but normal.

Gabri showed precocious signs of *unisexuality*, while her friends envisioned nothing more than "to be a pharmacist's wife, a baker's, a grocer's, the most daring ones dreaming of being a seamstress, a postal clerk or an elementary school teacher." Gabri told them she would be a sailor and dreamed of the sea, the ship dancing on a wave, the golden islands, the tropical fruits — "all that came as a background for the navy blue blouse, the beret with a red pompom"[111] of the French navy. She often dreamed of being a boy and sailing the seas like her grandfather and great-grandfather. In her late twenties she had a series of photographs taken of herself dressed as a sailor. Colette constantly stressed her masculine traits and her bisexuality. As a child she felt in herself "the extraordinary soul of an intelligent man and of a passionate woman."[112]

From eleven to fourteen, Gabri was enthralled by her mother's friend Adrienne de Saint-Aubin, who looked somewhat like George Sand. Her home was carelessly filled with piles of books, baskets of mushrooms, berries, truffles, fossils, and stale dishes of pet food. Gabri was seduced by Adrienne's lazy charm. She, like Gabri, had a drop of African blood, which showed in her kinky black hair, yellow eyes, and dark skin. She wore a ring inscribed with the words *ie brusle ie brusle* (I burn I burn).

The older woman artfully pretended not to notice Gabri's confusion; Gabri perceived her indifference as "the most extreme harshness."[113] At times she called Gabri "you whom I fed at my breast," referring to a day Adrienne and Sido had exchanged their suckling babies. The mere mention of the event triggered in Gabri's mind an erotic vision of "Adrienne's dark breast with its hard, purple nipple."[114]

Sido's attitude toward Gabri's emergent sexuality was ambiguous. Sometimes, when she found Gabri looking unusually pretty, she would put a pale blue ribbon in her daughter's hair and a large bunch of freshly cut flowers in her arm, and send her to visit her "strange friend." Nothing escaped Sido's "lucid gaze"; it was hard for Gabri to untangle her motives. Sido could look at her and say, "How stupid you look today! You are prettier when you look stupid; it is a pity it happens so seldom."[115] Colette countered her mother's probing by keeping to herself. Hurt by her "celestial cruelty,"[116] she was nevertheless mesmerized by her mother. Whenever Sido came back from a trip to Paris, Gabri was overwhelmed, unable to move, unable to speak, intoxicated by her mother's perfume and the fragrance of her fur coat.

It Is the Story of This Man That Should Be Told

In the summer of 1887 Achille came to Saint-Sauveur with "his best friend," whom Colette called Maurice in "L'Ami," specifying that it was not his real name. Who was Maurice? Her description points to Henry Gauthier-Villars (not yet the famed Willy), who, like Maurice, had just finished his law degree, and who shared Achille's passion for music. With his caressing gaze, doe eyes, blond mustache, small goatee, and beautiful hands, he looked like "the baritone Taskin," and had the refined and genteel sweetness that earned him the nickname *Doucette* (Sweetie). Henry Gauthier-Villars was the heir of a prestigious scientific press. In the story, Maurice's wealthy parents sold "chemical products wholesale,"[117] — a rather derogatory way for Colette to describe the scientific publishing house, but when "L'Ami" was published in 1922 Colette and Willy were divorced and had relentlessly attacked each other for years in the press. In a letter to the feminist writer Rachilde, Henry Gauthier-Villars said that he had known Colette since she was about ten. Colette said she had first known Willy when she was reading the avant-garde literary magazine *Lutèce* on the sly. *Lutèce,* founded by Henry Gauthier-Villars and two of his friends, Léo Trézénik and Rall, was published from 1883 to 1886.

Henry had come to Saint-Sauveur after a much-publicized duel. He was in love with Marie-Louise Courtet, the wife of his friend Emile Courtet (known as Emile Cohl), a talented caricaturist, one of the first to draw comic strips and cartoons in the early stages of the motion-picture industry. Henry was twenty-seven, Marie-Louise twenty-three, Emile Cohl twenty-nine. Husband and lover were determined to settle their claim on Marie-Louise by drawing blood. Duels were forbidden by law but were nonetheless fought and reported in *Le Gil Blas* and the penny press. Henry was scratched above the eye; Cohl had won the duel. Henry left Paris for a while.[118]

Gabri fell in love with Henry and started to steal sentimental memorabilia from him: "naughty magazines, Oriental cigarettes, cough tablets, a pencil with his toothmarks, and empty matchboxes with pictures of famous actresses, Théo, Van Zandt, Sybil Sanderson"[119] (Henry knew all these women and mentioned them casually). At night in her room she draped herself in a veil stolen from her mother, leaving one shoulder bare like the actresses on the matchboxes. Soon she found a better way to attract his attention: "To seduce him I became perfect simplicity in appearance, exactly as I ought to be: a slim child with long braids, waist nipped in by a ribbon with a buckle, hiding under a large straw hat like a watchful cat."[120] She let him see her kneading dough in the kitchen, pretending to dig up a flowerbed in the garden. That summer she discovered that her most winning charm for this sophisticated Parisian intellectual was the illusion of rusticity.

Over the years Henry came and went, bringing Gabri presents — "a toy monkey, a small turquoise purse, sweets . . . and the latest Parisian gossip."[121] He enjoyed chatting with her; she had a refreshing provincial accent, rolled her r's, and had a quick wit. Besides, she was quite lovely to look at — slim, with a triangular face, long blue-gray eyes, and an ambiguous smile — was it innocent? Was it ironic? And she had the longest braids ever seen, tidy tresses of light chestnut hair streaming down to her ankles, "which he held like reins when they walked."[122]

—⁓—

Henry-Jean-Albert Gauthier-Villars was born on August 10, 1859; his family was upper middle class, conservative, and Catholic. Henry's father, a graduate of the prestigious Ecole Polytechnique, was proud to be able to trace their printer ancestors back to the seventeenth century. His printing company, known to book collectors for the quality of its work, printed for Hertzel (the publisher of Balzac and Jules Verne) but specialized in scientific works. Jean-Albert Gauthier-Villars invented the G-V typeface and perfected the printing of algebraic formulae. From this press came the highly respected *Journal de l'Ecole Polytechnique, Les Nouvelles Annales de Mathématiques* and scores of scientific journals. La Librairie Gauthier-Villars at 55 Rue des Grands Augustins counted among its regular authors Auguste Comte, Camille Flammarion, Louis Pasteur, Henri Poincaré, Charles Cros, and Pierre and Marie Curie. Their catalog included the works of foreign scientists, Jammes Clerk Maxwell and William Crookes among others.

Henry was brought up in a strict and intellectually demanding atmosphere. His only recreation was music; his mother was an accomplished pianist. Henry knew most of the works of Schumann, Schubert, Chopin, and Beethoven by heart before he could even spell correctly. Blond, delicate, and intellectually brilliant, Henry was a seducer "with the caressing ease of a son who has seldom been far from his mother."[123] He had a younger sister who married General Etienne Saint-Claire Deville, and a brother, born in 1861, who was as serious and hardworking as Henry was talented and unpredictable.

When Henry was eleven the Prussian army besieged Paris, and he was sent away to his aunt in the country. Away from his mother, he started to lead a covert life — at school he only attended the classes he liked and spent his free time playing lotto for money with the wounded from an African regiment. Having exchanged his lycée cap for a *chéchia* (a close-fitting, cylindrical cap with a tuft of tassel), he caught lice. A barber shaved his head while his cousins watched and his aunt, in tears, predicted that he would end up *sur l'échafaud* (on the gallows).

War was a shattering experience. Paris was bombed, and shells fell on hospitals, churches, and schools. Under siege, Paris went hungry, and the zoo animals were slaughtered. Later Henry wrote that during this time he vividly pictured his father eating camel, his mother eating zebra, and everybody catching cats, dogs, and rats for dinner. People went begging in the streets; even ladies, wearing heavy veils to hide their identity, sang on the sidewalks and asked for alms. The Second Empire had collapsed. The war had a lasting impact on Henry; ever afterward he felt that life was absurd, that the pursuit of artistic and physical pleasures was the only thing worthwhile. He did not end up on the scaffold, although at one time the conservative press wanted to see him there because of his love for Wagner.

He went to school at the Lycée Fontanes, now Lycée Condorcet, then to an exclusive Catholic school, the Collège Stanislas. An erratic student, he excelled in literature. One contemporary recalled that he puzzled his professors by sitting motionless and transfixed while others wrote their papers and then suddenly, minutes before the time was up, writing an elegant, stylish essay, as if copying some written text from an invisible source. He had a gift for languages and, thanks to his mother's tutoring arrangements, was fluent in German and English. He had a passion for Greek and Latin and proved his excellence as a classicist by winning a gold medal for the translation of a Greek poem at the age of thirteen. Never a systematic student, he was considered rebellious in ways unique to an elitist Parisian lycée in the late nineteenth century. For instance, once he used a decadent Latin expression in a classical poem, defending it with a long Latin tirade. He peppered his articles with Latin expressions and wrote a critique in Latin of Gabriel Mourey's play, *Tennis Lawn* (directed by Antoine) that stirred up the Parisian avant-garde. He also wrote a review of *Lysistrata* in Greek for *Le Chat Noir.* He envisioned the walls of Paris covered with advertising in Latin — he thought it would be supremely elegant and spoofy. He was known for his marked talent in drawing, which can be seen in the series of virtuoso erotic etchings he made of Colette. Sophisticated and learned, his most celebrated talents were his humorous parodies and erudite puns. To celebrate the students' patron saint, Charlemagne, he wrote a parody the vice-principal found offensive. Forbidden to read it at the school banquet, he went outside and read it on the steps of the college. The students carried him on their shoulders in triumph as far as the Saint-Lazare railroad station.

At Stanislas Henry was slowly accumulating the elements of his future fame: his contempt for conventional morality, his love of practical jokes, his dandy demeanor, his love of linguistics, and his search for unparalleled literary expression, which he would find in *Le Style Rosse.* He earned his baccalaureate with great ease, by discussing the respective merits of Heine and Schiller in fluent German.

The Gauthier-Villars family never suspected that this polished adolescent, with his "ravishing voice," winning smile, and dreamy blue eyes — the image of youthful innocence — was leading a double life, and that his secret one was spent almost daily in a brothel. Henry Gauthier-Villars would always live an intricate covert life, impersonating the different aspects of his complex personality, giving them a name and a background, and using them as characters in his books: Renaud, Henri Maugis, Gaston Villars, Jim Smiley, Robert Préville, Maurice Lauban, and Tardot. "No one has ever known his true personality," noted Colette, who called him "this Balzacian genius of deceit."[124] Henry strongly disliked his chubby appearance, the fairness of his skin, his blond hair, and his medium height; he would have liked to be "tall, dark and thin."

In 1925, at the age of sixty-five, Willy gave a cool description of himself: "Abnormal, I have always been abnormal; from the time when I was very young and still in college, I loved very young girls." He went to a brothel in Montmartre that provided older men with teenage prostitutes. Two of them, bored by their usual performances with older clients, joined Henry for the sheer pleasure of it, and after that the brothel owner never charged him a penny, provided he kept his college cap on his head. "I understood much later that old men must have watched a trio's youthful frolic through some hole, and paid for the peep show."[125]

At eighteen Henry enrolled in law school. He published a few serious articles in a newspaper founded by his grandfather, *La Liberté du Jura,* and a book of sonnets printed on rare and elegant Japanese vellum. Given to bouts of depression, Henry was the image of the decadent aesthete. His budding career was interrupted by the draft; he spent one year in the Thirty-first Artillery Regiment. He preferred discussing Baudelaire with his friend Adolphe Brisson to doing the military drills, so for weeks he played the complete simpleton so convincingly that the drill sergeant asked him the bare minimum only. "He was comforting me: Come on, don't be afraid . . . and he chided my comrades delighted by this trick: Don't make fun of him. Don't you see he is a duffer."[126] The joke ended when a general, a classmate of his father's from the Ecole Polytechnique, came unannounced to review the troops. A frequent guest of the Gauthier-Villars, he knew Henry well and gave orders to make him work overtime. Henry was discharged a year later as a second lieutenant with a very honorable mention.

While taking his law degree Henry joined the avant-garde movements. He was one of the most active of the bohemians and one of the leading decadents. His two most quoted aphorisms were "art is erotic" and "art is autobiographic." His friends called him Willy (a nickname probably derived from Villars and given him because of his Anglomania). It was de rigueur for *les jeunes,* or decadents, to wear extremely refined costumes; Henry had his shirts and tailored suits made in London and adopted the flat-brimmed tophat and monocle of the aging prince of aesthetes, Whistler.

After 1880 Parnassians and naturalists, who had dominated French intellectual life for two decades, were violently denounced by newcomers on the scene. New aesthetic manifestos and a welter of short-lived magazines — one hundred and thirty of them from 1880 to 1895 — came briefly into being. The decadents were a small but highly visible and rowdy group. In the never clear-cut literary panorama, two events gave rise to the movement: the 1881 law regarding freedom of the press, and the reemergence of Verlaine who, after two years of prison in Belgium and several months of self-exile in England, was back in Paris. (Verlaine was imprisoned in 1873 for having shot and wounded his lover, the poet Arthur Rimbaud.) Early on, Henry Gauthier-Villars, a young lion of Parisian society and one of the rising stars of the decadents, gave a virulent lecture denouncing *Les Parnassiens* in the elegant Conférences Ollivaint. That evening Henry called for the liberation of the imagination and the rejection of everyday prosaic reality.

He was a member of La Société des Hydropathes, a club founded in 1878 to give young poets an opportunity to meet a public of connoisseurs. It was the crème de la crème of Parisian circles, the hotbed of *la décadence. Hydropathe* meant "sick of water," therefore "thriving on wine." The Tout-Paris took a liking to *les Hydropathes,* whose success was as enormous as it was short-lived. At one time their club was dubbed an annex of the senate. There Sarah Bernhardt presented her latest protégé, "one of the curiosities of Paris,"[127] the poet of *Névroses,* Maurice Rollinat, who so fascinated Oscar Wilde. Rollinat's neurotic poems included themes such as murder, rape, parricide, suicide, disease, hypochondria, cadavers, embalming, live burials, specters, madness, diabolism, and putrefaction.

Gauthier-Villars's sponsor was the poet-scientist Charles Cros, inventor of the *paléophone* (the first phonograph) and color photography.

Cros, later reclaimed by the surrealists, was a sensualist haunted by erotic images. He had founded Le Nouveau Cercle des Zutistes. The *zutistes* then split into several groups, among them the Jeunes and the Je M'en Foutistes.

Léo Trézénik, Alphonse Allais, Georges Rall, and Willy founded *les ironistes,* a group committed to the denunciation of all the flaws of human nature by making fun of everything, including themselves. That year Willy discovered Mark Twain, who was all but unknown in France. He wrote a 112-page essay to explain Twain's particular sense of humor and was immediately rebuffed by Guy de Maupassant, who snubbed him: "Mark Twain! You devoted a book to this humorist? That's a mistake, young man, no American writer, you hear me? None has the slightest talent."[128] Henry, outraged by the arrogance of the "great man," picked the name of the owner of the "Jumping Frog," Jim Smiley, for one of his numerous pen names. Gabriel de Toulouse-Lautrec congratulated him for having introduced Mark Twain to Paris and dedicated his translation of *Selected Tales* by Mark Twain "To Henry Gauthier-Villars" — quite a recognition.

In 1882 *les ironistes* founded *La Nouvelle Rive Gauche,* which after a few months was renamed *La Lutèce.* This four-page review became the official publication of the decadents after Verlaine published *Les Poètes Maudits.* The three founding members took turns as editor in chief. Henry signed "Henry Maugis," a name that became as famous as "Willy." The three ironists joined *La Revue Indépendante;* its new director, Félix Fénéon, had attracted a brilliant staff: the Goncourt brothers, Huysmans, and Verlaine. Soon *La Revue* became a symbolist periodical under a new director, Edouard Dujardin, creator of the elegant *Revue Wagnérienne,* a monthly that lasted two years. Henry Gauthier-Villars, a passionate Wagnerite, was on its staff and wrote in defense of the Wagnerian aesthetics. The two years he spent at *La Revue Wagnérienne* would establish his name as a music critic and decide the direction of his career. Henry and Trézénik remained members of *les hirsutes.* When *les hirsutes* left the Left Bank for Montmartre and their new home, *Le Chat Noir,* Paris' intellectual center shifted.

She Was a Terrible Tomboy

In October 1887 Gabri went back to school, where a revolution was taking place. Mademoiselle Viellard, who had no diploma at the age of forty, was forced to retire. She was replaced by a new principal, Mademoiselle Terrain, twenty-four, and her nineteen-year-old teaching assistant, Emma Duchemin. Both were part of the first avant-garde group of lay educators trained at the Ecole Normale and were in charge of the two newly created advanced classes. The new Mairie-Ecole (city hall school) had not been finished for lack of funds, so classes started in the old, battered, and rather unsanitary school building.

There were two students besides Gabri in the advanced section, Marie-Berthe Michaut and Gabrielle Duchemin, the younger sister of the new teacher, Emma Duchemin. Gabri cried when Mademoiselle Viellard was discharged. The first day of class she was in a rebellious mood, determined to intimidate Mademoiselle Terrain and assert herself. She opened *Le Temps* and started to read the Parisian newspaper. The new principal reminded her firmly that she was in a public school where everybody abided by the same rules. Gabri was nonplussed. The principal later told a journalist that she was "extremely intelligent, very gifted in French essays but not at all in sciences, extremely good in music, very witty and very naughty." Her yearly report on Gabri's performance, a requirement in French schools, read: "she is very imaginative but there is a deliberate will to be different." And different she was. At school "she was a terrible tomboy." Always perched on trees or walls, she "seemed to only want to show her legs . . . She never took the stairs, preferring to ride the banister."[129] "As a student Colette did not pay much attention to the given assignment, a quarter of an hour before the end of the class, she started to write a piece that none of us could have written in an hour and a half,"[130] said one of her classmates.

In *Claudine at School,* Claudine, Colette's avatar, is also a gifted student. But later Colette wrote that she never got top grades in French composition, that she was not a born writer, and that only circumstances had pushed her into becoming one. She complained again and again that she wrote slowly, with difficulty. Facts seem to show otherwise; Colette was a prolific journalist and it never took her more than a few months to write a novel. *Julie de Carneilhan* took five months, *Chéri*, started in September 1919, was published in January 1920. *The Ripening Seed* (Le Blé en Herbe) took her almost a year, but at the same time she was writing a play, *The Vagabond* (La Vagabonde), and her weekly articles and also giving lectures. *The Last of Chéri* (La Fin de Chéri) took a year and a half, but during this time she also wrote a play, poems for Ravel's *L'Enfant et les Sortilèges,* and weekly articles, as well as going on a theatrical tour. This does not even take into account her divorce, a breakup with one lover, and his replacement by a new one. Colette never changed the way she wrote, which so dazzled her classmates in Saint-Sauveur. Her magic was apparent very early. She once won a prize at a fair for speaking poetically about animals, charming her audience.

Gabri admired Mademoiselle Terrain as an educator but emotionally they were on a collision course. In *Claudine at School,* Colette wrote a story centered around a lesbian triangle. Claudine, smitten by the new young teacher Aimée (Emma Duchemin) lures her into her home on the pretext of private English lessons. She finds out that the principal, Mademoiselle Sergent (Terrain), is having a lesbian relationship with Aimée as well as a love affair with Doctor Dutertre (Doctor Merlou). Claudine, who was at first attracted to Mademoiselle Sergent, engages in a subtle fight with her to win over Aimée, while Aimée's sister, in love with Claudine, gratefully accepts kicks and abusive language from Claudine.

None of this was too far from reality. Mademoiselle Terrain made her career in Saint-Sauveur. Her assistant was Gabrielle Duchemin, Emma's sister, nicknamed "Duduche" by Colette. For nineteen years Gabrielle Duchemin remained an assistant teacher in Saint-Sauveur, refusing all promotion. When the novel was published in 1900 Saint-Sauveur recognized most of the characters in the book and talked openly about the unusual situation. Mademoiselle Terrain had already stirred up the town when it was rumored that she was Doctor Merlou's lover. She was respected despite her controversial behavior, since her school boasted a high rate of graduates. In 1898 Mademoiselle Terrain had an illegitimate child. After he was weaned he lived with his mother, who said he was an adopted relative. It was assumed that he was Doctor Merlou's son; the publication of *Claudine at School* left little doubt. After the disclosure of the lesbian affairs and illegitimate birth, Mademoiselle Terrain wanted to leave Saint-Sauveur, but was persuaded not to do so. Finally Gabrielle Duchemin married a colleague and left Saint-Sauveur.

Claudine at School was a vengeful book. Colette's targets were the people of Saint-Sauveur and Doctor Merlou, but essentially the revenge was aimed against Mademoiselle Terrain, "that ugly, passionate, and jealous woman."[131] Mademoiselle Terrain never forgave Colette for the book. Later in her fifties, Colette changed her descriptions and painted an idyllic rural life in Saint-Sauveur. She felt compelled to write to Mademoiselle Terrain, saying she was sorry for what had happened. She kept on writing to her old teacher who, somewhat surprisingly, reciprocated by saying nice things about Colette. In the last interview she gave, Colette disclosed that Mademoiselle Terrain was "one of her lasting remorses and one of her best memories."[132]

Captain Colette was selling off his farms and woods piece by piece. In 1888 he sold the La Forge farm; his bitterness at his impending ruin was offset by the receipt of a silver medal — la Médaille d'Argent de Première Classe — from La Sorbonne for his history of the Society of Topography. For the occasion the Colettes went to Paris, where they met General Desandré, Gabri's godfather, and Madame Cholleton, widow of a general who had been stationed with Captain Colette in North Africa. They visited Aunt Caro's salon on Avenue Wagram, described in *Claudine in Paris* (Claudine à Paris). Gabri and Captain Colette also visited Jean-Albert Gauthier-Villars. That year his two sons had become his associates: Henry, the lawyer, was editor in chief, while Albert was technical director of the printing company. Henry turned his office on the main floor into a literary salon, which became a meeting place for both the *vieille garde* and the new *avant-garde*.

The following year the Colettes were back in Paris after the captain sold the Pré Saint-Jean (some farmland) in Saint-Sauveur. France was celebrating the revolution's centennial with the Exposition Universelle, whose main display was the Eiffel Tower. (This engineering masterpiece was inaugurated to the acclaim of half of Paris and to the other half's utter disgust.) The trip was a reward for Gabri, who had graduated with both le Brevet Elementaire and le Certificat d'Etudes Primaires Supérieures. Only eight candidates out of twenty-six had been successful. School days were over for Gabri; she was only sixteen.

Before going to Paris the Colettes had attended the unveiling of Paul Bert's statue in Auxerre. Bert, appointed first governor-general of Annam and Tonkin in 1886, had died overseas. The town of Auxerre had commissioned Auguste Bartholdi, who had reached world fame two years earlier with his Statue of Liberty, to make a monument honoring Bert. Captain Colette was commissioned to write a poem to be engraved on the monument. In *Ode à Paul Bert,* the captain's reverence for Bartholdi almost overshadowed his admiration for Bert. In lyrical and enthusiastic verses he evoked the marvelous chisel that "elevated from the waves of the Atlantic the victorious beacon of freedom." But he also praised Paul Bert's social vision. Before a large gathering, on a platform decorated with flags and garlands of papier-mâché flowers and crowded with politicians who had delivered their panegyrics, Gabri recited her father's enthusiastic, rolling verses. The press praised her heartfelt rendition of *L'Ode à Paul Bert;* on stage she was always charismatic.

Little is known of Colette's life for the next two years. After graduating, it seems, she was an assistant music teacher. (In *Claudine at School* Claudine also gave music and voice lessons.) On September 28, 1890, Colette was chosen as the school representative to deliver the official speech for the inauguration of the new school buildings by the minister of agriculture; she eulogized Senator Merlou, who had broken the ground for the new school and put Saint-Sauveur within two hours of Paris with a new railroad station. "Easily reached Paris seemed to me closer, more intelligible than the unknown Burgundy,"[133] wrote Colette, who made the trip fairly often with Sido to visit Achille. In 1889 she was at the opera for Augusta Holmès's "great success" in *Ode Triomphale;* it was then that she met the singer whom she described as "blonde, a profile usually attributed to a goddess, she was not without affectation and casually sprinkled her champagne with rose petals."[134] A few years later she had an affair with her.

Colette wrote that at sixteen, love upset her life; it has been assumed she had fallen in love with Willy. But there is another version: Colette had eloped with her music teacher. Willy twice referred to Colette's elopement in his vengeful book, *Les Imprudences de Peggy.* In a letter he put it in musical terms — "a fugue with divertissements" — adding that after that Gabri was "unmarriageable." Colette attributed a similar episode in *Gigi* to Gigi's mother, who ran away with a music teacher. Unable to marry, she became a singer in the chorus of the Opéra Comique.

III

MADAME GAUTHIER–VILLARS

"The much admired friend who became my fiancé was now my husband."
"WEDDING"

$\mathcal{A}$CHILLE WAS FINISHING his medical studies. In February 1890 his doctoral dissertation, *Operating on the Kidneys*, dedicated "to my mother," was published in Paris by G. Steinheil. He received a bronze medal from the Assistance Publique, the administration overseeing public hospitals, and was appointed health inspector in a small town of 1,766 inhabitants sixty miles south of Paris, Châtillon-sur-Loing, where he opened a private practice. For Sido it was out of the question to live far from Achille. "She followed him," wrote Colette in *My Mother's House*. "He saw her every day since she had gone to live with him in the same village."[1]

Because they were to move to a smaller house, the Colettes decided to auction off some of their furniture. Adrienne de Saint-Aubin doubted that they would find appreciative buyers in Saint-Sauveur for the expensive and exotic furnishings. The house in Saint-Sauveur, which belonged to Achille, was rented rather than sold. Colette wrote in "The Green Sealing Wax" (La Cire Verte) that the house had been auctioned off after the complete ruin of the family. The legend was repeated by Maurice Goudeket, her last husband, and caught the imagination of her biographers. It was part of the carefully orchestrated image of Colette as a barely nubile, destitute village girl forced by circumstances to marry old, depraved, exploitative Willy. In point of fact the house was sold in 1925 by Achille's heirs.

In September 1891 the Colettes left Saint-Sauveur. Châtillon-sur-Loing was a *chef-lieu*, one of twenty-four administrative centers in the Loiret region. The Colettes had left "the bad lands" of Gâtinais and Puisaye to settle in a prosperous and historical small town. (Four years after their move it was renamed Châtillon-Coligny after its most famous citizen, Gaspard de Châtillon-Coligny, leader of the Huguenot party and the first to be murdered on the Night of Saint-Barthélémy, August 23, 1572, when three thousand Protestants were massacred in Paris and Châtillon was sacked. Three centuries later Republican France, in its conflict with the Catholic church, saw fit to rename the city in honor of the Huguenot martyr.) The house in Châtillon was smaller but more comfortable; each bedroom had a dressing room with a washstand. The water for the tub was brought in by their live-in maid. There was a drawing room, a dining room, Achille's office, and a waiting room. A walled-in garden full of lilacs, tarragon, and gillyflowers sloped down to the river Loing, which meandered through the town with wild radishes and saponaria on its embankments.

No sooner were the Colettes settled in Châtillon-Coligny than they became involved in Henry Gauthier-Villars's tragic love imbroglio. Despite having lost his duel with Emile Courtet, Henry had moved with Marie-Louise Courtet into an apartment on the Left Bank at 22 Rue de l'Odéon. She had changed her name and become known as Germaine Villars; he signed his articles "Gaston Villars." On September 19, 1889, they had a child. Henry moved his family to a larger apartment at 99 Boulevard Arago and lived in blissful pseudomarriage for five years. Sadly, however, Germaine fell ill; for months Henry tried to find the right doctor, the right cure — to no avail. In desperation he turned to Achille, who was just about to receive his medical degree. As Germaine's pain became more severe, Henry thought she should receive larger and larger doses of morphine, so he asked Achille what dose would be safe. Germaine died at three in the afternoon on the last day of December, 1891. It was New Year's Eve and the streets were crowded; trotting horses pulled cabs full of parcels, and there was music and singing throughout the night. Champagne was flowing all around town; there were masquerades, balls, and banquets; it was *Le Reveillon*. For

Henry the night ticked away minute by slow minute, full of heart-breaking memories.

New Year's Day brought him a few friends, still dizzy from le Reveillon and of small comfort to Henry, who did not know how to announce the death of the woman who was still legally Madame Emile Courtet. Finally, ignoring her husband, parents, and any formalities, he sent out cards announcing the death of "Germaine Villars" and had her buried under that name in the Bagneux cemetery on January 4, 1892. (A few years later her family had her body removed and buried under her legal name.) Henry was having a hard time pulling himself together; he wrote to a friend: "I am weeping helplessly over my loss and I curse this obligation to write funny articles, when my heart is bursting with tears."[2] Years later, Sido would accuse Henry of having stolen morphine from Achille to murder Germaine.

Henry was left with his two-year-old son, and Achille came to the rescue. As health officer, he recommended a good nurse. In a letter dated January 24, 1892, Sido wrote to Juliette that Henry Gauthier-Villars had arrived with his little boy, whom he placed in a house next to hers under Achille's supervision and care. As she explained the situation to Juliette, the child had been declared Willy's son, with no mention of the mother's name. Sido added a very surprising remark: "It is this child, who without doubt will open the gates for Gabri's entrance into the Gauthier-Villars family, because the grandfather is madly fond of this little one and will have to give his consent to his son's marriage with a dowerless girl for the child's sake. If not, the *sommations respecteuses* will be the only recourse."[3] Sido had a scheme in mind; she was infatuated with Henry, dazzled by the rebellious Parisian socialite, the wealthy publisher, the successful journalist. In the ten years she had known him, Sido had detected in this complex man a gentle, weak, and sentimental streak.

Gabri's future looked bleak, since she had no dowry. Sido was quick to see an opportunity. Henry had always been very fond of Gabri; he liked her boyish personality, her conversation, her quick but rather rough wit. Sido felt she could maneuver grief-stricken Henry into marrying Gabri, thus giving his son a mother.

In March Henry traveled to Brussels, where he was in contact with the group of symbolists who were to publish *La Revue Blanche*. Sido knew she could somewhat offset Gabri's lack of dowry by introducing Henry to her Belgian family. He met Sido's brother Paul, director of the

Kursaal, the plush Ostende casino. (Henry was a gambler, a member of the private clubs that were replacing cafés as meeting places for decadent society.) He met Sido's nephews, Eugène II, Raphaël, and Jules, all three journalists. Eugène II, born the year Sido married Jules Robineau-Duclos, was a friendly man with sparkling blue eyes, a short beard, and a winning smile. A brilliant conversationalist, he had a doctorate in law from the University of Brussels. He had made his career in journalism, and at thirty was editor in chief of *Le Précurseur*. In 1895 he became editor in chief of the newly founded *Le Matin d'Anvers* in Antwerp; he loved to say that his task was to whip every mind into a froth. He wrote light comedies with ease and charm, was a compulsive worker, and had the reputation of being a great wit. Henry belonged to Tout-Paris, Eugène II to Tout-Brussels.

Raphaël and Henry struck up an enthusiastic friendship; Henry recognized an alter ego. Raphaël was four years his senior, a slim, handsome man who appeared in the cabaret *Le Diable au Corps* (The Devil in the Flesh) — an intellectual, satirical cabaret, the counterpart of the Parisian *Chat Noir*. Raphaël chose to sing and write under the preposterous name of Rhamses II. The Landoys' Caribbean blood had given him doe eyes with long lashes, an olive complexion, and raven hair; according to his daughter, the novelist Jenny Landoy, he looked like a North African. Raphaël wrote a collection of hilarious tales to which Henry volunteered a preface signed "Willy," which was published in 1894. The stories were dedicated "To my excellent aunt Sidonie," "To Willy," "To Léo Colette," "To Doctor Achille Robineau-Duclos," and "To Jules Landoy, my uncle," but there were none for Gabri. Henry shared with Raphaël a fascination for etymology, philology, and linguistics. Fluent in French and Flemish, he played with literal translations that sent Henry into hysterical fits of laughter. But Raphaël had another side: he was a serious mathematician and high-ranking civil servant. He worked at the Ministère des Chemins-de-Fer, where he was in charge of all international problems arising from the movement of people and goods. Jules, the youngest Landoy brother, was also a successful journalist. The facts actually measured up to Sido's glowing description of her family. Henry started a lasting relationship with the Landoys, but — however glamorous the Belgian family — he still did not propose to Gabri.

In April 1892 Achille and Captain Colette sold the Lambert farm and its extensive woods for a very good price to an investor from the

Nièvre region; the last of the Robineau estate was now gone. That same month Gabri, now nineteen, went to Paris as the guest of General Cholleton's widow, whose husband had been Captain Colette's friend from their days at Saint-Cyr. Gabri was almost certainly under instructions from Sido to push a reluctant Henry into marriage.

Madame la Générale Cholleton, born in Oran, Algeria, lived comfortably at Rue Gaston-de-Saint-Paul. A converted Jew, she never missed Sunday Mass, while remaining faithful to her blue worry beads and her North African cultural traditions. Madame la Générale did not adhere to the strict code of the French bourgeoisie; she had been an opera singer in Algeria and kept the flamboyant manners of a diva. She showed Gabri how to make up her eyelids with kohl, explaining that kohl was the therapeutic antimony used by North African women to protect their eyes and even those of their newborn babies. But Paris was not Oran and no respectable woman wore makeup, however therapeutic. She taught Gabri "some of the manners of the harem."[4] (In Gigi, Colette would describe the education of an adolescent coached by her aunt in the subtle art of seducing wealthy Gaston.) Madame Cholleton once startled Gabri by her unseemly behavior with a manservant who was perched high on a ladder, cleaning windows. As Madame la Générale passed by, she gave him a strong slap on the buttocks and laughed. He laughed too, jumped down from the ladder, and responded with as strong a slap on her derrière.

Madame Cholleton never chaperoned her charge. This was inconceivable in any bourgeois family; strict social etiquette forbade any appearance of impropriety between fiancés, who seldom wandered away from their chaperones. Yet Gabri was left free to go where she pleased with Henry — who wasn't even her fiancé — to concerts, plays, and afterward, to late dinners. To the people they met she could only seem his latest conquest.

One evening at the Brasserie Poucet they were spotted by Catulle Mendès, the literary editor of L'Echo de Paris, who was dining with Eugènie Buffet, an eccentric Algerian cabaret singer notorious for her private life. The two were so impressed by Gabri's youthful looks, with her two fair braids reaching to her ankles, that both felt compelled to remind Henry that the law was very strict when it came to the seduction of underaged girls. After dinner, in the cab that was taking them back to Madame la Générale Cholleton's apartment, Gabri, who was a little tipsy, threw herself into Henry's arms and declared, "I shall die if I don't become your mistress!"[5]

This very same scene would be pivotal in the novel *Claudine in Paris.* Five decades later Colette repeated it, barely modified, in *Gigi,* whose heroine tells the blasé boulevardier Gaston she would rather be his mistress than lose him, which prompts him to marry her. Henry placed the scene in the comedy *Claudine;* at the premiere he whispered to his adolescent son as they sat in a box watching the play, "that was your little mother."[6] In a letter published after his death Willy replayed the scene to a friend, stressing that Colette was not the mythical, innocent country girl portrayed later: "There is more fact than fiction in *Claudine in Paris.* The day Colette, to my utter surprise, was tipsy after drinking two glasses of Asti and I was taking her back to la Générale Cholleton, who was her chaperone, she told me, 'If I am not your mistress, I will die.'[7] She did not die and Sido had the pretext she needed. Captain Colette went to meet with the Gauthier-Villars "who had not given hope of marrying Henry to an heiress," but it was now a matter of honor for their son to marry Gabri. They reluctantly agreed, but refused to have anything to do with the Colettes.

So "the friend of the family" finally became Gabri's fiancé. She did not see him any more often; when he came to Châtillon he brought books, magazines, and candies and was always busy with an article to finish, puns to find, or a review to write. The captain and Achille contributed ideas and soon the whole family would be writing, exchanging notes and sugestions. When Henry left, Gabri went to the railroad station to see him off.

In the five years since his first visit to Saint-Sauveur, Henry Gauthier-Villars had become one of the most formidable Parisian journalists. After writing in short-lived publications, he became the music and literary critic of a new monthly, *Art et Critique.* He wrote a byline signed "L'Ouvreuse du Cirque d'Eté" (An Usherette of the Summer Circus) and created a new style of criticism. Historians of that period recognized the unique place the Usherette held in contemporary intellectual trends.

The "Letters of the Usherette" were closely followed by composers, music directors, writers, and, to everyone's amazement, the public. The magazine's sales shot up and major newspapers took note. *Le Figaro* was the first to offer Henry a position as music and drama critic; two months later *L'Echo de Paris,* one of the three most important dailies, came up with an extraordinary offer — Henry was asked to join the editorial board, with the astronomical salary of fifteen thousand gold francs. In 1891 the yearly salary for a college teacher was six hundred francs. Gauthier-Villars was credited for a fifty-thousand-copy jump in the circulation; Paris had fallen in love with the Usherette.

The "Letters" showed an impeccable knowledge of music but were incredibly impertinent. The Usherette played with words, language, double entendres, context, and infratext, mixing wit, jokes, and erudition in such a way that the readers were overwhelmed and stirred to laughter. The cafés buzzed with her latest puns, and the musical establishment respected and feared the formidable Usherette. Henry Gauthier-Villars dominated musical criticism for twenty years. He supported the new composers — Claude Debussy, Emmanuel Chabrier, Vincent d'Indy, Gabriel Fauré, César Frank, Ernest Chausson, and, above all, Richard Wagner — with absolute disregard for any accepted opinion.

Henry always took his stand fearlessly. The war of 1870, which cost France Alsace and part of Lorraine, had made it hard for the French to accept Richard Wagner's music. But Henry supported the German master, putting art and genius above national feelings. When necessary he upheld his opinions sword in hand; he fought his first duel on October 25, 1886, to settle a dispute about a decadent poem. The publisher Ollendorff, owner of Gil Blas, a naughty daily aimed at boulevardiers, asked Henry to contribute short stories, essays, and his stunning reviews of concerts and plays.

During that busy year Henry joined the editorial staff of the newly created Mercure de France, founded by Alfred Valette. While Henry and the ironists were creating Lutèce and Le Chat Noir, another group led by Alfred Valette and his wife Rachilde had put forth their own publications: Le Scapin, Le Décadent, La Pléiade, and in 1890, Le Mercure de France. In a few months Valette transformed the thirty-two-page publication into a three-hundred-page journal and started a publishing house. Le Mercure de France became the most important liberal press in France for half a century, equalled in its importance only by Les Temps Modernes, after Jean-Paul Sartre appeared on the literary scene following World War II.

That year Ollendorff published the first book signed "Willy," Histoires Normandes, a collection of jokes coauthored with Léo Trézénik. Letters of the Usherette were released annually by Vannier, and Delagrave published Willy's first Année Fantaisiste, which appeared yearly until 1895. In 1892

Willy published *Comic Salon* with cartoons by Christophe but he signed historical articles in *La Revue Bleue* as Henry Gauthier-Villars. As director of his publishing house, he translated and revised the *Manuel de Ferrotypie,* under his full name, Henry Gauthier-Villars, but with a preface by Willy — thus splitting his personality, which he would fragment even further. He signed his multifarious productions with scores of names.

Who was Willy? The question was carefully orchestrated by the penny press and was giving rise to a myth. Willy (two syllables pronounced "Villy") was suddenly appearing everywhere — in sophisticated journals, popular dailies, risqué magazines, paperbacks sold in railroad stations, and avant-garde leaflets concocted at a table in the Chat Noir or Rat Mort. It was a literary blizzard. Who was Willy?

In his column, "Men of Today," Georges Lecomte described Henry Gauthier-Villars: "He rises with the sun, starts by reading everything his valet brings him: newspapers, journals, scanning through articles on philosophy, art, music, history, poetry . . . sends ten telegrams, twenty letters to friends, women, scholars . . . statesmen, producers, professors of the Collège de France; he jumps into a cab, takes notes on his way to an exhibition, a rehearsal . . . a concert, stops at the officers' club for a game of whist, writes five or six articles for various newspapers . . . dines with friends, goes on to an opening night, writes a review, sweet for his friends, harsh for his enemies . . . then comes sipping, supping and kissing."[8] He sleeps a few hours and is back in the Parisian whirlwind. A perfect gentleman, ". . . he never forgets to send flowers to the hostess, tickets for the latest show to friends, and fight a duel when necessary. He helps his friends in case of lawsuits, he goes annually to Bayreuth and more often to the Venusberg."[9]

Who was Willy? He seemed to cast a spell on his colleagues; T.H. Rosny, author of *The Quest for Fire,* wrote, "His ascendancy over others was extraordinary, besides he had such an appealing flair for art that he mesmerized his peers."[10]

Willy was also an irresistible charmer and had the reputation of being the gentlest of ladykillers. Five foot seven, with "the naive eye of a virgin from a German ballad, the caressing gaze so tenderly vague . . ."[11] He had a light tenor's voice which allowed him to sing at the piano with unerring skill. Colette was seduced by his "ravishing voice," "a feminine voice, frail under the terrifying bush of the moustache."[12] He grew a short beard to hide a dimple on his chin and wore a monocle. His discretion and tactful attentions made him the darling of Parisian hostesses. Rachilde hailed him as the epitome of the Parisian epicure: sensuous, dangerous, and famous.

In July 1892 Willy came to Châtillon to fetch his son and took him to Passy, where his parents lived in a large house. Sido was unhappy; she wrote to Juliette that Willy was in Bayreuth, "He is really in poor health, Gabri's lover, and I fear this will not end well at all. Consequently, I am very worried."[13]

Sido's uneasy feeling grew worse when anonymous letters trying to prevent the marriage from taking place were mailed to Captain Colette and to Achille. They had no idea who could be blackmailing them. Willy's family and friends had not yet been informed of his plan to marry Gabri but the Colettes had spread the news in Coligny and in Saint-Sauveur. Sido suspected that the blackmailer was Jules de Saint-Aubin, the son of her best friend Adrienne de Saint-Aubin. Three months older than Gabri, he had grown up with her, and, most probably, is the lover with whom Gabri ran off to Auxerres for a few days. Thirty years later, Willy would tell that, when he married Colette, no one would have married her in Saint-Sauveur. Because of this escapade Gabri had lost her reputation, if not her virginity. (Collette insisted this in *The Innocent Libertine* [L'Ingénue Libertine], the story of a teenager who ran off in search of sexual adventures and when confronted with reality ran back home, unscathed. She had to undergo a medical exam to make sure nothing happened, but her reputation is marred forever.) To stop the threatening letters, Willy responded in style in his book, *L'Année Fantaisiste,* a compilation of articles and poems. He made fun of Saint-Sauveur, which he called "Something by the Forest." He had come there to breathe clean air, he said, to drink fresh milk and enjoy the pure morality of country folks; instead, he found milk as bad as water drawn from Parisian street fountains and village morals so corrupt his readers "will be grateful to [him] for not describing them."[14] It sounded like a veiled threat, but nothing stopped the sender of the mysterious letters. The blackmail forced the Colettes to take extreme measures; they announced that Gabri's engagement was broken, and the anonymous letters stopped coming. "I suppose," wrote Sido, "the announcement of the cancellation of the wedding plans satisfied the letters' sender."[15]

In fact, the plans were speeded up; the captain and Gabri went to Paris, where Willy was to introduce her officially to the Gauthier-Villars. Sido wrote to Juliette that Gabri "was terribly frightened to meet Willy's family,"[16] as they had still not given up hope of finding a more suitable match. Willy had planned to travel with them, but earlier in the month he had been wounded in a duel and carried his arm in a sling; he used this as a pretext for not coming to Châtillon. The fiancé was showing no eagerness for the marriage. Yet in her next letter to Juliette, Sido wrote that Willy had surprised Gabri by taking her to their future apartment on the Rue Jacob; everything was ready, including the pots and pans, shining and lined up "as if someone was going to cook there tomorrow." There was much relief and elation in this letter, but Sido added, "Keep it to yourself! I have received another anonymous letter and so has Willy."[17]

In January 1893 Willy transferred his shares in the family business to his brother, Albert. Willy was starting to engineer the news of his marriage to make it sound like a daring social act: "You will see, I will end up by marrying a girl without a dowry."[18] To his friend Marcel Schwob, Willy announced, "I am overwhelmed by the fleeting grace of my pretty little Colette. A month from now I will have married her. And I won't have a penny. All right!"[19] writing "All right" in English. Strangely enough, he had not yet told his brother of the impending marriage.

At last, on April 21, he wrote, "Just a note. I was unable to reach you to inform you of a future event you may have heard mentioned at home, I mean my marriage. I am marrying the daughter of Captain Colette (of Châtillon), happy to prove my deep gratitude to this family who showed the utmost kindness to Jacques. She has no dowry, which does not make our parents happy. Upon my conscience, I could not act differently. Please share this information with Valentine, whose family, I believe, will scream to high heaven . . . It is seldom that in a marriage one can combine, as in your case, the most exquisite love and . . . how should I say? serious comfort. You have combined love and money in your marriage. Almost unique good fortune! For my part, I am not marrying money, oh no! When I ask myself to what point I have the right to say the words, "I marry for love," I may also say, "No." Love the great, the burning, the devouring love is, I believe, a novelist's joke. When one has a fragment of this ideal thing, one buries it in the Bagneux cemetery. One does not replace it, my dear brother. But I believe that a sound affection may still have some value, isn't it so?"[20] After this paean of love for his son's lost mother, Henry Gauthier-Villars wrote the following day, April 22, to the mayor of Châtillon to officially announce his intention of marrying the captain's daughter. He asked him to publish the banns in the minimum time prescribed by law, apparently to prevent any reaction from the blackmailer.

An unpleasant letter from his brother prompted Willy to answer sharply, "You say that this young girl will have a very difficult position? But where? You don't believe that I am foolish enough to impose her presence on our family. Come on! My parents are convinced that my marriage is to be deplored. I am less convinced. If they change their minds, it will be for the better, and she will do all she can to modify their opinion. If they keep on rejecting her, when she does not deserve it, I will not even try to change their attitude . . . Finally, you say I marry without great joy. You are right, it is true, I can do nothing about it. Everyone thinks I have forgotten the wound I suffered, it is wrong. Farewell. There will be some hard times ahead."[21]

To make things even more unpleasant, on May 4, eleven days before the marriage, an article appeared in *Gil Blas,* full of lewd innuendoes: "In Châtillon, there is gossip about the intense flirtation between one of our wittiest Parisian clubmen and an exquisite fair girl, famous all over the province for her marvelous hair. Nobody said that the word marriage had been pronounced, therefore we seriously warn the owner of the two incredible golden tresses, to give her kisses only when she will have the golden band on her finger." The article was unsigned; it implied that Willy was a Lovelace and that Gabri was his mistress.

Achille received the article in the mail, as did many others in Châtillon and Saint-Sauveur, including the mayor. Willy challenged the editor of *Gil Blas* to a duel and wounded him in the stomach. Sido wrote to Juliette's husband, who had eagerly mailed a copy of the article to his mother-in-law, that Gabri was as upset by the duel as if Willy had been the one with a slash in his abdomen. The scandal spread in a malicious way. On May 9, the Colettes went to Paris to sign the marriage contract in the notary's office of Maître Masson at 4 Rue Perrault. Willy's estate was three thousand francs in furniture and personal belongings, two thousand francs in cash, and a draft on his family's press for one hundred thousand francs. Gabri's dowry was five thousand francs in furniture and personal belongings and a note for three thousand francs.

The marriage took place on May 15. After short civil formalities at the Châtillon town hall, there was a benediction at the church at four o'clock in the afternoon. No professional photographer was hired; a single snapshot taken from a window remains the only souvenir of the event. Gabri's foster sister, Yvonne, who had come with her parents, was maid of honor. Gabri's witnesses were Achille and her Belgian cousin, Jules Landoy; Henry's were the writer Pierre Véber and Adolphe Houdard, Jacques' godfather. None of Willy's relatives were present, nor were Juliette and her husband. Sido wrote an embarrassed letter to her son-in-law a few days before the marriage: "Charles, you know that I would have been extremely happy to see you, Juliette and your daughter at Gabri's wedding, and Gabri would have been happy also, but what can be done? They don't understand."[22] "They" meant the captain and Achille. "They don't understand," lamented Sido, "and then you know we have been living in Achille's house for the past two years and without him, without his help, this marriage would never have taken place."[23]

The celebration, which Colette recounted in "Wedding" (Noces), was kept to a minimum; before dinner Gabri, who wore a white muslin dress and a white ribbon around her head, picked up the train of her wedding gown and took refuge in the garden. She sat down on the stone steps, breathed in the balmy air, and listened to the river. She had spent the preceding night imagining her future life and was feeling tired. Through the open windows of the drawing room she could see the captain in his armchair, reading *La Revue Bleue*. Sido was resting on the sofa. Léo had taken the two Parisian witnesses to the café for a game of pool. Willy and Achille had taken off their morning coats and sat at the table scribbling funny verses for advertisements and competing for the best line. From the garden steps, Gabri volunteered a pun on Baudelaire. "Great!" came Willy's voice, "You're a darling little pal."

"Petit Camaro" (little pal) was the nickname Willy gave her when she was sixteen; he never called her Gabri. He loved the sound of her patronymic name, Colette, which had a musical connotation for him. "Colette" is a comic opera by Justin Cadaux about a pretty country girl turned impromptu comedienne for one evening. It opens with a pastoral romance composed by Monsigny: "A girl is a bird." In eighteenth-century songs and comedies, Colette was a favorite name for country girls. For Willy it must have evoked the lovely, youthful shepherdesses in paintings by Boucher, Greuze, or Fragonard.

At six the captain announced that dinner was ready. During the meal Gabri fell asleep on her chair, but woke up to cut the Savoy cake. The wedding day drew to an end.

The following day Colette, Henry, and his two friends boarded the train for the one-hour ride to Paris, where she would be confronted with the problems of having married a celebrity. His friends were already writing about his strange marriage.

> *O povero mio! Cry, O' literature*
> *Cry, O' Muses . . .*
> *Willy is married!*
> *Cry, O' his friends . . .*
> *Willy is putting on weight*
> *and will never be slim again.*[24]

After much ado, Sidonie-Gabrielle Colette was now Gabrielle Gauthier-Villars. She was twenty, Henry was thirty-three — thirteen years' difference was the norm rather than the exception. Later Colette would create the legend that she had been a very young girl married to an old man. Gabri's "tender admiration" for "the prestigious Parisian journalist" had turned into "the rapture of a girl in love."[25] Seventeen years later she would write, "My God! How young I was and how I loved that man!"[26] Thirty-five years later yet, reminiscing about Sido, who had called "the first man the direst danger in a woman's life," Colette added, "One dies only of that one."[27]

About the night when she "traveled thousands of miles, crossed abysses, and underwent irreversible metamorphosis,"[28] about the most analyzed wedding night in French literature Colette commented, "I was grateful to him, I was extremely grateful to him later, for such an active abnegation, for a patience prolonged with such stoicism."[29]

Henry played the virtuoso with his young wife's senses. For him, "sensuous pleasure is made of desire, perversity, merry curiosity, libertine insistence."[30] This sophisticated relationship was underscored by the fact that he always addressed Colette with the elegant, formal "vous," while she used the intimate "tu." In *Claudine in Paris* and *Claudine Married* (Claudine en Ménage), she reverses this; Claudine addresses Renaud as "vous" at all times, even when "the exquisite torment of waiting" changes her voice to a halting "staccato."[31]

No sooner had she discovered physical love than Colette discovered her own power: "Alas, he has no authority except in his caresses . . . If I have not found my master, I have found my friend and ally."[32]

Henry, with his ravishing voice, dreamy blue eyes, and gentle, subdued manners, was nicknamed "Doucette" by Colette; a great tenderness bonded them together. This tender love is expressed in letters to her close friends, Marcel Schwob, Jeanne Muhlfeld, even Marcel Proust. When she cried over Schwob's heartbreaking *Le Livre de Monelle,* Henry rocked her to sleep. Alone in the country, she complained that without Henry's right shoulder and without being safely tucked in his arm, she found it difficult to go to sleep. How complex, how feminine he was; how much more brutal, more saturnine, more passionate she felt. She also felt more honest, more straightforward, truer than Henry. He had taught her the secret of rapture, given and received, and she enjoyed it passionately, "like a child playing with a deadly weapon."[33]

She refused to set boundaries between good and evil. "In this I did imitate my mother who with her peculiar candor was inclined to deny that evil existed, however her curiosity made her look for it . . . and look at it fascinated."[34] In 1936, still unable to overcome her passionate resentment against Willy, in her scalding autobiography called *My Apprenticeships* (Mes Apprentissages), Colette described her sensuous exploration as a form of courage. "Among those courages which defy reason, the courage of young girls is remarkable. Without it we would have fewer marriages."[35] She presented the book as the truthful account of her early married life, stating forcefully that she was the innocent victim of a depraved old husband. "In barely a few hours an unscrupulous man turns an ignorant girl into a libertine prodigy, who disregards any disgust. Disgust was never an obstacle. It is a feeling which comes later, like honesty."

She spoke of herself as a "child of twenty." She conceded that she started her new life with "a guilty rapture, a horrid, impure, adolescent impulse" and justified herself by saying, "there are many barely nubile girls who dream of becoming the showpiece, the toy, the libertine masterpiece of a middle-aged man. It is an ugly craving which they pay for by its fulfillment, a craving which goes along with the neuroses of puberty, the habit of nibbling chalk or coal, of drinking mouthwash, of reading dirty books, and sticking pins into the palm of the hand."[36]

Colette did not put all the blame on her husband; she admitted candidly that if she trusted her own memory "the corrupter does not even have to buy it dearly, his prancing prey fears nothing at the beginning, even often she is surprised: 'Is that all there is to it? At least, do we start all over?'" Colette summed up her awareness in one line: "How many contradictory riches, what a wealth of traps."[37] Traps Colette was set on exploring.

When I Was Very Young, I Hoped That I Would Become Somebody

A hectic life began, which was to draw Colette into a whirlwind of dinners, plays, concerts, exhibitions, literary salons, and friendships with Parisian trendsetters. The first invitation to dinner came from the socialite painter Jacques-Emile Blanche, Henry Gauthier-Villars's cousin; the occasion was the premiere of *Antonia,* written and produced by flamboyant Edouard Dujardin, founder of *La Revue Wagnérienne,* in an attempt to create a Wagnerian theater in Paris. The whole staff of *La Revue Wagnérienne,* including Henry Gauthier-Villars, had invited "everybody who was anybody . . . all the bluestockings of Jewish finance as well as the Faubourg Saint-Germains. The matinees attracted so many wealthy people with carriages"[38] that the performance had to be postponed until the boulevard had been cleared in front of the Théâtre du Vaudeville, one of Paris' most fashionable theaters. *The End of Antonia* was the last play in the trilogy *The Legend of Antonia,* inspired by Wagner's mysticism and Mallarmé's poetics. Dujardin's goal was to express the totality of human emotions. Antonia, the symbol of humanity, fell in love, betrayed her lover, returned to him as he lay dying, became a prostitute, repented, and, in the last episode, abandoning her quest for purity and ideals, gave birth to a shepherd's son and was redeemed by maternal love. Lugné-Poë, who launched Colette's acting career ten years later, staged the play with minimal action and, to convey its symbolic aspect, asked the actors to deliver their lines in a monotone reminiscent of Gregorian chants. For the very first time the auditorium was plunged into darkness, while the stage alone was lit. This was Lugné-Poë's lasting innovation; the play itself was by no means a landmark of dramatic creativity. "The uproar caused by the extravagance of the production of *Antonia,* by the protests and laughter in the audience who thought they had been made fools of, all led to scuffles. The police intervened . . ." Lord Lytton, the British ambassador, asked

Jacques-Emile Blanche as he was getting into his carriage, "Are you sure Monsieur Dujardin has genius?"[39]

After the play Jacques-Emile Blanche organized a party in a *brasserie*. Brasseries were all the rage; they stayed open all night, attracted artists, actors, singers, and the demimonde. Around the clock they served everything from sauerkraut and beer to elaborate meals. As French as cafés, they had terraces and basements that were the refuge of the literati. They were places in which to watch others watching you. That night Colette, in her burgundy dress, was observed not only at the table where she sat as a guest, but by everyone in sight, curious to size up "the prince of music critics'" wife.[40] Colette listened to the passionate discussion of the Wagnerians, a small, well-to-do group of intellectuals and artists, on how they could translate the continuous, ceaseless ebb and flow of Wagnerian music into the arts. Art was an expression of higher reality, they said; the true artist, the true individual waged war against philistinism, vulgarity, and bourgeois values. They argued that the absolute nihilist was the truest genius, superior to the messianic one. Did Wagner's leitmotivs translate Schopenhauer's archetypes? They extolled *Antonia* and Edouard Dujardin's methodical transposition onto the stage of Wagner's musical drama. (Colette loved the German romantics — Schubert, Weber, Mendelssohn, and Schumann. She would become infatuated with Wagner and embrace him fervently but impermanently.) She joined in the debate, Willy watching the reactions to his wife's comments. Colette was a sharp critic; she had seen *Antonia*'s excesses, the flaws of the play. She became nervous and bored by the discussion; "She started to shred her roll on the tablecloth in tiny pieces and looked at us perplexed."[41] Willy scolded her discreetly; one could say the most outrageous things, but bad manners were unacceptable. Colette looked enraged; she stopped and turned her head away. All this was noted at several tables.

At the premiere of Rostand's *Les Romanesques* Colette created a sensation. She was very bright, very quick to ridicule, had a sharp tongue, and used picturesque words from her native province. Willy's Parisian friends loved it — she was different, she had personality, *un tempérament*. Jules Renard, the cantankerous writer, noted "she had a braid of hair long enough to dip a bucket in a well";[42] Georges Courteline, the satyrical playwright, wrote that she had a "poetic quality" about her, and the word spread through Paris.

—m—

After a few busy days, Colette and Willy were off to spend their honeymoon in the Gauthier-Villars's family estate in the Jura, a hilly country close to the Swiss border.

The family had accepted, as graciously as it could, the inevitability of their bohemian son's marriage. Now Colette started to win them over. There is a photograph of her playing the piano with her sister-in-law and another with the family seated at a table. The women are dressed in dark, modest dresses — Colette, with her long braid and tiny waist, looks like a teenager lost among adults. They were kind to her, but a little disturbed by her free speech and her enthusiastic consumption of jam and butter. They kept calling her Gabrielle, and Colette watched them in their daily living as if she had landed on another planet.

On June 28, Henry and Colette settled in their apartment at 28 Rue Jacob, where they lived for three years. The building had a courtyard and its north side overlooked the Rue Visconti, next to the Abbaye de Saint-Germain-des-Prés, bordering on the aristocratic Faubourg Saint-Germain. It had a dining room, a salon, and a bedroom with dressing room facing south. Colette liked this room, wallpapered with red-and-white striped Pékiné and furnished with a huge Norman wardrobe and a bed in the Empire style, with white chintz curtains printed with red-and-yellow flowers and fruit. A small mahogany desk faced the bed. There was no carpet, but "a large white poodle skin," two stuffed armchairs, and a small wicker table: "What an array! but I find it exquisite."[43] In her bathroom, she put a rare Louis XV console "which should be in the drawing room — How wasteful! How foolish! I know it, but I am my father's daughter."[44] Across the landing were a large kitchen and a pantry; the servants' rooms were on the top floor. It was a diminutive version of a two-winged mansion. Colette had a cook, Juliette, and a personal maid, Joséphine; Henry had a valet and a hired coachman. The apartment was rented for fourteen hundred francs a year. It was a bourgeois apartment, comfortable by 1893 standards. Colette thought it was dark, "However I found it pleasant."[45] From her window she could see Rémy de Gourmont's garden. Willy described it to Guillaume Apollinaire as "a bleak house waiting for my death to be adorned with a votive tablet."[46]

Colette and Willy were seldom home. "We are invited all the time, dinners and luncheons too, parties, theaters, etc. . . ."[47] Henry and Colette were an odd-looking couple. During Germaine's illness, Henry had started to become bald and put on weight; he did everything to look older than his thirty-three years. "I have never known anyone who tried so hard to look older than his age,"[48] said Colette, who took credit for changing his appearance. She looked younger than her twenty years and made herself look even younger by wearing button boots, large, muslin collars, and a long braid — a fin-de-siècle Lolita.

They were *un ménage d'artistes,* a decadent couple in Parisian society; their friends were the small but highly visible group of decadent artists and writers whose immorality horrified the middle class and titillated the imagination of foreign visitors. "The fact that adultery featured so conspicuously in French plays and novels convinced many foreigners that Paris seethed with immorality and was a haven for the debauchee."[49] However, only a limited, sophisticated upper stratum of society flaunted its indifference to adultery and its tolerance of lesbianism, homosexuality, and other sexual deviations, and they exercised extreme circumspection. From the start, Colette and Willy "were a pair of comrades. Ill-tempered people find them bohemian, all the others find them charming. I believe the former are jealous,"[50] wrote Jean de Tinan, a close friend of the couple. He found Colette bright, witty, graceful, and pretty, and was amused by the number of pet names she called Willy: "The Sweet Master," "The Big Cat," "The Sweet One," "The Blue One."

They were different because they went everywhere together, from the editing rooms of *L'Echo de Paris* or *Le Journal* to the most exclusive salons and the pleasure haunts of Montmartre or Montparnasse, where married men were never seen in their wives' company. The "pleasure capital" was first and foremost a man's world. Only a very few artistic couples shared their uninhibited lifestyle: Paul Adam and his wife Juliette, who wrote under the pseudonym of Count Paul Vasili; Henri de Régnier and Marie, whose pen name was Gérard d'Houville; Vallette and Rachilde — all had anarchistic leanings.

As the wife of the most sought-after Parisian critic, Colette soon knew everyone in intellectual, artistic, and journalistic Paris. The Paris press was the most varied, influential, and uninhibited in the world. "Its press was also reputed to be one of the most corrupt. It was notorious for the way it accepted subsidiaries from various quarters, for its openness to bribery, its use as a political weapon, and its ferocity in attacking individuals."[51] Libel and slander were daily fare, with no recourse other than the right to reply or fight a duel, for legal protection against personal attack was practically nonexistent. It was a highly regarded, highly powerful, and self-seeking world of intrigues and scandals — brilliant, intense, pyretic. Politicians, writers, theater personalities, and the powers-that-be often contributed articles. Journalists wielded great personal power; they had their entrées into high society; they were revered and feared.

Willy's milieu was foremost the music world. At first Colette, used to a temperate dose of music, felt assailed, overpowered by the many concerts — so intense was her intercourse with music that her nerves were shattered and she had to learn to discipline them to withstand "the assault of the strings, the shock of the orchestra force."[52] At night she would lie awake watching the fleeting shadows of the street gaslights on the ceiling of her room and replaying the concert through her mind, marking the tempo with her toes and jaw muscles. Music, she said, is always new; words are used and misused and lose their power in constant handling.

All her life she composed music, of which almost nothing remains. There is a study to be made of the use of musical structures in Colette's works, particularly motets, fugues, and cantatas. "Musical motifs and sentences are born from that immortal and evasive couple: note and rhythm,"[53] she said. Colette first found the musical line before finding the words; she struggled to transcribe on paper the music in her mind. It was a painful process and Colette complained of the task's difficulties, "To write instead of composing music is to go through the same quest but with a less lucid trance and a smaller reward."[54]

Colette credited music as her passport to the Parisian world during the first years of her marriage. In some literary groups she felt "invisible and a nonentity";[55] she had no classical education, and discussions on the emerging science of linguistics, the recital of Latin or Greek poems, or the search for Indo-European roots so dear to Willy made her feel an outsider. Colette could never accept not belonging, not excelling. Her pent-up energies propelled her into fits of intellectual or physical activity. She read voraciously, took voice and piano lessons, improved her English, learned Spanish and Italian. Colette did not focus on her achievements but on her stumbling blocks; they were the catalyst of her creative process. It is characteristic that music, which she knew so well, is hardly mentioned in her writings. But she felt at home in the musical world; within a year of her marriage she signed music reviews for *La Cocarde,* then for *La Fronde,* Colette Gauthier-Villars.

On Fridays, without fail, Colette and Willy were at Madame de Saint-Marceaux's, a citadel of music. Madame de Saint-Marceaux gave carefully planned dinners followed by concerts in her hotel at 100 Boulevard Malesherbes. In between galas, her salon was a music work-shop, and she added a special charm by demanding that everyone be casually dressed; tails, tophats, and evening gowns were strictly for-bidden. The hostess intended her Fridays to be a reward for a hard week's work, not an exercise in social graces; she asked her guests to come as if they were simply going home and inisisted on being called Meg. It took Madame de Saint-Marceaux twenty years to convince all her friends that they should feel comfortable in a relaxed atmosphere and join in, no matter how early or late. A female marmoset moved about daintily, accepting a morsel of cake here, a slice of banana there, and wiping her tiny fingers on a handkerchief. There was also Waldine, a small basset hound who would listen to the music with the attitude of a "connoisseur."

Madame de Saint-Marceaux's salon embraced a circle of intimate friends bound by no rule. Meg would often read a book while her guests broke into small groups — Emma Calvé sang without leaving her chair; Prince Edmond de Polignac, a woolen shawl draped over his thin shoulders as a protection against imaginary drafts, made sketches of everyone (Colette lost the "flattering, so pretty cartoon" made by the prince); Gabriel Fauré listened and made sketches, too. Debussy, Chabrier, Messager, Schmitt, Chausson, and Louis de Serres would sit at one of the pianos and improvise, challenging each other to continue an interrupted melody.

Colette was not a silent partner; she intervened "in their dialogues . . . so they would not think I was deaf, impervious to their brilliance, ban-ished."[56] They dwelt on the importance of musical technique, neoclassi-cists and atonalists arguing about whether or not they should maintain an aesthetic distance from the emotions portrayed, rather than using the direct expression of dynamic emotions. Technically, these composers broke up the relationship between the elements of traditional musical discourse and recombined them with a greater freedom. They liberated musical elements from past limitations to bring out their particular ex-pressive qualities. Gabriel Fauré was pressing his students to look back to the polyphonic elements of Gregorian music; Vincent d'Indy, Charles Bordes, and Alexandre Guilmant created the Schola Cantorum to restore the Gregorian tradition and rediscover unpublished works by Monteverdi, Campra, and Schütz. Colette remained a pillar of the Schola and to her last years seldom missed the Saturday concerts given at the Conservatoire, although she complained at times of having lost her acuity of hearing, finding some notes blurred, which prevented her from following the score in her mind, missing the evolution of the thematic line. "She could have conducted Beethoven symphonies or *La Damnation de Faust*." Her ear "was faultless and she was never mistaken as to either the key or the tone of what she was hearing; she was particularly sensitive to the exactness of the movements." Except for Bach, whom she called "a sublime sewing machine," she did not greatly value the preromantics. "Mozart left her cold, Brahms did not touch her in any way. But Fauré, Debussy, Ravel . . . drew tears to her eyes."[57]

Gabriel Fauré, who liked "to seduce and be seduced," thought highly of Colette. He sent her "playful, gay and tender notes." In a letter he wrote a little score on the theme "kisses in the ear, oh yes!"[58] Fauré's legacy went beyond those facetious quotes. In Colette's style there is the same quality of unexpectedness, compression of meaning, sinuosity of the theme or melodic line, constant indecision of tonal modalities within a well-structured form, and dynamic sensuality tinged with melancholy as in Fauré's work. At Meg's, Fauré and Messager, both from the Niedermeyer School, played improvisations on *The Ring of the Niebelungen*. The two musicians challenged each other to "catch this one" or "fend off that one." "Colette sat in the back, listening intently and taking notes."[59] She sang songs she had learned from her nurse to Julien Tirsot, the music historian and librarian at the Conservatoire de Musique, whose passion was collecting popular French songs.

Colette's kindred spirit in the group was Claude Debussy, who credited Henry Gauthier-Villars with launching his fame and the understanding of his music. Debussy was working on his revolutionary aesthetics and his impact on Colette's own aesthetics would be overwhelming. He was awed by Colette's ability to faithfully recall a piece she had heard only once. She shared with Claude Debussy the same "inner frenzy." "Music seemed to intoxicate Debussy," she noted. He shut off the outside world and became cross-eyed, like "a hunting animal on the watch."[60] The world of musicians is an exclusive fellowship with little room for amateurs. Colette knew its language. She had learned it with her brothers and with her aunt Caroline de Trye, the interpreter of

Chopin. She felt free and at ease in this euphoric ambiance. "To consent, as I did to a sudden and total gift of myself to music, to close my eyes on two impending tears, to relax a lump in my throat with a sigh, resembles a voluptuous surrender in the dark."[61] Colette preferred the informal setting of Meg de Saint-Marceaux's to the rival salon of Madame de Saint-Paul, a good pianist with a scathing wit that earned her the name "the rattlesnake." She was born Diane de Feydau, which prompted the no less caustic Count de Montesquiou to say "It is unfortunate for Paganism and Christianity that she should be both Diane and Saint-Paul."[62]

Willy and Colette spent most evenings at 16 Rue du Croissant, in the editorial room of *L'Echo de Paris*, where the staff worked through part of the night; Colette was learning the trade. She would orrect some of Willy's proofs, then retreat to the director's empty private office and lounge on the comfortable red couch, waiting for Willy, a finicky editor, to finish up.

After midnight or later Willy, Colette, and journalists from *L'Echo* and *Le Journal* congregated at the Brasserie Gambrinus, Pousset, or Le Napolitain around marble tables loaded with glasses of beer and sundry cold cuts, sauerkraut with sausage, loaves of bread, and mustards, to which Colette preferred a lemon sherbet. One night she listened to Catulle Mendès, the senior literary editor at *L'Echo,* who had drawn the best and the brightest to the Parisian daily; his reputation as a great seducer had not abated, but he was no longer the handsome Don Juan of yore — he looked "like a crossbreed between a lion and a turbot."[63] He had a satanic strain and was said to have influenced d'Annunzio's *Poema Paradisiaco.* Mendès confabulated over his review while he wrote it, undisturbed by the conversations around him. "His sharp and useless intelligence"[64] did not impress Colette. Around one o'clock Georges Courteline arrived: "Ma p'tite Côlete," he shrieked with a popular twang in his raspy voice. "You have a bat's voice," retorted Colette, who liked his strong and mordant friendship. He was "tiny and essential" like "the pit in a fruit"; extremely funny, he always kept a straight face. Colette, who loved to dissect the people around her, to get to "the pit" of their personalities, thought that Courteline hid "a fundamental and secret melancholy."[65]

No one was more entranced by Colette than the twenty-six-year-old Marcel Schwob. Colette was equally fascinated by the coeditor of *L'Echo de Paris* literary supplement; she found in Schwob her most congenial friend. He came from a prominent Jewish family of rabbis and doctors and like Colette, he had been raised on Fourierist principles. His father, who as a young man had mingled with Banville, Gauthier, and Baudelaire, was an impassioned advocate of Fourier who became a high-level official in Egypt, then the owner of a newspaper in Nantes. His mother traced her ancestry to the Cayms, who fought in the Crusades with Saint Louis. Marcel Schwob was the *wunderkind* of this highly intellectual family. His brother became a businessman and owner of several newspapers; his sister was a concert pianist. Marcel was to enter "the Sacred Arch," as his father called the university. For that purpose, he went to live in Paris with his scholarly uncle, the head librarian of the *Bibliothèque Magazine*.

Marcel had a penchant for literature and wrote articles and short stories in *La Lanterne* (a leftist review); he also coauthored a major study on the evolution of French slang. Verlaine dedicated a sonnet to him, which was Marcel's anointment in decadent circles; he was soon one of the most prominent literary Young Turks. Extremely erudite, an existentialist even before the word came into existence, he shared Schopenhauer's nihilistic sense of life. Passionately Anglophile, he socialized with the London literati and thought of emigrating to England; George Meredith was extremely fond of him. Marcel, along with a handful of Anglophiles and Americanophiles that included Henry Gauthier-Villars, was an active promoter of all things English.

He and Willy shared the same interest in dead languages, medieval slang, and erotic literature; their discussions often centered around the meaning of irony. Under the Racinian pseudonym "Loyson-Bridé" (The Shackled Bird), Schwob wrote scathing satires of the journalistic world in *Moeurs des Diurnales* (Morals of the Dailies), describing the ongoing saturnalia in the editorial rooms. His friendship with Willy went beyond literature; they confided in each other and exchanged notes, sometimes several times a day.

Marcel shared with Colette an ideological background, if not the same outlook on life; he was one of the most vulnerable and pessimistic of the decadents. But she recognized that he could open new literary horizons for her; although her reading had been broad, she had entirely missed English literature. A quick learner, she needed someone to point out what was important to know. There was no better guide through the literary jungles than Marcel Schwob, a trilingual scholar who had read everything from ancient history to folklore, from Hebrew tradition to the Elizabethans, from the slang of medieval thieves to children's stories. Colette had acquired another master critic. For three years Schwob came regularly — "he talked, translated for me . . . I treated him as if he belonged to me."[66]

The Midnight Angel

Colette and Willy spent some evenings in Montmartre, with the ever moving crowd of their night-prowling friends: Henri de Toulouse-Lautrec, Steinlein, Degas, Forain (who greeted Colette, "Here comes my Midnight Angel!"), a coterie Willy described in *En Bombe* and *La Môme Picrate* (The Wino Kid), a *roman à clef* featuring Jane Avril, Toulouse-Lautrec's famous muse. Montmartre had been incorporated into the eighteenth arrondissement and was now part of Paris, but it remained a village with steep, winding streets, small gardens, run-down houses, and a half-rustic, half-bohemian population. Montmartre was a refuge for penniless painters and destitute poets. Willy was on the staff of *Le Chat Noir*, the official journal of the celebrated café; he would become its editor in chief in 1897. This publication more than any other exemplified the intellectuals' preoccupations in the Gay Nineties. Its tone was seditious and antibourgeois; *Le Chat Noir* published bitter social satires illustrated by Forain, Steinlein, and Toulouse-Lautrec and abrasive cartoons by Emile Cohl. It featured songs, typical of the new realist style, about the plight of the homeless and unemployed, mixing popular jargon with street argot. The tone of the cabaret Le Chat Noir and its journal was resolutely defiant — they ridiculed and jeered at politicians, high society, and the demimonde.

The cabaret Le Chat Noir was the creation of Rodolphe Salis, a mathematician and artist who produced religious paintings. Bohemians from the Left Bank came to recite poetry and sing satiric songs in his studio. In 1880 Salis opened a cabaret in Montmartre among the easels and canvases, featuring a few musicians and a few unknown writers of enormous wit and zest. They adopted a black cat as their mascot. Customers flocked to the cabaret, which had to move to larger quarters. Salis dressed his waiters in green-and-silver uniforms and cocked hats (the uniform of the Académie Française) and the headwaiter in the

striped uniform of a papal guard. The cabaret was fitted out in the Louis
XIII style. There were two other cabarets on the hill, La Grand' Pinte and
La Nouvelle Athènes, which were both frequented by local poets, artists,
and bohemians. At the Chat Noir Colette met the old group of *les hydropathes*, now all established journalists and writers. Toulouse-Lautrec
immortalized the most ebullient singer of the Chat Noir, Aristide
Bruant. Bruant would stroll into the smoke-filled cabaret in high boots, a
black velvet suit, a black felt hat, and a long red scarf flowing from his
neck. He would walk up and down between the tables singing — in a
rich, resounding voice — dirgelike melodies about the misery of the
Montmartre prostitutes and about assassins, thieves, pimps, lecherous
monks, and wicked rich people. He also sang about the guillotine, called
"the red widow." (Executions were still being carried out in public, and
the executioner, Monsieur de Paris — as all executioners were called —
was a dreaded and much lampooned character of Parisian lore.) Bruant,
interrupting his songs to insult a customer in evening clothes, would
erupt with scorn, mockery, and four-letter words in a frenzy of abuse, to
the absolute delight of the aristocrats, millionaires, and tourists, who
shuddered with excitement, feeling that they were part of a revolution.
The cabaret, which served beer only, was the most expensive in Paris;
Bruant himself collected the money for the drinks as he moved among
the tables, repaying his bewildered customers with outrageous remarks.
Colette greatly enjoyed Bruant's daring, aggressive songs and sang along
with gusto.

Other musts for the partygoer were the Jardin de Paris and the Moulin
Rouge, where the girls danced the cancan and kicked the customers' hats
off with their shapely legs. They had hair-raising nicknames: *La Goulue*
(The Gulper), *La Mélinite* (Dynamite), *Grille d'Egout* (Sewer Grill), *La
Glu* (Glue), and *La Môme Fromage* (The Cheese Kid). Toulouse-Lautrec's
licentiously truculent paintings captured the atmosphere of the Moulin
Rouge, with its hard-drinking crowd, prostitutes, and dancers. Willy's
friends surrounded Colette and she retorted to the witty and salacious
remarks with which they pelted her with innate brilliance. They agreed
that she had a "piquant," "spicy" quality that made her quite astonishing.
Colette summed this up as being "outlandish, spiritless, secretive and
attractive."[67]

Her vocabulary was a matter of constant surprise, mingling as it did
provincial expressions with popular street talk straight from the Paris

sidewalks and the "extraordinarily crude terms"[68] she had picked up from her father's bawdy songs. She had such a picturesque way of putting things together and such a sense of humor that she could get away with any nasty innuendo, slashing remark, or biting comment. Premeditated gaffes and scandalous speech were appreciated by the capricious and blasé Parisians, to whom teasing and mocking was a way to feel at home with their peers.

Willy would tell Colette, "Do read this, the author will be at *Le Mercure,* you should be prepared to talk about it."[69] So Colette prepared; stretched out on the couch with her beautiful Chartreux cat, Kiki-la-Doucette, eating an inordinate number of chocolates and confectionaries (her main diet), she read swiftly and with great intensity, scribbling down a few notes. Every Tuesday she and Willy went to *Le Mercure de France,* on the Rue de l'Echaudé and crowded into the small office of Alfred Vallette and his wife Rachilde, who greeted her guests in a black woolen dress, with two white mice on her shoulder.

Rachilde welcomed Colette; a yet deeper friendship developed when Colette found her voice as a writer. The outspoken Rachilde did not understand why Colette, whom she so admired, refused to acknowledge that she was the author of *Claudine at School.* She heralded her friend's talent; for years Colette kept an article by Rachilde in her purse as a good-luck charm. Rachilde was hard to impress; born in a prosperous provincial family (her father was an army officer), she had been educated by a private tutor, a Jesuit priest, and published her first short story at the age of twelve. She fled to Paris to avoid an arranged marriage and took refuge with a female cousin, director of the feminist review *L'Ecole des Femmes,* who gave her a position and published her first novel. She cut her hair short, dressed like a man, and changed her name from Marguerite Emmery to Rachilde. On her visiting card she signed "Rachilde, *homme de lettres."* She spent her evenings in cafés on the Left Bank, defying conventional standards. In the twenty years since George Sand wore men's clothes to be able to go unescorted to the theaters and restaurants, where women unchaperoned by a man were refused admission and equated with prostitutes, nothing had changed.

Rachilde's second novel, *Monsieur Vénus,* stunned everyone by its audacity; inverting traditional gender roles, she described the sexual adventures of a woman using a young man as her plaything. The main surprise was that such a licentious novel was signed by a woman not hiding behind a masculine pen name. Refused by Parisian publishers, the novel was printed in Brussels, caused a stir, and was dubbed obscene. In an unprecedented move in a city where erotic and pornographic novels and postcards were printed for shipment to gay Paris, Rachilde was sentenced in her absence to two years in jail and a large fine. In Paris Verlaine, no stranger to the censors' wrath, acclaimed her. She was called the "Princess of Darkness," "Mademoiselle Baudelaire." Barbey d'Aurévilly, scandalous author of *Les Diaboliques* and already frail and dying, undertook her defense: "Pornography, so be it! But so *distinguée.*"[70] The Paris police tried to confiscate the shipment of *Monsieur Vénus;* Rachilde persuaded the poet Jean Moréas to hide the books in his garret. A decade would pass before the book would be printed in Paris.

Monsieur Vénus was a catharsis; Rachilde had fallen in love with Catulle Mendès, who had a taste for bisexual women. His wife, Judith Gauthier, and two of his mistresses, the opera singer Augusta Holmès and the actress Marguerite Moréno, were known for their ambiguous personalities. Flattered by Rachilde's worship, he let her think he was not indifferent, then turned his attention elsewhere; this unfulfilled love led to a depression so deep that Rachilde was temporarily paralyzed in both legs. She later wrote that, anticipating Freud, she had studied the problems of hysteria caused by paroxysms of chastity in a corrupt milieu. Recalling her madness and her love for Catulle Mendès, she commented that to become his mistress one had to humiliate oneself again and again and again.

Nono and *La Marquise de Sade* followed in rapid succession, like cannonballs aimed at destroying the Baudelairian myth that "woman is natural, which is to say, abominable." Baudelaire asserted that spiritual life was closed to her, that "she is simplistic like the brute beasts,"[71] and wondered why women were even allowed to attend church. Love, he contended, was satanic and perverse and women contemptible, but necessary. The essence of women was animality, and sexuality brought with it guilt and self-abasement. Rachilde's female characters, for whom sexuality was essentially a power game, more cerebral than physical, were strong, manipulative, and domineering — the antithesis of the Baudelairian women.

Aesthetes and symbolists scurried to become Rachilde's friends. At first they were at a loss to reconcile their expectations with reality, since when she was not cross-dressing she looked like a girl just out of the

convent, rather slim, even frail, with incredible hands and a classical profile. Her most striking feature was her eyes. Oscar Wilde, who worshipped *Monsieur Vénus,* was stunned by the unassuming looks of
Rachilde, as was Maurice Barrès. Together they gave rise to a minor literary trend that dealt with sexual manias, suggesting that only the abnormal and unnatural were interesting. Rachilde, in men's clothes, took
Barrès to anarchist meetings, where discussions turned to brawls. At Le
Boulant a seditious group was rampaging one night, overturning tables
and chairs during a heated debate. Barrès, who had a speech impedi-
ment, would have liked to address the crowd; Rachilde listened to his
arguments, then jumped up onto the table and injected some sense of
direction into the chaotic jumble of ideas. The police stepped in and arrested her. It was her first but not her only ride in the prison van.

"You were not even convinced of what you told them," marveled the
aesthete Barrès.

"That was why I was so successful; I could watch my diction,"[72] retorted Rachilde.

Countless tributes have been paid to Rachilde's kindness, her lucid
intellect, her acumen for spotting talent, her generous disposition for
helping writers in need. When she found Verlaine drunk, sick, and destitute, lying on the pavement, she brought him to her apartment and took
care of him.

This unorthodox woman fell in love and married Alfred Vallette, the
scion of an old Parisian family, director of a lithographic printing press.
Vallette always dressed in tightly buttoned dark suits; he wore his dark
auburn hair in a strict crewcut and had a stern, classical face with a serious
expression underlined by a neatly trimmed moustache. He met regularly
with five or six friends at the Mère Clarisse to reshape literature; their discussions were extremely serious. Alfred Vallette promoted *synthetism,* a
new form of realism, the literary vision of a lithographer. He rejected the
idea of a novel reflecting the single vision or state of mind of a writer; instead, the psychology of a character should emerge by means of minute
descriptions of his physical gestures, described in the most intimate details
as seen from a multiplicity of points of view. Vallette never succeeded in
writing the great synthetic novel, but with Rachilde he created an intellectual center, sizzling with talent and daring ideas.

Le Mercure de France was at the crossroads of modern literature. Alfred
Vallette and Rachilde kept it at the forefront of all avant-garde movements.

At the *Mercure's* weekly meetings, they discussed woman's role in society, environmental issues, population control, workers' rights, children's rights, animal rights, freedom of the press, and the ongoing struggle for the abolition of censorship. They discussed Ibsen, Strindberg, Sjoernson, Bakunin, Gorky, Tolstoy, Rudyard Kipling, Stevenson, Mark Twain, and Oscar Wilde.

They were obsessed by questions about consciousness, dreams, sensuality, and aesthetics. "The conversations were highly technical . . . I scarcely saw any women," wrote Rachilde in her memoirs, recalling the crowd of "men of letters, some extremely bohemian, others already famous or on their way to fame, some poor men of genius, some too wealthy and amateurish to have any talent."[73] It was a man's world where women were expected, at least intellectually, to behave like men, debating, arguing, and putting forward ideas.

Colette, one of these few women, found a congenial group ready to listen to her. She felt inexpert at pushing herself into the limelight. However, she so impressed Alfred Jarry that in 1894 he inscribed *Minutes de Sable Memorial* (Moments of an Hourglass) "To glorify Madame Colette Willy." Marcel Schwob sent her his highly praised *Mimes* and wrote, "To Madame Willy, so she can imagine she is eating a Sicilian cheese. Her admirer." Pierre Louÿs sent her *Poétiques* with these words: "To Madame Willy. Why? To teach her how to write." Colette was not Henry Gauthier-Villars' silent shadow.

Willy was aware of Colette's potential as a writer; she had written an abundant correspondence, and he had probably read her diary, "those piles of notes"[74] she turned into *Claudine at School*. In a photograph taken during their honeymoon in the Gauthier-Villars' estate Colette, slouching over the table, rests her her left elbow on a folder and there are two other folders in front of her, dispelling the myth that she accidentally started to write eighteen months or two years after her marriage. The other women in the photo are busy with some embroidery; an ordinary young wife would have been, too, but Colette was not just another young wife. She was a writer, and it is as a writer that Willy, certainly enjoying his part as Pygmalion, nurtured his "child-genius." He was looking after her, recalled Rachilde, the way a gardener coddled a rare flower in his conservatory. So did his friends; no woman writer had so many talented godfathers monitoring her debut: the outrageous Jean Lorrain, the scholarly nihilist Marcel Schwob, and a curator at the Bibliothèque Nationale turned literary impostor, Paul Masson.

Willy called Colette "Ma Huronne." The nickname was a sophisticated, witty way of introducing his wife to his Parisian friends. *Le Huron
ou l'Ingénu* is a philosophical tale by Voltaire about a young man who
spent his life among the Hurons before coming to Paris. Untainted by
any prejudice, he expressed opinions that seemed reasonable and fair, but
outrageously out of context in a society governed by taboos, the intrusion of religion into the private life of the individual, and the social abuse
of power and authority. The Huron was the natural being making a stand
against the rules imposed by civilization and not justified by reason. "Ma
Huronne" was a nickname every Frenchman could understand.

For the initiated, who could grasp its deeper connotation, Colette was
introduced as "La Tahitienne avant l'arrivée du Missionaire" (The
Tahitian before the Missionaries). In Fourier's utopia Tahitians were
models of free, autonomous individuals. Descriptions given of Tahitian
life and mores by the first navigators to land there — Simon Wallis, Cook,
and Bougainville — had caught the imagination of the eighteenth-
century social thinkers. The Tahitians knew no prejudice, no repression,
and no sexual taboos. Their longevity was remarkable and their strength
and health led them to lust, orgies, incest — to the most lascivious customs. But love in its many manifestations was never a crime; according to
Fourier the Tahitians, isolated on their island, had attained a higher social
level than any civilized society.

Colette was "La Tahitienne"; healthy and unfettered, she was the ab-
solute opposite of femininity as defined by the decadent imagination.
"It is not in a single day or on a single impulse that a thoughtful
'Polynesian' like D. or a 'child of nature' like me are made,"[75] wrote
Colette in *The Pure and the Impure*. In calling her "La Tahitienne," Willy
was discreetly placing Colette at the forefront of the avant-garde.
Gauguin, back from his self-exile to Tahiti, had persuaded a hesitant
Durand-Ruel to hold a one-man show for one month, exhibiting
thirty-eight paintings he had brought back from the island. The exhibition, held in November, was controversial; the impressionists were
shocked, and only the symbolists enthusiastically defended Gauguin.
Willy was well acquainted with Gauguin's message that the artist must
express nature as he felt it; Gauguin had made his famous proclamation
that "a painting is essentially a flat surface spread with colors organized
in a specific order"[76] in *Art et Critique,* when Willy was on its editorial
board.

Willy reinforced Gauguin's ideas in a manifesto he wrote on the literary trend he called *Le Vivantisme,* which he elaborated to give more
credence and weight to Colette's singular style: *"Vivantisme* is the opposite of Paroxysm. . . . It aims to convey the sensations and the passions in
their nakedness, in their stirrings, with poetic and unaffected words, free
from rigid phraseology and oppressive syntax." He advocated the use of
images vivantes (living images), conveyed by the living rhythm to translate
the movements of the heart and mind."[77] Images should carry the
meaning; in the corrections he wrote in the margins of Colette's manuscripts, he always suggested making the images more precise. This advice
was not lost on Colette; in a rare allusion to the art of painting, she
wrote about Gauguin, "We can feel the breeze on a beach on the notch
in a cliff hewed by Gauguin."[78] She noted that except for one who "es-
capes and paints Tahiti," French painters achieved their revolution from
within the limits of their gardens and villages. This could be a description of Colette herself. No one ever claimed to belong to *Le Vivantisme,*
but it is still the best description of Colette's magical style.

Colette spent many "sweet" evenings at the Café Vachette or the Café
d'Harcourt on the Place de la Sorbonne, where the literary youths gathered. These young men brazenly cultivated outrageous public personnae.
Alfred Jarry wore a bowler hat with an oversized top that looked like an
observatory and a cape so long it dangled to his heels; he sported a cyclist's suit and a fabricated accent, hammering out every syllable and
sounding like an automaton. Pierre Louys, extremely elegant and handsome, wore the high collar fashionable during the French Revolution.
André Lebey, the seventeen-year-old poet, a fringe of ash-blond hair
half-hiding his eyes, astonished Colette (who wore a man's shirt with a
stiff collar and a tie), for he was the first man she knew to be interested in
furniture, interior decorating, and art deco. They were Oscar Wilde's and
Mallarmé's admirers, but twenty-seven-year-old Marcel Schwob was
their idol; Schwob had displaced Jean Lorrain and Barrès in the literary
pantheon of the Left Bank.

Sponsored by Willy and Schwob, Colette was genuinely adopted into
the group. Henry Bauer, Alexandre Dumas's gifted illegitimate son, was
struck by Colette's intensity. In the general discussion she favored tête-à-
tête and would listen critically, her impassioned gaze never leaving the
interlocutor's face. "I rely on the literary youths of the d'Harcourt,"
wrote Colette; a book was worth reading when they spoke of it "with

respect and venom."[79] In *My Apprenticeships,* Colette recorded only the sexual attraction she felt for "these upcoming, virile youths."[80] One of them in particular was "a peril" for Colette; she called him "Marcel" in *Claudine in Paris* and depicted him as a homosexual.

Colette was very fond of Jean de Tinan (who later collaborated on Willy's *Maîtresse d'Esthètes*). Tall, slightly stooping, with long, thin legs and delicate hands, the nineteen-year-old baron de Tinan (nephew of the countess de Greffulhe, Proust's model for the countess de Germantes) draped himself in a cape lined with purple satin and wore a black velvet vest with thirty silver buttons, a bunch of violets in a pocket over his heart, and a loose, romantic necktie. He was a disillusioned young man working on his first novel, *Un Document sur l'Impuissance d'Aimer,* based on a devastating love affair. He wrote on café tables, restaurant tablecloths, or on his heavily starched cuffs (a fad in those times), jotting sentences and notes down everywhere, even when with a courtesan in a private dining room at the sumptuous restaurant Paillard. He so impressed Valette and Rachilde that they created a new section in *Le Mercure de France* on "cirques, cabarets, concerts" in which Tinan discussed the world of entertainment. He did not blend in with the bohemians. The Montmartre period was ending, to be replaced by the hyperrefined new wave of aesthetic young men looking for artistic pulsations in the modern world. Whistler and Oscar Wilde had made way for Ruskin, Pater, and the pre-Raphaelites; Sören Kierkegaard had anatomized "aesthetic man," who, unlike "ethical man," was caught up in a succession of moods to which he surrendered. Jean de Tinan lived only for mood moments; he moved from sensation to sensation. His modern apartment near the Luxembourg became the meeting place for Colette, Rachilde, Pierre Louÿs, Henri de Régnier, Léon Blum, Jean Lorrain, and even Alfred Jarry, although de Tinan intensely disapproved of his lack of hygiene.

The charismatic personality that magnetized the group was Pierre Louÿs. Louÿs was recognized early; in his final year at the lycée, he had produced *Potache-Revue,* a fortnightly magazine that folded after three issues. One of the three cofounders was André Gide, who struck up a friendship with Pierre Louÿs that lasted seven years despite bitter quarrels. In the literary fashion of the day, they took pseudonyms: "Stello," "Claudius Ocello," Gide signing "Zan-Bal-Dar." They adopted Henry Gauthier-Villars's battle cry, "Death to the Parnassians!" Pierre Louÿs, who had published only a few poems, was the new Rimbaud. Schwob introduced him to Oscar Wilde who, during his three-week visit to Paris in 1891, met Louÿs almost daily at parties or for dinner at the Café d'Harcourt with Schwob, Aristide Bruant, Stuart Merrill, and, once, with Gide, who fell in love with Oscar on the spot and was unable to eat his dinner. Wilde admired both Schwob and Louÿs, inscribing *The House of Pomegranates* to the latter in florid terms: "To the Young Man who admires Beauty. To the Young Man whom Beauty adores. To the Young Man I adore."[81] As if this were not enough, he dedicated *Salomé* to Louÿs, whose help he sought along with Schwob's and Retté's for the play, which he wrote in French. The following year Louÿs was invited to London for the opening night of *Lady Windermere's Fan*.

Two portraits by Jacques-Emile Blanche consecrated him as a rising star, since Blanche never painted anyone who was not assured of success (he painted his cousin Colette only after the publication of *Claudine at School*). In the autumn of 1893 Louÿs's intimate friend was Claude Debussy; they wanted to share an apartment but then decided that friendship could not survive daily chores. The self-righteous Gide castigated Louÿs for his life of pleasure and debauchery.

Colette and her friends from Café d'Harcourt shared a common interest in bisexuality, which was being scientifically studied in medical circles; they turned to the Hellenistic theme of the androgyne, the hermaphrodite, the perfect being, a notion at the core of Colette's philosophical essay *The Pure and the Impure*. "I have the privilege of being only halfway a woman,"[82] wrote Colette to the poet Saint-John Perse. Théophile Gautier had opened the gates to a vogue of bisexual characters with his androgynous heroine Renée de Maupin. The hermaphrodite, the daughter-son of Hermes and Aphrodite, was "one of the sweetest creations of the pagan genius. Nothing more ravishing could be imagined in this world than those two bodies, both so perfect, fused together,"[83] wrote Pierre Louÿs.

Decadent literature coincided with the first works of Sigmund Freud. Far from the vulgar current of erotica, which exists in any age and borders on pornography, erotic literature at the turn of the century was produced by major writers, who described abnormal, deviant, even monstrous sexual behavior. Sadism, sadomasochism, hermaphroditism, even bestiality and necrophilia were the themes treated by literature as well as the plastic arts. Most aberrant forms of sexual behavior appear in Rachilde's *La Princesse de Ténèbres* and *L'Animale*. Although Rachilde and

Jean Lorrain were deliberately out to shock their contemporaries, some of their works might be taken as the fictional investigation of cases of sexual psychopathology. On different levels of bravado and provocation, some writers played a purely cerebral game like Rachilde, some integrated the flights of their investigation into their daily lives like Jean Lorrain. All fought against the constraints of bourgeois respectability. They also defied the rules of classic literature: the imitation of nature, decorum, moral justification of all human actions through reward and punishment, and ultimately *catharsis*, when it dealt with certain hideous forms of behavior encountered in mythology: incest, cannibalism, bestiality, parricide, and infanticide. The House of Atreus, where a brother feeds his brother his dismembered children; Pasiphaë, who makes love to a bull; Zeus, who turns himself into a swan to impregnate Leda; Oedipus, who marries his mother and kills his father; Prometheus, condemned to have his liver eternally devoured by a vulture — the list is as long as anything the decadent imagination could devise. But the decadents offered no redress, no punishment, no catharsis, no moral outcome; they vied with the decadence of the Asian and Roman Empires in their combinations of pain and pleasure, death and procreation, murder and debauch, torture and the delirium of power.

Meanwhile, Colette was creating herself; she began under the influence of the decadents and gradually passed into simpler blends of aesthetics. She tried to resolve her own contradictions but gradually came to see them as a source of strength. Her paradoxes would be a constant reminder of what lay behind the conventional. She would fervently embrace various styles of behavior, to conclude that hermaphroditism in its duality was the only mode capable of unshackling the total diversity and wealth of human nature: "I aim at the true mental hermaphroditism, which burdens certain strongly endowed beings."[84]

Willy introduced Colette expeditiously to all the literary circles that mattered. Mallarmé was the object of a cult; to be invited to his apartment amounted to a literary endorsement, since Whistler had proclaimed, "Mallarmé's *mardis* are historical, exclusive and reserved for artists who are honest. Entry to them is a privilege and a proof of worth — a distinction that makes us proud."[85] To step into the modest apartment was a privilege enterprisingly sought after; strangely enough, brilliant, witty conversationalists who outdid each other in salons slipped into Mallarmé's small dining room as if into a church. Seated around the table, they listened with reverent silence as the Master, standing in his accustomed place in front of the stove, launched into a long monologue interrupted only by his blowing a curling, blue haze of tobacco smoke from his perennial pipe. They listened, awed by the splendor, the exquisiteness of the improvisation, "by the magnificent symphony in prose." Colette was taken by his "sweet voice," but no more than Pierre Louÿs did she enjoy Mallarmé's pontificating. The Young Turks were becoming irreverent. "I have not seen him often, the gray chinchilla,"[86] said Colette, who never went with Willy when he spent weekends with the Mallarmés.

There was, too, a quite different and very important part of society to be conquered: the people who gathered on given days in a salon and gravitated around a hostess to debate, exchange ideas, recruit followers, and wield power. The turn of the century saw the last of the typical French salons, when on a set day a wealthy and talented hostess would attract her coterie of celebrities and carefully selected women. The most successful ones had a star guest and made every effort to keep him with the fierce determination of a lover, which was sometimes the case. There was rivalry, even warfare between them; there were spies to watch and spies to send out to other salons.

The salons were places of intellectual exhibition. The *hôtel particulier,* or *privé,* had a ballroom that could turn into an auditorium in addition to the vast drawing room, the salon proper, and a large dining room. Concerts, plays, or lectures were given to an audience seated on gilt chairs, the men in white tie and tails, the women in silk and tulle displaying their jewels. But the regular weekly gatherings depended exclusively on conversations, speech as fine art. Conversation was the salon's touchstone and it made or broke a new guest. Some hostesses directed the conversation with the firmness of a moderator; Madame Aubernon had a silver bell, which she rang whenever the conversation threatened to break up into pairs. This bell was surmounted by a small statue of Saint Louis (Louis IX), with the king's words inscribed around the edge: "If you have something to say that will interest all speak up . . . otherwise remain silent." There was the salon of Armande de Polignac, comtesse de Chabannes-La Palisse, who composed music to lyrics by Willy. There were the lavish parties and avant-garde concerts in the Parisian mansion of the princess Edmond de Polignac, born Winaretta Singer. She was the sewing-machine inventor's heiress who, with her fathomless fortune and discriminating taste, did more to promote contemporary music than any other patron. The comtesse de Martel who signed her popular novels, which Willy would turn into plays, "Gyp," had one of the most lively salons.

Willy was a member of Madame Arman de Caillavet's — a formidable Parisian hostess — inner circle and a regular at several other gatherings; however, this did not mean that Colette would be automatically accepted as a member herself. She did have a pedigree as the niece of Caroline de Trye, who had a salon in Brussels and attended the Paris season, but her sparkling intelligence was the reason for her immediate acceptance by Madame Arman de Caillavet. Prizing Colette's social charisma, Willy admired her for belonging to high society without being affected by it.

At forty-four, Madame Arman de Caillavet was a dynamo with curly hair and blue eyes. Impatient with dull people, she had tried to get rid of her little brother when she was three years old by throwing him through the window, because "he was such a bore." Born Léontine Lippmann, she had married Albert Arman, who had added the name of his château, de Caillavet, to his patronym. She was restless and opinionated: a staunch Republican, she always signed her name "Madame Arman," rejecting the aristocratic "de Caillavet." Her salon at 12 Avenue Hoche was a modern, liberal powerhouse, the gate to the Académie Française. She gave weekly dinners on Wednesdays for the happy few and receptions on Sundays attended by as many as one hundred guests; some evenings were devoted to conversations on lofty topics, others were frivolous. At a Wednesday dinner on November 6, Colette wore her first low-cut evening dress; she told her mother that she was nervous "to have to bare her shoulders under everybody's nose."[87]

Madame Arman wanted to leave her mark on French letters; unlike other hostesses who had their star intellectuals, she maintained that people who were already famous were usually passé and set out to create a new literary giant. In 1883 she spotted Anatole France (François Anatole Thibault) who, at thirty-nine, had published two small volumes of poems, a moderately successful novel, and a novella. He was awkward and lacking in social graces, but talented and ambitious. For the next twenty years Madame Arman devoted her energy to the creation of a great writer. She decided that what he most needed was strict discipline, so every day she locked him up in his study and only set him free when he had written his daily assignment. She edited what he wrote, gathered research material, and, being fluent in several languages, translated books and articles for him. At one time Willy and Schwob were Anatole France's ghostwriters. Willy could be trusted — he never mentioned his secret collaboration. Under Madame Arman's rule Anatole France turned out masterpieces at such a rate that it seemed miraculous. She enjoyed his fame vicariously, orchestrating her receptions around the great man.

Sundays at five, Madame Arman's guests would enter the long gallery. Only women were seated; men came and went like butterflies. She sat on the right side of the tall fireplace; Anatole France invariably came in with a bunch of violets, which he presented to her before taking his own place in front of the fireplace. When he spoke, everyone listened; when he hesitated, Madame Arman prompted him from her chair and the speech went on — politics, literature, ethics. Authors were expected to read from as-yet-unpublished books, composers to play their works in progress.

The regular guests were Alexandre Dumas the younger, the critic Jules Lemaître, Jean Jaurès, the radical leader who would be murdered in 1914, Raymond Poincaré, future president of France, and Georges Clémenceau, the left-wing politician who would become "The Tiger" and "Father Victory" in World War I. Madame Arman's son, Gaston de Caillavet, later a successful playwright, brought his friends, the twenty-two-year-old Marcel Proust, Jacques Bizet, and Fernand Gregh. The next generation of French writers — Colette, Proust, and Valéry — were carefully nurtured in Madame Arman's salon. Charmed by Colette, Anatole France also highly valued her opinion. In the spring of 1895 he sent her the first set of proofs of his novel, *The Well of Saint Clare,* inscribed "To Madame Colette Willy, before anyone else." Quite a compliment, coming from *le grand homme.*

Colette, talking with gusto, could be abrasive, aggressive, and funny. Hers was *le genre rosse,* and this nastiness was very much part of the cutting Parisian wit, which ridiculed the weakness of a character and brought it in a one-liner into the limelight. These *mots* would be repeated over and over again. Colette fascinated everyone with her stories about the provincial town of Saint-Sauveur. Her accent, carefully preserved throughout her life, and the patois dialect she integrated into her Parisian French added a special flavor to her risqué anecdotes about teachers and schoolgirls. Her education at a "godless" school made Colette an example of what lay education could produce; no other woman in her Parisian milieu had gone to a lay school. Colette was seen as the explorer of a terra incognita and made the most of it. Her remarks sent people around the dining table into fits of laughter. At one Wednesday dinner, Marcel Proust seated next to the slim, androgynous Colette, compared her to all the androgynous literary characters he could recall, finally naming Narcissus and concluding, "Your soul is like his, full of voluptuous sadness." "Not so," answered Colette, playing the candid, outspoken Huronne, "My soul is presently full of beans and morsels of bacon."[88] The incident remained famous and was still quoted years later. It was already known in the charmed circles that Colette Gauthier-Villars was an "amphibian," or the mannerly Marcel Proust would never have dared compare her to some ambiguous characters of antiquity.

Colette and Willy were also part of a quite different set who met in the salon of the Baronne Marguerite de Pierrebourg at 1 Avenue du Bois de Boulogne; the baronne wrote poetry and novels under the name of "Claude Ferval." After a tumultuous divorce, she braved disapproval and scorn by openly living with the writer Paul Hervieu.

It was very fashionable for le Tout-Paris to be free of censorship, cant, and moralistic attitudes. Beauty, talent, and wit were good tickets to Tout-Paris, as were political power, wealth, and an aristocratic name; but they were only potential introductions to this closed world, which selected its members. In its mysterious circle, Tout-Paris recognized its own; allusions were instantly grasped, first names instantly identified; a silence, a smile were worth a thousand words to the initiated. Doctors, newspapermen, lawyers, designers, couturiers, or actors could be part of Tout-Paris — why some were "in" and others "out" remained a mystery.

In one night Tout-Paris could "make" a playwright, actor, singer or composer; a single exhibition could launch a career. Tout-Paris saw itself as the creative elite and acted accordingly. It was ebullient, flamboyant, provocative, and baroque. Colette was one of its most noticed sophisticates. Paris had become so exciting for Gabri that Sido felt she had to calm her down: "There you are! So proud of living in Paris from your wedding day! You are like a lout strutting on your hind legs because you have married a Parisian."[89]

It was a splendid time. The gaiety of Montmartre, the sophistication of the salons, and the wit of the great cafés gave the 1890s their highly colorful atmosphere. High society went riding in the Bois de Boulogne, but so did the courtesans, competing with each other in their satin-lined *calèches*. One could see the actress Réjane in her carriage driven by twelve white mules and Liane de Pougy, the mistress of kings and bankers, wearing fortunes in diamonds and pearls. At night everyone flocked to the Moulin Rouge to see the cancan and listen to Yvette Guilbert singing the poetry of the street, or to watch Loie Fuller, who had conquered Paris with her shimmering display of gauze-and-silk billowing wings, as she performed her innovative dances under multicolored lights.

It was a splendid time to break the rules and everyone who was anyone did so in the most outrageous ways possible. Oscar Wilde broke the rules of heterosexual matrimonial decorum; artists and writers allowed people to guess their secrets. Pierre Loti wore rouge and high heels; Count de Montesquiou wore delicately hued coats and practiced the fine art of arrogance to the limit of decency; ladies from the wealthiest circles started Sapphic clubs. To be different was all that mattered.

What fun and what a challenge for gifted Colette, who had more than enough brains and talent to impose her uncrushable personality and unquenchable thirst for earthly delights on a society eager for new laws, new ethics, new art, and new literature! It was the turn of the century and the century was turning giddily; spectacular controversies in the arts, political tensions beneath the city's mask of frivolity, a formidable struggle between the old and the new was taking place. Everything was in turmoil under decorous but skin-deep manners. The young Republic was assailed on all sides by militarism, royalism, Bonapartism, and anarchists' bombs; religion was under political siege.

It was best to have an opinion about everything and let it be quotable. The Gauthier-Villars were seen everywhere and were in demand in every salon, eagerly expected in every café, theater, and concert hall. Colette acknowledged that they were "a typical Parisian curiosity."[90]

Private Life

At Rue Jacob, the atmosphere was a heady mixture of scholarship and pranks. "The prevailing atmosphere was extremely merry, even farcical, Colette and Willy carefully kept it so to the utter delight of their guests, writers, musicians, artists, actors."[91] Jacques, brought there once a week by his English governess, later recalled the laughter and the childish games. He adored "his little mother"; he was too small to understand the jokes but old enough to feel extremely comfortable in the mischievous atmosphere. Pranks were an integral part of the parties. Pierre Véber would rush out of the apartment and call "Monsieur Willy" from the courtyard, threatening to file a lawsuit because he had not been paid. Willy and Colette would then bend over the windowsill and engage in an extravagant dialogue that brought out the neighbors and janitor to listen. Meanwhile, bearded, satanic Paul Masson would hand out erotic postcards to the assembled crowd, not excluding the children.

Marcel Schwob came with an actress from La Comédie Française, Marguerite Moréno. At that time Catulle Mendès' official mistress, she was in love with Schwob, whom she eventually married. She wanted to meet Willy's wife and was surprised to find "an adolescent with a five-foot-four-inch tress of hair, curled around her like a snake."[92] Marcel threw a new book teasingly at Colette, who was kneeling in front of the fireplace roasting chocolate on a skewer; she retaliated by slinging a thick blob of melting chocolate at his white, starched shirt. The scholar and the imp were entranced by each other. He called her "Lolette." Sido traveled to Paris frequently; Marguerite Moréno remembered her sitting on a couch, carrying on a heated discussion while twirling her eyeglasses on a long ribbon.

Colette dressed with flawless chic and had a carriage, the fashionable victoria, at her disposal. Juliette, her cook, was an expert cordon-bleu, so dinners at the Gauthier-Villars were a combination of bohemian atmosphere and gourmet dishes. Whenever Juliette had her day off and the maid was in charge of the meal, Colette would joke that the Gauthier-Villars had more to offer than their cook's talent: "You have to come," wrote Colette to Curnonsky, "Willy's beauty, my wit should make you forget a mediocre dinner; it is a matter of allegiance, not fine dining."[93]

Curnonsky, not yet the "prince des gastronomes," remembered Colette's extraordinary knowledge of wines; originating in Jules Robineau-Duclos's cellar, it had increased with Willy's patrician tastes. Colette and "Cur" would rhapsodize about wines and cheeses. Once the impish hostess vanished into the kitchen to make what she called her "speciality," a baked crêpe made with two or three eggs, a few tablespoons of sugar, and a little flour; it was done in minutes. "This is not honest baking, it is make-believe,"[94] hinted Willy, who never adhered to the Fourierist fare of the

Colettes and loved nothing more than *gâteau de Savoie,* especially served after mushrooms in heavy cream; he ended up weighing 231 pounds and going to dietary clinics and spas to drink water and lose weight. Colette gave her crêpe, *la Flognarde,* literary immortality and herself, who was never without a maid, the reputation as a fine cook. Once, at an epicurean Parisian banker's house, she went to the kitchen, told the chef to add garlic cloves to the roast, and gave the guests the impression that she, herself, had created the recipe.

While Gabri was turning into a Parisian, Captain Colette was enjoying his own moment of prominence. Marshal Mac-Mahon, the former president of France and the national hero who had led the captain's regiment to victory, died and was honored with a state funeral. The Colettes had been invited to Mac-Mahon's country estate near Châtillon and Captain Colette was chosen to deliver the eulogy at the Montcresson cemetery on October 21, 1893. The captain made an impressive appearance; as the disabled veteran spoke, his beautiful voice quivered with emotion.

Colette and Willy spent a few days at Châtillon in the fall of 1893. The captain was at work on Mac-Mahon's biography, *A Soldier's Life: Edmé Patrice Maurice de Mac-Mahon, Duke of Magenta, Marshal of France, 1808–1893.* A picture taken in Châtillon shows the captain with a paper in his hand and Willy with a pen, looking at each other as if exchanging ideas. Colette, seated between the two, looks straight into the camera, her elbow on a pile of papers, the table overflowing with manuscripts and books. In the background Sido holds a manuscript in her lap. Photographs taken indoors required special lighting and a long exposure; the little scene had been carefully staged to show a family of writers. It also gives an idea of the opulence of the Colettes' residence at that time. The walls are covered with raised velvet, the lace curtains are richly embroidered, the tablecloth is an Oriental silk carpet, and the stuffed chairs and sofa are upholstered in cretonne with a printed pattern of large flowers.

The year ended with the death of Sido's friend Victor Considérant, one of the most popular characters of the Left Bank. He used to dresse as a Texas frontiersman, wearing a broad-brimmed sombrero, a black velvet serape, and boots. At the Café Soufflot, where he played dominos, he would captivate his audience with discourses on nonviolence and the meaning of democracy. In 1891 he granted a rare interview to *L'Eclair*, re-iterating his faith in a neverending movement toward social perfection, appealing for a peaceful, voluntary, and evolutionary democracy, and ar-guing for a federated European Republic, which should include the United States. Paris gave "the Pioneer of Socialism" a funeral almost at state level. To allow a large public to attend, the government decided he should be buried at noon at the Père Lachaise cemetery, not in Besançon. From the posh Avenue de la Bourdonnais, where Considérant had lived, to the working-class neighborhood of Ménilmontant, large numbers of Parisians lined the street. Every school of radical thought sent a delega-tion: syndicalists, revisionists, anarchists, and Marxists. Eugène Landois II came with the Belgian delegation. It is probable that Sido also attended; no letters of this period remain to ascertain the fact, but she was so fiercely loyal to her friends, her past, and her Fourierist principles that it seems un-likely she would not come to Paris to attend the funeral.

IV

"Of the first, the second year of my marriage, I have a vivid, fantastic recollection . . ."
MES APPRENTISSAGES

WINTER CAME. Colette suffered the first of a long se-
ries of bronchitis attacks, and Willy upset her by indulging the secret side
of his complex personality; he did not tell her that Marcel Schwob's
mistress Louise, a poor teenaged working girl, had died in a private
clinic, where Schwob had placed her at his expense. Hiding Schwob's
telegram in his attaché case, Willy went to the funeral by himself.
Colette found out and immediately sent Schwob an apology, complaining that Willy should have warned her "instead of wrapping himself
in useless mysteries as he always does."[1]

Willy was torn between bohemian behavior and upper-class mores.
He did not think it proper for Colette to attend Schwob's mistress's funeral; he also knew that his reasoning would be torn apart by Colette,
used to an intellectual environment where everything was discussed in
the open, albeit in stormy encounters. Colette could never fathom
Willy's penchant for secrecy; she felt the need to share in his life.
Claudine, her heroine, went to extremes to be informed, retrieving letters from a burning stove, opening drawers to read private correspondence. Willy envisioned the world on a multitude of separate levels

that never mixed, while Colette's vision of human relations was holistic.

After a few months of married life, Colette noticed that something was going wrong. In Colette as well as in Willy's novels, one can detect their doubts, their hopes, their disappointments:

Colette: "He loves me but if the lover does not understand me anymore, he remains my refuge, my understanding friend."

Willy: "She had adored her husband but only for a few months. She had been then 'the most devoted and faithful wife.'"

Colette: "He is hurt because I can read a book when he is in the room or because I can remain silent."

Willy: "I have the pathetic hope that it is not too late, that she will discover something wonderful in me and will become my Friend."

On a cold January day in 1894, seven months after her marriage, Colette received an anonymous letter informing her that Willy was betraying her with Charlotte Kinceler, a demimondaine, and that she could find him at the Rue Bochart-de-Saron; it was the second time someone had tried to destroy her relationship with him. Colette instantly hailed a cab, which drove her to a dilapidated district not far from Montmartre. Without stopping to think, Colette opened the unlocked door of a small apartment, walked in, and stared at Willy, who was seated at a table next to a woman with remarkably small hands; an open ledger was on the table and they were going through columns of figures. Willy, always the cool gentleman, asked quietly, "Did you come to take me home?" and because cool manners can be contagious, Colette answered, "Well, yes, precisely."[2] Meanwhile Charlotte, scissors in hand, was ready to stab her.

Willy had known Charlotte since "the death of Victor Hugo (1885); in those days I had hair and a little mistress called Lotte, because her name was Charlotte, and she called me Kiki, I don't know why."[3] "Kiki" was also the nickname Colette gave him, when it was not "Kiki-la-Doucette" (Kiki-the-Sweetie) — a name he shared with the household cat, who would become famous in Colette's *Dialogues de Bêtes.* Willy mentioned this affair in his *Souvenirs.* In *My Apprenticeships,* Colette described Charlotte as a tiny woman, four-feet-nine-inches tall, "not pretty, but full of fire and charm."[4] She was a prominent muse of the bohemian world and her sister had risen to the demimonde.

Kinceler had seduced not only Willy but the actor Lucien Guitry; she dazzled Jules Lemaître and many other famous men, who lavished attentions on her. The playwright Eugène Brieux based his play *Les Hannetons* (The Beetles) on her personality, showing her oppressing her lovers with her devouring passion. Willy took her to dinners, listening to her love stories. Over the years she had become his confidante and he her financial advisor of sorts, hence the ledger Colette saw on the table when she entered. Charlotte had an herbal store in the Rue Pauquet in Montmartre, where she sold herbal teas, contraceptives, and diverse erotic paraphernalia.

When Colette discovered Charlotte and Willy, not in a classic intimate situation but going over some accounts, she felt more betrayed by Willy's friendship with Charlotte than she would have by a physical relationship. She had married Willy well aware of his reputation as a lady-killer, one shared by Achille and Captain Colette. It was a masculine trait extolled by Sido, who recounted her father's, brother's, and son's amorous exploits, bragging about their illegitimate children, whom, unlike Willy, they never legitimized.

When they married, Colette expected that Willy would devote a great deal of time to her. She was disappointed, for Willy's philanderer's routine was inflexible. Colette knew that he was smitten with her, but not deeply in love; she also saw that he was vulnerable. The Kinceler episode gave her "the will to last and protect herself."[5] At first she was devastated. The trust she had in Willy, her longtime friend, the man she passionately loved, had been shattered. She preferred, however, "to willfully suffer because of love rather than to renounce it."[6] There is a recurrent regret in *Claudine Married* and *The Vagabond;* Colette would have preferred to be Willy's mistress rather than his wife. They were, she said, magnificent lovers, but as soon as they stepped out of their bedroom they fought "like rival college students."[7] Drama came naturally to Colette, while Willy loathed confrontation.

Determined to overcome her pain and her jealousy, Colette turned to Charlotte to learn the art of "becoming a woman." Charlotte was the first demimondaine Colette studied; they became "courteous like two reconciled rivals after a duel." Charlotte admired Colette for having kept her cool; Colette admired Charlotte's glib tongue and immense self-assurance. She frequently stopped by Charlotte's store and told her that, as a woman, she had everything to learn. Charlotte was delighted to tutor Colette. Invited to the Rue Jacob, she came, "very ladylike," in a karakul coat with a bunch of violets at her belt and wearing a hat with a tight veil over her face. She enjoyed showing off her expensive lingerie with Belgian lace inserts. "This young woman taught me a lot,"[8] commented Colette. Among the new acquisitions at the Bibliothèque Nationale in Paris there is a collection of letters from Colette and Willy to Charlotte Kinceler, showing the trio on excellent terms.

From the day she met Charlotte, Colette learned to make a pact with Willy's mistresses. Jealousy, said Colette, is always physical; to abate its effect, she converted Willy's mistresses into her own lovers: "All the little Loute and Moute and Touffe from the Latin Quarter, nothing was easier than to laugh with them."[9] Colette also had her own affairs. Not a year into her marriage, she felt a pang of love for her piano teacher, Augusta Holmes, who was a composer and singer, César Franck's favorite student, a formidable redhead with green eyes always dressed "in aquarium colors."[10] Augusta had lovers of both sexes and had been Wagner's mistress. She had four children, whom she never acknowledged, by Catulle Mendès, who had squandered her fortune and left her.

That spring Colette fell dangerously ill, suffering an attack of syphilis, a disease almost endemic among the Montmartre crowd.[10] According to statistics published in 1895, twenty percent of the Parisian population had syphilis in one form or another. As a doctor's sister, she knew the devastating effect of the unmentionable disease. It was a crushing blow that sapped Colette's will to live: "There is always a time in the life of the young when dying seems as normal and as enticing as living, I vacillated." Doctor Jullien, her attending physician, was prompting her to fight back: "Help me, I cannot cure you by myself."[12] Professor Louis Jullien was the leading specialist on venereal diseases, author of an authoritative and monumental study, *Traité Pratique des Maladies Vénériennes* and head physician in charge of the syphilography section at the Saint-Lazare Hospital.

Mercury tablets were the most common treatment for syphilis, but Doctor Jullien was experimenting with "the fever treatment," which lasted two to three months. Colette was put in a tub and her body temperature raised to 40° C (104° Fahrenheit) — every five or six days a copper tub was brought to the apartment, cushioned with sheets, and filled with steaming water. "Four strong arms lifted me, deposited me in the hot water, where I shivered with fever, exhaustion, physical misery, and a need to cry."[12]

Colette was on the brink of death. Doctor Jullien wrote to her mother that he feared he could not save her, asking her to come to Paris immediately. Sido arrived and nursed her daughter back to life. The disease was halted but not completely cured; for two years afterward Colette suffered from severe headaches and took ether to alleviate her discomfort. She had acute pains in her eyes and would remain in a darkened room for hours. She continued the hot tub treatment, which left her with an aversion for baths; as a journalist she wrote that baths weakened the organism and recommended sponging oneself off instead. For years, though, baths were a part of Colette's routine. In *L'Age d'Or,* Fernand Gregh recounts having stopped by the Rue Jacob to persuade Colette to be less harsh in her criticism of Saint-Saëns. Willy casually told him that Colette was in her tub, did he want to talk to her? Not knowing that only Colette's head was visible, the elegant young man beat a hasty retreat.

During Colette's illness Madame Arman de Caillavet climbed the three flights of stairs at 28 Rue Jacob several times, an unmistakable sign that Colette belonged to the inner circle of the powerful Parisian hostess. She brought rare delicacies — a pineapple, ripe peaches, or loads of candies "in a scarf tied as a bag, and summons to get better promptly." Paul Masson came every day to help Colette stay absolutely still and bear the pain of two plasters meant to raise blisters on both sides of her abdomen. She lorded over him as "an autocrat." Marcel Schwob came two or three times daily. At twenty-six, racked by ether, already frail, walking with difficulty, he arduously climbed the three flights of stairs. He translated English or American tales for her, Jerome K. Jerome, Dickens, or *Moll Flanders;* he proselytized about English literature, which he would translate "in a slow delivery, a *mezza voce,* which after a while had the lilting charm of a cantilena."[14]

She called him "Mon Schwob." He introduced her to the sophistication of Oscar Wilde, the rakish literature of the eighteenth century, and his own works, written with a scholar's mind and a poet's emotion. A passionate writer, he vented his violent feelings through cruelty and perversity on paper. Like Jean-Paul Sartre, Marcel Schwob was obsessed by his ugliness and circumvented it by seducing a number of women and using it as a literary theme. Inverting the myth of Narcissus, in *Le Roi au Masque d'Or* Schwob imagined a king who wore a golden mask from childhood; he lived confined in his palace like a Chinese emperor in the Forbidden City and everyone who approached him wore a mask. After the dire prediction of a blind beggar, the king searched for a reflection of his face, which, like Narcissus, he found by looking over the bank of a river. He screamed in despair as he saw his reflection: "a pallid swollen face, its flaking skin distended by hideous protuberances, and he knew, by what he had read, that he was a leper."[15] Behind the literary metaphor was Schwob's philosophy, that the revelation of man to himself was tragic and destructive.

Colette and Marcel challenged each other constantly. Following the Fourierist credo, they were both environmentalists, but they could not have been further apart in their outlook on the world. Her pantheistic celebration of life was antithetical to Schwob's gloomy view. In *La Mort d'Odjigh* he imagined a universe evolving into mineral chaos, an illustration of the theories of the astronomer Camille Flammarion: "A perpetual winter was cracking the earth open . . . these prodigious crevasses, gaping suddenly, destroyed everything above their level . . . the dark air was spangled with tiny, transparent needles; a sinister whiteness covered the countryside; the world seemed sterilized by a universal silver radiance, emptiness, nothingness slowly taking over."[16] Colette had a strong sense of what she wanted and never wavered. Literature had to carry, hidden in its midst, a positive message. Her model was and will remain Balzac. From the start she opposed Schwob's nihilistic theory: "I don't even want to answer your stupid stories about the abyss and the blatant uselessness of life, it is too silly!"[17]

Schwob initiated Colette in intellectual sadism. There was now a noticeable subterranean influence of the Marquis de Sade, as his works slowly emerged from clandestinity after their publication in Belgium. Sadistic themes increased and descriptions of sadistic acts proliferated. Huysmans in *Certains,* a volume of critical essays, wrote with an insistence bordering on relish about the tortures depicted in Jan Luykens's engravings. In *Là-Bas* he described in minute detail Gilles de Rais, the aristocratic mass murderer, as he tortured children. Jules Laforgue imagined Hamlet amusing himself by torturing helpless animals: a caged canary, beetles which he impales, and toads, whose feet he hacks off. From those victims that could not manage to drag themselves away he extracted a pound or so of pierced eyeballs and rubbed them into his fingers. No literary work was immune from Sadian revisionism: the Sodomites in Rachilde's *Les Vendanges de Sodome* (Wine Harvest in Sodom), having rid the city of their wives, find one who refuses to leave, stone her to death, put the body in their winepress, and trample and crush it out with the grapes.

It was sophisticated to experiment on animals in private gatherings. There is no indication that Colette attended any of these seances, but she boasted to Schwob about sadistic acts on animals: in Britanny she bought a knife to dig out seashells just to watch the "painful little ones shriveling up when they are yanked from the rocks"; she frightened little lizards and watched them fall from the roof "and I liked that." She described to Schwob how she would like "to draw some animals with a scalpel on the skin of his back, a terrible thing because it only draws white blood."[18]

What remained of Schwob's "boundless presents," which Colette "accepted as a queen would,"[19] was his praise of Oscar Wilde. The year when Schwob, at twenty-three, became editor of the literary supplement of *L'Echo de Paris,* Oscar Wilde blitzed the French capital. Schwob introduced the author of *Dorian Gray* to the literary circles. Schwob was so obviously fascinated by him that Jules Renard nastily noted that he seemed to confuse Wilde with Shakespeare; never short of vicious remarks, Renard added that he kept Wilde's photograph on his drawing-room mantlepiece. With unflinching enthusiasm, Schwob guided Wilde through Tout-Paris and took him to Montmartre to meet the Chat Noir group. There Aristide Bruant gave him a book with this unexpected inscription: "To Oscar Wilde, the merry 'fantaisiste anglais.'" Toulouse-Lautrec portrayed Wilde with his coattails showing from under his overcoat, his tophat revealing the center parting of his hair, which extended to the nape of his neck.

Wilde was received with excitement as the messenger of the new English trends; the House of Liberty, Morris, Walter Crane, Aubrey Beardsley, and Burne-Jones created a magic aura around the prodigious conversationalist. For his French admirers Wilde was not only the leader of the aesthetic movement, but an arbiter of vice, a pioneer of free expression.

Schwob amused Colette with the gossip surrounding Wilde. At a dinner he had startled the guests by saying quite casually: "I have been married three times in my life, once to a woman and twice to a man."[20] At one of the Tuesday gathering at Mallarmé's, Lorrain refused to shake hands with Wilde saying: "You are not one of my friends." Wilde retorted: "Ah my dear Jean, you are right, when one leads the life that you and I lead, one no longer has friends — only lovers."[21]

Schwob filtered down to Colette what he admired in Wilde. For instance, he put words into the mouths of animals. So did other writers such as Edmond Rostand and Jules Renard, but Wilde made the farmyard talk in the drawing-room style. His geese spoke like ladies, his dogs like subtle diplomats, while the hens' dialogues were worthy of Sheridan's comedies. When Colette wrote *Dialogues de Bêtes,* Kiki-the-Cat and Toby-Dog dealt with human problems in pure comedy style, witty, charming, delightfully socialized. Schwob liked to quote Wilde's remarks — "to get into society nowadays one has either to feed people or shock them, that's it," a notion as akin to Colette as Wilde's concept that "it is one's duty to be always seeking for new sensations, to have the courage to commit sins."[22]

For Colette, nobody embodied that notion more than Paul Masson. Colette admired outrageous personalities and none was more twisted and complex than the strange demonic scholar "with the satanical twinkling eyes of a bureaucratic devil." Ten years older than Willy, an admirer of Poe and de Quincey, he was an opium smoker. At forty-four he was reaching his life's end and Colette was his last love. He came every day to see her. "I don't know what he did to me but I am defenseless against him,"[23] wrote Colette. He is one of the models of Hamond in *The Vagabond,* he is Masseau in *Recaptured* (L'Entrave), he is himself in *My Apprenticeships* and *Le Képi.* She called him her "bodyguard." A drawing by Forain shows a very young Colette in a tight dress and straw hat facing an elderly, bearded Paul Masson, smiling a satanic smile across a café table. She is leaning toward him, her left hand reaching out to his. "He looked," she said, "like those devils whose mission is abusing teenage girls, transforming the lord of the manor into a wolf, the respected lawyer into a vampire."[24]

He was born in Strasbourg, the son of a trader. After taking a law degree he was appointed at thirty to be a judge in Algeria, then in Chandernagor. Less than a year later he was an attorney general in Indochina. He sometimes lived ostentatiously — he imported a gondola from Venice, for instance, with which to navigate the Ganges — but at times practiced yoga with a guru in an ashram, living half-naked under a tree. He later wrote *Les Pensées d'un Yoghi* (Reflections of a Yogi). After a minor but complicated political scandal, a reassignment to Tunisia, and a failed marriage, Masson resigned, a deeply disillusioned man. He built a villa in Meudon-Bellevue to house a rare collection of Indian art and Oriental rugs; in the hall, hanging from the ceiling, was a woman's skeleton facing his own portrait in which he is dressed as a judge in full regalia. His neighbor was the painter Garnier, famous for his erotic,

morbid paintings. Masson was in good company to launch "his enterprise of demoralization and cretinization." He called himself "Lemice-
Terrieux" (The Mysterious) and indulged in maddening hoaxes. Once
he had several music shops deliver grand pianos to the same address at
the same time. Another time he mailed over a hundred letters to cancel
an invitation to a party; the hosts waited in vain in their mansion in
front of the loaded buffets. He did the same in reverse, sending invitations to a nonexistent party, so that Tout-Paris in evening gowns and
coattails faced a closed gate. The banker Osiris, sponsor of literary foun-
dations, had to publicly disavow a letter written by Masson and addressed to the painter Meissonnier, announcing the creation of a grant
of fifty thousand francs for young artists. In the billionaire Cernuschi's
name, Masson mailed a letter to the striking workers of the Compagnie
des Omnibus saying that he would contribute one hundred thousand
francs if they kept on with the strike, because the street was too noisy
when they worked.

Masson devised a literary theory. He believed that readers could be
manipulated into accepting the most outrageous stories as long as they
looked serious. To test his theory, he published a treatise on how to prevent trains from crashing into each other. He turned *mystification* into a
philosophy. The psychology of the *mystificateur* is similar to the vandal's,
for he is not there to see the results of his carefully plotted hoax, nor does
he derive any recognition from it — the *mystificateur* remains anonymous.
Paul Masson wrote *The Intimate Meditations of Général Boulanger* and the
apocryphal *Carnet de Jeunesse de Bismarck*, (Bismarck's Early Diary), which
created a flurry of activity in the diplomatic corps and almost a diplomatic crisis. Masson had handwritten the manuscript in German, and
graphologists confirmed that it was Bismarck's own writing. "Many of
his mystifications — the best ones never having been discovered — are
an integral part of history. Now considered as certain, unquestionable
sources, they will help researchers . . . to distort completely the meaning
of events . . ." wrote Willy in 1894.[25] "He liked only involved mystifications with an international outcome," said Colette, who was charmed by
the man whose self-assigned mission was "to demoralize the provinces, to
plunge them into dementia."[26] Marcel Schwob dared Masson to create
an incident that would start a new war. Paul Masson was not only playing
God with history; as appointed curator of the medieval manuscripts at
the Bibliothèque Nationale, he invented imaginary titles whenever he

felt the holdings were inadequate, with the intention of confusing future scholars. He had admirers and some disciples; literary hoax emerged as a highly praised genre. It took erudition, a sense of style, and a total contempt for ordinary mortals. In December 1894 Pierre Louÿs anonymously published *Les Chansons de Bilitis Translated from the Greek for the First Time by P.L.*, preceded by a biography of "Bilitis." He told the story of the poetess's childhood in Pamphylia, of her time in Lesbos and her friendship with Sappho, of her life as a sacred prostitute in the service of Aphrodite at Amathus in Cyprus. Louÿs said that her tomb, which contained the text of the songs, had recently been discovered by a German scholar, Professor G. Heim, the first editor of the Bilitis poems published in Leipzig in 1894. Professor G. Heim (Geheim, or The Mysterious) was none other than Paul Masson. Readers and many critics were taken in by the hoax; a distinguished Hellenist declared that the Greek poet was not unknown to him. This Caligula of French letters had but a handful of friends with whom he was "sweet, attentive, and dangerous by his affectation of simplicity."[27] Colette and Willy were his constant companions. He used Colette as the model for the heroine, "half Froufrou, half Renée Mauperin," of a pseudo-Ibsenian play he wrote in 1895.

Masson and Schwob were both courting Colette. They pretended to hate each other, then, forgetting their rivalry, indulged in palaver. "I warmed up between these two refined and fallacious minds."[28]

On May 21 *L'Almanach de Paris* mentioned Colette's presence at the Theatre Sarah Bernhardt. A few days later, she opened the exclusive yearly ball of the prestigious Ecole Polytechnique with her father-in-law, Albert Gauthier-Villars, who was president of the Alumni Association. The event was attended by the most entrenched of the grande bourgoisie. Colette wore a pale green gown with a large lace collar floating over her thin shoulders. Lentheric had done her hair à la Vigée-Lebrun with a ribbon around her forehead and had let her five-foot, four-inch braid of chestnut hair stream along the fold of her train. She was still feeling weak and very pale — "as green as her dress" — but the ball was a personal victory. It meant that the Gauthier-Villars had accepted Gabrielle (as they kept calling her). She played her part as "Gabrielle"; she was eager to please. If it took some theatrics, it came easily to her. She was atuned to people and would offer them the image of herself they were most likely to accept.

—⸿—

In 1894 Paris was jolted by a series of anarchist bombings and stunned by the repeated calls, in *La Révolte,* for a class war and the overthrow of society. Grave's book *La Société Mourante et l'Anarchie,* with a preface by the journalist-novelist Octave Mirbeau, was seized by the police, who confiscated the subscription list of *La Révolte.* The list read like a "Who's Who" of the progressive intelligentsia: Anatole France, Alphonse Daudet, Huysmans, Mallarmé, Pierre Loti, Rémy de Gourmont, and Jean Richepin. It included all Colette's friends, starting with Henry Gauthier-Villars himself. Lucien Muhlfeld, Tristan Bernard, Laurent Tailhade, Paul Adam, and Paul Masson had all also sporadically contributed to the other anarchist publication, *En-Dehors,* edited by an ex-deserter who took the strange pseudonym of "Zo d'Axa."

Félix Fénéon was arrested. He was a civil servant at the ministry of war with a deep interest in poetry and painting who had known Willy since the days of *La Revue Indépendante.* He adhered to anarchist ideals and made no secret of his political leanings. His house was searched and the police discovered a suspicious-looking metal flask, which could conceivably be used as a bomb. He was jailed at Mazas, the sinister Parisian jail. As this news spread, there was a sudden rush of intellectuals toward the provinces.

In June Colette, Willy, and Paul Masson left to spend six weeks at Kernic-en Trédez, a manor on Belle-Isle-en-Mer, a resort island off the coast of Brittany. While Willy wrote, sending off scores of letters and telegrams, Colette, escorted by Paul Masson, took long walks. They visited the fort that Sarah Bernhardt had bought that year and was turning into a castle.

Masson was a drug addict. He was "feeble and seldom tired, capriciously high or down because of 'the drug.' "[29] Drugs were pervasive in intellectual and artistic circles. The increase of drug use in the decadent era was partly due to the use of morphine as an anesthetic during the Franco-Prussian War. It became a panacea as a painkiller and was even prescribed to relieve patients suffering from nervous disorders. Despite warnings stressing the dangers of addiction, the use of morphine was as common as the use of Vichy water, wrote Léon Daudet, whose father depended on it. At first restricted to the upper class, morphine spread through all sections of society across Europe. In France there was a second factor — many of the expeditionary forces stationed in Indochina had become opium addicts and had brought the practice home. Clandestine opium dens multiplied during the last two decades of the 1800s and at the turn of the century there were thousands. Drug abuse fitted into the decadent mood of escapism and craving for acute sensations. With Paul Masson as mentor (not to mention Schwob and Jean Lorrain), Colette experimented with opium. *Ces Plaisirs* starts with a visit to an opium den and Willy, in *Lélie, fumeuse d'opium*, described Colette — under the name of the baronne de Bize — smoking opium in Paul Masson's den, yet taking great care to state that she was never addicted. She could walk on the edge of an abysmal drop without ever falling.

Colette wrote to Schwob from Belle-Isle. These letters, signed "Lolette," have all the sweetness of a child-woman but the tone of a zealous student of evil. She would like to wrap Schwob in an enormous flypaper and watch him "struggle into total inertia" like the flies which "must suffer tremendously."[30] But on the whole her letters to Schwob indulge in charming descriptions and silly gossip.

What emerges from the correspondence is a watchful Willy, who doesn't want Colette to write too much to avoid straining her eyes. At Belle-Isle Colette read Schwob's latest book, *Le Livre de Monelle*, dedicated to "My dear Willy and my dear Colette." She was so moved that she had a "big sobbing fit."[31] The book was heavy with symbols: Monelle's sisters were named "Perverse," "Savage," "Faithful," "Disappointed," "Dreamer," and "The Chosen One." Colette loved "Cice," who begs for a seat in the sumptuous hearse — she named a jewel Madame de Caillavet had sent to her "Cice." But of all Monelle's sisters, Colette preferred "the horrid and delectable little Madge, who eats plaster,"[32] which may have reminded her of the sealing wax she liked to consume.

Le Livre de Monelle was Schwob's treatise on aesthetics. "Destroy, destroy, destroy, destroy yourself, destroy around yourself, make room for your soul and the other souls, destroy all good and all evil." It was a handbook on literary anarchy, compared to Dante's *La Vita Nuova* because of its complex symbolism. Schwob was referred to ever afterward as "the author of Monelle." Monelle's philosophy became the credo of a whole generation:

> *Look at all things as momentary ...*
> *Live moment by moment ...*
> *All love that lasts becomes hatred ...*

All sincerity which lasts becomes a lie . . .
All justice which lasts becomes injustice . . .
All action which lasts slips into death,
All happiness which lasts becomes unhappiness,
Every moment is a cradle and a tomb.

Colette invited Schwob to come to Belle-Isle, since he refused she asked him to join them in Châtillon. She was feeling well again and up-braided Schwob for his nihilism: "Are you the Insane?" She made fun of him for being lost in an intellectual fog and told him she was leading a healthy life, driving around Châtillon with Achille when he visited his patients. On the way they sang arias and gathered wild berries. The old mare loved Achille so much that she would press her head against a pa-tient's cottage door to listen to his voice. Why doesn't Schwob come? He came. Why doesn't he come again? asked Colette.

As Colette was recovering from her illness, she was also building up her self-confidence. This turning point was very apparent in her letters to Schwob that summer. When Colette learned why Schwob did not come to Belle-Isle (apparently he was afraid that she would make him suffer too much), she commented, "I don't know if I would have hurt you as much as Masson." She concluded: "Willy is a sensitive beast and you, you are a sensitive idiot. What am I supposed to do between the pair of you?"[33]

In the fall *Une Passade*, the first novel signed "Willy," hit the Parisian bookstores. It was a roman à clef cowritten by Willy and Pierre Veber. The heroine was based on a nymphomaniac from Montmartre obsessed with writers and painters who hated Pierre Véber and wrote Willy thirty-page letters. (She was temporarily committed to an asylum after firing a shot at a senator, Lazare Weiller.) Mina Schräder's many brief love affairs allowed Willy and Véber to poke fun at the literary world, particularly at Rémy de Gourmont who transposed rather than trans-lated the poet-monks of the eleventh and twelfth centuries, arguing that the decadent Latinists were a distant mirror of contemporary deca-dents. Henry found the symbolism of the occultists and mystics vapid. He and Véber made the most of their heroine's aspirations and her lovers' high-flown literature. *Le Journal* reviewed it as a novel glittering with wit.

Une Passade would be at the core of the controversy over whether Willy did or did not write his novels. Véber and Willy had already coauthored and cosigned *Les Enfants s'amusent* and *Contes Fantaisistes*. According to Henry's biographer, when *Une Passade* was published Pierre Véber was engaged to the daughter of the playwright Tristan Bernard and did not want to upset his in-laws with a naughty, autobiographical story full of unabashed attacks on the mores of writers who might be their friends. Willy signed the novel to shield Véber from controversy but unmasked himself; the cover bore the name "Willy" and underneath, in parentheses, "Henry Gauthier-Villars." With *Une Passade* Willy had found his formula: the storyline would be loosely naughty to appeal to a large public and the characters would be thinly veiled portraits of contemporaries; the infratext would be a social satire.

Une Passade and its two sequels satirized mystic symbolism. On the positive side, Willy endorsed what can be loosely defined as "modernity": he supported Paul Valéry, the mature Mallarmé, Jean-Paul Toulet, Pierre Louÿs, Alfred Jarry, and Apollinaire, who stood by Willy when he came under attack. Willy never failed to support all his collaborators, whose names regularly appear in his novels.

In 1894 Willy published five books, all compilations of his articles: *Rythmes et Rimes* and *La Mouche des Croches,* both signed "The Usherette"; *L'Année Fantastique* and *Soirées Perdues,* both signed "Willy," and *Les Enfants s'amusent,* cosigned "Willy" and "Pierre Véber." Willy also wrote a preface to Jossot's *Artistes et Bourgeois* and another to *Récits de Rhamsès II* for Raphaël Landoy, Colette's Belgian cousin. A glittering production, but no major breakthrough.

My Exquisite, Loving, Depraved Kid

At the end of the year Maurice Barrès asked Colette and Willy to join the staff of the newly created *La Cocarde,* a Republican newspaper. Barrès wanted to open his columns to other intellectual movements. "The social question" was debated everywhere; the upper middle class spoke of reaching out to the people, but it was a fad rather than a commitment. Jean Huré summed up this affectation in *Le Figaro:* "The Pope is socialist, William II, Emperor of Germany, is socialist, Maurice Barrès is socialist . . . Mimi-Patte-en-l'Air (a cancan dancer) is socialist. The more you dress at Redfern's, the more your hair is done at Lentheric's, the more socialist you are."[34]

Colette contributed six articles to *La Cocarde,* reviewing four concerts, an opera, and an operetta. In a letter dated December 11, 1894 d'Indy asked her to suggest a tenor for his opera *Fervaal,* an indication that she was taken seriously in the world of music. Her musical criticism was straightforward. She used some of Willy's mannerisms in the first article, but freed herself of his influence in the following ones — no puns, the language and clarity are typically hers.

Charles Maurras remembered Colette at *La Cocarde;* she sat among the other journalists, a Basque beret rakishly drawn over one ear, her braids beating against her heels, and while she corrected or pretended to correct her own and her husband's proofs, she would not lose a word of the arguments flooding the editorial rooms.

At this time Colette was working on her first novel. In the summer or fall of 1894, a year or a year and a half after their marriage, she said, Willy asked her to write about her school in Saint-Sauveur. She scribbled the first lines of the book that was to change her life: "My name is Claudine, I live in Montigny. I was born there in 1884, I will probably not die there."[35] It was the birth of a literary legend. In a letter to Rachilde, which Colette may have later forgotten, she wrote, "For many years I had kept this heap of notes in diary form, but did not dare believe it was worth reading, but thanks to "Belle Doucette," who pruned and veiled some of the coarse expressions, much too Claudine-like, Claudine became acceptable — and so did Colette."[36] A letter to Rachilde by Willy echoes Colette's: "It would really amuse you to see her notes, which, believe me, I had to "feminize" and deprive of some of their flavor . . . In the original form, before I toned them down, they had the spontaneity and coarseness of a tomboy's diary."[37]

Nothing was spared to help Colette write her book. Gabrielle Duchemin, the model for Luce Lanthenay, was invited to spend a few nights with her, but Colette could not recreate in her Parisian apartment the ambiance of her relationship with Gabrielle. After one day she sent her back to Saint-Sauveur, declaring, "My Willy, in Paris it is not the same."[38]

In May Colette and Willy decided to go to Saint-Sauveur. She wanted to revisit the town, for she had not set foot in it for five years. She wrote a letter to Mademoiselle Olympe Terrain signed "Your ex-Plague," begging for gossip from Saint-Sauveur. She described her life in Paris, dazzling the provincial teachers with tales about theaters, restaurants, dinners, and lunches with the stars of the day. Life was one great party with a single inconvenience — she suffered from terrible migraine headaches. She assured Mademoiselle Terrain that she was still the tomboy she used to be and bragged about a new affair with a wonderful young girl exactly like Gabri before her marriage, "except that she may be worse, more disheveled, ill bred, and prettier."[39] Colette and her new friend held somersault competitions. A few days earlier in Colette's apartment, they beat up their two boyfriends before throwing them out onto the stairs. Wouldn't Mademoiselle Terrain have approved? asked Colette. Now one of the boys was madly in love with her girlfriend and Colette drew the conclusion that blows were like Cupid's arrows. A strange letter to a school principal! Colette seemed to be trying to bring back memories of things past, of her fistfights at school and her involvement with Gabrielle Duchemin.

In Paris Colette had fallen under the spell of Catulle Mendès's mistress, the slim, pale Marguerite Moréno, a young actress from the Comédie Française "who seemed to have stepped out of a Burne-Jones painting."[40] It was love at first sight: "We were young enough to feel a flaming schoolgirl crush."[41] In Moréno Colette had met "her soul," her alter ego; bisexual Moréno would become the model for the perfect being in *The Pure and the Impure.* Their friendship through their strangely parallel love lives never waned. Moréno, barely two years older than Colette, had long experience in gallantry, like any young actress who needed protectors. She left Catulle Mendès, confiding to Willy, "Listen, discreet bald man for whom I have no secrets, Mendès reads me poetry all night and in the morning, can't deliver."[42]

Colette's visit to Saint-Sauveur looked like a fit of nostalgia; neither the school principal nor the teachers suspected the practical purpose behind the letters and visit. To recreate the atmosphere in a girls' dormitory, Colette not only wanted to see it for herself; she wanted Willy to spend two nights at the Saint-Sauveur school. Mademoiselle Terrain welcomed the Parisian couple but did not ask them to stay, expecting them to spend the night at Juliette's. But Colette and Willy asked to sleep in the school dormitory. The request was unusual, for men were not allowed in the girls' quarters. But Colette's mind was set and she charmed Mademoiselle Terrain, who lodged them in her assistant's room next to the dormitory. The students were dazzled by Colette and her famous husband, a *boulevardier* of such sophisticated reputation.

That evening the principal and her guests sat at a small table set apart from the long one reserved for the teachers and girls. After dinner Colette went to the piano, Willy sat on the bench, she knelt next to him, and they played a duet. Early next morning the Parisian visitors walked into the girls' dormitory, Willy carrying an enormous bag of candy. Raised on Spartan fare, the sight of the candies melted the girls' shyness. Willy poured generous heaps into the basins. Colette, her hair curled in tight locks over her forehead and wearing a fine blouse of sheer linen, came and kissed the girls. This visit is recounted in *Claudine Married*. Claudine, who has made a deep impression on pretty Hélène, "wraps her arm around this silent little girl who has the fragrance of a pencil made of cedar and of a fan made of sandalwood. She trembles, then yields, and it is on her soft lips that I say farewell to my past."[43]

In July they were back in Saint-Sauveur. Willy wrote to Curnonsky, saying they would spend two days there and that he anticipated the fun of caressing the students and kissing the young teachers; "it amuses me madly and amuses even more my exquisite, loving, depraved kid."[44]

Colette's libido was a constant marvel for Willy, who made it the topic of several of his novels. He never interfered with her inclinations. He wrote to Charlotte Kinceler that he let Colette have any lesbian relationship she wished and even provided occasions. Colette referred to this marital arrangement in *Claudine Married* and *Claudine and Annie* (*Claudine s'en Va*); it appeared also in Willy's *Maugis Amoureux*. Willy shielded Colette, whom he encouraged to explore the realm of the senses; he was extremely careful that her reputation and his own should not suffer. When a cab was to take Colette and Schwob to Madame Arman's, Willy suggested it would be wiser if Schwob left the cab before reaching 12 Rue Hoche and walk the last block to avoid arriving together, "so people won't say too much that we 'flaunt' our liaison. You do agree?"[45] joked Colette.

Willy advised Colette not to waste her time in futile feminine friendships and introduced her to the flamboyant world of the courtesans, the world of *Chéri*. Willy was boosting the Parisian career of "La Belle Otéro"; in 1889 he had enjoyed a liaison with the Spanish dancer, which he publicized in one of the first letters by the "Usherette of the Summer Circus." In his self-deprecating style he wrote a portrait of himself — "Peculiarity:

speaks Spanish (doesn't he Nina?), which does not help him to understand Wagner." "Nina" was Caroline Otéro's nickname. Colette credited her with having been one of her role models in the art of being a woman, and it is not coincidental that she started *My Apprenticeships* with a long chapter on her friendship with Caroline Otéro, dubbed "the most scandalous woman since Helen of Troy."[46]

Caroline Carasso, born in 1868, the illegitimate child of a Spanish gypsy and a Greek nobleman, started to dance at the age of twelve; at fourteen she was kidnapped by an amorous chief of police, then rescued by a young gentleman whose family had her put in jail to prevent their scion from marrying her. At fifteen she married an Italian charmer who exploited her; she had three Spanish grandees as lovers. She shed them all and fled to Marseilles, where she danced in a *café-concert* by the sea. She heard about the gambling casino in Monte Carlo, went there, and walked up to the gaming table. Not knowing how to play, she placed her accumulating winnings back on winning numbers and walked away loaded down with a hundred and fifty thousand francs. With this fortune she went to Paris and set herself up in luxury. By 1892 she was the star of the Folies Bergère. She became the mistress of William II, the Prince of Wales, Alphonse XIII, Grand Duke Nicolas, Gabriele d'Annunzio, and Aristide Briand. She lived in a sumptuous *hôtel particulier* next to the Bois de Boulogne, built for her by a prince to thank her for a dinner given in his honor. She had a staff of sixteen and for secretary a Spanish grandee, former consul to Lisbon. Her carriage was an eighteenth-century landau upholstered with blue satin and pulled by four black horses. Her jewels were famous: her first row of pearl necklaces had belonged to Empress Eugénie, the second to the empress of Austria, and the third to the courtesan Léonide Leblanc. Once, as she was dancing, her necklace broke and the pearls scattered all over the stage; the audience immediately demanded that the show be stopped and a search went on until each pearl had been recovered.

She had eight bracelets made of rubies, emeralds, and sapphires, ten enormous ruby clips, and a pearl-and-diamond tiara. She also owned a unique diamond bolero, a masterpiece by Cartier; when he put it on display, people crowded the Rue de la Paix to look at the marvel. It was valued at two million two hundred seventy-five thousand gold francs and was kept in the vaults of the Crédit Lyonnais; whenever Otéro wanted to wear it on stage, it was brought to her in an armored carriage by two gendarmes who stood guard in the wings. Willy wrote in *Un*

Petit Vieux Bien Propre that she could not tell which of the stones of the bejewelled bolero were true or false, for she kept losing them at the gambling tables.

Otéro used the familiar "tu" with Colette instead of the formal "vous." They played cards together. (As her correspondence shows, Colette was an eager cardplayer and, if we are to trust Willy, she lost a great deal of money.)

Otéro gave intimate dinners for women only — limited to a friend or two and Colette. They ate Spanish *puchero,* then Otéro, dressed in her petticoat or a floating gown, would pick up her castanets and dance for pleasure until the wee hours. Like most courtesans, Otéro had lesbian lovers. *Truth* of New York wrote, "She prefers the company of women . . . Just like men, women want to pay tribute to her beauty."[47] She came back from the United States with one million seven hundred thousand francs. Over the years in Caroline Otéro's entourage, Colette met the most aristocratic and wealthy of the lesbians.

Jean Lorrain

One of Colette's favorites as a friend and literary mentor was Jean Lorrain. "He is as strange as crime,"[48] wrote Marcel Schwob. He wore heavy rings and his hair was dyed a garish gold with red, black, and white coming through in surprising locks. Colette called him "a Portuguese cat" because they come in three or four colors; he loved it and signed many of his letters to her, "your Portuguese Cat." His cheeks were touched with rouge, his large blue eyes rimmed with kohl, his athletic chest held tightly by a corset, which gave it the bulge of a bosom. He was the most highly paid journalist in Paris, an admired critic and a feared gossip. He wrote poems, strange tales, and romans à clef about the private lifes of Tout-Paris, which was terrified by his fearless nastiness and the poison he could spill through his chronicles. Between 1885 and 1905, he was the Petronius of a modern *Satyricon.*

The writer was a master stylist, the man a rake. Born Paul Duval, he came from a bourgeois, provincial family with a mansion near Fécamp in Normandy; his mother indulged her son's every whim. She decorated his room with a sea green ceiling between dark beams and walls covered with an antique pink cloth embroidered with silver thistles; his bed was draped in green curtains lined with pink flowers. When the pampered young man decided to go to Paris and start a literary career, his father gave him a large allowance. He chose "Jean Lorrain" as his pen name and joined the *hydropathes'* club, where he met Willy. Both wrote for *Le Chat Noir,* both spent hours drinking and talking at the Rat Mort café, where homosexuals of both sexes met. Lorrain adopted the role of a homosexual with all the bravado and panache he could project. The dying nineteenth century was festering in its taste for perversity and its love for the gutter's picturesque. Lorrain liked to prowl around the La Villette slaughterhouses where he met with prostitutes and tough butcher boys. He craved violent, hideous adventures, basked in the scum of Montmartre, and enjoyed a special status in brothels, fearlessly confident in his bulk, his muscles, his swordmanship, and his wit. Lorrain haunted every red-light district and told his friends, "You see, I can go everywhere safely, they admire me, I am their Sarah Bernhardt."[49]

His articles were read by politicians looking for ammunition for mudslinging. Lorrain disliked the Bonapartists, ridiculing Napoleon III's nephew, the duc de Morny, whom he described in an article on transvestites as indulging in the luxury of robes by Worth or dancing in a pink tutu, bare-legged in ballet shoes. He relentlessly attacked the duke's daughter, the marquise de Belbeuf. When Colette became her lover, Lorrain branded her "la sous-Belbeuf." He used transparent names that Tout-Paris immediately identified and he spared no one. Yet he had very loyal friends — Willy, Masson, Schwob, Rachilde, and Vallette — who saw beyond the ruffian and the aggressive satirical journalist to the true artist, a man with an unerring taste for beauty and style, quick to grasp the real personalities of people beneath any disguise. Marcel Schwob was his close friend; both used ether and opium and shared a passion for medieval literature, in which they could find a distant mirror for their ribald lives. They liked to eat fried fish and drink white wine on the banks of the Seine, to hear stories from tavern owners about corpses found in cabs and thrown into the river, pimps getting even, or knife fights between the gangs, the *Pschutteux,* the *Urphs,* and the *Vlans.*

Lorrain was racked by syphilis and alcoholism. When he was very ill he repaired to his mother's home for help, then rushed back to his devastating lifestyle as soon as his massive body overcame the illness. In search of the unusual, Lorrain was drawn to the occult. His apartment near the Boulevard Saint-Germain had three large rooms bathed in sunshine and did not seem to harbor evil spirits, but he created a theatrical set worthy of a gothic novel, complete with drapes and mirrors and a Renaissance replica of a decapitated woman's head, her hair and lips painted gold and bloodstains where the sword had struck. He called her "Our Lady of Silence," for silence is golden. Her eyes were white enamel, her face green bronze; she was placed on an ebony stand draped with pink and blue silk. When Oscar Wilde saw her, he exclaimed, "It is Salome's head . . . It is John the Baptist's revenge."[50] Antique painted heads became a fad, a strange metaphor of femininity.

When Lorrain served tea to his visitors he casually added a dash of ether to the cup. Ether, combined with his obsession for spiritism, made him neurotic. At night he saw mysterious shapes, felt pains in his chest, was afraid of having a heart attack, and drank more ether for relief. Hallucinations and obsessions tortured his mind. His hearing and vision were distorted — he could hear and see evil creatures ripping through the silk of the drapes and, although he left his lamps on all night, what he saw terrified him until daybreak.

Such was Lorrain in 1893 when he met Colette and became her friend; he remained very close to her until his death in 1906. He was only four years older than Willy but his way of life had taken its toll. He trusted Colette, complained to her about his physical miseries, and confessed how naive and young he felt in spite of his way of life. She loved his astonishingly beautiful blue eyes; she loved to listen to his anecdotes, read his letters, go with him to places off-limits for decent women. She was in her early twenties, discovering with curiosity the secret world of dissolute men.

Jean Lorrain was surrounded by a group of young men and women he called *la petite classe* (the kindergarten kids), linked by a way of life on the fringe of accepted morality and extremely self-protective. He took Colette and Jean de Tinan under his wing. Lorrain was the indispensable guest of the courtesans, called the *grandes horizontales;* without his wit and refinement, a supper was never quite a success. They needed his discerning taste in clothes, interior decoration, and good manners, since, except for Liane de Pougy, they came from very humble families. The stars of the demimonde professed an adoring friendship for Lorrain, whom they called "Notre Jean" (Our Jean). He could be their best agent — a mention from him in an article meant publicity and money. Even Sarah Bernhardt courted him, since he could "make" or "break" a play.

Jean Lorrain introduced Colette to Liane de Pougy. An officer's daughter, she had been brought up in the renowned Catholic boarding school, Le Sacré Coeur. Married at nineteen to a naval officer, she had a son and many adulterous affairs while her husband sailed the seven seas. He returned and shot her, wounding her in the derrière, and she divorced him. To survive she gave English and piano lessons, then managed to be hired for a show at the Folies-Bergère. She could neither sing nor dance, but was very beautiful and clever. Reading that the Prince of Wales would be in Paris, she sent a short letter to the future king: "Your Highness, I am about to make my first appearance at the Folies-Bergère, if you come and applaud me, I shall be famous immediately."[51] The prince, amused by this incredible gall, went with some friends from the Jockey Club and applauded her. Liane became a celebrity overnight, and was launched on her career as a courtesan and shrewd businesswoman. She managed four steady lovers concurrently: Maurice de Rothschild in Paris, Lord Carnavon in London, the banker Bleichröder in Berlin, and the aristocratic Count Strozzi in Florence. Visiting princes and grand dukes also showered her with jewels, a fortune she carefully managed. One of her first admirers, the playwright Meilhac, paid eighty thousand francs just to watch her disrobe — a very expensive striptease.

Liane de Pougy had literary ambitions and wrote successful novels. Who can recall, wrote Colette in *De ma Fenêtre,* that the literary event of 1898 was a novel by Liane de Pougy? Liane was "an amphibian" — a queen of Sapphic Paris, she publicized her affair with the American heiress Natalie Clifford Barney in *The Sapphic Idyll* and much later in her carefully arranged memoirs, *My Blue Notebooks.* Jean Lorrain considered a visit to Liane a necessary part of his protégée's *éducation sentimentale.* To complete her education as *"un homme de lettres,"* Lorrain took Colette to visit brothels. He showed her the red-light districts, the meeting places of the dropouts from society: thieves, pimps, prostitutes of both sexes, drug addicts, alcoholics.

In *La Petite Classe,* Lorrain wrought a charming portrait of Colette as the beautiful Madame Gabrielle Baringhel, who loves *Pelléas and Mélisande,* prefers the iris, that orchid of the poor, to the newly imported Japanese flowers, and speaks in lyrical terms of fruits and plants. She is not a Parisian; she comes from Momigny, as Claudine came from Montigny. The narrator takes beautiful Gabri on a grand tour of *les fortifs* before she retreats to her village for the summer. It was in *les fortifs,* the old fortifications of Paris where the prostitutes operated, that Colette made a field of dreams for Minne, her innocent libertine.

A new fad emerged: Satan was *à la mode* in songs, poems, novels, and paintings depicting creatures and activities of the lewd and bloody kind. The diabolical tradition seemed innate in Lorrain. In 1895 a critic compared him to Poe, Petronius, and the Florentines of the Renaissance, who dealt in mysterious poisons with magicians and alchemists and created sinister shadows and tragic beauty. Jean Lorrain wrote about the afterlife till he wavered on the brink of a nervous breakdown.

He took Colette to the high priestess of the occult, daughter of the poet Théophile Gautier and the opera singer La Grisi. Judith Gautier received her guests on Sundays from two to half past seven at the Rue Washington. She was the main attraction of her salon; extremely beautiful, her father called her "the most perfect of my poems." He had a Chinese friend who had taught Judith Chinese; at eighteen she had published an admirable translation of ancient Chinese poems. She shared with her father the belief that she was the reincarnation of a Chinese princess. Victor Hugo wrote a rapturous sonnet for her, and she was Richard Wagner's last love and his inspiration when he composed *Parsifal*. To enter Judith's salon was to step into an Oriental dreamland: she welcomed her guests wearing floating Chinese robes and Oriental jewels, and an antique statue of Buddha occupied a whole wall. A refined dinner was served on low tables; a Chinese butler glided silently among the carefully selected guests. Oriental atmosphere was a euphemism for opium smoking. Around 1890 opium was not yet illegal, and opium smokers gathered in large artists' studios, where Oriental servants in Oriental dress brought the green paste and pipes and lit the charcoal burners. Because of their special skills, they were in high demand. Marcel Schwob, Pierre Loti, and Claude Farrère were all waited on by Chinese butlers.

Lorrain taught Colette how far one could go too far. His frank approach to any pleasure "pure or impure" and the strength and daring of his vocabulary have more kinship with Colette's writing than Willy's subdued, subtle, witty, rather light style. Willy played with licentious situations, but in a veiled manner, a pun always playing the part of gauze thrown just in time over some shocking scene. Willy is light comedy, light operetta; Lorrain is life, fire, and thunder, jewels and flowers, admirable landscapes, horrible, heartwrenching scenes. His blunt, aggressive way of stating facts for what they were had a distinctive twentieth-century flavor — something of Jean

Genet, something of Sartre, something of their ruthless handling of the reader's sensitivity and their equally ruthless handling of the subject matter. With Lorrain, Colette learned secrets generally reserved for men, and her intrepid approach to social taboos owes much to him.

In May of 1895 Colette and Willy were invited to the home of "the painter of roses," Madeleine Lemaire. On Tuesdays between April and June the surrounding streets were jammed with carriages. She received guests in her studio on the top floor, which had the only glass roof in Paris. She painted roses, only roses — roses on ladies' fans, roses on book covers, roses on stationery, enough framed roses to hang on all the boudoir walls of Paris. The least of her paintings sold for five hundred francs. Dumas the younger called her "the woman who, after God, created the most roses." Madeleine Lemaire wore large hats to hide her acne-pocked face and gowns with trains to hide her large feet. When Redfern tailored suits made trains and flounces old-fashioned, Madame Lemaire resorted to costume balls. She surrounded herself with fledging writers, whom she called her "pages." That day in May she had invited a small group to a reading of *Portraits de Peintres* by the twenty-four-year-old Marcel Proust. Overwhelmed by emotion and never an actor, he did not particularly enhance the quality of his text. But Colette was impressed and she wrote to Marcel that she found the poems subtle and beautiful. "But you should not spoil them as you do by reciting them very badly, this is very unfortunate."[52] Proust took her criticism seriously. A few days later he paid a small fortune to have the most elegant actor of the Comédie Française, the dashing Le Bargy, recite his poems accompanied at the piano by Reynaldo Hahn.

In May Proust wrote to Willy to express his admiration for his style. He was trying to have his poems published and Willy, who patronized many poets like Saint Pol Roux or Georges Fourrest in his columns, could launch his career. Colette answered for Willy. She told Proust that he and Félix Fénéon were the only ones to have seen clearly "that a word written by Willy is not the mere representation of something, but a living thing, and much less a mnemonic sign than a pictorial translation." She added that she knew Proust would understand what she meant "because you are aware, your letter proves it, that my Willy is unique (although he tries to hide it). Trivial expressions, clichés, or incoherent metaphors disgust him to the point of nausea, he is more prepared to transcribe his ideas into hieroglyphs, than into tropes."[53] It is interesting to note that Proust and Colette, both respected for their masterful treatment of the French language and the beauty of their style, admired Willy's craftmanship.

The article by Félix Féneon mentioned by Colette had appeared in *Le Nouvel Echo* in 1892 and was an analysis of Willy's style: "On music or books, on a play or about life, M. Willy writes 50 lines, but the meaning will be fathomless. He creates with words, with an infallible technique, a world teeming with images and ideas. His method is complex: he taps the vocabularies of science, arts, the Kabala, the boulevard. He peppers his text with Greek, English, German, sometimes Czech, more seldom, Syriac . . . and yet the style remains direct and sound, among so many hazards."[54] It was under Willy's guidance that Colette grasped the idea that a word should always be a pictorial translation; the fact that she referred to an article published three years earlier shows how drawn she was to the problems of style.

Colette deplored that Marcel Proust had missed Madame Arman's meeting the day before; she had half-expected him and hoped to see him the following Wednesday "to chat." "For it seems to me that we have many interests in common, Willy being one of them."[55]

Each year Colette and Willy went to Bayreuth, a must for the music critic of *L'Echo de Paris*. The Willys made this Wagner pilgrimage every year until 1902. The musical mayhem and lax mores of the European socialites in the Wagnerian town served as a background in *Claudine Married* for Claudine's love triangle with Rézi and Renaud.

Willy was Cosima Wagner's friend and undertook Wagner's defense in the article: "Bayreuth et l'Homosexualité," published in *La Revue Blanche,* when it was rumored that Wagner was homosexual. Colette did not like Bayreuth, which only came to life during the festival and had not enough hotels to accommodate the crowd, who slept in private homes; however she enjoyed the "three or four hours of music at the Festspielhaus and certain beautiful voices."[56] At a dinner in 1933 with Max Reinhardt, Colette, "whose memory is amazing, imitated a number of Wagnerian singers with their specific accents — Swabian, Scandinavian, or Viennese."[57]

In March of 1895 Colette was invited to a banquet at the Café d'Harcourt to launch a new review, *Le Centaure.* Colette, Rachilde, and Marie de Régnier, also known as Gérard d'Houville, were the only women among the fifty-five guests, who included Lord Douglas, Stuart Merrill,

Marcel Schwob, and Henri Gauthier-Villars. At the end of the banquet they signed copies of *Le Centaure;* was it Willy or Colette who inscribed them "Colette GV and her man Willy"? In a long letter to his brother listing some of the luminaries who attended, Pierre Louÿs named Madame H.G.V. "the new young journalist whose initials you will recognize."[58]

Colette was often at the d'Harcourt with Jean de Tinan and participated in the debate that led to the creation of the *Le Centaure.* Its only two issues dwelt on the nature and function of art and advocated the free expression of eroticism. Gide resigned because this review was "an invitation to debauchery," which prompted an ironical response from Pierre Louÿs describing Gide's "La Ronde de la Grenade," a poem published in it, as "excessively, even revoltingly lewd."[59] Colette consistently repudiated the romantic idea of art as an overflow of feelings; she insisted that she was not a born writer, and that to write was a craft. This concept of art was best expressed in Paul Valéry's "La Soirée avec Monsieur Teste," published in *Le Centaure.* What Colette, Valéry, Louÿs, and Gide — the four most important writers to spring out of the d'Harcourt group— had in common was the conception of art as artifice.

Colette finished the manuscript of *Claudine* in the spring of 1896. In 1936 she wrote in *My Apprenticeships* that Willy had read it, declared it unpublishable, and put it away in a drawer of his desk, where it lay forgotten for years. In fact, Willy took the manuscript of *Claudine* to his publisher. Simonis Empis, who had published eight books signed "Willy," refused this one on the grounds that it would never sell a hundred copies. Delagrave did not want it; Léon Vanier, who had published Willy's *Letters of the Usherette* and *Comic Salon,* offered to publish it at the author's expense. The six-hundred-fifty-six-page manuscript did not have the usual format of a novel. It was a satirical chronicle with no suspense; it had no chapters; and the philosophy underlying the text would shock a public that was becoming more conservative. Colette was disappointed; the literary world had slammed its doors.

Willy and Colette spent July in Uriage, a fashionable health spa, taking Jacques along to cheer Colette up. While Willy engaged in what was to be a lifelong battle against weight and tried to shed a few of his 231 pounds, Colette and Jacques took long walks with Kiki the cat. She had taught Kiki-la-Doucette to walk on a leash; the pair became celebrities. Colette was seen everywhere with her obedient pet, whom she even took to her box at the opera on opening nights.

Before going in August to the family estate in the Jura where Colette was already vacationing, Willy tried once more to have her novel published, asking the publisher Hetzel what his intentions were concerning the manuscript he had submitted. He tried to entice him to publish it by reminding him that he had enough friends in the press to enjoy free publicity, assuring Hertzel that he himself would write anonymous rave reviews which would launch the novel. Hetzel refused.

Colette's Salon

Back in Paris after the annual Bayreuth pilgrimage, Colette and Willy moved from the Left Bank to the newly built bourgeois district of La Plaine Monceau on the Right Bank; the apartment was on the fifth floor of 93 Rue de Courcelles. It was spacious and sunny, quite a relief from the dark Rue Jacob. The walls were painted a light green and white goatskins were scattered all over; artifacts signed "Bing" and a collection of tankards bought in Bayreuth added to the art-nouveau setting. A liveried concierge opened the door of the elevator, which was upholstered in red velvet. Like most French elevators, it only went up.

Since literature seemed to be evading her, Willy made sure that Colette was recognized as a Parisian personality; he prompted her to have a *jour*. The informal meetings of the Rue Jacob were replaced by *les dimanches de Madame Gauthier-Villars* after the Sunday afternoon concert. No Parisian of note would miss a visit at Rue de Courcelles. At one gathering the journalist Amory noted Gabriel de Lautrec, the fiery neo-royalist Léon Daudet, and the comtesse de Greffulhe, immortalized by Proust. Colette was in the public eye; Nadar photographed her and Fix-Masseau sculpted her bust, with her shoulders and her left breast bare. This bust, exhibited at the Galérie du Champs de Mars was the centerpiece of the 1896 salon.

That fall Colette's growing success as a hostess was a direct menace to well-established salons. A quarrel occurred between Madame Arman and the Willys when she alleged that Willy, for years an intimate friend, had breached etiquette by openly flirting with her daughter-in-law, Jeanne. Madame Arman, who could be blunt to the point of wounding, went straight to Colette, telling her that her husband was courting

Jeanne (Rose-Chou in Colette's *Claudine and Annie*). Another version of the feud is that Anatole France found Colette extremely attractive. Whatever the facts, the Willys were barred from Madame Arman's salon. After that Colette referred to Anatole France as "a noisy cad" in *Claudine Married* and described Madame Arman as an owl with "a crooked nose."

Marcel Proust, upset by this harsh banishment, acted as a go-between and tried to reconcile the two parties. Willy told him that Colette had reacted to this humiliation with such sorrow "she almost lost her eyesight"[60] and had to stay in a darkened room. Proust was upset and begged her to see his own ophthalmologist; Proust, himself, was under Madame Arman's orders not to see the Willys anymore and they avoided each other.

Meanwhile, Charlotte Kinceler brought her troubles to Colette and Willy. In letters written in common they gave her their advice — Charlotte was involved in the complicated breakup of an affair with a famous general. She had ordered ten thousand francs worth of linen from the outrageously expensive Grande Maison du Blanc while the general was her lover. Willy and Colette concocted a diabolical scenario to swindle the general: Charlotte was to return the linen to the store and the general was to give her the ten thousand francs, which would be pure profit if the scheme worked. On November 6, Colette's letter started with a sigh of relief — "Ouf!" — for their plan had worked. But she expressed disgust that the general had not paid the full amount, keeping back four thousand francs, which she felt was so little for so rich a man. The first part of the plot having succeeded, the next step was to return the linen to the store. Colette, who as Madame Gauthier-Villars commanded respect in upscale stores, went with Charlotte and persuaded the management to accept the return. The trio celebrated their triumph.

However, Colette was concerned about Lotte's poor physical state and reassured her by telling her that two years earlier her own womb had been severely damaged and that she was now totally cured. She firmly believed that Lotte would see the same happy ending. This correspondence sheds a vivid light on Colette and Willy's relationship with the demimonde.

Willy had invited the eighteen-year-old model Fanny, to their apartment. Painted by Léandre in a "black gown as the Angel of Darkness" and celebrated by Jean Lorrain, that year she was the rave of Montmartre. As Fanny stepped into the couple's bedroom, she explained "to Mr. Willy, to myself, to the birds through the window, her voluptuous preferences ..."[61] In a letter to Marcel Schwob, Colette made fun of the incident, comparing Fanny to her cat Nonoche, wild with love, with "rolling crazy eyes."[62] Colette put an end to the trio.

Something else was wrong; Willy was brooding. In his November 13 letter to Charlotte he insisted that he was bored to death, devoured by a boredom that crushed him, that he would do anything to lift himself out of it, but that nothing seemed to help. Then he made a startling confession to his "darling Lotte." Because he loved her so passionately, he never allowed her to have lesbian relationships, although he permitted them to Colette, encouraging her and even providing occasions. He asked Lotte to compare his love for her with his love for Colette and draw her own conclusions. He confessed he was in a web of problems, but when the three of them met, nothing in their behavior should betray anything confidential between him and Lotte. A few days later he complained to "My Lolo" about his lack of money — he was afraid he and Colette would not be able to pay the rent. He signed "Kiki" and Colette added an affectionate postscript. Their relationship seemed very relaxed; but they had settled for a way of life which did not exclude a great deal of pain, jealousy, and humiliation.

(In the last letter of their correspondence, dated February 16, 1897, Colette thanked Lotte for a ring so beautiful that she wore it to bed and showed it off by raising her little finger. Their friendship would last until 1906, when Charlotte, suddenly converted by a priest and seemingly well on her way to salvation, wrote on a large piece of paper left on a table on a gray day in November, "When it rains like this, everything makes me sick," then took a pistol and shot herself — "through the mouth,"[63] wrote Colette; "through the temple,"[64] wrote Willy.)

November brought more bad news. Paul Masson, who in his peculiar way seemed to be able to put everything into perspective, committed suicide: during a visit to his hometown, he stuffed his nose with cotton balls drenched in ether and drowned. His body was recovered seven days later. Colette was stunned when he died: "I lost my first friend, the first friend of my coming of age as a woman."[65] Colette had a serious breakdown with violent nervous fits; she remained in her room in total darkness, alone, with the door closed.

By December Colette was well again; she had heard Alfred Jarry read *Ubu Roi* at Rachilde's and did not want to miss the rehearsals. December 10 was opening night at the Théâtre de l'Oeuvre, which functioned like a club. There was no box office for the general public; seats were sold by subscription only. Its subscribers were the regulars of *Le Mercure de France* and *La Revue Blanche*. *Ubu Roi* was a savage farce, an apotheosis of defiant anarchy, a forerunner of the Theater of the Absurd. With the help of Vuillard and Toulouse-Lautrec, Bonnard created the set; his brother-in-law, Claude Terrasse, composed the music.

Jarry lived in a single room full of dried bones, since he fed carrion to his pet owls and considered his room the outdoors that he missed. He used to bicycle round and round the room, avoiding the rare furniture pieces. He was as pale as parchment, painted his lips a vivid red, and was a regular at the Gauthier-Villars'. Willy helped to boost his career, even coauthoring a play with Jarry that was never produced.

On opening night the lights went out. (Lugné-Poë was the first director to systematically darken the theater despite the public's violent objections — Parisians felt that if they could not see each other, they were missing half the show.) The short twenty-three-year-old Jarry appeared in front of the curtain, perched on a table covered with burlap, heavily made-up, his hair plastered down, and dressed in an oversized suit. He delivered the prologue in a hammered-out singsong, ending with, "the action takes place in Poland, that is, nowhere." The curtains parted. On one side of the stage snow fell on a canopied bed complete with bedstand and chamber pot; on the other a boa constrictor twisted itself around a coconut tree. A skeleton hung from a scaffold; owls perched on a windowsill; the actors entered and exited through an oversized fireplace. An actor posted a sign reading "This is the house of Mr. & Mrs. Ubu." Ubu entered, pearshaped and wearing a conical hat, and hurled his first word at the public: "MERDRE!" to the screams of an outraged audience and the wild applause of the *Mercure* clan. Colette was heard laughing so loud that her voice dominated the uproar; Georges Courteline shouted, "Jarry is making fools of us"; Willy rose to his feet and shouted to the audience, "Let the show go on"; Rachilde tried to stop the booing; the young poet, Fernand Gregh, insulted the audience, "You don't even understand Shakespeare," while his dissenting brother shouted at him, "You never read Shakespeare yourself." Ubu started a wild jig and Lugné-Poë turned the lights on; this silenced the crowd until he turned them down again. Savage shouts covered the voices of the actors as they went on with the play.

Not since Victor Hugo's *Hernani* had the Parisians enjoyed such a glorious intellectual riot; they would have to wait until 1913 and Stravinsky's *Le Sacre du Printemps* for another evening so wild. *Ubu's* name entered the language; his obscene statements became an assertion of free speech. Mallarmé, who did not approve of Jarry's anarchism and rowdy homosexuality, nevertheless sent him a congratulatory note and named his cats "Monsieur Ubu" and "Madame Ubu." The influential *La Revue Blanche,* with Willy on its editorial board, offered Jarry a regular salary; when *La Revue* folded in 1903 he was left destitute. Jarry drank two bottles of wine and three glases of absinthe as an eye-opener, according to Rachilde; according to Apollinaire, he drank a cocktail of vinegar, absinthe, and a drop of ink as a nightcap. When he died at the age of thirty-four, his last request was for a toothpick.

Ubu Roi was the culmination of the literary *pronunciamenti* made by the *hirsutes,* the *hydropathes,* the *fantaisistes,* and the *symbolists,* all groups which had shown a keen interest in the relationship between art and society, and who had proclaimed that art could play a part in reshaping the world. They defended the artist's right to express himself with limitless freedom; they championed individualism in the most outrageous ways, bordering at times on hooliganism, and scorned every established convention. *Ubu Roi* was the latest attempt of *Le Mercure de France* group to force the government to repeal the censorship law.

Her novel forgotten in a drawer, Colette went back to journalism. She and Willy left *La Cocarde;* Barrès had become an anathema to many after the publication of *Les Déracinés* (The Uprooted), a novel advocating an extreme nationalism that became the basis of his political platform. Colette signed theater reviews in *La Critique* and in 1897 joined the newly created feminist newspaper, *La Fronde.* It was the first daily entirely written, managed, set, and printed by women. With collaborators such as Rachilde, Juliette Adam, Gyp, and Colette, success was assured from the start; the first issue sold two hundred thousand copies. *La Fronde* declared war on "abuses, prejudices, outdated codes, arbitrary laws which do not reflect the present conditions." However, it was more informative than purely militant, publishing regular articles on the stockmarket and extensive coverage of national and international news. Colette wrote musical reviews; later Willy claimed that he was the author of the articles in *La*

Fronde, "because they were so bad."[66] It was a piqued response to Colette saying that she had been forced to work as a ghostwriter.

In February Willy was in a private clinic in Passy — officially to lose weight but more probably to be treated for a syphilis-related depression. Colette wrote to Schwob that Willy was very sick and in a state of total despondency, yet his latest book was taking off after a slow start. She was referring to Willy's second novel, *Maîtresse d'Esthètes,* whose hero was Masseau, the sculptor who had just finished the bust of Colette. He had given Willy the material for the book and showed him his correspondence with Henriette Maitland, the "Minna" of *Une Passade.* Armed with her correspondence, and completely without scruples, Willy and Jean de Tinan all but named the actual lovers of their heroine. They peopled the book with Willy's friends: Spéret, director of *La Revue Mauve,* was Alfred Valette; Jean Nancy was Jean Lorrain, the mistress of Jim Smiley (alias Willy); Clarisse-Sidonie was Sidonie-Gabrielle Colette.

Maîtresse d'Esthète caused a feud between Willy and Pierre Véber, who was mad at Willy for having recycled the character of Minna into a sequel written with someone else. Véber reclaimed Minna as his own. When he heard that Willy had refused to sign a petition asking for a retrial of Dreyfus, Véber said: "It would be the first time Willy refused to sign something he had not written."[67] Although their friendship overcame their bitterness and the following year *Une Passade* bore their two names, Véber's insult would be used as proof that Willy did not write any of his novels.

As a journalist, Willy surrounded himself with students, young writers who did the groundwork for him, and experts to advise him on technical points. Fagus described how Willy's everchanging collaborators worked: "It happened that we collaborated on one or two of the *Letters of the Usherette.*" After listening to a concert "we wrote a punctilious analysis," which Willy edited. What was only an ordinary review written by any conscientious amateur became, after his rewriting, "inimitable Willy." After *La Revue Bleue* published a review of *The Letters of the Usherette* naming Willy as sole author, he asked the director to rectify the statement: "I want to underline that the book was written in collaboration with my good friend Alfred Ernst."[68] For his reviews of concerts, he had the input of Claude Debussy, Gabriel Fauré, Vincent d'Indy, Gabriel Pierné, Louis de Serres, and Florent Schmidt; his most constant collaborator would be Emile Vuillermoz.

Willy was asked to rescue the sinking *Le Chat Noir*, which was having serious difficulties; a rapid succession of editors in chief had plunged the review into debt. Willy reduced its format and called his friends to the rescue. The first wave of collaborators was working for major papers and could no longer submit to the demands of cooperative works. Like many small publications, *Le Chat Noir* derived its success from a small clique who saw the review as a cooperative venture. Willy was unable to revive the review, whose anarchistic stance and particular wit were passé; however, he retained two of the team from *Le Chat Noir* as his collaborators: Paul Barlet, who wrote under the alias Paul Héon, and Maurice Saillant, who signed "Curnonsky." Paul Barlet was hired as secretary; Curnonsky remained Willy's collaborator and confidant until his death. He abandoned his academic career to work for him.

There is no doubt that Colette was part of the team. "I see myself working (I did not sign either) on the thin, crackling American paper which I preferred to any other."[69] Whatever articles or parts of novels she wrote can only be conjectured, but it was well known in Paris that Colette collaborated closely with her husband and many people made sure to send her their works, dedicated "To Colette Willy." Colette found Willy's style too elaborate; he found hers lacking in precision. When she wrote, "I put on my scarf," Willy wrote in the margin, "which one?"; then she added, "I put on my scarf of white tulle."[70] She mastered the masks and impersonations that were part of the mirror game that Willy played with the world; not only were the novels signed "Willy" the shimmering result of multiple collaboration, but they were also a reflection on society, as they mixed real people under easy-to-read fictitious names and fictitious characters. The team used their idiosyncracies to create multiple characters. Colette appears as a mistress under the names of Sidonie, Clarisse, or Marie. As a free teenager, she appears under the name Jeannette. As a bisexual, Colette becomes Claudine, as a nymphomaniac, she is called Annie. As an unhappy woman she is Renée. As a voyeur, Willy appears under the name of Jim Smiley, as a romantic writer he is Parville, as a loving husband he is Renaud, as a betrayed lover, he is called Tardot. It is obvious that their personalities are split into a variety of characters but remain easy to identify in the romans à clefs produced by the team.

After *Maîtresse d'Esthètes*, the group worked on *Un Vilain Monsieur*, in which some paragraphs are undoubtedly Colette's. The literary ricochet game was carried one step further when de Tinan, Curnonsky, and Héon included those characters in their own novels. It was unusual salesmanship; for years Willy and Colette used this device in a literary dialogue unique in the literary world. When Jean de Tinan died at the age of twenty-four, he left an unfinished novel, *Aimienne,* in which he described Willy and Colette under the names of "Silly" and "Jeannette." In *Aimienne,* the hero Vallonges meets Suzette, an avatar of Colette; they get along very well without being in love. They spend a month in Montigny, Claudine's birthplace, the literary mirror of Saint-Sauveur. This novel was written in 1897, while *Claudine* would not be published before 1900; only an intimate friend could have had access to the *Claudine* manuscript. In this creative entanglement Férier, Aimienne's father, reminds one of Captain Colette; like him, he is a Republican, who calls for social harmony in lyrical speeches. Tinan made fun of the way Willy worked: "He had found one of his sentences in a new book by Caublance, lifted from one of his own; then he remembered that he himself had lifted it from a letter received from Madame A . . ."[71] Willy always picked up every scrap of information that might eventually serve as the seed of a novel or article. His son recalled telling him about his experiences as a draftee and being urged to write them down, which he did. Willy then analyzed the paper and concluded that it was no good as it stood, but added, "I will keep this, I have read much worse. It can always prove useful, it is well documented."[72]

For the third year in a row, Colette and Willy went to Bayreuth for the Wagner festival. They attended the performances with Siegfried Wagner Wagnerisso and rode in his carriage. When they came back to Paris, they found themselves more "in" than ever. At the annual exhibit of French painters, Jacques-Emile Blanche showed a portrait of Colette and Willy (now at the museum of Barcelona in Spain) and Fernand Humbert a portrait of Colette with red carnations behind her ear, looking like a gypsy.

Colette stopped collaborating with *La Fronde;* she did not thrive at the feminist newspaper. Consistently albeit casually, she would later say that suffragettes should be burned at the stake or locked up in a harem. She had an aversion to political involvement and to any form of commitment.

New intellectual centers were emerging in Paris, and Jeanne Muhlfeld was replacing Madame Arman as the city's most prestigious literary hostess.

Born Jeanne Meyer, she came from an old Jewish family; one of her sisters had married Paul Adam, the other, the painter Leonetto Cappiello. She herself was married to the critic and novelist Lucien Muhlfeld, Willy's friend from university days. After a few years in Bombay, Lucien Muhlfeld had become "the king of the press." Tall and thin, with graying hair, he liked to say that literature did not exist, that it was either a work of art or a scientific product. He worked in a room without a window, lit day and night by an electric bulb, its walls covered in canvas with gold spangles.

Jeanne Muhlfeld abandoned the sacrosanct, appointed day for an open house; every day at five o'clock she received friends for tea. Cappiello, whose bright posters brought sunshine to the gray walls of Paris, decorated Muhlfeld's salon in pale yellow and white. There she reclined on a sofa covered with white furs, as she suffered from a crippling arthritis of the hip. Jeanne put her energies into making her salon a path to the Légion d'Honneur or the Académie Française: "She was a master at that game of chess which consists of turning a writer into an essential piece and moving it to the cupola of the Académie,"[73] wrote Jean Cocteau. She was beautiful and extremely amusing; she knew a genius as soon as she saw one and had a taste for beautiful, talented women. She was immensely captivated by Willy's nonconformist young wife; they became close friends. Colette renamed her *Fille du Fleuve* (River Maid) and threatened to cheat on her with Willy if Jeanne refused to ride in a cab with her — yet it was to Jeanne that Colette confided how much she needed Willy.

In April Willy's father, Jean-Albert Gauthier-Villars, died; Colette has left us an affectionate portrait of her father-in-law in *De ma Fenêtre*. Willy relinquished all claims to the family business; that same year, he became executive director of the very serious *Revue Internationale de Musique*.

On May 2 Colette and Willy attended Achille's marriage to an heiress, the aristocratic Jeanne de la Fare, granddaughter of the marquis de la Fare. Achille was thirty-four; he had led the life of a typical, wealthy, *fin-de-siècle* bachelor. He had many Parisian friends and had befriended Colette's new ones, particularly Schwob. In Châtillon he had had an affair with a farmer's daughter who, according to Colette, had come to his office to seduce him, after which they had carried on their silent love affair in the open fields. A child was born of the liaison; Sido said the girl's parents were so proud that their grandchild was Doctor Achille's son that they never created a problem, and even boasted about it. It was the world as seen by Fourierist Sido; in fact, to have a child out of wedlock carried a heavy social stigma.

According to Sido, the aristocratic la Fares were also proud to see their daughter marry her peerless son. The couple settled into a house of their own, but Achille came to visit his mother daily.

Colette was unhappy. She was afraid of "becoming herself, only herself, that is, a nice little woman who had no esteem either for her anonymous work or her submissiveness." Of all Willy's protégés, she alone had not yet published under her own name; she was falling into the stereotype of the writer's wife, becoming her husband's assistant. And Willy was ailing; he asked his readers to forgive him if his articles were not as witty as they should be. After *Un Vilain Monsieur,* no other novel was forthcoming.

Curnonsky was back from Persia with a new friend, the poet Paul-Jean Toulet, who led a bohemian life and wrote articles. Having met Curnonsky, he had taken him along to Asia. They coauthored two novels under the pseudonym "Perdiccas": *The Courtesan's Handbook* and *Love as a Profession.* Toulet lived in bed and only rose once or twice a week. He had been told by a doctor to avoid absinthe, an alcoholic drink known to have destroyed many excellent minds, including Verlaine's. Toulet retorted that he had personally experimented with a variety of alcoholic beverages and they had all had effects on his mind. Since the main ingredient they had in common was water, only water could be said to be detrimental; therefore he would drink only pure alcohol. These drunken aphorisms were widely repeated. Toulet was seven years older than Colette. She spent hours listening to him as he rambled on about opium and the strange meeting places of the weirdest people imaginable.

With Toulet and Curnonsky, Colette went to *Les Concerts Rouges,* where a philharmonic orchestra played Wagner, Beethoven, and Mozart while the audience drank beer or brandy with maraschino cherries for a franc and a half. Then the trio would go to the *Ball Bullier,* a dance hall where students, working girls, and store clerks danced the polka, the gallop, the spinning waltz, or the quadrille. Men from the upper class came to pick up pretty midinettes, or young seamstresses. Daring women came in with heavy veils drawn over their faces to avoid recognition; bisexual courtesans came in to pick up young girls. *La Belle Epoque* was fascinated with the dark and murky side of pleasure; scandal would be a constant trait in Colette's writing, always linked to paradox.

V

CLAUDINE

"Name Willy, only Willy, to him all the glory"
COLETTE'S LETTER TO RACHILDE, 1899.

ON THE 1899 cover of the annual compilation of the "Usherette's" articles, (titled that year *La Colle aux Quintes*) its publisher, Simonis Empis, announced a future release: *Claudine*. Strangely, the author was not named.

Times had changed, a new generation of naturalists critized the aesthetic of the symbolists and the decadents. They expressed contempt for a literature replete with the abnormal and the pathological. Mallarmé's aesthetic was seen as a literary dead end. In his *Essai sur le Naturisme*, Maurice Le Blond, the theoretician of the naturist trend, attacked the two mentors of the decadent generation: Baudelaire, neurotic and impotent, understood nothing about nature; as for Gautier, his taste for the odd, abnormal, and artificial led his followers into sterile ecstasies. In *L'Ennemi des Rêves*, Camille Mauclair scorned writers who rejected everyday life, exhausted their intelligence in byzantine analysis, and were doomed to intellectual death. The cult of the self was no more than a "moral narcotic." A return to nature would lead to the rediscovery of mental ease and physical well-being. Young André Gide had made that discovery in 1894 as he traveled through North Africa; he depicted his newfound *joie de vivre* in *Les Nourritures Terrestres*. Willy sensed the new trend and encouraged Colette to write.

Colette's friends — Masson, Mendès, Schwob, de Tinan, and Lorrain — had nothing to offer for the fulfillment of the heart and mind. According to them, man lived on the brink of madness in order to escape dismal *ennui;* they drove themselves to desperation in order to refine their consciousness. The decadent intellectuals felt they were part of an aging civilization, that physical and nervous exhaustion were the price paid for centuries of progress, that the human race had reached the age of decline. The Western world was old, suffering from the throes of exhaustion.

Colette reacted to this aesthetic with untamed energy; her critical intelligence led her to the very essence of literary modernity. Decadence constituted a spiritual crisis — Colette denounced "a pose that abhorred simplicity and even clarity."[1]

The abstract transcendence sought by the decadent intellectuals was replaced by a vision of the immanent wholeness of the world. Health and fulfillment replaced pessimism and decay. "Toute oeuvre est autobiographique," Willy had proclaimed. Autobiography, not confession with its moral implications, became the preferred mode of expression. This reconciliation with life led to the disappearance of misogyny, so characteristic of the decadent era. Woman was no longer seen as the cause of masculinity's disintegration, but she was redeemed in the new glorification of life. The turn of the century saw the flourishing of feminine and feminist literature.

Willy, with his flair for timing, knew the public was ripe for *Claudine*. He asked several writers and journalists to read the manuscript. In his memoirs, Armory recalled that one morning Willy gave him "a roll of papers" that Colette had written. He read the manuscript. "Well?" asked Willy. "Extraordinary! When do you publish it?"[2]

Willy felt he should do some editing; Armory advised him to change nothing. Willy asked Curnonsky if he could cut the 656-page manuscript to marketable length, then decided to edit it himself. Alfred Diard, one of Willy's secretaries, said that he proudly showed the manuscript of the first *Claudine*, entirely in Colette's hand, to his friends. In an interview with Pierre Varenne, Willy said once again that he cut Colette's original script in half. However, Colette never mentioned any cuts, and there can be little doubt that whatever was excised was reworked into *Claudine in Paris*.

Colette gave two versions of how she wrote her first novel; in the most widely recounted one, Willy asked her to jot down her memories of the days when she loved to tyrannize the Saint-Sauveur schoolgirls. He was not impressed with the results and put Colette's notebooks in storage. Some five years later, after a vacation in Franche-Comté, he stumbled upon them and exclaimed, "Damn it! I'm a jerk,"[3] which Colette watered down in the 1948 edition of her collected works to "I'm a fool." But in an interview in 1907 Colette said, "He (Henri) wrote books and that did interest me. One day, I told him that I, too, could write a book. He burst out laughing and made fun of my pretensions and inexperience. However, without saying a word, I jotted down whatever went through my mind, when there was enough material, I showed it to him; he was flabbergasted, amazed, dumbfounded."[4]

This destroys the image of Colette locked up by Willy. In 1948, in an interview, Alain Parinaud asked her to expand on how she had been ordered to write the *Claudines*. Colette replied that Willy had never ordered her to write, that he had asked her to write a novel about growing up in Saint-Sauveur and she had seen no reason not to do so. Parinaud made another gaffe. He mentioned again the books ordered by Willy. Colette rebuffed him. He then asked Colette how Willy spiced up her text, and gave as an example the seduction of Aimée by Claudine. In that scene, according to Parinaud, Claudine behaved like a boy, therefore it was written by Willy. An ironic Colette asked: Why would not a girl have the same feeling as a boy? She added to the journalist's surprise, stating that when she did not agree with Willy's suggestions she simply ignored them and he trusted her judgment. Parinaud was blocked by the myths surrounding Colette's debut as a writer and kept prodding. Did Willy let her go out alone? Did he not keep her under lock and key? Never in Paris, retorted Colette, but maybe sometimes when they were at their country estate he had to coax her back to her writing table. She had worked out her own rules, setting everything aside to write several hours a day. When she could write no more, she did some gardening or some carpentry but, all her life, she had to force herself to write and always longed for the break. Parinaud commented that Willy had signed her first novels unfairly. Colette set things right: she did not want to sign the risqué *Claudine* and demanded to sign Colette Willy only after her separation from her husband for financial reasons. She added that her divorce had nothing to do whatsoever with her literary production.

Simonis Empis did not publish *Claudine in School*. Encouraged by the enthusiastic reactions from his entourage, Willy negotiated a better deal with Ollendorff, the owner of *Gil Blas*. He had help from Lucien Muhlfeld, who on January 10, 1900, sent him a *pneu,* one of those messages written on special blue paper and placed inside a cylinder propelled by compressed air through a tube from post office to post office throughout Paris. Muhlfeld's message held information that Willy was to keep to himself: Ollendorff's influential reader, Pierre Valdagne, had given a favorable opinion of the book and had said that it was good, witty, and very well documented, but would stir up a storm. People would object to such a description of a village and its lay school. However, Valdagne concluded this would not hamper its sales. Muhlfeld warned Willy that Ollendorff was going to call him and instructed him to act like an author who knew what a commotion his book would create. He should ask for a first printing of three thousand copies, not the usual five hundred, and demand twelve centimes on every franc. He insisted, "Stand your ground, don't give in."[5]

Next came a letter from Pierre Valdagne asking Willy to change the preface. Willy had written that "an unknown girl" had sent him the manuscript tied with a pink ribbon. Valdagne thought this could lead the public to believe that the book was not by Willy, while they needed his name to ensure a best-seller. Willy refused. *Claudine at School* was released in March with its ambiguous preface pointing to an "unknown girl" as author of the manuscript. For weeks the sales were flat; the book was lingering in limbo. The daily newspapers listed or reviewed the book only briefly in their weekly or monthly book sections — Willy's hopes that Ollendorff's *Gil Blas* would publicize the novel proved wrong. It was barely mentioned.

In May Colette was in London with Sophia Van den Brule, the Calliope Van Langendonck of *Claudine in Paris* and *The Sentimental Retreat* (La Retraite Sentimentale). Colette had a pang of passion for this Greek beauty married to a Belgian businessman. Together they visited Colette's stepson in boarding school and witnessed celebrations of the British victory over the Boers at Mafeking.

Back in Paris, Colette grew impatient, for her book was not moving. On May 18 she turned to Lucien Muhlfeld, asking for help: "repeat and repeat again that *Claudine* is very good, oh very good! . . . even if it is not true, but it would help a great deal."[6] Muhlfeld put his journalistic might to work, as did Willy, who promoted *Claudine* in every possible article signed by any pen name other than Willy. He paid to have reviews inserted — a common practice of the time. He gently reminded anyone who owed him a favor that it was time to oblige. In May two friendly articles put the book on its road to success. The first was by Rachilde in *Le Mercure de France*. Before writing it she told Colette that she intended to name her as the author. Colette immediately replied, asking Rachilde not to do so for family reasons, for propriety's sake, because of "certain friends," and so forth. She never imagined that her book would become one of the greatest hits ever in French literature.

Whatever her reasons for remaining incognito, *Claudine*'s authorship was soon an open secret. One day at a luncheon Catulle Mendès turned to her and said, "You wrote *Claudine,* you needn't overdo the bashfulness."[7] Jules Renard, a constant guest at Colette's Sundays, wrote in his *Journal,* "Claudine is a delicious creature . . . and Willy *have* lots of talent," deliberately using the plural.[8] Rachilde all but named Colette in her review:

> Written by Willy, this book is a masterpiece; written by Claudine, this same book is the most extraordinary work which could come from the pen of a beginner, it promises more than glory to its author: martyrdom! Bravo Willy! Thank you Claudine. But if you ever produce an ordinary book after this one, beware!

In her review, Rachilde, an outspoken feminist, declared that it would have taken a "stroke of genius" for Willy to have written *Claudine.*

> Here is *a true book.* The dazzling light of a living being has fallen on me. I am thunderstruck by this discovery . . . Oh, dear old Willy, I am happy I have no favor to ask from you so I can speak my mind: *Claudine* is not a novel, not a thesis, not a diary, nothing usual, this is a person, a live person, a *terrible* person. Yes, she may be a small person, fifteen years old, her hair in braids, her fists on her hips, but she is the total woman screaming at the top of her voice about her puberty, her desires, her will and, yes, her crimes. Whether by a stroke of magic, Willy, the *boulevardier,* the gossipmonger, the brilliant writer, the most delicate virtuoso has created this character, Claudine, or whether he really took these pages from the hands of a beloved woman, as one would take flowers to place them in a precious vase, I don't care.

Here is an astonishing work and that is all that counts . . .
Claudine is modern, she is a rascal, she is classic, she comes straight
out of the eternal . . . *Claudine* is at school in her wooden shoes.
She forages around in her small hell with all the glee demons find
in existing, corrupting, vanquishing with a sad and mysterious
grimace. Vice? No, vice is an invention of civilization . . . It is the
first time a woman dares to speak simply about unnatural love as
of natural paganism.

Claudine says, 'I like to torment her, to beat her, to protect
her when others bother her.' The sadism and kindness of love are
included in this one sentence.[9]

The next enthusiastic article came from another friend at *La Cocarde,*
Charles Maurras, in the *Revue Encyclopédique* of May 9, 1990: "The most
discreet confessions in this book bear witness to the fathomless experience
of Claudine. This schoolgirl has to be a woman of thirty."[10] Reviews followed like a flash flood; there was a rush to the bookstands, and forty thousand copies were sold in two months. As there was no mass readership in
1900, these sales were unprecedented. Jean Lorrain was happy to write that
Claudine sold as much as Zola. Under the pen name "Willy," Colette had
reached her own status as a writer, however ambiguous it might be.

In the Catholic press the reviews were scathing; the author was accused of immorality. A provincial newspaper, *La Croix de Reims,* attacked
Willy who, using his right of rebuttal, wrote an article twice as long as
the review, making fun of the conservative, religious paper. In
Republican newspapers, Willy was blamed for his lewd description of a
lay school and branded an adversary of state education. Now Willy appeared not only as a witty, amusing writer, but as an immoralist and
enemy of the state. He capitalized on the scandal with enormous flair,
having carefully watched Madame Arman, a wizard in promotional
techniques, as she took the career of Anatole France into her hands and
steered him towards the Académie Française.

What was *Claudine at School*? What made it such a best-seller? Was it
a novel? Not in the traditional sense. Colette's true diary? No, it contained too much fiction; yet Colette and Claudine seemed to be the
same person. Colette defined it as "a landscape" and asserted "It's me and
it is not me."[11] The village called Montigny is a replica of Saint-Sauveur;
the school is the old Saint-Sauveur school of 1890. Claudine, like

Colette, has long braids of chestnut hair. Both write their essays in class without a draft in just a few minutes, "the way you fry an egg,"[12] both are excellent musicians, and the parallels go on. The only difference is that Claudine has lost her mother, but she has a father, an absentminded scholar called Claude. The principal, Mademoiselle Terrain, who welcomed Colette and Willy in 1895, was Mademoiselle Sergent; Captain Colette's opponent, Doctor Merlou, was easily recognized in Dutertre. The obscure villagers depicted in vitriolic terms were so true to their models that today their real names and biographical notes are published in the *Cahiers Colette*. The novel is the scandalous chronicle of a provincial lay school, where everyone is immoral. The narrator describes with great gusto and glee the inspector's corruption, the principal's immorality, the various love affairs and the lesbian tendencies of the students and teachers. An unsophisticated perversion permeates the whole book, yet something extremely strong comes through all this lewd hanky-panky — the talent of a great writer. The readers, starting with the critics, felt the heartbeat, the rush of blood, the flow of emotions. Here was something Parisians recognized with unforeseen nostalgia: the rush of fresh wind through the unpaved streets, the hazy dawn, the heat of summer, the bracing winter, the whisper of a tree, the call of a bird. A spell was cast on the reader. *Claudine* was capturing everyone's fancy. Some compared this book to the *Confessions* of Jean-Jacques Rousseau. Most simply fell in love with Claudine.

In *Claudine at School,* lesbian overtones dominated the overall scandalous and satirical atmosphere. Willy reminisced twenty years later how the whole region of Saint-Sauveur was in a state of shock. Its representative, Doctor Merlou, was hounded by his portrait as Dutertre, and the local press described the book as a political attack. Critics failed to see that in *Claudine at School* Colette had begun her reflections on the pure and impure, on the protean forms of love as seen from her particular point of view. In its preface Willy warned the reader that the heroine of the book was not raised according to the common concept of good or evil, but without any principle at all. The result of a truly unfettered education, Claudine was free to be her own self, between a father who pursued his own interests and her nurse Mélie, who provided for her material needs. The adolescent was exploring her awakening senses, experiencing her lesbian leanings, playing her abusive games without any guilt or remorse.

Colette saw love as the pivot of human freedom; from *Claudine* to *Gigi,* she relentlessly pursued her own analysis of the human heart and of a new order based on Fourier's utopian dreams. The works of Colette's maturity — *Sido, The Break of Day, The Pure and the Impure, The Other One* (La Seconde), and *Duo* — contain elements of her philosophy. There is an ideological unity in her work, which comes from the core principles learned from her mother and which Saint-Sauveur, the village without a steeple, allowed to flourish. Whenever Colette felt she was losing her difference, her principles, she went back to those two focal points — her mother and her village.

On September 2, 1900, Colette and Willy bought a century-old estate, Les Monts-Boucons. The estate was in joint ownership, which was unusual since under French law the husband was the sole owner. Colette never loved any home more than the Monts-Boucons. She redesigned the park planted "according to the rules of Louis XIV." Colette "abhorred from childhood straight alleys and square gardens. I wanted them following the curbs and always on some slope . . . facing south or west." Around a house, she also did not like "a sumptuous landscape entering by its doors and windows." A garden was a separate world. Colette planted large beds of flowers in the alleys to stop the eye from wandering down panoramic views. She cleared the underbrush around some old trees, but turned the three terraces into little jungles. "In the garden which I oversaw disorder was always a simulation, an entanglement achieved only with the collaboration of the shears."[13] Captain Colette wrote a poem for the occasion celebrating the Monts-Boucons, a place that gave birth, not to children, but to books. A series of photographs shows a happy-looking Colette dressed in a velvet pre-Raphaelite dress in her wildflower garden in front of some large greenhouses, with a group of friends serenading her.

The estate was bought for forty thousand francs. At the end of the year, the royalties from *Claudine* amounted to forty-five hundred francs. The Willys wanted to capitalize on its success; Colette went to work at a frantic pace and *Claudine in Paris* was released in March of 1901, exactly one year after the publication of the first *Claudine.* The sequel focused on male homosexuality. Once more Colette wrote about her own experience, describing people she knew, telling a story close to her own. In 1931 Willy would write that almost everything in *Claudine in Paris* was true.

The originality of this book lies not in the story — Claudine falls in love with a forty-year-old man and marries him — but in the discovery of Parisian society by an adolescent raised in the country. The novel was in the tradition of Montesquieu's satire, *Les Lettres Persanes,* in which two visitors from Persia, amazed by what they see, describe the Parisians' customs, behavior, food, and pleasures. It is in the best satiric tradition of Voltaire and Swift, with the added spice of Colette's fascination with homosexuals.

Rachilde wrote that everything was delightful, if not extremely moral, in *Claudine in Paris.* She was the first to notice "the exquisite stories about cats"[14] that were to develop into Colette's special genre. André Beaunier commented, "Claudine is extremely quick to see through matters and people, she notices everything with unshakable common sense. She may be viewed as a sort of moralist, a very experienced one, very up-to-date and at the same time, a libertine, quite indulgent and not in the least dogmatic."[15] Moralist, immoralist, amoralist — the press would play with these definitions whenever a book by Colette was released. The sequel was also signed "Willy," but Colette had dropped the mask for her own entourage. She wrote to Rachilde, "You prefer *Claudine at School* and do me the honor of telling me so. I am extremely flattered, believe me, to be treated as a professional writer, *un homme de lettres.*"[16] Sacha Guitry always referred to her as *un homme de lettres,* stressing her peership with male writers rather than restricting her to the "less glorious" world of female literature.

Georgie Raoul-Duval

In January of 1901, while dining at the Muhlfelds', Colette fell in love with the socialite Georgie Raoul-Duval. "I loved her, if love is to desire until it burns . . . to dream of running away with her, to dream of her voluptuous sequestration."[17] Colette courted Georgie with the impetuosity of an irresistible passion; it was an ardent, obvious, tenacious courtship. "It scandalized Paul Adam, Henri de Régnier and their wives, all the literary couples we knew, Georgie was dangerously seductive,"[18] commented Willy. She was one of the most winsome beauties of the international set and one of the most venturesome. Men as well as women fell for her; Marie de Régnier (Gérard d'Houville) was one of her lovers. But discretion was still the rule, and Colette's open burning love was seen as abnormal behavior.

Georgie Raoul-Duval, born Georgie Urquhart, was the wife of a French-American millionaire busy prospecting oil fields all over the world. She was born in Vienna and educated in France and belonged to the cosmopolitan society that gathered in Paris with the sole object of spending money and finding amusement. Spendthrifts and scions of the great European families were recklessly vying with each other to squander colossal fortunes. The most extravagant was one of the models for Gaston in *Gigi,* Max Lebaudy, heir to a fortune made in sugar, who, whenever he won a race, celebrated by having his fleet of cars washed in champagne.

Georgie wrote poetry and novels: *Little Miss, Shadows of Old Paris, Written in the Sand.* Jean Cocteau, who went to the same private school as Georgie's son, saw her as "a noble and mysterious woman." In Edouard Boudet's play *La Prisonnière* she was the model of the seductress from whom a young woman tries to break away in vain. Neither her family nor her husband can free her from the love that cannot tell its name.

Colette was Georgie's passionate *prisonnière;* she followed her everywhere, to the couturiers of Rue de la Paix, to Worth's, Doucet, Rouff. She watched Georgie gracefully slipping into lovely dresses, expensive furs, and diaphanous lingerie. They rode together in the Bois de Boulogne, met in Willy's *garçonnière* at Rue Kléber, not far from Georgie's apartment at 107 Rue de la Pompe. Colette dreamt of going away with her. They made at least one trip to London.

In August Colette, Georgie, and Willy went to Bayreuth for the Wagner festival. Colette and Willy arrived on the twelfth, and Georgie appeared the following day for propriety's sake. Colette spent hours watching her curry her beauty; she even adopted her diet of stewed fruit, salads, and cucumbers, but found solace in thick, gooey ice cream. She quipped that a country where one could find ice cream for ten cents was not forsaken by the gods. In a postcard to Jeanne Muhlfeld, she told her that in spite of *The Flying Dutchman,* the mood was pleasant. Georgie was cheerful, while Willy went from lyrical joy to fierce indignation, which he expressed in the most horrid terms. After the festival, the trio took a trip through Austria.

The Gauthier-Villars were now part of the circle of the Raoul-Duvals, which included the irresistible pleasure-seeker Count Boni de Castellane and his American wife, Anna Gould. But Colette wished she could wipe out humanity and remain alone with Georgie on planet Earth. Georgie was flattered, amused, and unfaithful — she seduced Willy. She relished danger, and her greatest pleasure was to make appointments at hour intervals with Colette and Willy. When Willy realized what she was doing, he warned her that Colette, who always carried a revolver, would shoot her if she ever found out. "Wouldn't she rather shoot you?" asked a puzzled Georgie. "No," replied Willy, who explained that Colette would feel betrayed by Georgie and not by him, with whom she shared everything.[19]

As Willy had predicted, Colette was deeply hurt by Georgie's betrayal. "She was a wicked and seductive girl, that Rézi, who wanted to put her fair naked grace between Renaud and me, and indulge in the literary pleasure of betraying us both."[20]

In the afternoons Colette worked on *Claudine in Love* (Claudine Amoureuse), attempting to chart her marriage and its near wreck in the unforeseen undertow of a love that was more than a passing fancy. The "Inexorable," as she would call the senses in *The Pure and the Impure*, had done their devastating work, reaching to the core of her being. She examined what had happened to her through Claudine, who felt that since she had married Renaud, "a slow and pleasant corruption" had progressed in her. She sensed a rift in their relationship without being able to identify the cause.

Renaud, the husband, is first seen as a father figure. He calls Claudine "my darling little girl" and gives Rézi to her as he would a box of candy. Claudine resents his interference; she wants to be free to love Rézi. She feels his "loving fatherhood,"[21] his impatience to know every detail as intrusive, overprotective, and burdensome. When she goes to meet Rézi, Renaud straightens her hat and hands her a bunch of Rézi's favorite red roses. The affair amuses him, which leaves Claudine puzzled. He tells his wife that a lesbian couple is a pair of "pretty little animals"[22] looking for a diversion from men, that it provides women with a true mirror, and that some women need women to retain their taste for men. He explains that she needs him, that he is her shield against a world that might not understand her bisexuality. When Claudine and Rézi look for a place to meet privately, Claudine goes to her complacent husband, who arranges for the two women to meet in the safety of his bachelor apartment. He drives them there himself and then leaves. Claudine feels that she has a natural right to love, and that all loves are equal and good. But her feelings are ambivalent; she would like to be free in her passion for Rézi, and at the same time she resents that Rézi is disrupting her life with Renaud.

A few days later Rézi meets Renaud in the same apartment. Claudine happens to pass by, notices a curtain moving, has a sudden suspicion, rushes up to the apartment, and finds Renaud apologetic and Rézi undressed. She vows to escape forever from Parisian corruption and seek sanctuary in her native village. After a few days of grief, she asks Renaud to join her in the innocence of her rural life. Again she refers to herself as Renaud's little girl, "his spoiled child," and the story ends very morally, with Claudine begging Renaud to be less permissive. In her third novel, Colette was coming to grips with her vulnerability and with her passion for love — "Food of my pen and of my life, love."[23]

In February 1902, despite the unprecedented sales of the two former *Claudines*, Ollendorff refused to publish *Claudine in Love;* some scenes were too risqué, and he was sure the censors would stop publication. *Claudine in School* was already on the blacklist of diverse leagues for the protection of public morals. Witty but harsh rebuttals by Willy in the provincial press had boosted sales but irritated politicians, both right and left.

Pierre Valdagne came to see Colette and asked her to delete some scenes, particularly those in which Renaud takes Claudine and Rézi to his own bachelor apartment. Colette, in distress, turned to Lucien Muhlfeld, asking him to judge whether the passages that had so stunned the publisher should be expunged; she defended her book by saying that there was not a single word in it that could be subject to censorship. Lucien Muhlfeld supported her and intervened. Ollendorff was reassured, the book was printed and bound. But someone tipped off Georgie Raoul-Duval that her portrait was so thinly disguised that she would be recognized by all her friends — that her affair with the Gauthier-Villars had been told in detail. Her lawyer went to Ollendorff and offered to buy the whole edition on condition that the book be destroyed; Ollendorff accepted. Today only four copies are known to have escaped destruction; one is in the Bibliothèque Nationale.

Willy demanded and received a large compensation for breach of contract; he was in a rage and took the manuscript to Alfred Valette, who agreed to publish the dangerous book to make a point against

French censorship of literature, instituted in 1894 after terrorist attacks by anarchists. *Le Mercure de France* group had never stopped fighting for the abolition of censorship; Valette and Willy agreed that *Claudine in Love* could be a test case. *Maîtresse d'Esthète* had already enraged the conservative right, who had denounced the censors' laxness; *Claudine in School* had further exacerbated the debate. There must have been little doubt in Willy's mind that *Claudine in Love* would be seized. Willy and his friends had already testified in favor of several books seized by the censors, but the sleazy material had so little literary value that they lost their case every time. *Claudine in Love* was different; it was a literary masterpiece of erotic writing. Valette changed the title to *Claudine Married*. Willy started beating the publicity drum: "My dear colleague, you know the place *(Le Mercure)*, they have no advertising budget, can I count on you?"[24]

Colette was appalled by what he was doing. At a weekly meeting at the Muhlfelds, she felt so tired and in such a state of "moral liquefaction" that she could not bring herself to speak to Jeanne Muhlfeld. As soon as she reached home, she dropped into bed, exhausted; Willy stayed up all night, as he often did, and worked on *Claudine Married*. When Colette discovered what he had done to her manuscript, she sent an s.o.s. to Jeanne Muhlfeld: "This resentful man, extremely angry with Georgie, is turning Rézi into a glaring portrait" of Georgie Raoul-Duval. The new version was much more revealing than the previous one; no one could fail to recognize Claudine's lover. Colette thought this unworthy of Willy, unworthy of any decent person. She pleaded with Jeanne Muhlfeld; just one word from her or Lucien would be enough to halt Willy's rampage. She asked Jeanne to let Willy know that she was the one who had appealed for this intervention. It would be a great service and relief for Colette if the Muhlfelds could stop him. Willy thought Colette was protecting Georgie; they quarreled. Colette could not convince him that she was only trying to avert a libel suit. Weary, she once again called the Muhlfelds, party to all her secrets, to the rescue.

Colette also asked Rachilde for advice, as she valued her criticism. "I feel flattered, when you tell me 'I like that and that but I don't care for that.'" Rachilde thought that "a naughty little boy" should have been added to balance the story. Colette toyed with the idea and agreed that a boy was very tempting — "Willy was all for it." The book "would have been more logical," she conceded, but she felt the story "would have contained too many horrors." Afraid she might have hurt Rachilde, she pleaded, "you will keep loving your Claudine, won't you?"[25]

Rachilde never liked Colette wholeheartedly, finding her cruel, abrasive, and too exhibitionist. Rachilde herself was extremely discreet; she enjoyed the circle of friends, artists, and intellectuals who attended her literary Tuesdays, but closeted her private life. Through *Le Mercure* she wielded an enormous power. Colette courted her friendship: "Rachilde, for heaven's sake don't die now. Now that I have been lucky enough to please you, give me time to love you more intimately and see you often next season, wait at least until I have no appeal left for you." Colette gave Rachilde some advice on how to react against critics, "My dear Rachilde, I am so touched you thought of me. Why were you so down? Is it because of some nasty people? If so hit them hard. It is my remedy, but maybe, it is not a panacea, what a pity!"[26]

Colette herself was swaying between an urge to fight and moments of depression. The book was not yet off the printing press and already some critics were clamoring for its censure. Willy could be brought before a court of justice, and Colette was aware of the threat. At a party given by *Le Mercure de France,* a journalist who had read the manuscript asked her what she thought of certain "risqué" scenes. She answered with admirable poise that she was a slow reader, adding, "I have not reached that page yet."[27]

The manuscript was heavily revised; there are 176 corrections, replacements of words, additions, and suppressions; fifty sentences have been rewritten.

Claudine Married was released on May 15, 1902. Jean Lorrain defined it as the *Liaisons dangereuses* of the twentieth century. Of the three novels, *Claudine Married* is the most audacious study of various facets of physical attraction. In spite of or because of the scandal surrounding it, the novel reached its hundredth edition.

In *Le Mercure de France,* Rachilde wrote that *Claudine Married* was a revolutionary work, in no way revolting to those who loved naked truth: "It is an honest work, so beautiful, so delectably written that it brings tears of joy to the eyes of lovers of natural art. Of the three *Claudines*, this one is certainly the most daring and the most well written and it places Willy in the forefront of French writers."[28]

Marcel Boulenger asked readers, who were buying the book as fast as it came off the press:

Do you like Boissier candies? Do you relish cream chocolate? Crave sherbet, meringue and mousse? Would you enjoy a whole dinner of sweet dishes and sweet wine? Then read *Claudine Married* . . . The book starts with caresses, followed by caresses, winds up with caresses, and hopes for more caresses . . . I must say you have to be sophisticated, or elegantly permissive. The love of two scatterbrained young women does not strike me as the ultimate chic, and the voyeur, that third woman Renaud, the feminine husband, is not more guilty than we are since we read *Claudine*. The characters are as depraved as we are.

As for the book, it brims with talent, it is a succession of enchanting scenes, a harmony around one motive. It is extremely pretty and certain sequences, like the seduction of Claudine, are written with an art that reaches perfection.

It is impossible to forget certain lines. The writing is light, skilled and what can surprise all of us today, the syntax is impeccable.[29]

Critics agreed: amoral, yes, but what talent and what perfection in the art of writing! One critic, charmed by the rhythm of the prose, said that the *Claudine*s were classics. It was the ultimate compliment. The *Claudine*s were written by a born writer, just as Mozart's first works were composed by a born musician. The circumstances and choice of subject matter had no real impact on the deep appeal of the books. It was not their eroticism that fascinated the critics, who maintained that the novels were amoral, but the extraordinary quality of their style. The day would come when Paul Valéry would write about Colette, "She is the only woman who knows that to write is an art."

Reactions against *Claudine Married* were violent. Not everyone separated art from morals and tolerated freedom of expression. Although the Republic had eliminated religion from its schools, the government was still the guardian of civic virtues, and the emancipation of women was frowned upon as a danger to the family structure. The *Claudine*s, with their brazen daring, proclaimed the sexual complexity of women and their right to happiness. Senator René Berenger, a self-appointed watchdog and staunch champion of public morality nicknamed "Father Modesty," denounced the book and tried to have a formal complaint filed against it without success.

Polaire

The Gauthier-Villars were spending more than they earned. They thought that the stage could make them rich, so nothing was spared to make *Claudine* a hit. Willy asked Lugné-Poë and Charles Vayre to cowrite with him a musical comedy with a prologue. The production was controlled entirely by Willy and Colette.

As soon as word spread that the candid and lovable character was to appear on the stage of the Théâtre des Mathurins, actresses hounded Willy and Colette to play the part. They laid siege to their table in restaurants, rang their doorbell, and forced their way into the apartment. But even sharing Colette's or Willy's bed was not a path to the coveted part. It was the music-hall idol Polaire who would get the part, which she frantically wanted, since she had read the *Claudine*s and experienced a shock of recognition.

Her name was Emilie Zouze-Bouchaud. Born into a family of eight children in Algeria, she was illiterate when she came to Paris at fourteen to join her brother, the comedian Dufleuve. He bought her a song, coached her, and introduced her to the director of L'Européen, who hired her immediately and told her to come back with a name. She walked home in the night, watching the stars. Why not pick the name of a star? Why not "Polaire," the north star? In 1895 Toulouse-Lautrec made a lithograph of her for her posters. She had an intense personality; high-strung to the point of being unable to stand still, she sang with such emotion that the audience, mostly working men and women at the rowdy L'Européen, cheered her wildly. She had the same pathetic quality that would later rivet Edith Piaf's fans. She became a trendsetter. In a time when every woman took pride in the length of her hair, she cut hers short. She had sparkling teeth, a thin, pointed chin, and dark, melancholy eyes, but her most striking feature was her incredibly small waist, the size of a man's shirt collar.

Willy was the first critic to notice her; he wrote that her waist could make a bee jealous. Jean Lorrain raved about her eyes, which he described as those of a *fellahine*. Marchand, director of the Folies Bergère, offered her one hundred fifty francs a day; she had a three-year contract with the Ambassadeurs which she did not want to cancel, so she sang there for ten francs, then took a cab followed by an escort of cars and carriages to the

TOP: Henry Landoy, grandfather of Colette. Courtesy of Harlingue-Violet.

MIDDLE: Adèle Sidonie Landoy (Sido) at 28. Courtesy of Drouts Réservés.

BOTTOM: Eugène Landoy journalist, writer, editor. Courtesy of D.R.

The house where Colette was born. Courtesy of D.R.

The Family: [first row, left to right] Juliette Robineau-Duclos (Colette's sister),
a friend, Sido, the Captain, Gabri at eight years, Marthe Landoy, two friends.
[second row, left to right] Léo Colette, Jules Landoy, a friend, Raphaël Landoy,
s friend, Achille Robineau-Duclos (Colette's brother), a friend. Courtesy of D.R.

Henry Gauthier–Villars (Willy). Courtesy of D.R.

Willy, Colette, Sido, and Captain Colette in 1893. Courtesy of D.R.

Colette and Willy's Family in 1893. Courtesy of D.R.

Colette and Willy in 1894, rue Jacob. Courtesy of D.R.

TOP: Colette, Willy, and Toby-Chien during the days of *Claudine*. Courtesy of D.R.

MIDDLE: Mrs. Colette Willy. Courtesy of D.R.

BOTTOM: Willy and Colette. Courtesy of D.R.

BELOW: The Celebrated couple of the Belle-Epoque. Courtesy of D.R.

RIGHT: Marcel Boulestin, the Willy's, and their coach. Courtesy of D.R.

ABOVE: Colette at thirty.
Courtesy of D.R.

RIGHT: Colette in her gymnasium-studio-loft at Rue de Courcelles.
Courtesy of D.R.

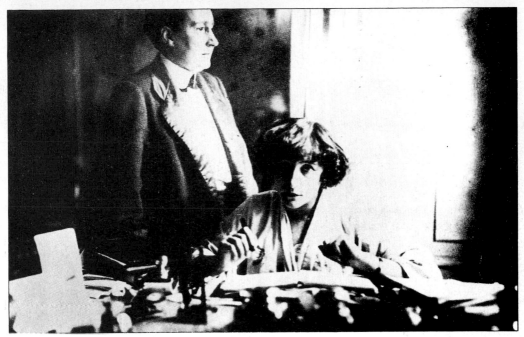

Colette and the Marquise de Morny. Courtesy of D.R.

Colette and Missy in *Rêve d'Egypte* (A Dream of Egypt). Courtesy of D.R.

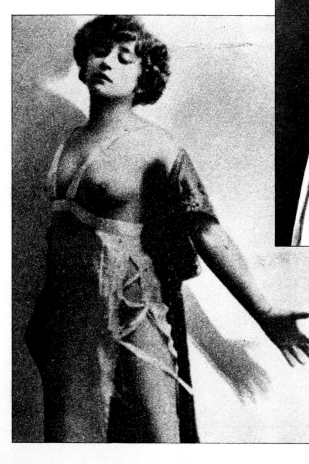

Mademoiselle
COLETTE
de "Bataclan"

ABOVE: Colette at the Ba-Ta-Clan.
Courtesy of D.R.

RIGHT: *La Char* (The Flesh), 1907.
Courtesy of D.R.

Folies Bergère, where the wealthy courtesan, Emilienne d'Alençon, who had a music-hall sketch with tame white rabbits dyed pink, became infatuated with her. She was the first woman to own a racing stable. Emilienne, like most courtesans, was an "amphibian" (the turn of the century term for bisexuals); she sent Polaire a full-sized horse made of rare flowers. The heir to a sugar empire, Max Labaudy, gave Polaire an enormous crescent of diamonds and a whole batch of pearls. One of her lovers commissioned Lalique to make a belt for her tiny waist.

As soon as Polaire appeared, the audience showered her with violets, while a procession of delivery boys brought gifts to her dressing room. In 1902 she was the toast of the town. The banker Jules Porgès was her main protector and kept her awash in money. She kept beautiful young boys and owned a mansion near the Place de l'Etoile, where her portraits by fashionable painters hung on the walls between mirrors and sumptuously draped windows.

Polaire's agent Pierre Mortier tried to secure the part of Claudine for her. But Lugné-Poë, the director, wanted Eve Lavallière. Willy did not want Polaire either; he preferred the established and popular actress Hélène Réyé. He told Mortier that Polaire's mannerisms prevented her from performing in *Claudine* and that the only thing she could do was show off her legs and waist. Informed of Willy's comments, hot-tempered Polaire flew into a rage, jumped into her victoria lined with blue satin harnessed to her famous team of white horses, and ordered her coachman to gallop to the Rue de Courcelles. Arriving unannounced at the Willys', she marched into their salon, saying "I am Claudine!" Colette was there, dressed in a tailored suit, with her pointed chin and her eyes that could drill your very soul. Polaire was so forceful, so convincing, so inspired when she said "I am Claudine!" that she became Claudine on the spot. She rehearsed with Colette, who had a whole gymnasium in the rooms above the apartment, where she worked steadily. A photograph shows Colette holding the trapeze on which Polaire is sitting, very much at ease. Colette hoped the play would be a popular success; "I need the money," she kept repeating. Polaire did not understand her concern and told her, "We are making art," to which Colette drily replied, "I am only trying to please my creditors."[30]

Colette wrote to Lucien Muhlfeld, "I beg you, Muhlfeld, to review the play — it has nothing to do with art or literature. It is stupid, please say so. But please add that it will make a lot of money. It has to make a lot of money, because I need money."[31] Colette had no illusions about the play's artistic value. She knew art had nothing to do with financial success, but that brazen publicity would attract a large public.

The play opened on January 22 at the Bouffes Parisiens. Polaire stepped onto the stage looking like a fifteen-year-old schoolgirl, a small bow in her short curly hair, wearing a black smock barely reaching her calves, a round white collar with a soft checkered bow tie, socks, and button boots. The audience, accustomed to long gowns, flounces, garlands, bows, plumes, and mountainous hairdos, started to boo. Willy stood up in his box and shouted, "Proceed, Polaire, pay no attention to these idiots."[32] The evening turned into a success, and 123 performances followed. When a previously signed contract forced Lugné-Poë to end the show, the theater was still sold out. Every evening Willy went to the theater and checked the money at the box office; he also read the stacks of letters in Polaire's dressing room, which the star did not bother to open.

Claudine had created a new kind of sex symbol; bordellos added a "Claudine" to their personnel, a girl dressed in a black smock with socks, button boots, a round white collar, checkered tie, and short hair with a bow — a replica of Polaire on the stage. In her memoirs Polaire recalled that Willy, who "went to brothels to observe characters for his novels,"[33] had seen an oversize picture of Polaire dressed as Claudine on the wall. Music halls, cabarets, and café-concerts had to have sketches about Claudine: "Claudine on a Rampage," "Claudine and the Apache," "Claudine at Two Schools," "Claudine has Fun," "Claudine Arrested," and so on. Teenagers dressed like Claudine.

Colette had mixed feelings about *Claudine in Paris* on stage. The character called Maugis made her uneasy — he was a carbon copy of Willy, complete with the famous tophat and balding forehead. During the second act, which took place in a brasserie called "The Convalescent Mouse" (after the famous Dead Rat, a meeting place for homosexuals of both sexes), Maugis was on stage uttering some disillusioned aphorisms on love, life, and literature. True to life, too, was the scene in which Claudine, tipsy after two glasses of Asti, declared to Renaud that she wanted to be his mistress. It was a replay of the actual scene in the cab when Colette, also after two glasses of Asti, told Willy she loved him and wanted to be his mistress.

The play was a personal success for Polaire and eclipsed the novel; this was not to the Willys' liking. Polaire was drawing all the attention and they decided to reclaim *Claudine* and the profit that went with the ever growing popularity of their brainchild. Since Polaire had become the perfect image of Claudine, Colette had to become the perfect image of Polaire and reclaim Claudine for herself. First, Colette cut her long hair and curled it exactly like Polaire's. Colette welcomed her new look and never expressed a regret at having cut her long braids. "All I felt was the joy of tossing a head freed from its mane, to sleep untangled."

Willy had thousands of postcards printed as publicity flyers, which were distributed in bookstores, theater lobbies, and fashionable stores; Colette used them as stationery. The concept was new in France but not in England, where, at the turn of the century, it was fashionable to keep a velvet-bound album on the parlor table containing photographs used as calling cards by theater celebrities, popular hostesses, and even royalty. Photography was very much the craze, and aristocrats like Lady Dudley, Lady Randolph Churchill, Lady Helen Vincent, Mrs. Cornwallis-West, and other young socialites known as "the Professional Beauties" allowed their photographs to be sold in stationery shops. The Anglophile Henry Gauthier-Villars picked up on the idea, and had photographs of himself and Colette spread around. (He also had his stationery printed with his picture.) The postcards represented Colette in Claudine's black smock, looking like Polaire, Colette with her bulldog, or with Willy in carefully staged scenes stressing the image of the old man and the young girl; the captions read "Claudine and Toby-Chien" or "Colette and Toby-Chien," "Willy and Colette," or "Colette Willy." Polaire had similar postcards made; the confusion was complete. The image of Claudine Colette-Polaire became one in the public eye. The author and actress looked like twins and incarnated two sides of a creation that had come into being thanks to Willy, who always referred to himself as *le père des Claudines* (Claudines' father). He had three suits made for his "twins": a blue-gray tailored suit with off-white stripes, a lovely white muslin dress with lace, complete with a large lace bonnet, and another tailored suit, checkered in green, brown, and black — all very smashing. Willy and his "twins" were seen everywhere, at the restaurant, at the races, at the opera.

The "twins" were the subject of endless gossip; the latest was that the famous couple Willy and Colette had added "a hyphen" to their name. Polaire resented this. "I was not even Willy's mistress,"[34] she wrote in her memoirs. Polaire had fallen for Colette instead.

During that time the drama that would serve as the catalyst of Colette's *Claudine and Annie,* and Willy's *Le Retour d'âge* was unfolding. During a trip to Bayreuth, Colette had found Willy in bed with Liette de Serres (Marthe Payet in *Claudine and Annie*), the wife of their friend, the composer Louis de Serres. She felt betrayed by both of them and could not bear the fact that Willy had a hidden life, one he did not share with her. Colette immediately boarded a train for Paris. She pried open her husband's desk and found out in "an indecent correpondance" that Willy had also been for many years the lover of Madame Chausson, the wife of another of their musician friends. Colette left the correspondence on the floor and moved out of their apartment to L'Impériale Résidence, Rue Marguerite. In *My Apprenticeships* Colette clearly states that her relationship with Willy started to deteriorate in 1902, "The year Polaire was on the stage playing Claudine." However, they made up and Willy described L'Impériale Résidence as a blissful place. At forty-four Henry Gauthier-Villars was afraid to lose his little Camaro; he became obsessive and jealous. Colette was surprised by his reaction, "your belated, awkward and retrospective jealousy. It came to you without knowing why or how, just like love itself."[35]

As for Colette she had always had violent fits of jealousy which surprised her friends. Jacques-Emile Blanche remembered that when he was painting her portrait, she kept jumping up at the sound of an approaching cab and ran to a window. Willy was coming to fetch her, and when she saw that he was riding in the carriage of the countess of Guimont-Fautru, she fainted. The maid had to wrap her in a blanket and bring her some smelling salts. As soon as she regained consciousness, Colette's first words were "Was he kissing the Countess?"

The Willys left their third-floor apartment to move down the street to 177*bis* Rue de Courcelles. They rented the second floor of a mansion; the previous tenant had been the minister of labor. On the first floor lived Prince Alexandre Bibesco, a bibliophile married to the actress Hélène Réyé, who had triumphed in the parts of Gavroche and Claudinet.

The apartment was spacious and sunny with deep sofas, very modern and elegant. Everywhere were portraits, pictures, and statues of Colette, Willy, and Polaire as Claudine. Modern paintings hung on the walls, including a large portrait of Colette and Willy by Pascau, representing an elegant, refined, older Willy towering over a very young and tired-looking Colette. Neither of them were fond of it. Books and journals were scattered all over the thick carpet. In Willy's office there were more photographs, statues, and paintings, and a bust of his father on the mantlepiece. The bathroom had a mammoth tub and a water tank the size of a bastion. The bedroom was white with an enameled white bed covered in white satin, a large wardrobe, a vanity, and several white arm-chairs. The Willys had the latest luxury, a telephone: 556-86.

The third floor, which Colette called "my garçonnière," was her private place. There was a bedroom and a studio, in which she installed a complete gymnasium, as she had at Monts-Boucons. Colette had a sports trainer who coached her in acrobatics. She took riding lessons with an officer from the Cadre Noir de Saumur and rode in the Bois de Boulogne. She was a trendsetter; to walk her three bulldogs in the Bois de Boulogne she wore button boots, and exercised regularly when women barely risked a few steps in their thin slippers with high heels before getting back into their carriage. She wore tailored suits and small hats. Ten years later, when Coco Channel was changing women's looks, Colette described in *L'Entrave* the stares and comments she provoked as she entered a restaurant dressed in a strict suit — tailored suits still connoted a *déclassée* woman, an artist, a lesbian.

Colette's gymnasium-studio-loft had a private entrance and here she received her own friends, many connected with the theater, like Robert d'Humières and Hélène Réyé. Polaire came here to rehearse. Colette was pursuing her goal to become an actress, to be famous in her own right.

Colette never wrote in her den, she had a small desk with a lamp under a green shade to protect her eyes in a corner of the living room. Throughout her life she recreated the tiny corner she had so loved in her father's library; all she wanted was a lamp and a desk placed far from the windows, sometimes in her living room, sometimes in her bedroom. More than the comfort of an office, Colette needed a reassuring presence next to her; at first it had been her father working on his articles while she read, daydreamed, and held imaginary dialogues with Marie, her other self. Colette's need for a reassuring figure is captured in photographs of her as a writer. The setting is always the same: Colette is seated at a desk with a manuscript in front of her, and behind her, as time brought them into her life, are Henry Gauthier-Villars, the marquise de Morny, Henry de Jouvenel, and Maurice Goudeket.

If Colette-the-writer needed a protective cocoon, Colette-the-woman, at the age of twenty-nine, wanted the same freedom as a man. Her role model was none other than Willy himself. Georgie's betrayal had provoked a crisis, subconsciously a welcome one, enabling Colette to assert herself. The immediate aftermath was complex; she had to satisfy the duality of her own nature; she became more conscious of her "virility" and described Willy as feminine, even physically, his voice delicate and mellow. Colette had a pang of passion for a young actress, Renée Parry, with whom she liked to wrestle; Willy found them on the floor one day exchanging punches. Renée was a member of Sarah Bernhardt's troupe and her particular protégée; in 1901 Sarah cast her as *La Dame aux Camélias*. Colette maintained that a little roughing up made for a better relationship. Willy understood Colette's androgyny and stood by her. They went to dance halls together, both cloaked in black and looking more like father and son than husband and wife. For Mardi Gras at the notorious Bal Wagram, they appeared dressed alike, without masks, escorting a young girl with blue eyes and curly hair.

In 1904 a journalist wrote, "How disconcerting and strange this woman with the body of a slim urchin, who dresses indifferently as a woman or a boy and looks in either attire an androgyne, a creature of undetermined sex."[36] Because of Colette's short hair and indifference to their advances, men declared she was interested in women only; however, her ambiguous charm attracted the attention of men and women alike and she called it "a deadly weapon."[37]

In April, still troubled and upset by the events in her marriage, Colette went to Châtillon for four days, taking along her stepson Jacques. To cheer them up, Achille took them on a ride in his De Dion-Bouton. (Colette took her responsibilities as Jacques's *petite maman* seriously; when he left to go back to his English public school, she always went to see him off. She visited him several times in England, always escorted by strikingly beautiful women.) Early in June Colette and Willy were back in Châtillon. She was unhappy, and Willy hoped that four days there would cure her of her melancholy and put some distance between her and Georgie Raoul-Duval.

Then they left for Marseilles with the cast of *Claudine in Paris*. The play's success was as great there as in Paris. Willy paraded his "twins," dressed in identical tailored suits with white collars and wearing identical boaters. People in the street often mistook Colette for Polaire and called out to her, "Hey, Claudine!" Colette could have taken over Polaire's part without the public, who had been deluged with postcards, being able to tell the difference.

Jean Lorrain met them in Marseilles. He was now living on the Riviera, covering the social scene for several southern and foreign newspapers, and had reached the last stages of addiction. Colette was happy to see him and Jean did everything he could to amuse her. They visited the "Inferno" of Marseilles, the picturesque bars and cafés along the shore and the red-light district behind the municipal theater. Polaire, who berated drug users and decadent millionaires in her songs, was not interested in the seamy side of life; her tragic childhood had given her an outlook that did not match that of her blasé companions. She preferred the luxury of boat rides and plush hotels and refused to join them when Lorrain and Colette went to a bordello. The girls paraded in front of them and Colette "called them back several times" to check out their uniforms, the required stiff muslin gowns over nude bodies, black stockings, and elaborate hairdos. She was fascinated by a haggard girl with "a mane like a cloud" who did not speak French. The madame declared this girl unworthy of her guests' attention, as "she is one we took for the colored sailors." They left after ordering drinks for everyone and went to dine at Basso, an elegant restaurant overlooking the Mediterranean. Colette tried to forget the haggard girl, but Lorrain, amused by Colette's fascination, improvised several biographies of her "and disgusted me completely."[38]

Lorrain introduced Colette to a transvestite florist, Baptistine, a pimp who was making a fortune while the play was in Marseilles. He once came on behalf of a "rich man, who would be very generous and was even prepared to offer Monsieur Willy an expensive tiepin"[39] if he would arrange a gallant encounter with Polaire. The immorality of the whole situation delighted the entire group, always in search of racy material and situations.

Paris-Lesbos

Colette and Willy left for Monts-Boucons. Willy bought a farm and twenty acres of vineyards and fields adjacent to their property on August 27, 1902, hoping that the management of the estate would occupy

Colette and make her happy. Colette spent the summer at Monts-Boucons; she worked on a fitness program in the open-air gymnasium, rode her horse, and drove her new present from Willy, a light carriage with a harness of fine English leather and drawchains of pure silver. She worked in her garden and picked fruit to make jams, remembering her childhood in Saint-Sauveur, those opulent days when she felt "like a queen," "a free spirit." She was never happier than when at Monts-Boucons. Friends came to visit, and Willy was put on a strict regimen of healthy foods and long walks. They spent hours creating projects, correcting proofs, reading to each other, and writing their correspondence. In September Colette remained at Monts-Boucons while Willy accompanied Polaire to Berlin for several performances of *Claudine in Paris;* he was now managing her acting career.

By fall the trio was inseparable. They could be seen at Le Palais de Glace, the skating rink on the Champs-Elysées, after five o'clock, that magical hour when dutiful bourgeois sons and daughters went home and the courtesans made their entry. It was the hour of the *cocottes,* the *demicastors,* the *grandes horizontales,* the cream of the ladies of the night. Liane de Pougy glided by on sterling silver skates, her hands in a silver fox muff. Instructors in green uniforms with golden frogs and loops guided beginners across the ice. The adolescent Jean Cocteau spotted "at one table, Willy, Colette, and her bulldog; Willy with his large moustache, bright eyes under heavy lids, a wide necktie, a tophat . . . with hands as white as a bishop's resting on his cane. Next to him Colette . . . a slim, very slim Colette, a sort of little fox dressed in a cyclist's garb, a lock of dark hair tied back on the temple with a red ribbon." Then Polaire appeared and stole the show: "she dominates fashion, she exasperates women, she excites men,"[40] said Cocteau, who made a sketch of Willy, Polaire, Colette, and Toby-Chien. Sem made caricatures of the trio for several newspapers. The penny press implied that Willy mistook one for the other and snickered about the trio. Rachilde, a staunch ally, nevertheless expressed some criticism of "those two young and very pretty women who are alike in their love for the stage and their maniacal exhibitionism."[41] The reason behind the unrelenting publicity was to set a framework in place for putting Colette on the stage.

When Willy came back from Berlin he found that Natalie Barney, whom François Mauriac called "the Pope of Lesbos," was attracted by Colette and willing to help her with her stage career. Willy encouraged the relationship, for he felt that Colette needed strong, protective companionship; he also hoped that Natalie would cure her of her love for Georgie.

Three years younger than Colette, Natalie was the heiress of a fortune described as "fabulous" by the Goulds. Her friends called her "Moonbeam" because of her silver-blond hair. She was slim and athletic, played tennis, swam, and was an accomplished equestrian. She told Colette that she used to run barefoot in the dew and swim at Bar Harbor, where only the Vanderbilts and Pulitzers had private swimming pools.

At fifteen, Natalie had fallen in love with Eva Palmer, heiress to the Huntley and Palmer biscuits fortune. Fascinated by Greek sculpture, they cavorted in the woods of the Barney estate at Bar Harbor, taking pictures of each other as naked nymphs. They conceived their love affair as an expression of art. Traveling in Belgium with Natalie's mother and sister, they saw a milk cart pulled by a woman and a dog while the man walked alongside, contentedly smoking his pipe: "that is when we became feminists."[42] They understood feminism as the freedom to live as a man of the world. Nowhere was it easier than in Paris, where Mrs. Clifford was working with Whistler, who had accepted her as one of his very few students.

One evening at the notorious Bal Bullier, where the wealthy and wicked met with hustlers and prostitutes, and young working men and women went to dance and watch the cancan, Natalie spotted Liane de Pougy walking in with three men and vowed to conquer the courtesan. She had a costume made by Landolff, an almond-green page's outfit embroidered with a white lily over the heart. Every day she sent a bouquet and a poem to Liane. One morning in the Bois de Boulogne she noticed one of the irises she had sent the day before in Liane's belt; it was the signal she awaited. She put on her almond-green page's outfit and, with a bouquet of irises in hand, rang at Liane's door. But she found, reclining on a couch, not Liane but Valtesse de Bigne — a courtesan who had known her days of glory during the reign of Napoleon III and was now Liane's business advisor. She deemed Natalie worthy of Madame de Pougy, who wrote an autobiographical novel, *L'Idylle Saphique,* as their love story was unfolding. When *L'Idylle Saphique* was published in 1901, *Le Gil Blas* noted that "in such a time of progress towards feminism, even her critics will not deny that she is a born writer with a delicate sensibility."[43]

Natalie Barney lived with total but prudent freedom. In what some called "Paris-Lesbos" and others "Paris-Mytilène," it was understood that love was free and that all that was required was either extreme discretion or such daring that it gained the admiration of those who wanted to be above social taboos at any cost. In the self-protective, self-centered high society whose public image and private mores rarely coincided, very few broke the law of silence.

In the fall of 1902 Natalie was invited to Rue de Courcelles. She noted in her diary that Colette was training herself with method and discipline, "maybe with the music hall in mind." She also noted, "the Willys have no private life."[44] She described Willy as a master in public relations and promotion and Colette as a young woman with strong legs and a round derrière, her manners as direct as her language, but — when silent — as enigmatic as a cat, with her triangular face, her beautiful gray-green eyes, and a gaze that had the power to seduce or subdue.

That fall Colette was still in love with Georgie. Georgie was angry with Colette, but did not hold Willy responsible for the publication of *Claudine Married*. Colette was the writer; it was she who had chosen to tell their story, not Willy. Natalie was apprised of the situation by Willy, who asked for her help. On November 10, he had received a long, feverish letter from Georgie without a single mention of Colette; he construed this omission as an obsession and concluded that Georgie was still dangerously in love with Colette. He told Natalie that the opening night he was to have attended with Colette was postponed, so Colette was free, and urged her to invite Colette to her apartment in Rue Lapérouse. Willy explained that Colette did not have to save her energy for the evening and so could dine with Natalie.

Willy was carefully monitoring Colette's recovery from her passion for Georgie. In a letter to Natalie later that year, he reflected on the remembrance of past loves, noting that half-dead memories have a stubborn way of popping back up. He told her of Colette coming back from Natalie's home still feverish and thrilled. She had talked about her friend tenderly, very gratefully, but while speaking of their afternoon together, her tongue had slipped and twice she had said "Georgie" instead of "Natalie." Teasing Natalie in a satanic way, Willy added that he, too, was unable to forget Georgie — her slow diction, her eyes, her soft undulating movements — but did not tell of his lasting entanglement with her.

Colette's affair with Natalie was not without its problems. In one letter to her Colette referred to a bungled experience, said she would come to dinner, and asked Natalie to give her another chance, since the previous day she had not been up to her usual self. Natalie classified Colette as "a half-love." She resented Willy's interference and was puzzled by the intimate friendship that bonded the couple together. She found Colette too devoted to Willy but saw that she had an instinct that kept her free from domination.

Her influence on Colette was deep and far-reaching; she brought her a new outlook on life, an assertiveness unknown to French women. Her indomitable personality impressed so many writers that she pervades the literature of the first half of the century. She is Flossie in Colette's *Claudine and Annie*, Evangeline in Djuna Barnes' *The Ladies' Almanac*, Laurette in Lucie Delarue-Mardrus' *The Angel and the Perverse*, Valerie Seymour in Radclyffe Hall's *The Well of Loneliness*, Miss Retchmore in Fitzgerald's *Tender Is the Night*, the Amazone in Rémy de Gourmont's *Letters to the Amazone*, and "The Woman" in Renée Vivien's *Une Femme m'apparut.*

With Georgie and Natalie, Colette entered the international literary world of lesbian writers centered around Natalie Barney, whose *Portraits — Sonnets of Women*, illustrated by her mother, Alice Pike-Barney, had just been published by Ollendorff.

Feminine literary circles were determined to discover their identity and a literary voice of their own. Repressed by laws dating back to the *code Napoléon*, women found in androgyny a way to assert their independence. Since business was off-limits, and fashion creators like Landolff, Coco Chanel, and Germaine Patat who broke into the stronghold of haute couture were noted exceptions, Paris-Lesbos challenged the status quo on sexual and literary grounds. It was an intricate, closed society, most of whose denizens were heiresses — Princesse de Polignac, Baroness de Nyevelt, Marquise de Morny, Baroness Deslandes — and controlled enormous wealth. They found in sexual braggadocio a means to proclaim their equality with man, to challenge him on his hunting grounds: the demimonde, Montmartre, the bordellos, or the *fortifs*. Having affairs with the great courtesans seems to have been the ultimate statement of equality.

Women also turned to arts and letters to redefine themselves: "The Amazons are retaliating, they appear from all sides: from high society, from the demimonde, from the New World."[45] The cutting-edge literary figure of Paris-Mytilene was the now forgotten Franco-German baroness Deslandes, whom Colette called "Ilse," the title of one of her novels. She wrote in long, circumlocutory sentences covering full pages. A member of Jean Lorrain's *Petite Classe*, Baroness Deslandes was a muse of art nouveau. Her tiny feet and hands delighted Burne-Jones; his portrait of her reflects the strange, dusky pre-Raphaelite atmosphere in which she lived. De Graux painted her as Edgar Poe's Ligeia; Barrès, Bataille, Forain, and Wilde all wooed her. She had red hair and was extremely pale, even sallow, from insomnia and soporifics. Her boudoir was lined on all sides with white bearskins long before Mae West's. She abhorred anything trivial. For her private needs she used an alabaster vase, which her butler filled with orchids. She had been married and had a son; looking at him, she would say, "I can't deny that my husband raped me." She felt a brief flash of passion for a lion tamer she saw at the Neuilly fair, and Boni de Castellane made it the main attraction of a charity bazaar he had organized: *"une femme du monde dans la cage aux lions"* (a lady in the lion's den). Never shy when it came to grand gestures, Baroness Deslandes, dressed as a druid priestess, entered her lover's lion cage, and surrounded by lions, recited a poem written for the occasion by Jean Richepin. Bisexual, she cross-dressed whenever she made love to her own sex. She was surrounded by the most gifted *femmes de lettres,* whom she promoted.

Colette also met the violent, provocative marquise Casati, a Swiss-Italian aristocrat and friend of d'Annunzios. She lived at Le Vésinet in a palace bought from Robert de Montesquiou; she had all the furniture removed and ambled from room to room dressed in the strangest costumes, wearing a lion's muzzle as a headdress. She made up her face with black powder. A leopard, a dove, and a boa she fed two sheep a month shared her empty lodgings. Intimate friends were treated to visits to a built-in armoire containing the wax likeness of the seventeen-year-old baroness Veczéra, who died mysteriously a few days after becoming Archduke Ruldoph's mistress. Marquise Casati spent her entire inheritance of forty farms and ten mansions in *fêtes,* in a metaphoric quest for ideal purity and art.

In 1901 Colette Willy published *Claudine in Paris,* Renée Vivien *Etudes et Préludes,* Lucie Delarue-Mardrus *Occident,* and Anna de Noailles *Le Coeur Innombrable.* "Women used to have a salon, now they have a publisher. The most striking fact is that they have talent" wrote the historian Casella. "'Modernity' is breaking through tradition, the new century is heralded by women. Nietzsche predicted it, Madame Rachilde set the example ten years ago."[46] According to Stendhal, women seldom wrote well because they did not dare to be sincere. The turn of the century saw a change in women's attitude. "An explosion of sincerity is taking place,"[47] noted the critic. Who better than Liane de Pougy could describe love-making? Who better than Renée Vivien could describe the feelings of women in love with women? Women's writings, said Colette's neighbor Rémy de Gourmont — not too kindly — were their polite way of making love in public. Léo Taxil blasted the tribade, who "in search of her kindred has a distinctive sign, the magnificent, curled, bedecked and pret-tified and sometimes even beribboned poodle, which accompanies her in her outings . . ."[48] Lesbos or Gomorrah, pagan freedom or biblical sin, Sapphic love was part of the texture of *La Belle Epoque*.

The return to Mytilene was spearheaded by British-born Pauline Tarn. Raised in France, Tarn first wrote under the masculine pseudonym René Vivien, then feminized her name to Renée. Very thin, tall, and graceful, Renée reminded one of a weeping willow. Her shoulders never retained shawls, which slipped off them constantly; she lost her gloves, dropped her umbrella, and had the bashful charm of a teenager. With her ash-blond hair, soft brown eyes, dimpled cheeks, small mouth with a short upper lip, and tiny nose, Vivien was Barney's *grand amour*. She wrote childish and sweet letters to Colette, but she was a sad, desperate poet, obsessed with a death wish.

Vivien lived on two different levels: true love was poetry, but the senses were the domain of sadomasochism. She was quite wealthy and kept the sweet-faced, gentle courtesan, Emilienne d'Alençon. Vivien, the slender muse who loved violets, would ride in Emilienne d'Alençon's electric au-tomobile to the Moulin Rouge ball, dressed as the revolutionary Camille Desmoulins. Liane de Pougy liked to go to whorehouses and often took Renée and Natalie to humbler prostitutes. Between Liane, Emilienne, Natalie, and Renée, debauchery took on the form of orgies.

Renée Vivien left Natalie and turned to another woman: the baroness Zuylen de Nyevelt, born Hélène de Rothschild, one of the most famous cross-dressed patrons of Paris-Lesbos; she wrote novels and some poetry. Hélène Zuylen and Vivien coauthored four novels, signed "Paule Riversdale." But Natalie was not easily put off; she asked the fa-mous opera singer Emma Calvé, just back from a triumphal tour of *Carmen* in the United States, to help her. Dressed as buskers, they drove to Vivien's house, where Emma sang the magnificent lamentation of Orpheus in Gluck's opera, "I have lost my Eurydice . . ." Vivien opened a window and Natalie threw a poem and a bouquet over the railing. But

Vivien still refused to meet Natalie, who stalked her to Bayreuth. Eventually she persuaded her to go to Sappho's isle of Lesbos to found a literary community. The colony did not succeed, but Barney wrote *Cinq Petits Dialogues Grecs* in praise of Sappho. Renée Vivien wrote a new translation of Sappho's poems. Lucie Delarue-Mardrus wrote *Sappho in Despair.*

Scholars still refused to admit that the fragments of Sappho's passionate poetry were addressed to women. Hellenists asserted that Renée Vivien, that "misled creature," had no idea of what she was doing, and rejected what they called her "naive" interpretation. A long tradition of scholarly criticism had altered texts alluding to homosexuality; in the Middle Ages the monks had changed Alcibiades into a woman. Greek and Roman antiquity, so liberal when it came to heroes and gods and their male lovers, made no mention of feminine homosexuality; the only exception was Sappho. Lesbos, the island where she lived, became the symbol of feminine unisexual attraction.

Colette's *Claudine* told her contemporaries that there was nothing abnormal in their longings, nothing to hide. The paradox was that Colette was hiding behind one of her husband's pen names, while her new circle of friends — Lucie Delarue-Mardrus, Natalie Barney, and Anna de Noailles — refused to use pseudonyms like the older generation of women writers. Colette became aware of the contradictions of her own situation.

Between January and June Colette wrote reviews for *Gil Blas:* "Claudine au Concert," followed by "Claudine au Conservatoire" both signed "Claudine." The reviews, written from the mischievous Claudine's point of view, were very similar in style to her novels: "I plan to bring to these reviews my good faith and the bad education that has made me so many enemies. But my solid friendship with the *Usherette* will hopefully save me from glaring gaffs . . . I take notes, but I scribble so poorly I cannot read them, zut!" Colette created an odd, seemingly autobiographical dialogue with her readers; her fictional characters were taking over reality. The egomaniac Claudine set her own standards; of Fauré's music she said it "had no more morals than . . . myself . . . I adore Fauré, he looks a little like Renaud and, like that womanizer Renaud, he knows how to charm a woman."

Colette constantly referred to the Gauthier-Villars' other selves — the Usherette, Willy, Maugis, Renaud, and Claudine. Colette and Willy were enlarging their mirror game to such a point that even Sido wondered how much was autobiography and how much was fiction. Colette's promotion of her character was unrestrained; her review of a night at the opera on January 26 became an account of the Claudine craze that had overtaken Parisian life and fashion. In the audience she counted "143 Claudines," in black smock, short skirt showing naked calves, black socks, and the ruffled petticoat of a *cocotte*. "If you knew — Claudines fit for Mardi Gras — how little you resemble me and how your disguise as little girls waiting for old men is far from the woolen skirt, the pleated blouse, the hood, the wooden shoes of the real Claudine."[49] (The latter was not the portrait of Colette at Saint-Sauveur but a description of the cover illustration of *Claudine at School* by Emilio della Sudda, who had depicted Claudine looking like a perverted version of Little Red Riding Hood.) Reviews containing such constant interplay between fictional characters and the author of the article were unusual.

On January 2 Colette was in Brussels at the Théâtre Royal de la Monnaie for the premiere of Vincent d'Indy's *L'Etranger,* an opera based on Ibsen's play, which had not found a sponsor in Paris. Colette liked d'Indy's lyricism and she joined a group of admirers who went to Brussels for the occasion: "the reporter of *L'Eventail* mistook me for Polaire because of my short hair."[50] The next concert Colette reviewed was quite different; the aristocracy of the Faubourg Saint-Germain applauded a *Passion,* by Prince Edmond de Polignac. Colette noted the presence of "princesses, countesses, marchionesses and duchesses too, yes five or six." In June she reviewed a concert of works written by Armande de Polignac. "a serious *quattuor,* variations for a cello, choir music, and ravishing melodies with lyrics by Henry Gauthier-Villars."[51] Using a literary device that became her stylistic hallmark, Colette removed herself from her friends and milieu, looking at them from a distance and leading the reader to believe she was not actually one of the elite, but one of the readership itself.

But the "Claudine" style of criticism did not sit well with readers; *Le Gil Blas* did not renew her contract after July. For the second time Colette had failed in her attempt to become a music critic like her husband. In 1933 she would write in *La République* that she had wanted to become a journalist since her early twenties, and that "this temptation" had never died.

If she was disappointed, there is no trace of it, for the Willys were dominating the literary scene. In January *La Maîtresse du Prince Jean,* the new novel signed "Willy," gave Senator Berenger his chance to bring Willy before a judge. The characters were easy to identify: the mistress was the courtesan Léonide Leblanc, the prince the deceased son of the exiled king, Louis-Philippe. As in the *Claudines*, the pervasive theme was that any form of love was acceptable and that the mores of the upper class were as dissolute as those of Claudine's village school. *La Maîtresse du Prince Jean* had already been published in installments in *La Vie en Rose* before being released by Albin Michel.

Senator Berenger, who had been lampooned by Willy for years, was determined to see him brought to justice for his novels past and present; since the censors had not acted, he asked The League Against Indecency on Public Streets to file suit. Willy was charged with a misdemeanor and accused of having written a pornographic novel. In the name of freedom of speech, the intelligentsia rallied to Willy's side; a renowned lawyer, Joseph Paul-Boncour, undertook his defense. The hearing was set for April 1, 1903. Not even Willy could have chosen a more propitious date. Many believed it was a publicity stunt. When asked to be his witness, the poet Viellé-Griffin answered by telegram, "Congratulations on your extraordinary April Fools' Day joke." Two weeks before the trial, the fourth *Claudine* — *Claudine and Annie* — released on March 17 by Ollendorff, compounded the outrage.

On April 1 the group from *Le Mercure* and journalists from *L'Echo de Paris* and *Gil Blas* came to testify in Willy's favor and defend writers' and artists' freedom of speech. The historians Casimir Stryienski and Funck-Brentano praised his historical books; Huysmans declared that he wrote interesting documents on contemporary mores; Jules Renard, well aware that the *Claudines* were the real target, sent a glowing appraisal of their artistic value; Catulle Mendès spoke of Willy's generosity — as "the Usherette" he had helped scores of poets and young musicians. Willy was fined one thousand francs, the newspaper *La Vie en Rose* three hundred; Albin Michel was to delete certain names.

Willy, in a defiant mood, had an outrageous cover made for the next edition of *La Maîtress du Prince Jean;* it showed Willy at his desk with an arm around Colette's waist. On the first page there was a photograph of Polaire dressed as Claudine with the words, "Vive la Vie en Rose" and signed "Claudine." Paul-Boncour's speech for the defense was published separately, although Willy wanted it included as the book's preface. In his scholarly work *Réflexions sur l'Amoralisme du Roman,* Alfred Adams ranked André Gide's *Les Nourritures Terrestres* and Willy's *La Maîtresse du Prince Jean* on the same level.

The Willys' spirited defense was a *cause célèbre*. In a poem published by *Gil Blas*, Willy and Colette both assumed responsiblity for having coauthored the *Claudine*s and *La Maîtresse du Prince Jean,* which proves once again that they made no secret of their collaboration. Colette felt that she had also been the target of the lawsuit. The poem read, "If I had been slinging mud to make money / I would blush / But I never tarnish anything pure / I write literature, sorry, but that is my profession." For the first time Colette signed "Colette Willy." Until 1923 she would use that pen name, which she later called "my fantasy name."

The Crazy Tandem Never Hesitates to Cross the Limits Beyond Which No Limits Are to Be Found

The Willys were the Parisian phenomenon, *les Enfants Terribles* of Tout-Paris. Five hagiographic biographies came off the printing press in quick succession. In 1903 Eugène de Solenière wrote a *Willy* inscribed "To Colette." Willy was lucky "to have met a pal as attractive as a mistress, as mischievous as a kid, as sweet as a devoted companion. Colette is more than his wife . . . she is the one who shares everything, knows everything, understands everything, and is also the coauthor who intelligently adds wit and grace to her husband's prose. O exquisite Colette, how truly you are Willy's perfect counterpart."[52] Henri Albert, who had just published a biography of Nietzsche, followed with a *Willy* in 1904 for the series "Famous Contemporary Men." Jean de la Hire started the series "Couples of Artists" with *Willy et Colette.* On the cover Colette, dressed as Claudine in her black smock and button boots, is sitting on the floor at Willy's feet in the company of Toby-Chien. A postcard was made of the cover.

Colette and Willy were the entertainers *par excellence* in their own salon as well as everywhere else they went. At a party given by Countess de Chabannes La Palice in her art-nouveau *hôtel privé* in the Rue Dosne, Willy led the cakewalk with Prince Scipion Borghese. For several weeks Count Etienne de Beaumont and the marquis de Montebello had rehearsed on the Rue de Courcelles and learned from Willy and Colette how to do the highstep to the music and move in a square formation.

Colette, a crimson carnation in her hair, danced with sensuous grace and won the prize — a highly decorated cake. Etienne de Beaumont noted that when she stopped dancing, she became very subdued and watched Willy "with the eyes of a tame panther."[53]

With the Beaumonts the closed society of the Faubourg Saint-Germain, or at least its most liberal wing, opened its doors to Colette and Willy. In its wake, millionaire aesthetes crowded Colette's salon, particularly "the numerous clan of foreigners."[54] The Spaniards were led by the aristocratic painter José-Maria Sert, the Italians by Count Primoli, the Anglo-Americans by the Raoul-Duvals and Natalie Barney. The foreign press also paid court. The Willys' every move was reported in *La Revue de Paris et de Saint Pétersbourg* and in the *London Referee*. In their apartment one could meet "a strange medley of characters: actresses, great or struggling, writers of all sorts, artists of all kinds and women who belong to high society thrilled and deliciously ashamed to visit this scandalous couple, who are a well-established part of Tout-Paris. They almost swoon at Claudine's remarks, wonderfully indifferent to the opinion of these silly hypocrites, because of her free speech and the flabbergasting frankness of her diary published in four volumes."[55]

Colette's manners were as direct as her language; she could be coarse and intimidating. The first time the author of *Occident,* the shy, introverted poet Lucie Delarue-Mardrus, came to the Rue de Courcelles, Colette, always quick to grasp people's weak spots, exclaimed, noticing that her guest was quivering with embarrassment, "What's wrong, Lucie? Do you need to go pee?"[56]

Marcel Boulestin, a university student and author of a play that had caught Willy's attention, recalled the day he stepped into the salon:

"Bonjour Monsieur, and who are you?" asked Colette curtly.

"I am Boulestin."

Colette turned to her guests and announced mockingly, "Let us say no more, he is Boulestin."[57]

Colette's *jour* since she moved to the 177bis Rue de Courcelles was Wednesday, a more fashionable day than the proletarian Sundays. Colette's *mercredis* dispelled the Victorian atmosphere of nineteenth-century bourgeois salons. Colette rejected "any kind of discrimination," and illegitimate couples, courtesans, and transvestites were welcome around the buffet of "foie gras, beluga caviar, ham club sandwiches, strawberries, ginger, tiny French pastries, and an international selection of spirits." The guests were encouraged to mix their own Jézebels, that is, any mixture of liquors. "A hairy southern poet" composed one "with Kummel, cognac, Cherry Rocher, and Russian anisette."[58] Jean-Paul Toulet and Renée Vivien added ether to their powerful cocktails. Colette and Willy "displayed a peaceful indifference toward the weirdest people, in their salon a few morphomaniacs feel at home — and in that blessed abode teatime is the pretext for a display of alcohol from every part of the world."[59]

On Wednesdays a valet would announce some forty guests, who entered a hall crowded with antiques, its walls covered with paintings and drawings, including one by Ingres. Catulle Mendès quipped that he had to enter the salon sideways. In the salon, painted a light green, bearskins were spread over the couches and books overflowed everywhere. Three "lions" of Tout-Paris society could be seen at Colette's mercredis: the indisputable queen of the courtesans, Liane de Pougy, the trendsetter Count Robert de Montesquiou, and Natalie Barney, "the wild girl from Cincinnati."

Colette attracted the most daring of the sophisticates; one of them was José Maria Sert, who remained her friend until his death in 1945. His works include the gigantic frescoes for the Vich cathedral in Spain, the ballroom of the Waldorf-Astoria, and decorations for Rockefeller Center. He was ugly and short but very seductive; he came from an immensely wealthy Catalan family of textile manufacturers and was a favorite of the Spanish royal family.

Sert settled in Paris in 1899 and dazzled Tout-Paris, who nicknamed him "the Tiepolo of the Ritz." Picasso scoffed at his huge frescoes as "gilt and merde."[60] Sert dressed in a cape and sombrero, spent extravagantly, drank heavily, and took morphine. In his sumptuous studio in the Rue Barbet de Jouy, which had belonged to Horace Vernet, he gave roaring parties among his gigantic canvases.

Colette liked Sert both as an artist and as a man; they shared a common taste for life and its pleasures. Colette's letters to Sert are full of lighthearted banter and suggestive imagery. His studio was hard to heat? She suggested a harem to keep him warm in bed. She described to him her first trip to Bayreuth, how she had enjoyed lying naked in the sleeping car while Willy fumed about the rough sheets and overheated compartment. She made some coarse jokes about the Wagnerian singer Delmas, whom she had spotted as he emerged in his pink nightshirt from his compartment and waited for his turn at the toilet door. She imagined him seated on this most private of thrones, brandishing his *papier hygiénique* like Wotan's spear. In Bayreuth, she had hated the art-nouveau paintings of Wagnerian Rhinemaidens, with large breasts and fat derrières, cavorting in milky waters.

Colette invited Sert to her *mercredis* to meet some Parisian beauties and a growing number of delicate young men. She confessed to him that she was enthralled by one of them, the eighteen-year-old exquisite blond, black-eyed, red-mouthed aesthete known as "Natalie," who wore an irridescent Lalique necklace. She also invited Sert to stay at Monts-Boucons, which, she said, was so sad and peaceful that she could not wait to be there.

Colette and Sert shared a taste for the unconventional. At the end of one dinner in a private dining room at a famous restaurant, a dinner that Sert had organized for a group of friends who all had theatrical connections — actors, directors, and playwrights, Willy among them — the doors opened and four waiters marched in, bearing an enormous platter supporting a mountainous cake topped with frothy meringue and whipped cream. The cake was set in the middle of the table, and two giggling faces popped out of the frothy cream — Polaire and Colette, stark naked, bursting with laughter, and kicking meringue all over with their pink, bare feet.[61]

As the literary myth of a teenaged Colette/Claudine was solidly taking root — carefully tended by Colette and Willy — the real Colette, now thirty years old, had an intense private life. Polaire found out that in Colette's love life there was no rule but her own pleasure. She broke up with Colette the day she left her lover, a rich playboy, alone with Colette, and returned to find them making love. Polaire grabbed Colette, they fought, and Colette left with a black eye.[62] But Polaire was incapable of holding a grudge and they resumed their lesbian relationship.

Colette's escort and confidant was Marcel Boulestin, Willy's secretary. He came from a well-to-do family from southern France, but was an orphan with an inheritance insufficient for his expensive tastes. As a student he had had a drama performed in Toulouse and asked Willy to write a preface for it; Willy saw some promise in the play and obliged. Boulestin was the critic for *Le Courrier Musical,* published in Bordeaux. He had had a good introduction to the Parisian musical milieux, was a protégé of Madame Mulhfeld's and was not yet twenty when Cappiello made a drawing of him.

Boulestin was a homosexual dandy who wore makeup and earrings in private. He was a great storyteller; his best tale was the murder of his uncle, who was stabbed to death by his mistress with a carving knife. Colette found him irresistible and used to take gold coins from Willy's pockets and give them to Marcel, who spent extravagantly. Soft-spoken Marcel enjoyed the company of the robber gangs known as *les apaches,* who operated on the outskirts of Paris; he was also partial to butcher boys and other toughs. Willy tried to dissuade him from such dangerous encounters and suggested he meet elegant and graceful young men. Boulestin answered dryly, "I am not interested in toothpicks."[63] He would become Hicksem in Colette's *Minne* and Blackspot in Willy's *Une Plage d'Amour* (Love at the Beach).

Boulestin was Colette's companion in the afternoons, while Willy ran off to his rendezvous and business appointments. He described his role and Colette's status when he pleasantly referred to himself as "the young attaché escorting the ambassador's wife on her shopping sprees."[64] Colette and Boulestin went to buy Turkish delight, sweet potatoes, and the still rare and exotic banana. At Smith's or Brentano's she bought reproductions of Aubrey Beardsleys, copies of the *Studio,* and fairy tales illustrated by Kate Greenaway and Walter Crane. They would stop for tea at l'Elysée Palace, at Colombia, at Rumpelmayer on the Rue de Rivoli, or at a bakery on the Rue Royale famous for its sandwiches. They sipped whiskey and soda at Fouquet's on the Champs-Elysées. Usually Toby-Chien, the much photographed bulldog, would ride in the victoria and sit on a chair in cafés and pastry shops. Colette liked to go to American bars like the Eureka or Calisaya, paneled in mahogany, where they could drink mint juleps, stars-and-stripes, and manhattans, which had begun to compete with French drinks in the nineties, and swallow prairie oysters. Colette and Boulestin also went to the less chic Brasserie des Hannetons, the first lesbian-run café, or the Thé de Ceylan, with its infamous back rooms and discreet studios, where they met delicate youths, transvestites, and drug users.

Colette was leading the complicated life of Paris-Lesbos, spending lavishly on herself and on some brief encounters. She had a fancy for the poet Lucie Delarue-Mardrus, "the child Muse." Lucie's poems had mesmerized Doctor Joseph Charles Mardrus, an Orientalist raised in Egypt famous for his translation of *The Thousand and One Nights.* They had met at a literary gathering and were married ten days later; she was nineteen and looked fourteen; he was forty-two and a defiant nonconformist. He took charge of the marriage ceremony, commanding her to appear in the garb of a bicycle rider: checkered bloomers, a blouse with enormous sleeves, and a small straw hat. Dr. Mardrus covered his wife's fingers with jewels he had brought back from Ceylon and perfected her adolescent looks; she had to wear her cyclist uniform or skirts that barely reached her ankles.

Lucie had been madly in love with a baroness twice her age. She confessed this infatuation to her husband and showed him the picture of the beauty who had meant so much to her. Dr. Mardrus laughed and, with a twinkle in his eye, tore up the picture, explaining to Lucie that "sapphic" loves were totally devoid of any kind of interest. She could indulge in them; anything that nurtured the poet in her was good. He had an intellectual attraction to and passionate love for her talent and saw to it that her poems were published. The Mardruses lived in a large pavilion, where each of them had a personal office. In the evening, Lucie sat at her desk and wrote while her husband went to bed; in the morning he rushed to her desk to see if she had written anything. When he found a poem, he would come bouncing into the bedroom and, seated between the twin beds with tears in his eyes, rapturously read it. "This is when I felt the happiest,"[65] wrote Lucie in her memoirs.

Lucie was seven years younger than Colette, but they moved in the same circles and Lucie became a regular at Colette's *mercredis*. She was impressed by her hostess's physique and noticed "the dark blue sparkle of her eyes in her triangular face"[66] but thought she was acting the part of Claudine out too much. They engaged in one of those affairs which for Colette started with a sensuous attraction and developed into a lasting friendship. It had been this way with Marguerite Moréno, Lucie, Natalie, and Eva, and the pattern would be the same with Meg Villars, Musidora, Claude Chauvière, Germaine Beaumont, Thérèse Robert, Renée Hamond, and Annie de Pène (who left her husband for Colette's sake), Hélène Picard (who did the same), Germaine Patat, the marquise de Morny, and princess de Polignac.

Few *ménages d'artistes* lasted. Lucie left Dr. Mardrus, wrote *Sappho's Despair,* and acted the part of Sappho on the professional stage at the Théâtre Fémina. Another *ménage* was splitting up in the midst of a scandal: Colette's friend Juliette Adam was suing her husband for stealing her literary production. She had published a successful novel, but Adam claimed the book was his, and the second printing came out with only his name on the cover. Juliette filed a lawsuit and lost — a wife had no right to property of her own, literary or otherwise.

The claim to authorship was as yet no concern of Colette's; she was afraid that Willy was slipping away.

In March of 1903 Willy's *P'sitt,* a one-act play, opened at Les Mathurins, Polaire was playing *Claudine in Paris* at Les Bouffes-Parisiens, and the fourth *Claudine* — *Claudine and Annie* was released. The cover, signed "Pascau," showed a young woman in a traveling suit, and behind her two posters. One read *Claudine and Annie,* the other *Claudine at School.* On the back cover of the book was a caricature of Polaire.

Claudine and Annie was a catharsis. In the last pages of *Claudine Married,* Claudine looks back and wonders what she has accomplished in her married life. She feels happy because Renaud loved her, sad because of his unfaithfulness, and shocked by his secretive nature. Claudine expresses the desire to be the faithful wife of a faithful husband.

In the sequel centered around the emotional shock of discovering that Willy had a secret life, Colette wondered why she had been acquiescent, so blind, so submissive. In *Claudine and Annie* Colette created a new avatar of herself, Annie, the antithesis of free Claudine. Colette felt that she and Willy were slipping into banality, that "From every corner rose a bourgeois threat."[67] Annie was the literary incarnation of that fear. The threat was not that Willy was a womanizer, but that he led the life of the typical philandering husband, hiding his affairs from his wife. He was destroying the core of their relationship, the trust in a pivotal love around which everything else evolved. Colette turned the book into an argument for divorce and an explicit warning to her husband. She first gave the novel the ominous title *Je m'évade* (I escape). In the background the couple Claudine-Renaud is a constant reminder of their ideal marriage *en camarades* and of days gone by. In contrast the couple Annie-Alain, the epitome of a bourgeois couple, is a mirror of Colette's fears. Annie is the submissive wife of a self-centered, demanding womanizer. When he goes on a four-month trip to South America, Annie discovers that she is an individual with a life of her own and cannot envision going back to her previous life. This metamorphosis occurs when Annie meets a group of liberated women — including Claudine, herself, and Marthe, her sister-in-law, the cynical mistress of Maugis. To her new avatar, Annie, Colette gave what she loved most, Monts-Boucons, called "Casamène," and her bulldog, Toby. Annie's life is a travelogue through Colette's life: her trip to Uriage, a trip to Bayreuth with Polaire and Willy, an evening at Madame Lemaire's, a concert of music by Fauré, a pantomime based on Verlaine's *Les Fêtes Galantes,* with the guests in eighteenth-century costumes performing *tableaux vivants* of paintings by Fragonard.

Annie's metamorphosis from compliant wife to emancipated individual goes through a last temptation of ordinary womanhood, the desire to have a child. This notion is quickly curtailed by Claudine: "Bouac! Never!" Annie should stay slim and delicate. Colette concluded her novel by sending Claudine back to Montigny with Renaud, "her nonchalant, complacent friend from other days," to whom she promised not to be tempted any more by beautiful women.

Colette's message to Henry was clear; either they reverted to their previous understanding or Colette would flee. She could survive on her own, even financially, having a three-thousand-franc dowry and fifty thousand francs stashed away. She did not care if the divorce laws, then so unfair to women, declared her the culprit for abandoning her home. To explain her decision to her husband, Annie leaves his desk open, his love letters spilling over the floor. In *My Apprenticeships* Colette described the same scene. In "Letter from Claudine to Renaud," she again warned Willy, "Beware that Claudine does not recall her memories of the past. If not, like Annie, she would leave taking Toby with her as well as her revolver, hoping to find somewhere 'a little piece of paradise.' "[68]

The novel had none of the style, wit, and brio of the three former *Claudines.* "*Claudine and Annie* gave me a lot of trouble,"[69] wrote Colette, who had written her manifesto of independence while wavering between rebellious and perplexed states of mind. Willy, who made very few corrections to the manuscript, wrote to Alfred Valette that the novel was poorly structured and that he washed his hands of the book. For commercial reasons the title referred to Claudine, even though she was not the main character and was signed "Willy."

Willy wrote to Marchand that Colette wanted to make it a "revenge novel" and to "drag in the mud, all the women with whom she went to bed."[70] It was also a revenge novel against the women she suspected of having had love affairs with Willy. There was Candeur, "the child poet" (Lucie Delarue-Mardrus), "who voluptuously bites her lower lip as if it were that of another woman."[71] Colette inserted Lucie's poem "Pour le

Chat" in her text. There were Miss Flossie (Natalie Barney), "as supple as a silk scarf"[72] and her red-haired friend, Eva Palmer; there was La Rose Chou, Madame de Caillavet's daughter-in-law (Jeanne Pouquet), who had been courted by Willy. It was a galaxy of glaring portraits: of Henry's mistress, Liette, the wife of the musician Louis de Serres and Colette's friend; of the composer Ernest Chausson's wife, who had had an affair with Willy in the past; and of Sophia Van den Brule, who had also fallen in love with Colette and Willy.

In spite of its weakness, the book received some good reviews: "Never has libertine literature been more serious, never has it been more honest and more pure in its intentions . . . I have read the *Claudine*s with the same aesthetic awe with which I study sketches by Fragonard,"[73] wrote Miomandre.

Ex-lovers were not the only targets; Jean de Mitty, editor in chief of the tabloid *Le Cri de Paris* had been insulted and his newspaper called a rag that profiteered in blackmail. Jean de Mitty sent Willy his witnesses and a duel took place on April 3, 1903. In a state of fury De Mitty attacked Willy, and his sword entered Willy's chest; the red spot on the shirt grew large, but Willy wanted to fight on. The witnesses declared the encounter over and dragged Willy away. The sword had entered at an angle and gone through five inches of fat without reaching the stomach. The following day all the press reported the duel in great detail. Two weeks later Willy fought another duel; in one of his articles in *Gil Blas* he had insulted Samuel Larray; they fought in the Count de Chabannes' park, and Larray was wounded in the stomach. Colette was upset by Willy's duels and roamed aimlessly from room to room, dizzy with anguish; when her legs could no longer carry her, she dropped onto a sofa. Boulestin noted with amazement Colette's despair at the idea that Willy could be hurt.

Colette was also fighting for her name, or rather her pen name; the pseudonym "Willy" had become extremely popular, particularly with women who borrowed it to sign their own articles and confessions. In a courteous and witty letter to the director of a daily, she voiced her concern that so many women were using her pen name. She asked the director to take her modest claim into account, hoping that from now on she would be the only one to sign "Colette Willy."[74]

—⁕—

Show business was becoming more and more attractive. Three of Willy's plays were produced at the same time: at the Théâtre Moderne, it was *Serments d'Ivrogne* coauthored with André Tremisot who signed "Andrée Cocotte"; at the Bouffes Parisiens, it was *Claudine in Paris,* followed on April 18 by another hit, *Le P'tit Jeune Homme,* coauthored by Willy, Lugné-Poë, and Charles Vayre, with Polaire as the lead. She was dressed as a boy, and Willy had pictures taken of him helping Polaire adjust her pants. He also had pictures taken of Colette in the same attire; both photos were distributed in stores and by mail, pursuing the deliberate plan of identifying Colette with the extremely successful Polaire.

At no time was the public allowed to forget that Colette Willy could lay claim to the fame of Claudine. The Claudine mania was not subsiding; from Latinville (the best ice-cream parlor) came *la Glace Claudine;* then came *le Gâteau-Claudine,* a cake that could still be bought forty years later in a pastry shop in the Rue de la Boétie, *la Lotion Claudine, le Parfum Claudine, le Parfum Colette,* and the *Willy* face powder. The *Claudinet,* a round collar for ladies and children, could be bought by mail order in the catalog of La Samaritaine (a large department store); *le Col Claudine,* a round collar with a checkered scarf, became so common that even today a *col Claudine* is synonymous with an Eton collar. Lewis made the *Claudine* hat; even the state capitalized on the craze — a new brand of cigarettes called Claudine could be bought from tobacconists. Colette and Willy found another source of profit in advertising; Willy was a patron for garters, Colette Willy for *Claudine* socks, lighters, and toothpicks. Colette, a fitness enthusiast, also sponsored gymnastics.

Willy's idea of capitalizing on the Claudine fad came from America. When Sarah Bernhardt went on tour in the United States, manufacturers produced Sarah Bernhardt perfume, Sarah Bernhardt candy, Sarah Bernhardt cigars . . . even Sarah Bernhardt eyeglasses. A brewing company brought out large billboard posters representing Sarah as she was and then Sarah with hips and a bust *à la mode,* stating in bold letters, "Sarah before and after six months of drinking our bitter." But the Willys used publicity to a previously unprecedented degree; Colette's and Polaire's appearances as twins intensified, yet Polaire's part in *Le P'tit Jeune Homme* was demanding and Colette was busy. So Willy invented look-alikes, young actresses impersonating Colette and Polaire. The twins caught the popular imagination, and it became fashionable to dress alike. The twin phenomenon lasted for years; the upstart Coco Chanel caught the attention of Tout-Paris ten years later, when she appeared with "a twin" in the same evening gowns.

In May Willy managed to surpass all his previous pranks. Edmond Rostand, the immensely popular author of *Cyrano de Bergerac* and *L'Aiglon,* was elected to the Académie Française. The glorified "Immortal," dressed in green with silver embroidery around his collar and on his lapels, wearing an eighteenth-century hat and a ceremonial sword, gave a speech reproduced in every newspaper; it was stated that Rostand had been asked to deliver it, not in verse as he had intended, but in prose. On the first of May Willy, signing "Gauthier-Villars" because this was an important matter, published an article including a long excerpt of Rostrand's original speech in verse in *La Nouvelle Revue.* The poem was superb; the press picked it up and it was reproduced everywhere. Jules Clarétie, the literary critic for *L'Echo de Paris,* noted the marvelous grace, the irony, the caprice, the dream "of this enchanter who opened the gates to a fairy palace with these verses like rose petals thrown to the wind."[75] The next day, Paris and Edmond Rostand himself roared with laughter when Willy published a letter to Clarétie confessing that he had written the Rostand masterpiece.

In July Colette reviewed the competition finals at the Conservatoire (the national school of music and drama), the last event of the Parisian season. She signed her articles "Claudine au Conservatoire." The *Revue Théâtrale* noted that Willy, Colette Willy, and Polaire, "the sacred trio," attended the competition together.

As the season was over, Colette went to Mont-Boucons for what she called "a life as solitary as that of a shepherd."[76] (Colette's idea of solitude was her own. In a letter she once lamented that she knew no one in Paris, as she could barely name two hundred people.) It was a peaceful summer; she wrote to Marguerite Moréno that she worked in her gymnasium hidden by trees — "a trapeze, parallel bars, poles and ladders . . . I am proud of my work on the trapeze. Toby-Chien has learned to climb the ladders in two lessons. I keep this in store for hard times."[77] Colette was haunted by the fear of losing Willy and being left destitute. Asked why, at the time of *Claudine and Annie,* she did not go back to live with her mother, Colette retorted that she would not "go back totally bereaved, go back as someone who had failed albeit by her own fault . . ."[78] Polaire joined the couple "to have some fresh mountain air"[79] before starting a grueling tour of the provinces organized by Willy.

Kiki-la-Doucette, the cat Colette took to opening nights and walked on a leash, had died a few months earlier, "We lost him without knowing why. He became flat, flat and that was it."[80] In 1902 Colette had published a song written for her cat, *Minet,* music and lyrics by "Madame Willy." She liked Kiki-la-Doucette's universal contempt, the quality she so admired in her mother, Sido. "Kiki is our big loss. Willy loved him so much,"[81] and "to amuse Willy" she wrote *Dialogues de Bêtes,* four dialogues between the cat Kiki-La-Doucette and the bulldog Toby-Chien. Henry anwered with some love poems that would be inserted into his novel *Maugis Amoureux.*

The Novel Factory

These literary love games could not finance the Willys' ritzy way of life. That summer they put together a "novel factory," which Colette later called les Ateliers. It is hard to assess today how much Colette contributed to the factory in writing, rewriting, and editing. The Willys' five biographers all agree that the couple collaborated. Colette easily imitated her husband's style. "If you need me for Maugis," said Mr. Willy, "leave some blanks. I left none . . . My pastiche stood up very well, my Maugis expressed himself in pure vintage Maugis."[82]

By 1903 the Willys, under several pseudonyms, appeared in at least forty-nine newspapers, dailies, weeklies, magazines, and journals; they contributed feature articles, poems, reviews, and short stories. France was flooded with newspapers; 3,342 were printed in Paris alone. The Willys were masters at repackaging articles, a practice Colette followed during her journalistic career. Three full-time secretaries — Boulestin, Diard, and Héon — and a score of talented writers supplied the material; Willy, or at times, Colette, gave it that distinct "Willy flavor." After the unexpected phenomenon of the *Claudine*s, Colette's part in the enterprise was substantial; the ghostwriters called her *la Patronne* (the Boss). The main collaborators remained Curnonsky and the poet later rediscovered by the beat generation, Jean-Paul Toulet. It is hard to tell how many writers collaborated with Willy, Inc. The best man for descriptions was given a novel's plan, with specific indications of the descriptions he should write; the one who wrote the best one-liners was put in charge of dialogue. The manuscript was sent back and forth, and often the ghostwriters did not even know the story line. All of them were pushed, pressed, and requested to work at full speed; then Curnonsky, Willy's trusted backup, put the manuscript together, and Willy edited the final draft — he never wrote a novel from scratch. This method compares today with the collective work involved in the production of a movie, soap opera, television program, and even popular best-sellers. Willy was decent, even generous with his "coauthors"; Curnonsky received on hundred gold francs for one contribution, Jean-Paul Toulet twenty-five hundred gold francs for a book. Curnonsky defended his ghostwriting: "If I had signed my name, I would have sold three thousand copies, Willy's signature made us sell two hundred ten thousand copies of *Maugis en Ménage.*"[83] The ghostwriters also had their own works reviewed and promoted by Willy.

The novels that came out of Les Ateliers were romans à clefs, light, licentious, and semiautobiographical. Lovers, husbands, wives, and courtesans pursued each other in a swift choreography of catastrophic encounters. Always on the brink of indecency, always suggestive, never gross, and avoiding censorship skilfully, they managed to skirt the code of moral decency. From 1904 to 1907 Les Ateliers turned out fourteen titles. The name "Gauthier-Villars" all but disappeared from the publisher's lists, except for a biography of Bizet, articles on musicology, and some opera lyrics. Only the famous "Usherette of the Summer Circus" did not give way to "Willy."

At Monts-Boucons that summer Willy and Colette organized the output of Les Ateliers: five titles for 1904. It was obvious that the Claudine character had run its course. Colette had written a short story, "Minne," about the fantasies of an adolescent girl. Willy saw in "Minne" a potential successor to Claudine and asked Colette to expand the tale into a novel. However, the true counterpart of Claudine was Henry Maugis. Colette collaborated on the *Maugis* books, a series that became as popular as the *Claudine* tetralogy. The name Maugis, like Renaud, came from the twelfth-century epic poem, *Doon de Mayence.* The protean magician Maugis, through his magic and medicine, cured his cousin Renaud, the perfect *chevalier.* Maugis was an autobiographical portrait of Willy, who cured the ills of his contemporaries through his witticisms and brilliant improvisations: "My latest volume, *With Open Sheets,* was selling as much as a politician's conscience, since an enemy had denounced the profound immorality of the novel in a newspaper, which has made money by declaring three bankrupcies in a row."[84]

In their intertwined creations, Colette and Henry constantly gave the feminine and masculine versions of their marriage.

In French society, where money was never discussed and salaries never quoted, Willy dropped all pretense and told his large following, "I write only for money." It was as daring and avant-garde a statement as Claudine's admission of her own bisexuality. "How will posterity appreciate my production? I couldn't care less. It has given what I wanted in my lifetime. A few hours spent virtuously every day on my well-planned work allow me to me to satisfy my expensive tastes. I am invited to dinner to amuse the guests. I am quizzed about Wagner, about the opera, about the draft, about air-ships, about the immortality of the soul and the size of Polaire's waist. I gossip to their heart's content and this public, full of truffles and extra-dry champagne, acclaims with laughter the palest witticism. If I ask the waiter for some cheese, they think it is some kind of joke and applaud . . . I hate, I detest this chatter, I hate to recite my next article, I hate to hear, 'Maugis has said, Maugis will say' . . ."[85]

In *Maugis Amoureux* Willy praised Colette's charms, her intelligence, and her wit:"her attitude enchants me, to belong to high society without stooping to its rules and not caring about it!" He knew that Colette did not like his womanizing "but I rule it out because, as everybody knows, she does not like men very much, although they do not reciprocate . . . if she adores her husband, it is because he is more feminine than all the pretty women like Rézi put together." Willy also painted Claudine (Colette) and Renaud (himself) as the ideal couple, since they flaunted "their double egoism which they honestly proclaim . . . and their nastiness, strictly defensive but many times helpful to friends."[86]

Maugis Amoureux was part of the literary dialogue Colette and Willy carried on for the rest of their lives. They treated the events of their lives as raw material for their novels. They were writing and enacting their own legends. Maugis and Claudine transcended all the other literary selves created by this couple; they were perceived as their true likenesses.

Colette wrote in a portrait of Willy in *La Revue Illustrée,* "Claudine and Minne are my daughters as well as my husband's . . . ." Colette concluded her portrait of Willy: "close to him animals become sentimental and women cynical."[87]

In order to make Maugis a household word, Willy used the same promotional techniques as for Claudine; he repeated Maugis's name and deeds in articles, in prefaces, in novels. Willy-Maugis had his picture on postcards with a bunch of flowers wishing "Happy Birthday" or "Happy New Year," in tophat and tails, on horseback, on a bicycle. He was a favorite with painters and caricaturists. Jules de Goncourt once said, "Glory is a name repeated over and over." No one succeeded better than Willy, "the best known name after God," quipped Sacha Guitry.

In March *Le Mercure de France* published Colette's first book signed "Colette Willy," *Dialogues de Bêtes.* As soon as the *Dialogues* were released, friends expressed enthusiasm. Catulle Mendès hugged Colette in public, saying, "Once more I have found the poetry of the *Claudines.*"[88] Colette had found her poetic voice in the *Dialogues:* music for the ear, emotion for the heart, witticism for the mind, and a pagan kinship with all living things. The slim book was reviewed by Rachilde:

> Madame Colette Willy reveals a naive soul and a complex mind, a very interesting combination. A feminine writer by her careful choice of details, a true "man-of-letters" by the all-new approach and the new metaphor she uses to study people, and she is simply a woman by the genuine admiration she has for her animals. She is right, our cat, our dog are really the best in our lives.
>
> . . . We hope Madame Colette Willy will not stop on this mysterious trail through little jungles. We guess this is the hors d'oeuvre of the full meal of a future book. We expect, we demand Kiki-la-Doucette in Paris, then Kiki-la-Doucette married . . . I believe the author can keep us eagerly interested in these heroes, because all said and done, the author has the stamp of a professional writer.[89]

Colette sent a copy of her book to Francis Jammes, a poet published by *Le Mercure de France*; he was regarded as a Catholic La Fontaine, the poet of the animal world. Jammes wrote emotional verse about overworked donkeys, miserable dogs, stray cats, all creatures great and small that suffer from man's unkindness — not at all Colette's animal world of purebred cats and dogs who drink from a crystal bowl. Colette wanted Jammes to write a preface for the expanded version of *Les Dialogues de Bêtes;* Marcel Schwob was entrusted with the diplomatic mission. Jammes's unenthusiastic letter to Colette reflects the ambiguity of Colette's and Willy's literary standing in Parisian letters: "Allow me to remain silent about this book, which I have read with affection. I don't want you to come to me from the depths of your Parisian legend . . . I want to see you as the blue cornflower in the rye or as the flaming marigold on the mystical whiteness of the path where Kiki and Toby dream your magnificent dream."[90] Colette was not deterred; she started to woo this Catholic poet who dressed as a monk. She asked him to autograph two of his books, *Clara d'Ellebeuse* and *Almaide d'Entremont.* Jammes's heroines were the purest of provincial girls, raised in "the mystery of convent life." They could not be farther from Colette.

To bridge the gap with the author of a *Prayer to Go to Heaven With the Donkeys,* Colette wanted to make him feel that they had more in common than he knew. In a letter dated October 16, 1904, she added a postscript, "You know my distant forebears came also from the hot islands from out there, far away, like your own, but mine must have been darker than yours. In my family we keep nothing, neither papers, nor souvenirs, nothing, but there remains a daguerreotype of my mother's father, a gingerbread gorilla, who traded in cocoa. Voilà, I have a black spot in my blood. Does it repel you?"[91] (In the first publication of her correspondence with Francis Jammes in 1945 she deleted this postscript; she was careful not to upset her readers, who had been subjected to racist propaganda during the war. The postscript was restored in the 1973 publication of her correspondence, *Lettres à Ses Pairs*).

Colette's correspondence with Jammes was an exercise in seduction and bargaining; coyly she wrote that Jammes should not be fooled — her Parisian legend was nothing but a legend. Everything was terrible for her in Paris; the leaves turned black as soon as they grew and the scent of lilies of the valley "drove her to despair." Luckily she had Willy: "Willy is a good squirrel master, the cage is charming and the door is open." He had even given her "very nice squirrel toys: a whole gymnasium and she can kick the back of her head with her heels."[92] She included two pictures of herself in tights and tank top.

Jammes answered with some curt compliments on her latest *Dialogues,* but was not mollified by Colette's letters. In October she dropped all pretense: Valette was ready to publish an expanded version of *Les Dialogues, Sept Dialogues de Bêtes;* would Jammes write a preface? Should he do so, it would distance Colette Willy from the *Claudines* and confirm her status as a poet. Jammes was willing to write if Colette met his conditions: "I am writing the most gracious preface for the *Dialogues*, but I would like to request the following from you and Willy, that it be published in *Femina* along with an article that a young girl is writing about me . . . Her name is Andrée Villiene, I would like her to have a position with *Femina*. This would be an excellent occasion . . . As soon as she arrives in Paris she will contact you. I appeal to all of Willy's 'journalistic' power and to his kindness to obtain publication of this article."[93] Colette, elated to have a preface signed by Jammes, promised everything.

Jammes was uneasy. His friends from the *Nouvelle Revue Française,* the emerging intellectual group, shunned Colette and Willy; besides, Colette's dubious reputation did not go down well with his Catholic readers. On October 17, 1904, Jammes wrote cynically to André Gide that he was working on a preface for Colette Willy. "You may answer that you would not have written a preface for that book, then I would reply that I find it perfect and that this preface is a wonderful opportunity to spread my name a little further,"[94] and no one could "spread a name" better than Willy.

The preface was a masterpiece of clever conceit; Jammes simply went through the looking glass and described Colette in reverse. Since she was known for her androgyny, eccentric behavior, and brazen rejection of all conformism, he denied the whole thing and gave his "true" version of the "authentic" Madame Colette Willy. He declared that she never had short hair, did not dress in men's clothes, did not take her cat to concerts, that her dog did not drink from a long stemmed glass, that it was not true that she worked on a trapeze and touched her head with her heels. According to Jammes, Colette had never ceased being the perfect bourgeoise who rises at dawn, gives hay to the horse, corn to the chicken, cabbage to the rabbits, seed to the canary, snails to the ducks, and water to the hogs. At eight she made coffee and milk for her maid and herself. She read *The Rustic Home.* She knew everything about bee hives, orchards, vegetable gardens, and greenhouses. He described her cheeks, pink as an apple, her lips like poppies, her grace, like that of a honeysuckle. He saw her leaning against the green fence of her yard. Transferring to Colette his own understanding of the relationship of animals with their cruel owners, Jammes said that Colette felt all the sadness of the dog victimized by his ungrateful master, the misery of the cat thrown out on the dung heap, hungry and shaking with fever, waiting

for the next human torture. This astoundingly misleading preface created an image of Colette as a peasant girl, which in time superseded all
others. Jammes declared Colette was a true poet: "She kicks down from
the slopes of Parnassus all the fake muses."[95]

Colette kept her side of the bargain. In December of 1904 she met
Jammes's young friend Mademoiselle Villiene, but expressed serious
doubts about her chances of becoming a journalist "if she has already
lost her courage after a half-defeat and one rude remark from an individual who should not even exist for her. One does not feel offended
when an errand boy or a hawker calls you a whore in the street. It is
exactly the same. In my opinion this cannot spoil the beauty of life."[96]
Jammes insisted on having the preface published in *Femina* with his
friend's article, but Mademoiselle Villiene was so taken aback by
Colette's bluntness that she pulled out of the deal. The preface was
published in *Le Mercure*.

Colette did not forget her exchange of letters with a man she would
never meet. In 1911 *Les Tablettes* asked her to contribute an article to a
special issue on Francis Jammes, and she picked up the conceit of the
country lass and went even a step further: if Jammes should raise his hand
holding a rose, she would instantly "lose her body like an empty dress"
and nothing would remain of her except "a little animal: a squirrel, a dog,
a cat or a hare with a velvety nose or maybe a spotty hen, or a shimmering pigeon, she would peck at the miraculous grain which pours
through the sun-rays in Francis Jammes' paradise."[97]

The four *Dialogues de Bêtes* became seven, then in 1930 twelve, published in *Le Mercure de France*. There would be other dialogues written
between 1909 and 1915, published under the title *Creatures Great and
Small* (La Paix chez les Bêtes). The little jungles of pedigreed animals
would become her most special domaine. In *The Cat* (La Chatte), a cat
would be the central character of a novel.

Les Dialogues de Bêtes established Colette Willy as a writer. "She has
the rare and awesome glory of having created a new literary genre,"
wrote Jean de la Hire in his biography *Willy et Colette*. *La Revue Illustrée*
said "it is one of the rare beautiful books — written by a woman — that
will last."[98] *La Vie Parisienne* praised "its so perfect perfection" and "its so
peculiar originality."[99] Colette's new status was evident when her name
appeared in *La Nouvelle Littérature 1895-1905* as author of *Les Dialogues de
Bêtes* and contributor to *Gil Blas, Revue Illustrée, Renaissance Latine*, and *Le*

Mercure de France. Colette was listed as Willy (Colette-Claudine-Colette, Mme Henry Gauthier-Villars).

In June *Minne*, signed "Willy," was published by Ollendorff. In a letter to Rachilde, Willy dismissed *Maugis Amoureux* as a commercial product and informed her that this time he was preparing *Minne's Marriage* in collaboration with Colette, a book she might prefer. He added that they yelled at each other every evening as two true collaborators should, since Colette insisted on including fistfights, sword fights, and a few rapes, and scorned and derided what she described as "Willy's virginal blushes."[100] The sequel, *Les Egarements de Minne,* was published in May of 1905. The critic Jean Ernest-Charles branded both novels as blatantly commercial. Colette herself was not pleased with them. She felt that Willy's inserts, usually aimed at satisfying some personal vendetta, distracted from her topic. In 1909 she fused them into one volume, *The Innocent Libertine,* eliminating Willy's inserts.

Freedom was the central theme of the *Claudines*; repression, a pivotal Fourierist idea, is the theme of *Minne. Minne* is a dogmatic novel based on Fourier's assumption that "the predilection for atrocity is but the countereffect of the suffocation of certain passions"; he explains that any repressed passion produces its counterpassion "which is as malevolent as the natural passion is beneficial."[101]

Minne, fourteen years and eights month old, is encased in a typical bourgeois family; Colette depicts the proper, stifling milieu with its disastrous consequences denounced by Fourier. She creates her first mother figure, Maman (the absolute antithesis of Sido), a young widow who gives up her youth to pamper her daughter and live vicariously through her. The father figure is Uncle Paul, a doctor suffering from tropical fevers who devotes himself entirely to the well-being and security of his sister and niece. He has a son, Antoine, seventeen years old, shy, respectful, and in love with Minne, whom he plans to marry.

Everything that Sido spared her "savages" is systematically applied to Minne with the direst consequences. What Colette calls "the insoluble problem of a girl's education" has never troubled "Maman's simplistic soul"; she smothers Minne with kindness and delicate attentions, while Minne is secretly brimming with passion, "of which she knows nothing, but she whispers the hissing word to herself, as one tries out the lash of a whip."[102]

To paint the picture of the typical, dutiful, bourgeois family, Colette had only to remember her in-laws, the respectable and well-meaning

Gauthier-Villars, who had raised so many safeguards, set such virtuous examples, and had such sweet manners that Colette thought it was enough to drive one to suicide. Free Claudine had no malice and no taste for crime; her mind was sound, her body healthy, her zest for life harmless. Minne, the pampered daughter of the archetypal bourgeois mother, craves violence, which she discovers with relish in the forbidden newspapers she reads on the sly, while pretending to do her homework. She laps up the gory descriptions of a gang of thieves and murderers and thirsts for evil in every form.

Minne, who does not have a moment without the smiling supervision of Maman, compensates for her permanent frustration with outrageous daydreams. On her way to the most snobbish and exclusive school, in the unavoidable company of Maman, an encounter with an old lady is enough to set Minne's imagination soaring. The old lady is carried away by a band of criminals: "let them draw mysterious signs on her buttocks with their knives! . . . drag her, yellow, like rancid butter . . . throw her into the limekiln."[103]

During Sunday dinner, while Maman listens with deference to her elder brother, the doctor, Minne imagines that "the windows are smashed, hands armed with weapons . . . turn over the table, slaughter indiscriminately . . . then in the darkness, touched by the pink hue of flames, carry her away, no one knows where." This daydream is shattered by Maman's sweet voice offering another piece of cake, and Minne, cool and composed, answers, "Yes, please."[104]

As soon as she has received Maman's goodnight kiss and closed the door of her pink-and-white bedroom, Minne runs to the mirror and does up her hair in a bun like a prostitute pictured in the evening paper. In her bed she listens to the shrill whistles in the distance and wonders if the gang that is terrorizing the newly opened Boulevard Berthier, where she lives, has murdered someone. She has memorized the details of the latest article: there has been a fight among the gangs; the police have picked up five of them; but their leader, Le Frisé (Curly), has escaped. She muses, "To be their queen, with a red ribbon around my neck and a revolver . . . Queen Minne!"[105]

But dreams are no longer enough. One evening, imagining that she hears Le Frisé's footsteps under her window, she ties the red ribbon around her neck and rushes out in pursuit of a vanishing shadow. Her quest leads her through dark, dangerous streets; she meets a scornful prostitute and is almost picked up by a half-drunk reveler; runs for her life; and manages to reach home and fall in through the open door, swooning and spattered with mud. She is carried to bed unconscious; Uncle Paul examines her while Maman, in agony, holds the lamp. To their immense relief, Minne is intact but cousin Antoine weeps "because she is lost, defiled, branded forever with the infamous seal."[106] Appearance outweighs reality; appearance is all that counts. On that ironical note, Colette concludes Minne's story.

After *Minne's* theme of repression leading to violence, its sequel, the novel *Les Egarements de Minne,* develops another Fourierist theme: forced monogamy leads to secret debauch, while freedom leads to love. As the story unfolds, Minne has been married for two years to Antoine and has had three lovers. She has been coerced into the marriage; on her deathbed Maman has begged Minne to marry Antoine, since no one else would marry her after her escapade. Maman assumes that Minne's reputation is lost, although Colette emphasizes that nothing happened and nobody knows about Minne's misbehavior except her close family and the maid. Uncle Paul assumes that Maman had died from grief and blames Minne for her mother's death. Convential motherhood leads to repression, a concept Colette would examine again in "Maternité."

Minne does not like to let her husband join her in bed but resigns herself to it, since that is the rule in married life: "Well, he is my husband. He is no worse than any other, but . . . he is my husband . . . with this conclusion which contains the whole philosophy of a slave, she proceeds slowly to her bedroom." Minne has given her body to husband and lovers alike "but has never thought that this gift implied a downfall";[107] since Antoine gives her no pleasure, Minne feels free to seek it in extramarital affairs, even with Maugis who gently sends her home.

Meanwhile Antoine, the unloved husband, does some painful soulsearching and comes to a Fourierist conclusion: "It is the greatest love that accepts sharing."[108] He realizes to his chagrin that he married Minne and used her like a smug pasha, without bothering to ask her if she wanted him or not. Now he admits to her, "I can't prevent you from loving someone any more than I can stop the world." He is ready to "give up his honor as a husband, to be her devoted accomplice." Antoine tells her, "I want you to love me enough to ask for anything that would please you, anything, you hear? Even the things that no one usually asks from a husband." This strikes Minne like a thunderbolt; she understands that Antoine is unlike her lovers. No man has ever said to her, "Be happy,

I ask nothing for myself. I will give you jewels, candies, lovers . . ." Antoine has removed the shackle, and Minne is out of the cage. As a free woman, she calls Antoine to her bed and for the first time discovers *volupté,* total sexual gratification. "Life comes to her, easy, sensuous, as commonplace as a beautiful girl."[109]

End of an Era

Although the marriage seemed harmonious, an undercurrent of sadness had invaded it. Willy was sick and spent most of the summer at Monts-Boucons in bed. He was in and out of bed for months and had surgery twice; he was probably suffering from syphilis. Colette had noticed a "sore" on Willy's leg and wrote to Comtesse de Martel that it was taking a turn for the worse.

Colette had reached "the age when one does not want to die for anyone or from anyone."[110] She was concerned for herself; she had never lost her childhood disgust for diseases, which had made her cross the Saint-Sauveur streets to avoid passing a house where someone was sick.

Willy was depressed; like his alter ego, Maugis, he had lost his lust for life and wanted to die. Colette had written *Dialogues de Bêtes* "to amuse Willy"; his answer, "to amuse Claudine," was *The Healing Suicide,* a surrealistic tale of a man who stuffs himself with matches to commit suicide and finds his flame rekindled.

According to his latest biographer, Willy, having used and abused his senses, was growing impotent. The fiery Colette had accepted Willy's way of life, but her own needs were demanding. More and more young and famous men and women, attractive charmers, "rakes," aristocrats, and millionaires were moving into the charmed circle of a sensuous, daring, self-assured Colette. They came to her studio without stopping to call on Willy, and "Willy took notice," wrote Colette. "He did not like me wasting my time with young men."[111]

For a while life reverted to a familiar pattern, *ménage à trois.* Colette and Willy added a new "hyphen" to their couple, an aspiring actress and student at *Le Conservatoire d'Art Dramatique.* Colette initiated her into the art of lovemaking in her studio. This aspiring actress with "very clear and beautiful eyes" "looked like the adolescent King Louis xv."[112] She amused

Colette, but Willy soon tired of her as she was lazy and untalented. Her successor was Marguerite Maniez, an alluring brunette with blue eyes; brought up in England, she was bilingual and later wrote some plays and novels both in French and in English. She became quite famous for her feature articles in *The Tatler,* which she signed "Priscilla." In 1904 she was studying to be an actress. Willy became her manager and lover and re-named her Meg Villars, pretending that she was his daughter and not his mistress. Colette cast her spell over Meg, who was "hypnotized," fasci-nated by her. Like many of her generation, she had first fallen in love with the fictional Claudine. Invited to climb to the third-floor studio to meet the real Claudine, Meg was totally confused. She wrote to Colette, "Your Meg who no longer knows to which gender she belongs."[113]

On the first of October in 1904 Willy had another hit play that ran to the end of the year. It was the stage version of a novel by Comtesse de Martel. A sentimental tearjerker, *Le Friquet* — slang for "the sparrow" — was the story of a young acrobat, superbly played by Polaire. Lugné-Poë, Vayre, Amory, and Colette all contributed to the stage adaption of *Le Friquet.* Then they adapted *Minne,* a play in two acts, which opened in February of the following year.

On December 2, 1904, Henry's mother died. Colette never liked this *grande bourgeoise,* who severely criticized their libertine novels; she thought her son was wasting his talent. Colette had noticed that Henry clipped out the pages he did not feel proper for his mother to read be-fore sending her their books. On December 8, Le Gymnase canceled *Le Friquet* for one night "because Mr. Willy is in mourning," an unusual gesture, considering the financial loss for the actors and the theater. But Willy was Paris's *enfant chéri,* and Tout-Paris grieved with him.

In May 1905 *Le Mercure Musical* published the first of six stories signed "Colette Willy," "The Vine's Tendrils" (Les Vrilles de la Vigne), the tale of a nightingale caught in the tendrils of a vine while he is asleep. He untangles himself in a panic and swears never to sleep as long as the tendrils grow and to sing until the safety of daybreak. As he sings through the night, his song becomes more beautiful and he begins to enjoy the sight of the stars and the moon. The snares of springtime, full of grasping tendrils, are no longer a threat; he discovers an unexpected happiness in the increasing splendor of his voice. The allegory was as beautiful as it was clear: Colette felt entangled in the uncertainties of her life — the love affairs, the financial problems, the couple's multiple plans. On the manuscript a crossed-out sentence expresses her anxiety: "I dare not fly away." In the margin Willy's handwriting encourages slyly, "Do continue, charming little horror."[114]

By now Colette had mustered enough courage to do what she had long wanted to do, go on stage. Colette's "maniacal love for the stage" had become her challenge. She took dance lessons with Caryatis, a modern dancer inspired by the rhythmic school of Jacques Dalcroze, who danced barefoot in a Greek tunic like Isadora Duncan, or half-naked in a leopardskin. She strengthened Colette's wish to dance unconventionally. Colette's flexible body allowed her to perform acrobatic feats. She appeared on private stages with her dog and turned down an offer to take over "an act with thirteen trained Russian greyhounds. Everything was ready, the tour's itinerary, the contracts, everything . . ."[115] but at the last minute she pulled out of the deal.

Colette wanted to be an actress, but with no classical training she would have been blocked if it had not been for the avant-garde theater, *le théâtre naturaliste,* a new trend pioneered by Lugné-Poë. He emphasized realism, simplicity, and a kind of diction that owed nothing to traditions going back to the seventeenth century, to the musical rhythm of Alexandrine verse, or to the strict technical discipline of the stars of the day — Sarah Bernhardt, De Max, and Mounet-Sully. Colette had the vitality, spontaneity, sex appeal, and daring that were the hallmarks of the new drama.

Franc-Nohain, a friend who had known Colette and Willy before the *Claudines,* wrote in 1906 that Colette could not be explained without Polaire:

> The key to Colette-Willy's behavior is Polaire . . . Before the success of the *Claudines,* Colette was a charming young woman simply more intelligent than most . . .When Claudine appeared in the bookstores, the author Willy did not make a secret of Colette's contribution to the best-seller; then Claudine went on stage and was suddenly identified with Polaire. Polaire-Claudine, Claudine-Polaire, suddenly there was no longer any reference to Colette Willy. It was very bitter to feel robbed of Claudine's personality — her own Claudine — by the triumphant Polaire. So Mrs. Colette Willy decided to recapture Claudine with Polaire's own weapons . . . Mrs. Colette Willy's first step was to

adopt Polaire's unique hairdo, Claudine's short, curly hair. Then came Polaire-Claudine dresses, next the movements, the attitudes; and it is exclusively because of Polaire's orientation to the theater and the thunderous applause which ensued that we owe Colette Willy's new orientation to the stage.[116]

There were other reasons. By 1905 *Claudine* had been upstaged by the *Maugis* series, the pseudomemoirs that sold over a half million copies. The forty editions of *Minne* could not compare with some of Les Ateliers productions. Les Ateliers was a money-making machine fueled by publicity, the end always justifying the means. Colette and Curnonsky did not always approve of Willy's ventures. Les Ateliers produced a biography of Jane Avril, *La Môme Picrate,* depicting the milieu of Toulouse-Lautrec, Degas, and the Moulin Rouge; Curnonsky complained that Willy was "messing up the chronology and the philosophy." "I told you a hundred times, I don't give a damn," answered Willy, "When I need money, I'll do anything. Don't nag me about it."[117]

Colette called these bread-and-butter books "the three francs fifty." She was tired of them; she never even considered the *Claudine* series very good literature. "I never found my first book very good, nor the the three others. With the years, I have not changed my mind and I judge the *Claudines* sternly."[118] Colette resented the frantic pace and the end-justifies-the-means mentality of Les Ateliers; she thought the theater would be an easier way for her to make a living without preventing her from writing what she wished. Willy had successfully managed Polaire's shift from the music hall to the stage. He would do the same for her.

By 1905 the Willys were living lavishly: they had horses, a carriage, and a car rented for six hundred francs a month; Jacques was being educated at an expensive public school in England; they had a very smart apartment at 177*bis* Rue de Courcelles, a country estate, and three full-time secretaries, soon joined by the musician, composer, and critic Vuillermoz. Their staff was unusual: an astonishing secretary who left Willy's correspondence to slip over to Colette's apartment to borrow mascara for his eyelashes, and a lesbian maid, Louise, who had a passion for hinges and locks. She would work on doors for hours and was a poet of sorts; she wrote lascivious poems and sent them to the young servants of the neighboring households. Colette's cook complained that she was being harassed; she had received an ode celebrating her beautiful hair along with a specific offer: "Antonine, I will pay you up to a hundred francs, and that is no joke."[119]

The round of dinners, opening nights, restaurants, and *fêtes* of all kinds intensified; Colette was now as famous as Willy. During his school breaks, Colette's thirteen-year-old stepson, Jacques, watched the couple in their everyday life. Willy, back from the theater, dinner, or some newspaper editing, still in his evening clothes (sometimes tails and white tie), would write until 2 A.M.; Colette would go straight to bed. She rose late and spent hours in her bathroom; meanwhile Willy, up at 9 A.M., had written letters, answered the phone, and received visitors in his glossy white office with short curtains over latticed windows, which "looked like a remodeled candy store."[120] His office overflowed with daily newspapers, English and German clippings, and books to review. He would joke: "I do not have the admirably tidy desk of those who never write." Colette wrote every day, four hours in the late morning and early afternoon.

Twice a week they went riding in the Bois de Boulogne; on those days Colette was ready at 9:30, elegant in her Redfern riding costume and large felt hat. They trotted down l'Allée des Acacias, where the rich and richest rode in carriages or on horseback. Jacques recalled that they were hunted by photographers as soon as they appeared.

They took their friends to the flashy Café de Paris, or to Maxim's, where Russian grand dukes, millionaires, and bankers would come to throw their gold away — no metaphor at Maxim's, where gold coins flew across the room like confetti in the grand Russian style. (When Maxim's was redecorated in the 1930s, and its seats were removed and the carpets rolled away, its nooks and crannies, cracks and crevices revealed hundreds of gold coins — a treasure trove.)

In February Colette and Henry joined the exodus to the Riviera. Aristocrats from the court of the tsar of all the Russias, nobility from the Balkan states, sultans and pashas from Egypt, Lebanon, and the Sudan with their harems locked up in luxurious villas, the listless heirs of Europe's greatest fortunes — all swarmed in the private and public balls. Some society hostesses kept up a pretext of intellectual life, patronizing concerts, plays, and poetry recitals. At one gathering Colette Willy read *Dialogues de Bêtes*. But, escorted by a decrepit Jean Lorrain, Colette loved best to plunge into the carnival dominated by the demimondaines. Willy joined in the entertainment *par excellence,* gambling at the Moorish-style, wooden casino on stilts in Nice or at the pink-and-white casino in Monte Carlo, only leaving the gambling tables for the racetracks.

They left the Riviera when they learned that Marcel Schwob was dying of pneumonia, attended by Marguerite Moréno and his Chinese companion, Ting, with whom he had sailed the southern seas.

During the funeral Colette and Willy had to support Alfred Jarry by his elbows when his knees gave way; he was devastated by grief and totally drunk.

VI

―――――――――――

THEATER AND MUSIC HALL

―――――――――――

"No actress has been promoted with such fanfare as Mme Colette Willy"
LE CRI DE PARIS

ON MAY 1, 1905, Colette and Willy legally split their financial assets. Willy, acting as his wife's impresario, started a press campaign to draw attention to Colette's new career. In June an anonymous article in *La Vie Parisienne* described a private party restricted to twenty guests given by Natalie Barney and Eva Palmer, of Huntley and Palmer Biscuits. "Electric cars brought from Paris, divorced princesses, very Parisian writers such as the Willys and Montesquiou . . . very Parisian Britishers such as Cosmo Gordon-Lennox and others with golden chains around their necks. If Oscar Wilde were still alive, he would be there."[1] They came to see Colette, in a skimpy earth-colored tunic, cast as the Greek shepherd Daphnis in a pantomime by Willy. Eva Palmer played a nymph and "Miss Gauthier-Villars" (Meg) was a flower girl.

The article had been leaked to the press. Next, Willy released a note stating, "I have decided to let the author of *Dialogues de Bêtes* start a career as an actress. To be exact, I am writing a one-act play in verse for her."[2] Nothing was left to chance; *Claudine in Paris, Le P'tit Jeune Homme,* and *Le Friquet* were playing in Paris, the provinces, and Belgium. Willy brought to bear all the weight of his popularity as a playwright to assure

Colette Willy a formula for success. With his instinct for what caught the public's fancy, Willy wrote one act with a faun as the main character. This part suited the author of *Dialogues de Bêtes,* and the faun was part of the symbolist mythology explored by Mallarmé and Debussy. Postcards of Colette Willy as "the Faun" or of *The Faun,* with Willy in coat and tails and tophat, flooded Paris. The play was performed in Natalie Barney's park; Colette, half-naked in goatskins, wore a crown of ivy and two tiny horns. "I am a faun, a tiny faun, strong and well built. I have sweet eyes and a witty smile, I know it, for when I drink in clear springs, I look at my reflection."

Natalie Barney's park was the stage for another sketch with Colette and Eva Palmer; Colette had asked Pierre Louÿs to write *Dialogue au Soleil Couchant* (Dialogue in the Setting Sun) for her. The author was among the guests. Colette, a Greek shepherd in a short tunic with naked arms and legs, was courting the shepherdess, Eva Palmer.

Colette was coached by Georges Wague, who had revolutionized the art of pantomime. Traditional pantomime, like Japanese *No* theater, used gestures and facial expressions codified and repeated by generations of mimes; Georges Wague broke with the tradition and invented a more realistic body language. He could make an audience weep for Pierrot dying of love for the unfaithful Columbine, shudder as he stabbed his rival and killed himself in a frenzy of jealousy, or laugh when he played the clown. Colette was interested in this form of silent art, part dance, part acting.

The first difficulty arose when Colette lost Natalie Barney's support. Flossie, Natalie's name in Colette and Willy's novels, was always careful not to spend money except on her own pleasures, and was reluctant to finance her lover's career beyond the walls of her garden and did not consider Colette to be a gifted actress. But Barney was not Colette's only sponsor; Renée Vivien took a keen interest in her stage career. She lived in a *hôtel particulier* that Colette described as "dark, sumptuous, everchanging,"[3] lit by candles even when broad daylight washed over its facade. Collections of antique coins were replaced by collections of rare jade, which vanished to make room for insects and exotic butterflies; only a collection of ancient musical instruments and a few precious statues of Buddha were permanent. Stained-glass windows allowed a rainbow of colors to filter through the half-closed drapes, and incense burners provided a heavily scented atmosphere. Purple was the predominant color for *la Muse aux Violettes;* her household livery was purple, purple satin lined her carriage, and purple-topped boots were worn by her footmen and coachman with white breeches and a mauve jacket.

Renée Vivien moved about draped in dark veils, like some spirit at large; she barely ate, drank ether mixed with alcohol, and used morphine. Sometimes she would leave her guests to drink alone in a closet. She would pass out suddenly, her eyes closed, her head drooping on her shoulder; then she would come out of her swoon and go on with the conversation. Colette, who feared that Vivien was destroying her health, tried to convince her to change her habits, but in vain.

Colette knew Renée Vivien quite intimately for five years; it always amazed her that Vivien never mentioned her work. Three or four times Colette caught her scribbling on her knee in the corner of a couch; she would jump up and excuse herself. Whenever she sent Colette a just-published volume of poetry, she would hide it under a bouquet in a basket of fruit. Colette never understood the deep, sad longing for death expressed in Vivien's poetry, "some of it beautiful, some less good, some magnificent, uneven like human breathing, like the rush of wind, like the pulsing of a powerful pain."[4] Few read her poems, which were on the Catholic church's index; reciting her poems on stage at La Comédie Française was still forbidden in the 1930s, since lesbian poetry was banned.

Colette sent some photographs of Renée Vivien to Sido, who was always monitoring Colette's adventures. She found her surprisingly beautiful, not at all the ugly woman portrayed by the press. Renée was agoraphobic and reluctant to meet journalists. She had asked Natalie Barney to let her former governess — a strong, tall woman — impersonate her, and word spread that the poetess was not a ravishing creature straight from Lesbos, but a horrid old hag. Renée Vivien carefully skirted scandals; in proper Edwardian style, Willy would chaperone Colette and Renée in Nice or London, where she had a flat. Colette briefly described a room she discovered in Renée's London apartment that was full of whips, chains, and other sadomasochistic paraphernalia.

Her mansion was a sapphic sanctuary. There Colette danced *La Danse du Sphinx,* Moréno recited Vivien's poems, Emma Calvé sang *Carmen,* and chamber music was played on a rare collection of ancient instruments. Masquerades and historical *tableaux vivants* were not taken lightly; when Renée Vivien decided to portray Jane Grey, Henry VIII's doomed wife, she thought she looked too fat — so she disappeared into a hotel in the Forêt de St. Germain and fasted for ten days, drinking only tea, while she walked in the woods six hours a day. Her maid, who followed her carrying coat and shawls, collapsed during the ordeal, but Renée Vivien lost ten pounds. She appeared in the tableau as a swooning Jane Grey, marching to the scaffold surrounded by her maids of honor. She had to be carried to be beheaded on a block draped with crimson silk. The executioner was portrayed by the marquise de Morny, quite convincing with an axe on her shoulder. The performance took place at the Théâtre des Arts, which Vivien had rented from Robert d'Humières.

Colette was building up a following in these amateur shows, but they were not what she had in mind. The previous summer she had tried out her dancing skills in a tour in the provinces, which had been mentioned in "Les Potins de Paris" (Paris Gossips). Vivien, even more than Barney, lived a sheltered life; neither of them liked the relentless publicity surrounding Colette and Willy. Colette finally found the right person in the marquise de Morny, Napoleon III's niece.

I Belong to Missy

Colette and Willy were on the editorial staff of a new lavish magazine, *Le Damier*. On March 27, 1905, they attended the first monthly dinner organized by the magazine. Its title was ambiguous; *le damier* meant "the checkerboard," but could also mean "pertaining to women." Willy was its music critic and signed "Henry Maugis"; Colette signed "Colette Willy."

The magazine was launched by an exclusive club, Le Cercle des Arts et de la Mode, patronized by courtesans, actresses, and members of the Jockey Club. This highly selective club was also known as Le Club Victor-Hugo. It had a large salon with a grand piano and a stage, intimate salons, and a casinolike gambling room where members played till the crack of dawn. Mathilde, the marquise de Morny, was the club's main sponsor. She was France's most notorious cross-dresser and was attracted to Colette, who reciprocated.

Sophie-Mathilde-Adèle-Denise de Morny, known as Missy, was ten years older than Colette; her family tree was a resplendent genealogy of illegitimate nobility. Her father, Duke Auguste de Morny, was the illegitimate son of Hortense, queen of Holland, and an illegitimate descendant of Louis xv. Her mother was Princess Troubetzkoï, rumored to be the tsar's illegitimate daughter.

Duke de Morny was an extremely successful businessman; there was no major commercial venture in France in which he did not have a financial interest. He created the Longchamp racetrack and the Deauville seaside resort. He loved the theater and wrote several light comedies and an *opera-bouffe* with Jacques Offenbach. He discovered Sarah Bernhardt and launched her on her career. He helped engineer the coup d'etat on December 2, 1851 that made his half brother, Louis-Napoleon, emperor of the French. When the duke de Morny died in March of 1865, he was buried with imperial honors. He left an enormous fortune to his two sons and two daughters. Missy, the youngest, was five when her mother remarried a Spanish grandee, the duke of Sesto, tutor of the boy-king Alfonso xii; Missy was raised with the royal Infantas. At eighteen she married the marquis de Belbeuf, one of the richest men in France, who reigned over an empire of textile industries. Missy had a string of highly visible lesbian affairs and she and the marquis separated after six years, agreeing never to meet again and to spend their fortunes as they wished. They did not divorce until 1903.

The marquise de Morny was the most visible cross-dresser of the lesbian establishment. She wore gray or navy tailored suits, ties, and a large pin shaped like a horseshoe, heavy with enormous emeralds. Her long legs gave her an elegant gait that could pass for a man's, but her tiny feet gave her away; although she put on several pairs of socks to fill her shoes, her aristocratic feet remained blatantly feminine. She wore a large gray felt hat and a monocle, carried a stick with a gold knob, and smoked cigars. She was perceived as outrageously shocking, yet took care not to shock; for social engagements she wore a long hooked-on skirt. When visiting friends she would take it off to reveal a full, tailored suit with pants; at her club she would unhook the skirt and leave it in the cloakroom, as a man would leave a cape.

The marquise's imperial background made her a favorite target of the Republicans and royalists, who hated this "Napoleonide." She gave them every possible cause to do so. Reckless, passionate, generous, she loved masquerades and living imaginary lives. She was one of Lorrain's characters in several of his tales and romans à clef. In an article, he showed her arriving with a retinue of women in a quiet resort by the sea. Every evening they strolled through the town smoking cigars, singing lewd songs, or staging such orgies that the residents could not sleep. In another story, in order to recapture a lover the marquise organized her own funeral, complete with flowers, candles, and notices of her demise. When her repentant lover, torn with grief, came to mourn, Missy threw aside the flowers and opened her arms to the weeping girl.

She was Catulle Mendès's *Mephistophela*, and Rachilde gave her a chilling name in her novel, *La Marquise de Sade*. "She was the erotic tourist who had seen it all, had sampled it all, haunted every flesh market, truly the slave of her eternal boredom more than her perverse tastes." She was said to have a harem, and to give fortunes to her lovers, including a copper factory to a working girl, where she came to make copper doorknobs and faucets in order to share her beloved's lifestyle. History and legend aside, Mathilde de Morny — Missy to her friends — was charming, considerate, and extremely well bred. Boulestin met Missy at the Rue de Courcelles when she came to visit the Willys. He felt he was in the presence of a woman "who without any pose had abdicated her femininity and behaved as a man quite naturally."[5]

She treated all women as a man of the world would, with indulgence, with a smile, with deference, with understanding for their weaknesses, always in a gallant and grand manner. The marquise had candidly crossed the gender border and forgotten all about it; her servants addressed her as "Monsieur le Marquis," and she liked to be called "Uncle Max" by her young friends, although she was referred to in the newspapers as "La Marquise."

She enjoyed throwing parties at which the guests wore fancy dress, all centuries confounded. Roses in large baskets were provided at each small dining table; before the hors d'oeuvres the guests would bombard each other with the fragrant ammunition. After dinner, in the mansion's spacious retreats, couples could join discreetly according to their sexual preferences.

Missy had a passion for theater and invited the leading actors and actresses of the day to perform on her private stage. She wrote plays and pantomimes, appearing as Nero (quite striking in a Roman tunic with a crown of gold laurel leaves), as an Arab sheikh, and as a Franciscan monk. She let no one forget that, although she had been raised in Spain at the strictest royal court in Europe, she had also played parts on private stages and danced the fandango. She understood Colette's longings for the theater; Mathilde de Morny became an easy pawn in the intricate game played by Colette and Willy to launch Colette's career.

On September 17, 1905, Captain Colette died. Colette and Willy drove to Châtillon for the funeral and arrived three hours late. They finally showed up at the cemetery at 5 P.M., having been delayed, they said, by mechanical incidents and because "their tires blew out three times."[6] The real cause of the delay was typical of the egotistical couple. On their way from Paris to Châtillon, Colette and Willy stopped for lunch at a country inn in Fontainebleau; the inn was pleasant, the food agreeable, and the couple felt such an irresistible urge to make love that they rented a room. They arrived just in time to see the captain's casket (covered with the Zouave's coat he had worn when he received the wound that turned a dashing thirty-year-old officer into a tax collector) lowered into the ground.

His death did not put an end to the siblings' feud; Achille prevented his mother from notifying Juliette of her stepfather's demise. Five days after the funeral Sido wrote an embarrassed letter to Juliette, lamenting that her daughter had learned about her stepfather's death from strangers. She ended her letter by reminding Juliette that she had lost her financial independence and had no personal income left. Sido pressured Juliette to give her a monthly pension and asked Colette to put pressure on her sister: "do it amicably, it is the best way to get results."[7] Machiavellian Sido instructed Colette not to tell Achille of their plan. Colette relinquished her share of her father's estate in favor of her mother; she agreed to send her one hundred francs a month. She — or Willy — faithfully carried out her obligation until Sido's death in 1912. However, ten days after her father's death, Colette asked her mother to let Willy manage her capital, as he would give her a high rate of return. "Yes, My Darling, I will entrust my funds to Willy,"[8] wrote Sido, but mused, how can Willy become rich if he pays such high interests?

Colette broke the news to her mother that she was rehearsing a play and would make her debut at the Théâtre des Mathurins. Sido was stunned: "So you are going to earn a thousand francs per performance every evening! Jesus-Mary! What a sum! I fear it will only serve to stop up some deep hole. Do tell Willy to write to me if he has a moment."[9]

The Willys had a grand plan, financed by his maternal inheritance. He was also talking to his friends about investing in his new venture.

The wealthiest of his prospective patrons was the marquise de Morny. In November of 1905 Sido wrote to her daughter in a panic, "Willy is organizing a theater of his own? Good Heavens! What a bundle he will have to put up!"[10]

The theater would be a showcase for Colette; for himself, Willy bought a racing stable with five purebred horses, including the racing champions, Rameau d'Or and Belhomme. He hired one of the best-known jockeys, Riou, but did some of the training himself, leaving Curnonsky more and more in charge of Les Ateliers. Colette and Henry were often at the races, very much at ease with the exclusive group of stable owners and breeders. Willy's passion for gambling and horses made news even in Belgium: "Today we see without any surprise, Willy the owner of Rameau d'Or and four other purebred horses, the start of his racing stable! If only Mrs. Colette Willy, the person who best knows how to make animals speak, would translate for us in a new *Dialogue,* the opinions and discourse of the horses from Willy's stable!"[11]

On February 6, 1906, Colette crossed the threshold between amateur and professional actress. She had the lead in a *mimodrame* by Francis de Croisset and Jean Noguès, *Le Désir, l'Amour et la Chimère,* at the Théâtre des Mathurins, whose director was the actress Georgette Leblanc, Maeterlinck's mistress and the Willys' old acquaintance. Boulestin played the part of an Athenian with nothing to do but walk across the stage as gracefully as he could, clad in a short Greek tunic, his arms full of flowers that he scattered on the god of love's altar. Boulestin felt terribly frustrated because his part was so short. "Never mind," said Colette, who was onstage all the time, "There is no such thing as a small part."[12]

Colette displayed her acrobatic skills, and Boulestin was awed as they rehearsed together in her studio; she would throw back her head, arch her back, and reach her ankles with her short hair. As opening night grew near everyone was in a state of excitement except Colette, who showed no sign of nervousness. Under pressure she never showed any sign of emotion; she concentrated her inner energy and unleashed it the moment she stepped onstage, determined to excel. Still, to appear before the critical audience of Tout-Paris was a challenge, and Tout-Paris was very eager to see what Colette Willy could do on stage. The curtain rose on a one-act play by Maeterlinck, *The Death of Tintagiles;* the sophisticated audience, a full house, chatted and greeted their friends, barely paying attention to the play, waiting impatiently for Colette Willy. The intermission lasted a whole hour and turned into a party. The Willys' clique was there *en masse;* a journalist noted that if an ordinary spectator had strayed into the lobby or hallways of the theater, he would have felt in the wrong place and crawled away. At last the curtain rose, revealing a Greek set. The program announced that the scene was set "in Greece in the days when mermaids haunted the seas and fauns roamed the woods."

Hidden in the bushes, the faun, Colette, watched two beautiful girls as they came with offerings of garlands and wreaths to the god of love's statue, followed by their pretty maid with baskets of blossoms. Two young Athenians tried in vain to seduce the girls, who fled; as they ran away, they dropped a mirror. The faun, in a tunic slit to his hips and barely attached to his shoulders, picked up the mirror and discovered his own beauty; he was as beautiful as the god of love himself. He decided to trick the maidens by removing the statue of the god and taking its place, carefully crowning himself with roses to hide his horns, and waited for his prey. In came the maidens with flowers for the statue; the faun leapt down and tried to kiss them. They fled; the two Athenians rushed in to their rescue, wrestling the faun to the ground and leaving him wounded and sobbing. One of the pretty maids felt sorry for the faun, knelt by him, and wiped the blood from his wounds. "Suddenly the faun seizes her and seals her lips with his brutal and divine kiss."[13] The maid rose to her feet, and her veil slipped from her head, revealing two little horns and pointed ears: the magic kiss had turned her into a faunness. The faun played his pipes and she followed him, dancing, as they both vanished into the woods.

Colette, ambiguous, intense, and passionate, seduced the audience. The marquise de Morny appeared in her box and very noticeably applauded the faun's dances. *Le Désir, l'Amour et la Chimère* was booked for twenty-one performances, a fairly long run. (Small theaters, including the Théâtre des Mathurins, changed their listings frequently, like today's movie theaters. They could be rented by private groups or by individuals who had financed a show.) After Paris, the entire cast was to give a performance in Brussels. When Colette, escorted by Boulestin, arrived at the railroad station, she found that the thrifty director, Georgette Leblanc, had bought them third-class tickets: "Art for art's sake,"[14] grumbled Colette, who paid the extra to travel first-class.

—∾—

Colette was more than ever in the public eye. On February 15, her portrait by Jacques-Emile Blanche was on the cover of *La Vie Heureuse,* a plush bi-monthly magazine. The painting itself was part of the exhibition of the *Cercle de l'Union Artistique;* it had a catchy name, *La Bourguignonne au Sein Bruni* (The Burgundian With Dark Breasts). Colette was presented as a sex symbol, with a lowcut dress about to slip off her left shoulder. Today the portrait hangs in Barcelona's Museum of Modern Art.

At the end of February Colette and Willy traveled to the Riviera; Colette was booked to dance *Le Faune* in Monte Carlo. They spent March with Renée Vivien in her Villa Cessoles in the hills above Nice. (A series of amateur snapshots shows Colette with Willy and Renée among the trees; Colette, a big bag on her shoulder, is gathering thyme and marjoram, fragrant herbs that grow wild.) She told Natalie Barney that her dance had been extremely well received in Monte Carlo. Renée Vivien, moved by Colette's beauty, wrote a poem inspired by the pantomime *La Flûte qui s'est tue,* which was published in *Flambeaux éteints* the following year. She mailed the manuscript to Natalie to give to Colette, for Renée was a very shy writer; she autographed *Une Femme m'apparut,* the book inspired by her affair with Natalie Barney, "To my little Colette from the deplorable writer, Renée Vivien." During this sun-drenched vacation Colette learned the lines of a one-act play written for her by Willy and Andrée Cocotte; in honor of their hostess, Willy named the main character, to be played by Colette, René.

In Monaco Willy spent most of his time at the gambling tables. On Mardi Gras night Colette went with Jean Lorrain and the playwright Henri Bernstein to the casino in Nice dressed as a yellow Pierrot; yellow and purple were the prescribed colors that year. The entire demimonde was there: la Belle Otéro, Emilienne d'Alençon, Liane de Pougy, and Suzanne Derval. Colette danced with Eve Lavallière, who was dressed as a purple Pierrot, until a gendarme stopped them "for propriety's sake."[15]

On March 30, she was back in Paris to act in Willy's play *Aux Innocents les mains pleins* (Fortune Smiles on the Innocents) at the Théâtre Royal at 23 Rue Royale. It was a typical *petit théâtre,* more like a cabaret with a minimal stage. The men who patronized these theaters came after dinner in black tie; at intermission the actresses joined them. It was smart to be seen in one of these little showcases, which attracted journalists for the latest gossip.

The show started at 9:15. The first turn was all songs by a chanteuse with her own following, which left with her. Then came a sketch full of risqué jokes, then a mini-operetta with romantic waltzes. The fourth turn was a comedy written by a young protégé of the marquise de Morny, the playwright-actor Sacha Guitry. At ten o'clock the curtain rose on Colette, who was scheduled as the star of the evening.

The scene was in a bar. Willy had written the part of a playboy for Colette; she came onstage as René in a brown suit from Savile Row. Boulestin, the bartender, was to speak in broken English. He introduced René to Suzanne, a pretty gold digger who seduced him. The public booed and cheered every time René kissed Suzanne; the direct allusions to Colette's way of life delighted the audience. Willy's dialogue was intended to be outrageous and indiscreet. Colette had her own circle of followers; however, certain days were stormy. Willy wrote to Curnonsky that the smart set of young men, who were accustomed to her private performances in chic drawing rooms, did not like to see Colette turning into a professional actress and had decided to punish her. They whistled and tried to stop the show, but Missy and Willy had put their own people in the audience and the show went on in an atmosphere of scandal.

The marquise did not like Colette dressed as an elegant gigolo. "I don't like to see a woman dressed up as a man,"[16] she told Colette, explaining that women did not know how to walk properly; they never swung their legs from the hip, they always bent their knees, and they did not take long enough strides. Nevertheless, she came several times and never passed unnoticed; the press never failed to mention that she was Napoléon III's niece and the queen of Holland's granddaughter.

The play, breaking with *travesti* tradition, was openly erotic; the two actresses performed the seduction scene with realism — that was the scandal, not that Colette played a man's part. On the French stage *travesti* had been an accepted theatrical convention since the eighteenth century, when Beaumarchais stated that the role of Cherubin in his *Marriage of Figaro* could only be played by a young woman. The *travesti* became extremely popular in the nineteenth century; on the French stage the actresses in "sexual disguise" remained so throughout the play, unlike "the breeches part" on the English stage, in which the character's gender was always revealed at the end of the play. Sarah Bernhardt gave the *travesti* its *lettres de noblesse*. She maintained that had she been a man, she would have had a greater career, since the most complex roles were written for men — with only one exception, Racine's *Phèdre*. She performed twenty-seven leading male parts from Lorenzaccio to Hamlet, excluding from her repertoire roles such as Don Juan or Romeo, for she insisted in her *Art du Théâtre* that *travesti* can be performed only if the intellectual dominates the physical.

Colette took the *travesti* one step further; she crossed the threshold Sarah refused to cross. Colette and her impresario husband knew that at thirty-three she could only succeed by blazing new trails. Colette exploited to the fullest what was then described as "her feline grace," what our nonmetaphoric age calls sex appeal. The provocation was glaring; "that exceptional couple" was teasing, taunting, and defying public morals by pushing even further the limits of tolerance.

Colette and Willy left for Monts-Boucons. Jacques did not see any change in his parents' relationship; the atmosphere was as relaxed and as casual as usual. In the evening Colette would read some new dialogues between Kiki-la-Doucette and Toby-Chien, or Willy would read Colette the first chapters of *Jeux de Prince*, the next best-seller from the novel factory. The Willys' way of life was draining all the money they made; Colette spent without restraint, Willy without concern. They did not pay their tailors or dressmakers; their credit was apparently unlimited, wrote Boulestin. There was never enough to meet postdated checks and promissory notes. Colette would later accuse Willy of hoarding money, but his secretary "could not think where and why."[17] Debts kept piling up: internal revenue demanded arrears of payment amounting to 475.87 francs. Willy's racing stable was an expensive venture and none of his horses ever won a race. His compulsive gambling made things worse. Creditors harried Willy in increasing numbers, but he was skilled at the aristocratic game of putting them off. Not paying one's debts was a sport practiced for centuries by the high and mighty; it had unwritten rules on when to refinance, when to pay a percentage, when to woo, and when to threaten one's creditors.

Colette was taken to court by the exclusive couturier Redfern; the judgment was in his favor and she was sentenced to pay 625 francs in principal plus interest, Redfern's expenses, and a daily fine until she had paid off her debt. She let things stand as they were and paid nothing.

Missy invited Colette, Willy, and Meg to Le Crotoy in Normandy. Missy was convinced that she lived at her villa Belle-Plage in casual simplicity. She would arrive in her red car with a chauffeur and two maids — the staff who had come by train was awaiting her. Missy had her favorite guests, whom she called her three sons: the young actor-playwright Sacha Guitry, who remained her devoted and lifelong friend; a Rumanian aristocrat, Prince Georges Ghika; and Auguste Hériot, a dashing millionaire whose family owned, among other assets, *Les Grands Magasins du Louvre*. Missy appreciated character and beauty. When she turned her attention to Colette, Willy remarked shrewdly that the marquise was old enough to adopt her.

Colette kept up her acrobatic training. There were parallel bars installed on the beach, and she and Missy proceeded with their body-tuning routine. (Missy had a set of parallel bars and a trapeze installed at the foot of her bed in each of her *garçonnières* and was known to impose her fitness program on her lovers.) There were very few bathers on the beach; the women wore long bathing suits with skirts and ruffles to hide the shape of their bodies. Colette shocked everyone by walking into the surf in a tightly fitting bathing suit while the marquise, in her usual breeches and jacket, waited on the beach, ready to throw a bathrobe over Colette's dripping body.

Not far from Le Crotoy a small wooden casino and two hotels in a pine forest formed a modest complex known as Paris-Plage. Willy negotiated with the casino management for a few performances of *Aux Innocents les mains pleines*. The marquise moved all her guests to Le Grand Hôtel. Since she had no social obligations in her summer residence, she wore only men's clothes — no hook-on skirt. She drank her favorite green Chartreuse as she smoked an afterdinner cigar, and the waiters called her "Monsieur." At dinner Frank Richardson, the theater manager, looked at Missy and asked, "Who is that elderly pederast?" When apprised of the situation, he said his party would go to the play "just to see Colette trousering."

It was the last summer of Paris-Plage. A few months later rows of luxury hotels, golf courses, and a new casino sprang from the lonely sand dunes. The fashionable resort of Le Touquet was born, financed by venture capitalists led by Paris Singer, heir to the sewing-machine fortune.

That summer Colette met Léon Hamel, who would appear as the fictitious character Hammond in *The Vagabond*. He was fifteen years older than Colette, tall, slim, and extremely elegant. A good tennis player and admirable dancer, he had traveled extensively in the Far East and had lived for seventeen years in Egypt, where he had been appointed by Le Crédit Foncier to supervise their interest in the *Deirah Sanieh*, the group that managed Ismaïl Pasha's holdings. He had just returned from Egypt to settle in the Rue de Florence in Paris. To be near Missy he bought a villa at Le Crotoy. He took a keen interest in Colette, becoming her confidant and financial advisor.

Colette's part in *Aux Innocents les mains pleines* had been too controversial, too far from mainstream naughtiness; it was a faux pas. Colette asked Count Montesquiou for his help in refocusing her stage image on the role of the faun. Robert de Montesquiou wrote, in a belated review in *Le Figaro,* that he had enjoyed the pantomime danced by Madame Colette Willy in February. He compared Colette's movements to the voluptuous and rhythmical ones of the paintings on Etruscan vases, describing her as being "extremely refined" and "a little frightening."[18] He praised the little brown faun, who vibrated from the tips of her painted fingers to the tips of her toes, but it was Colette's eyes — her strange, dark, inquisitive, and mocking glance — that struck him as extraordinary. He commented that pure artistic pleasure was seldom found on stage, but that Colette had given him one of those rare moments. Colette the dancer had found a champion in the most refined and sophisticated member of Tout-Paris.

She had met him in the salon of Madeleine Lemaire in the summer of 1895. Obnoxious and egoistical, the count, whose ancestors went as far back as the Crusades, maintained he was descended from the earliest kings of France and considered the Bourbons to be usurpers. Extremely handsome, thin, and nervous, he dressed in colors only he would dare: lilac, blue, almond, and white, with ties in shimmering pastel shades. After his thirty-fifth birthday he switched to shades of gray and kept only the muted rainbows of his ties and a few priceless rings. A descendent of d'Artagnan — that famous character from *The Three Musketeers* — he established a pattern of incredible refinement and lavish style, surrounding himself with writers and artists who imitated his manners and boldness. No one could outdo the count in sophistication; he was the perfection of French dandyism. He hated Oscar Wilde, "that Antinoüs of the ugly."

Montesquiou had liked young Colette from the start. The "Arbiter of Elegance," "The Commander of Suave Fragrances," as he called himself, the ultimate judge of excellence and propriety (or so he thought) stood by Colette when she was treading the slippery road that led her out of high society's fold into the wasteland of the outcast. He bowed to no one's opinion and did his best to impose his own. He was cruelly witty;

he would sacrifice a friendship for a *mot,* an epigram, a one-liner. He admired Whistler, "the Great Aesthete," and put into practice *The Gentle Art of Making Enemies.* He was addicted to the aristocratic pleasure of giving offense, and socially assassinated people with ridicule.

Always in need of money, he stopped at nothing to obtain it; when Verlaine was sick, destitute, and dying in a hospital, the count set up a fund and collected one hundred thousand francs — which he kept, giving Verlaine a beautiful cashmere scarf, because he was too sick to need money. But when he heard that Marcel Schwob's cat was ill, he dispatched Yturri, his private secretary, to visit the ailing pet and bring it delicacies. He used his knowledge of art and his name to swindle unsuspecting buyers. He had rare keepsakes of dubious origin: a birdcage that had belonged to the historian Jules Michelet, the bullet that had killed Pushkin in his duel, a tear shed by Lamartine in a vial, and a cigarette butt smoked by George Sand. One of his famous acquisitions was the pink marble bath of Louis XIV's mistress, Madame de Montespan. He claimed that he had discovered it in a convent garden, where the unsuspecting nuns washed their clothes in a tub full of sinful memories; he exchanged it for a pair of his own slippers, convincing the gullible sisters that they had belonged to the pope.

As art critic of *Le Figaro,* the count wielded power. When he brought an article to the right-wing newspaper, all the editorial staff rushed to greet him, and as he left, stopping on every step to tell startling stories about Tout-Paris, they followed him down the stairs. He helped promote art nouveau, which, after fading away around 1900, left in its wake the entwined entrances to the Parisian Metro, the Grand Palais staircase, and the works of Gallé and Lalique. Montesquiou discovered the short-lived Aubrey Beardsley, whose drawings of startling daring and perfection, inspired by Japanese art, became fashionable at the end of the century.

Colette had "an almost guilty passion" for Beardsley. The concept of androgyny, so central to her work, is the essence of Beardsley's art. She told Montesquiou, referring to *La Toilette d'Hélène,* an illustration from *Under the Hill,* published in *The Savoy* in January 1896, "the drawings of this rather mad and very young man correspond so closely to what is hidden deep in me."[19] In May of 1907 Montesquiou, stressing their common admiration for Beardsley, wrote to Colette, "I find, and please do take this as a compliment, singular similarities between your characters and his, the same bizarre elegance, the same apparent candor in their

perversity, the same way of obtaining by some graceful gesture the abso-
lution of what one was to blame."[20]

She was a frequent guest at Montesquiou's *Pavillon des Muses,* where
his taste for the bizarre led to many surprises; at one party the lights
were dimmed, gusts of perfume wafted into the room, and a turtle, its
shell encrusted with diamonds, traced a luminous trail. Montesquiou patronized Fauré, Debussy, Verlaine, and Mallarmé; Paul Valéry dedicated
Introduction to the Method of Leonardo da Vinci to him. Sarah Bernhardt,
sheathed in gold or silver gowns, recited the count's poetry, as did
Marguerite Moréno, dressed in Liberty style. Colette performed at least
once at the Pavillon des Muses and in a letter informed the count she
had perfected "a little act" he might find amusing.

A New Star

On the first of October Colette made her debut in *La Romanichelle* (The
Gypsy) on the stage of a big music hall, at Olympia. She was daringly
naked in the gypsy's rags. The public was not accustomed to bare skin;
dancers or mimes appeared clad in veils, their busts covered with jeweled
breast-plates and skirts split to the hips, presenting only "make-believe"
nudity. They wore pink cotton tights, flesh-colored leotards, and bodices
laced to the neck; some wore undertights with pads woven into the fabric
that added curvaceous forms to the leanest body. They were so modestly
covered from toe to chin that only by a stretch of imagination could the
public believe they were gazing at the actual body of the performer.

Willy had prepared the media beforehand for Colette's next move;
he had coauthored with Curnonsky *Chaussettes pour Dames,* pleading for
bare skin on stage. The book was illustrated with a photograph of
Colette Willy as the scantily dressed faun; Colette was the first dancer to
do away with tights and leotard on the stage of a popular music hall.

La Romanichelle was a *mimodrame,* a long and elaborate pantomime;
Willy had coauthored the text with Georges Wague and Paul Frank, a
mime who owned the Théâtre Royal; Edouard Mathé had composed
the music. Prompted by Willy, who mailed him a detailed letter on what
should be said, Curnonsky reviewed *La Romanichelle* in glowing terms
in *Paris-Qui-Chante.*

Madame Colette Willy will draw all Paris to the Olympia. Her famous name, her literary reputation, her social status, her talent, her beauty have made her one of the greatest stars any music-hall director has ever discovered. Nothing that Madame Colette Willy does can leave anyone indifferent, the passionate attention of the public is all hers. But many don't accept the idea that she is a dancer, a mime, because she is one of the most delightful French writers. Everyone knows the importance of her participation in the novels that are worldwide best-sellers, the *Claudines*, the *Minnes*, and she has signed the *Dialogues de Bêtes* which will remain one of the most original works written in our language ... The public considers her as a great author, a true master of the written word, one of our most perfect writers. Now here she is charming but unexpected, a savage little gypsy, barely covered with rags which let us admire her white flesh. That is enough to stun the cream of society.

Curnonsky underlined the originality of Colette's performance: "She appeared. She wore no tights and the public gasped. Her beautiful legs were bare. She is not the first to dare nudity, so does Isadora Duncan. Colette is beautiful, her beauty is strange, disturbing. She brings to her part as the gypsy, the keen insight which she has as a writer. She displays the animal sensuality, the savage tenderness of those wild gypsies who come and go as they wish." Curnonsky urged "all those who idolize Claudine to go and cheer Colette Willy in her new endeavor."[2]

The new trend on the Parisian stage was the *Théatre de la Nature* (Theater of Nature), based on the assumption that man was born to be naked; the great chic was to discard as many clothes as society would permit. Amateur performers appeared on private stages dressed in strips of fur, leopardskins being the favorite, or wreaths of leaves or flowers; to justify this nude trend, pantomime and dance themes were borrowed from antiquity or exotic cultures. This return to "the state of nature" promoted an escalation of eroticism, which slid from the wealthiest layers of society to society at large; Colette was instrumental in that process. By appearing "in the nude" at the Olympia she was doing nothing more than performing the erotic, private *fêtes* of Parisian high society for the general public. Still, their definition of nudity differed. In Renée Vivien's drawing room in the Avenue du Bois (today's Avenue Foch)

Colette danced *La Danse du Sphinx,* one of her great successes. If the evening was a private party for women only, she danced entirely nude; if not, she dressed in leather straps, jewels, and transparent veils.

Colette's success on the professional stage added glamor to her appearances in private salons; to *La Danse du Sphinx,* she added *La Danse du Serpent Bleu* (The Dance of the Blue Snake). She would arrive in a horse-drawn carriage at the gate of one of the Avenue du Bois mansions in the middle of a party. The butler would take her fur coat, while she remained in her blue veils, leather belt, and brassiere studded with jewels until the show began. Pantomimes had become as popular with the sophisticated crowd as chamber music, avant-garde recitals of poetry by stars such as Sarah Bernhardt, (who charged the stiff fee of fifteen hundred francs) or Mata Hari's Oriental dances, which she performed sometimes in turquoise-studded leather bands, sometimes in the nude. Yvette Guilbert, the witty chanteuse, would sing one or two of her satirical songs, lash out at high society, and leave with one thousand francs. No wonder the stage attracted Colette, who had a passion for money that Willy called "peasantlike." She wrote to Georges Wague, "I know I am a tough bargainer."[22]

Colette danced with a mesmeric animal vitality, noted by all who saw her; she leaped, twisted, crawled, glided. She knew everyone in the audience; all the men had met her in a salon, at a concert, at the theater, or at a party, where they had bowed and kissed her hand in the common gesture of polite greeting. They watched her with ambiguous feelings. Women sitting on gilt chairs, stiff in their corsets and long skirts, followed her movements with dismay. Colette was secure, healthy, strong, and free. The rhythm of the music, the soft light playing on her body, changing her into sculpture as she struck a harmonious attitude, gave her a sensuous pleasure. Controversial Colette was at the center of Tout-Paris's eternal gossip. She possessed a sex appeal that was hers alone. Writers sent her their books with flattering words. Abel Bonnard, an ultraconservative who would become the Vichy government's minister of education during World War II, sent her *Les Familiers:* "To Madame Colette who may sufficiently like animals to appreciate these." From the opposite side of the social spectrum came *Yvé Jourdan,* a novel by Liane de Pougy: "I offer this to Colette as a token of admiration for her beautiful eyes, so full of wit but reflecting her heart."

Colette encouraged Missy to take lessons from Georges Wague. On November 17, 1906, an article in *Le Journal* aroused the curiosity of

Tout-Paris: "The ex-Marquise de Belbeuf Plays a Part in a Pantomime."
The headline adroitly avoided printing Missy's name, so as not to antag-
onize the Mornys, but did antagonize the divorced marquis de Belbeuf.
The heading read: "In the marquise's mansion, a reporter from Le
Journal watches a rehearsal of La Romanichelle, in which she plays the
part of a painter."

The journalist Fernand Hauser, tipped off by Willy, came to Missy's
mansion in the Rue Georges-Ville. Colette met him in the drawing
room and in a carefully rehearsed scene, immediately attacked, asking,
"What does it matter to you if the marquise has decided to be in a pantomime with me? She is going to perform in a private club. It is none of
the newspaper's business." At this point the marquise, clad in dark velvet
with a palette in her hand, walked in and gently said in her sweet voice,
"Oh! This is the gentleman from Le Journal, what can I tell you? I play
tomorrow at the Cercle des Arts et de la Mode and Thursday at the
Cercle Charras. I enjoy it, it is very amusing, but why inform your
readers?" Willy walked in and chided the marquise: "Why try to resist a
reporter? If you do not give him your picture, he will find one anyhow."
Missy gave the reporter an interview; she loved to be onstage and had
often played in comedies in Spain. She was going to join Colette in La
Romanichelle to please friends who had begged her to do so, but only as
an amateur. Then she added that her stage name was "Yssim," her name
read backwards. The reporter had a scoop and questioned the marquise
further. Would she appear in a music hall before the general public?
Missy hesitated, then said, "I haven't thought about that." Colette inter-
jected promptly, "Write that she has not even thought of such a thing,"
hammering out every syllable. The marquise went on in her low voice,
"And what are you going to write about me? You are certainly going to
say that I am a very poor performer." The reporter replied, "That would
be unfair, I have never seen you on stage." Missy asked kindly, "Would
you like to see a rehearsal?"

In the drawing room, with Napoleon frozen in all his imperial glory
in a marble bust next to the piano, the rehearsal began, directed by
Georges Wague. Vuillermoz was at the piano and Willy, seated next to
the reporter, told him what he wanted Paris to know, emphatically
praising both women. Colette, thinking he was overdoing it, looked at
him sternly, and he quipped, "When she was married to me, she never
frowned at me like that."[23] Everyone laughed. Fernand Hauser wrote

that he could not help but sincerely admire their artistry; both were as good as professionals, both in command of their movements. He was impressed by the ease with which Missy wore her masculine attire and played her part. He had three words to describe her, "She is perfect." The reporter was given a picture to publish with his interview. This picture was to whip up a storm of gossip; Colette, her head resting tenderly on Missy's shoulder, looks at her; Missy, holding Colette's hand to her heart, gazes lovingly into her eyes.

In October 1906 *Le Cri de Paris* announced Colette and Willy's separation: "There will be good copy forthcoming for a new *Claudine,* no doubt: *Claudine Divorcée* and after that, certainly the two sides of this story, as when Alfred de Musset and George Sand split and we had two confessions, *She and He* and *He and She.* Or this time wouldn't it rather be *She and She,*"[24] a clear allusion to Colette's involvement with Missy. Boulestin gave an account of those days: "The autumn brought in its wake dark, alarming clouds. I soon realized a storm was brewing. It started, as these things do, by discussions, indiscretions, unpleasant paragraphs in the press . . . Colette was morose, Willy bad-tempered, our amusing days over . . . We had days and weeks of unsettled weather, so to speak, followed by a temporary calm. Then one day, without any preparation, Willy told me they had decided to separate and that Colette was leaving him."[25]

A month later, *Le Cri de Paris* carried an article on the couple's love affairs under the provocative title "All in the Family."

> At the opening night of *Mademoiselle Josette*, Colette, seated in the front row with La Marquise, was assailed by friends who enquired, "Where is Willy?"
>
> "There he is, a few rows behind us, with his young girlfriend."
>
> "???"
>
> "You will easily spot her, she is my exact opposite, a gorgeous, chubby blond."
>
> Thereupon, the girlfriend comes to shake hands with Colette and so does Willy, who brings a box of candied fruit, which is enjoyed by the family. The show goes on![26]

On November 5 Colette, using her right to respond, sent a letter which was published on December 5.

Sir,

I have always read your articles with pleasure, a rather frequent pleasure since you have been spoiling me for some time. What a shame you gave one of your wittiest papers the title, "All In the Family." This gives Willy, who is my friend, the Marquise and myself, as well as this peaceful and nice little dancer whom Willy calls Meg, the appearance of despicable philandering. You have hurt the feelings of at least three of us. Do not link in the minds of your readers in such an intimate way two couples who have arranged their lives in the most normal manner I know, which is, according to their pleasure.

I send you my regards,
Colette Willy[27]

Colette's relationship with Missy was now in the open, spread by *Le Cri de Paris*. Her cheerful acceptance of Willy's girlfriend, Meg Villars, was another shocking statement. No woman ever defied public opinion as directly as Colette. Her conclusion could have been a quote from Fourier's *Amourous World*. It was a statement of Colette's deeply felt philosophy that pleasure creates the only acceptable rule of behavior.

Colette was writing a new novel. She wanted to call it *The Vagabond* but settled for *Retreat from Love*, (La Retraite Sentimentale) a much more romantic title suggested by her publisher, Alfred Valette. It was the last of the *Claudine* ones, Claudine's farewell to Renaud. She has grown sadder and wiser; her husband Renaud dies; she stays alone in Casamène with her pets and feels her past slip away as she heals slowly with the blossoming of spring. The last pages of the novel are among the most beautiful Colette ever wrote. There is a poignant feeling of fleeting joys and discretion in the face of sorrow.

Willy had added in his tiny, thin handwriting a few corrections or suggestions on the manuscript begun in 1905 and completed late in 1906. At the end of the prologue, Willy indicated that a sentence should be cut, "Stop right here, my child-genius." At the end of the manuscript Colette wrote, "I have not lost my love." "Neither have I," wrote Willy in the margin. [28]

In some ways the book was prophetic; Colette killed off her hero Renaud, knowing that the character he embodied could never be revived.

Gone were the days of the bicycle rides along La Marne, the picnics, the nights spent in the clatter of *L'Echo de Paris*'s and *Le Journal*'s smoky editorial rooms smelling of ink, gone the vacations at Belle-Isle en Mer, gone the days of Renaud's passionate lovemaking, when at times Claudine wished that old age would mellow her husband's lust. Renaud had become sick and impotent, and "Here I am full of energy never entirely exhausted . . . He loves me and suffers in silence a pain which is humiliation because I don't want what he offers and I accept neither his tender, clever hands nor his mouth which gave me so many delights . . . My nerves and my decency are revolted when I imagine him acting for my sake the part of a complacent and insensible instrument." Yet Claudine did not want to leave him — "O my freedom which I refuse" — and hoped that in the end "everything will turn out right."[29]

For several years Colette and Willy clung to the belief that their love still endured; Colette offered Willy a chance to go to South America together to start anew and recapture the authenticity of things past. She wrote him letters telling him she could not live in the same town and yet be separated from him. They saw their separation as a charade, convinced they were acting for the press and their readers, that the lines of that story could be rearranged at will. After *Retreat from Love* and Renaud's death, Willy referred to Colette as "my widow" and to himself as "the late Willy."

In *Retreat from Love,* more than in any of her other works, Colette analyzed the antagonistic forces at work in the core of her personality: Claudine, "proud," "free," and "chaste"; Annie, the nyphomaniac "slave of [her] body," who confessed, "It's my body that thinks" and "my skin has a soul"; and violent, wild Willette Collie, the lesbian dancer who beats up her lovers or their boyfriends.

At the end of *Retreat from Love,* only Colette's and Henry's dark personae survived: Henry Maugis — libertine, manipulator, physically and morally ruined — and Annie, who revels in brief encounters with "Marcel, Paul, Chose, Machin, the little driver, the bellboy at the palace, the high school student from Stanislas . . . ,"[30] and a famous tenor, and a famous pantomime actor.

Back from Le Crotoy, Colette moved out of the Rue de Courcelles and rented an apartment at 44 Rue de Villejust (today's Rue Paul-Valéry) in an expensive neighborhood close to the Arc de Triomphe and next to

Missy. A year later a lease dated September 27, 1907, bore Colette's signature as renter and her brother Achille Robineau-Duclos's as owner. The quarterly rent of two hundred francs was extremely low for the location, and ownership by Achille, who lived in Châtillon, of an apartment in the backyard of Missy's residence raises questions. Either Colette bought it with her "stashed away fifty thousand francs," or, most probably, Missy bought it for her; Colette did not want Willy to know about it. She moved in with her maid, Francine. Missy paid Colette's rent and gave her five hundred francs a month as pocket money; most of the time Colette lived with Missy and used her apartment as a *pied-à-terre*.

The house's backyard bordered on the garden of 22 Avenue du Bois, Renée Vivien's residence; Colette had only to push a gate to reach Vivien's door. At the end of the garden, Vicomte Robert d'Humières had a small bachelor apartment. He was the director of the Théâtre des Arts. Edith Wharton, who had taken an immediate liking to him, revealed in *Backward Glance* that he was a circumspect homosexual, a fact known only to a few, including his somewhat nervous wife. Colette, who made no mystery of her bisexuality, never gave away any of her friends' sexual preferences, unlike Lorrain or Willy, who exposed high society's mores using barely transposed names. But she enjoyed provoking them. Colette described a dinner for twenty-four at which, taunting her audience, she bit into an apple, rejecting knife and fork, and intentionally sending shudders down the table. Turn-of-the-century society could accept any kind of debauchery, but never a breach of manners. The marquise and Renée Vivien, who had been presented at the court of Saint James, cheered; Liane de Pougy found Colette "vulgar." But Colette manipulated her entourage. Later she would tell young Francis Carco: First become famous, then do whatever you please. At another dinner Colette arrived with a lamp and placed it in front of her plate; Renée Vivien burst into tears and said she would never forgive her. A basket full of peaches arrived the next day with a letter begging forgiveness: "Come back for dinner, bring our friends."

Paniska

On November 28 Colette appeared in *Pan,* an ambitious three-act half-drama, half-pantomime written by the Belgian poet Charles Van Lerberghe, with music by Robert Haas. Opening night at the Théâtre Marigny on the Champs-Elysées was booked to the last *strapontin,* those uncomfortable, armless and backless folding seats.

Pan was a philosophical play, an attack on all taboos. The author, borrowing from Nietzsche the notion that Christianity had destroyed all the joy of the senses experienced in pagan antiquity, advocated a return to nature symbolized by Pan, the god of nature; he celebrated the rebirth of pagan rites and the eradication of all religious dogma. The play reflected Colette's own deeply felt philosophy; Van Lerberghe seemed to have written the part of Paniska just for her. The play was billed as "profound and daring"; the publicity was enormous, focusing on the fact that Paniska, the girl who falls in love with Pan, would appear in a bacchanal in the final act, crowned with vines and in the nude. Tout-Paris whipped up a maelstrom of gossip, since according to the daily *L'Intransigeant,* the marquise de Morny, under her stage name "Yssim," was to play the part of Pan. At the last moment, however, she panicked, and Georges Wague took over the part.

Lugné-Poë had cast Colette as Paniska without considering anyone else after seeing her in *La Romanichelle.* As for her Burgundian accent, Lugné-Poë said he could rid her of it in one day. He was convinced she was the only actress who could communicate the exhilarating joy of Paniska, wild with love and sensuous delight, as she led the dancers in a celebration of wine and roses after her wedding with Pan.

Intellectual Tout-Paris shared the theater with Tout-Lesbos. Boxes were filled with short-haired women wearing mannish tailored suits with flat skirts; some sported monocles.

The set revealed a hut in the woods. Pan was asleep; a shepherd and his wife were seated on two stools facing each other; Paniska, their daughter, stood center stage, lit by the fire of the stone fireplace; gypsies lay prostrate on the floor. "Paniska contemplates Pan and the slumbering gypsies; she raises her hands to heaven, then slowly brings them down to her temples; she goes to the door and gazes at the night." The dialogue started with mysterious hints about the death of God and the beauty of spring. Then a child entered, bearing a lantern in the shape of the moon, followed by three wise men bearing gifts of honey, wine, figs, grapes, and incense. A camel and two panthers, "animals dear to Pan," followed them onstage; the gypsies started dancing. Then philosophy took over in what the press unanimously described as "dull dialogues." A mayor, a priest, and a game warden, symbolizing the establishment, exchanged trite ideas. The ideological part of the play bored the public, who started to boo. Then Colette danced, and Tout-Lesbos cheered. Missy was very noticeable as she moved from box to box, kindling the enthusiasm of the supporting troops.

Everyone eagerly awaited the scene in which the gypsies would undress Paniska for her wedding to Pan. The text in the program was specific: "The gypsies take off the pantherskin worn by Paniska and throw a transparent veil over her under which she appears nude. She kneels before the god Pan."[31] Colette struck a few artistic attitudes; Tout-Lesbos went into ecstasy. The critic of *Le Rire* described the scene: "She made a last entrance in a very short pantherskin with a tail curled round her plump legs and then she danced one of her little dances for us — By Jove! — This was worth the trip! Never had I understood so clearly what the triumph of Nature was all about . . . There was applause and a few catcalls by some splenetic people who want success to be the reward of long years of studies, not of pure carnal appeal. *Pan* ended in an apotheosis." There were sixty-eight curtain calls. The marquise thought that was not enough; she would have liked to see "the curtain rise more than a hundred times."[32] The play was a flop, but Colette herself was a tremendous success.

After its Parisian debut, *Pan* went on tour to the Théâtre du Parc in Brussels. A Belgian paper published an interview with Colette:

> A strange little woman, a mane of hair hiding her forehead, a pretty face, a body beautiful enough to enchant the most blasé amateur of women. She told me, "In Paris I danced in a leopard skin but in Brussels the public demands a whole leotard from neck to ankles. I hate this artificial skin."
>
> "Are you afraid of a stormy audience?"
>
> "No, I was hoping for more noise in Paris. I am ready for any form of dramatic art: pantomime, dance, comedy, drama. I love the theater."
>
> Monsieur Gauthier-Villars's wife has earned a reputation in Brussels as a talented writer, as an actress, and even more as a very eccentric person, with all the gossip around her, with her legend as the true model for Claudine and Paniska.[33]

On December 4 *Le Patriote* warned its readers of the play's antireligious and immoral character and said that Colette Willy would appear without leotard or tights. The theater was besieged. Two long lines formed at the box office, people bought standing room, the theater overflowed, and police were posted to control the crowd. But Colette wore the legal cotton bodice and tights; the mostly masculine audience was disappointed, and some asked for a refund. Finally the dance, the music, and the dialogue overcame the frustration and the show turned out to be a success. *Le Patriote,* however, had reservations; Colette's dances were too lewd.

Colette's Belgian family was divided when it came to her new career, and Colette, escorted by Missy and several young actresses, blazed a trail of scandals in Brussels. Jules Landoy, her witness when she married Willy, refused to see her; Raphaël, who loved the theater and performed his own sketches in the cabaret *Le Diable au Corps,* enjoyed his notorious cousin's company and invited her to his home.

Success brought with it a new group of fans. Among the young men who fell in love with Colette was a Belgian count, Sylvain Bonmariage, whose father was a close friend of Georges Clémenceau's. He was nineteen when he saw Colette on the stage for the first time. The smitten Bonmariage wrote:

> When I first saw her, she danced. I use the word for its aesthetic meaning it implies that as an artist, Colette expressed herself by dancing. Exactly as David danced before the Ark, Colette danced before her contempories, or, to say it better, she danced before life. Colette's perverse and disturbing charm were the result of a constant arousal of her own senses. Her total lack of modesty set free her talent for introspection which I consider as even greater than the extraordinary introspective powers of Marcel Proust. Colette was the admirable, the unique, the sublime Paniska . . . She danced love the way she made love in reality.[34]

Fifty years later, after a long career in journalism as editor in chief of political newspapers and an honorable career as a playwright, Bonmariage published a book about his long relationship with Colette and Willy. He still cherished his memories: "After a passionate scene, Colette, who was half-naked, repaired to the wings glistening with sweat. She brought a strange odor with her, a fragrance that I had never noticed anywhere else and which still lingers in my nostrils when I think about it." Thérèse Robert, a young actress, all dimples and curls, and one of Colette's lovers, was quick to explain, "She has the unexpected odor of a man, and that makes her so thrilling. The magic of her seductiveness lies in this bizarre fragrance."[35] Bonmariage thought that her magic lay in her way of moving as if offering herself. Spellbound, he thought his friend, the sculptor Bourdelle, would be inspired by Colette and arranged a meeting, but Bourdelle, famous for his Rubens-like statues, was not impressed.

Colette placed Thérèse Robert in Bonmariage's care; she wrote her "passionate and indecent letters that sent Thérèse dreaming and sighing."[36] She joined the couple for a trip to Holland as a trio. Bonmariage had literary ambitions and was broke, so Colette channeled him to Willy to do some ghostwriting.

Willy had settled at 6 Rue Chambiges. He observed what was happening with mixed feelings; the music hall seemed to be paved with gold for his "dear depraved kid"; he had handed her himself over to Missy and did brilliant public-relations work for her, but he felt like the Apprentice Sorcerer. In a letter to Curnonsky he complained, "You are the only one who knows how much I am annoyed that Colette is in such idiotic shows. If I had the money, she would never appear in any of Paul Frank's plays. [La Romanichelle]."[37] To Vuilleremoz he wrote that, after all, he missed her terribly, much more than he dared admit to himself; he was bored without her. "Well, I hear our divorce is on its way," he told Curnonsky who, over the next two years, would be asked repeatedly to persuade Colette that a separation was enough and a divorce not necessary. Meg had moved in with Willy; he wanted to substantiate the fiction that Meg was his daughter and, in a barely coherent letter to Curnonsky, he wrote, "Old Pal, tell everyone that Meg is indeed my daughter, just as Jacques is my son." Then he added that Meg was "a little darling, who asked for a spanking whenever she spent too much time on her curls, or too much money on chocolates."[38] Willy slipped into some lewd details about the effects of spanking on their lovemaking.

Not everyone approved of what was happening to the famous couple; friends felt they were both on the wrong track and tried to bring them back together. Francis Jammes was concerned about their salvation; he sent them his latest book, *L'Eglise habillée de feuilles* (The Church Dressed in Leaves) and wrote that he could "indicate a refuge for Willy's and Colette's souls."[39] In April 1906 Colette replied she had stopped writing to him because of her career in show business, "and that humiliates me forever in your opinion . . . You see, I know my place. The fact that I have played a Faun at the Mathurins and a young rake at the Théâtre Royal makes me arrogant with some, humble with you. If you wish, I will send you my picture as the Faun, because of my beautiful muscles."[40] Colette could not resist teasing the poet who dressed in a monk's habit. "You know, I cannot say much about *The Church Dressed in Leaves* because I know nothing about God and don't know if I will ever understand much about God."[41] Jammes' reply was prompt, "Don't call me 'Monsieur' with such solemnity because you are an actress and don't 'yet' understand God." He concluded that a woman "reduced to her body" was a terrible thing, but he was convinced that there was "an impenetrable wall" between the life she led and her true nature.[42] That was the end of the correspondence between Colette and Francis Jammes.

Franc-Nohain also tried to prevail on Colette to abandon the theater; in a two-page article in *Fantasio,* which started abruptly by "And the terrible fact is that she has enormous talent,"[43] he lamented the fact that she was so good. Yet others could be as good as she on stage, while no woman was her equal as a writer. He tried to send her back to paper and pen, by urging the heroes of *Dialogues de Bêtes,* Kiki-la-Doucette and Toby-Chien to tell her also, "What a shame!"

Sido was aware that the marriage was disintegrating. Colette and Willy's theories concerning their relationship as a married couple upset her own. Although she had always felt that sleeping with one's husband "is neither clean nor proper,"[44] putting whole streets between husband and wife was going to extremes. She advised her daughter to resume her life with Willy; she told her how much she admired her sister-in-law, Caroline Landoy, for paying her husband's mistresses — Eugène Landoy was "handsome and a philanderer, but what can you do about that?"[45] — implying that Colette should do the same.

She was puzzled by Colette, who praised the charms of Willy's mistress, the young singer-dancer Meg. "Bizarre," wrote Sido, "Bizarre." Bizarre indeed! Meg was spellbound by Colette and, far from wanting Colette to remove herself from Willy's life, she offered her a warm friendship, extended it to Missy, and was disposed to extend it also to Sido, to whom she would soon be sending affectionate letters and photographs. Sido wrote that she found Colette's relationship with Meg "fantastic"; she also warned Colette to be practical: "What about your pretty Dutch drawing room? What about your furniture?"[46] It is impossible to know what Colette wrote to her mother in those troubled days; all her letters, hundreds of them, were destroyed after her mother died.

Sido worshipped writers. She could not understand what motivated Colette to become a dancer. A writer was welcome in the most exclusive intellectual milieus, while a dancer, especially a "nude" dancer, joined the ranks of the courtesans.

Sido's principles, her total disregard for religion, gave her enough tolerance to accept her daughter as an unsinkable survivor; her love affairs did not bother her. She believed in freedom and independence for women. Nevertheless, she found it hard to see Colette onstage. "You are planning to be on stage for good, so I suppose you like it and that you will make a lot of money. Well, I never thought you had what it takes to be an actress." She commented that one needed to be pliable physically and morally to be onstage and concluded sternly, "You have become pliable both ways, that is a fact."[47]

In December Sido came to Paris and met the marquise de Morny. After a few days spent with Colette and Missy, she realized that there was nothing she could do, that Colette's mind was set. Sido wrote with self-restraint, acknowledging that dance was a necessity "for some reason or other" and promised to say no more about it. She realized what an enormous support Missy's love was to Colette in a period when she had neither husband nor money of her own. She begged Colette, "Do tell Missy to take good care of you."[48] At the end of her letters she would send "big hugs" to "Madame Missy"; for Sido, there was no "Oncle Max" or "Monsieur le Marquis." Missy's generosity spread to the whole family; at Christmas she sent a nightingale and a music box to Achille's daughters and a box of exotic fruit to Sido. She also welcomed Léo Colette, Colette's indolent brother.

I Want to Dance Naked . . . I Want to Write Chaste Books

At the end of 1906 another scandal was brewing; for months Willy had tried to convince Missy to appear with Colette on the professional stage. At every rehearsal of *La Romanichelle* he charmed her with clever compliments; he had Vuillermoz engaged as the pianist for her performances at the Cercle Charras and the Cercle des Arts. Georges Wague, who directed the rehearsals, noticed Willy's and Vuillermoz's maneuvers. They took turns convincing the marquise to appear in public; they drew Mayrargue, manager of the Moulin Rouge, into their plot, and he begged Missy to perform on his stage. the Moulin Rouge, rebuilt three years earlier after it had burned down, was the high-society playboys' favorite music hall; like the Berlin Winter Garden, it had a large gallery built above the balcony and boxes, which overlooked the stage and the orchestra. Dinners were served at small tables in the gallery; the only drink was vintage champagne.

December 14, 1906, Colette and Missy were at the opening gala of the Théâtre Réjane. *Le Figaro* reported that never since the opening of the Suez Canal had there been such a sensational première. The French president, members of the cabinet, literati, and socialites mingled at the *bar américain* and in the smoking room lined with eighteenth-century antiques, a daring mix of new and old — the centerpiece was the giant *electrolier* with one hundred and twenty bulbs. Photographers blinded the celebrities with magnesium flares as they strolled to their "pullman seats" lined with white-and-gold brocade and the orchestra played "Fascination," that year's most popular song. The journalists spread the news that was the talk of the evening: the marquise de Morny was to appear with her lover, Colette Willy, in *La Romanichelle* at the Moulin Rouge.

The audience gazed in fascination at the three notorious women seated in the same box: the marquise de Morny, in a dinner jacket and silk tie held by a splendid pin made of a giant pearl; Liane de Pougy, beautiful in lily-white silk, with her famous rows of pearls cascading down her *décolleté;* and an extremely elegant Colette Willy, wearing the famous choker bearing the inscription "I belong to Missy" for everyone to see.

Scandal was the strongest ingredient of promotion. As a publicity coup, nothing could equal Napoleon III's niece on the stage of a music hall. On December 15 *Fantasio* came out with a cruel article against Missy, a masterpiece of negative publicity.

> Twenty-five years earlier, when the imperial and royal aristocracy had as yet no cause to band together to disown her, Mathilde de Morny was as beautiful as Diana, the hunting goddess, with her lily-white complexion, her fascinating eyes, and the pure profile of a Greek god crowned with curls the color of honey. Her disenchanted smile and slim, tall figure fascinated the painters. In those days she seemed to be bored to death and in search of illusions. She would mix subtle feelings with corruption. The letters she sent to her favorites had a touch of eighteenth-century ele-

gant depravity. They were the equal of the famous letters of
Mademoiselle d'Aïssé to her lover, the Chevalier d'Aydie. No
one could organize as well as she an intimate supper or some discreet debauchery.

Gossip about her would fill volumes. All that is gone. Now
Missy can be seen in special bars, her face as white as plaster, she
has the vacant stare of those who drug themselves with ether. She
is followed sometimes by a favorite poodle, sometimes by an aspiring actress. She has dropped out of her class. Most of her fortune is spent, she will end her life either in a convent or as the
hostess of some gambling den, some casino for women only.
Meanwhile she has started to appear in pantomimes in the company of a friend of hers who is already famous.

The article was illustrated by photographs of Missy and Colette with
the captions: "Pantomime on Stage, a scene from *La Romanichelle,*" and
"Pantomime in Town," showing Missy wearing breeches and Colette
clad in a long dress leaning against Missy's shoulder and gazing into her
eyes. "Colette Willy and la Marquise," explained the caption.

The marquise de Morny sued for defamation, demanding fifteen
thousand francs in damages; the judge sentenced the newspaper's director to pay the minimum twenty-five francs in damages and twenty-
five francs as a fine. The judgment, published in *Fantasio,* was even more
insulting than the article itself: "La Marquise is justified in complaining
that she has been represented as capable of indulging in all sorts of vices.
Damages are due. But these damages cannot reach the important sum of
15,000 francs when one takes into consideration the letter from Colette
W. . . . dated November 25, 1906, and published in *Le Cri de Paris* on
December 2, in which the latter shamelessly discloses her way of life. For
these motives, the damage is limited to 25 francs, the fine is limited to 25
francs also. There will be no other compensation."[49]

Willy exploited Missy's weakness. Besotted by Colette and befuddled
by her love of the stage, the marquise gave in. On December 20, Colette
and Yssim appeared at the Moulin Rouge in *La Romanichelle;* Yssim was
booked for one performance only. An attack was immediately launched
in *Le Rire* with a scathing article signed "Le Snob":

A new artist is born! Yssim! A name that some ladies only pro-
nounce on their knees. The program made our mouth water, it

announced that Yssim is a very famous socialite, an authentic
aristocrat with a coat of arms, who recently discovered her
artistic inclination . . . she stepped in, slightly middle-aged, . . .
paler than ever, with a long nose over her colorless lips. The
sketch should have been called "O My Forefathers!" and in fact I
can imagine the portrait of the noble father, the Duke, the Grand
Dignitary of the Second Empire, changing colors as he gazed at
his beloved daughter on the stage of a music hall.

Yssim started a sort of struggle with a scantily dressed gypsy,
while from every side of the house came encouragement, "Go!
Go! Good old Yssim! Take her! But go on take her!" And when
the gypsy went away, unseduced, maybe to join the Polar Star
[an allusion to Colette's affair with Polaire], Yssim dropped to
the ground in tears and all the public in a touching display of
empathy shared her sorrow with sobs, cries, shouts, wails. It really was extremely funny. The only people hissing and whistling
in the audience were the last representatives of the Imperial corruption.[50]

Christmas was spent at Missy's mansion, a quiet supper with pounds
of truffles cooked under the ashes for Colette, who ate an enormous
amount of her favorite dish. Willy, who was not feeling well, "ate none
and only drank Vittel water." "I particularly remember this meal as it was
very different from our previous suppers, quite like a simple family gathering, but with a kind of 'atmosphere,'"[51] recalled Boulestin.

A greater scandal was in the making; on the last day of December
1906 *Le Gil Blas* published a note denying that Willy had composed any
part of the music "to which Madame de Morny, Colette Willy, and
Dassan are going to appear in a pantomime at the Moulin Rouge." It
was a pretext for giving away Yssim's identity, a breach of journalistic
ethics and social convention. Colette had masterminded her next move
to stardom; she had signed a contract with the Moulin Rouge to act
with the marquise in a pantomime authored by Missy. In a fit of cold-
blooded jealousy, Willy was determined to mar Missy's reputation forever. He had nicknamed her "Le Minotaur" and felt that he was losing
control of the situation. In giving away the marquise de Morny's name
he had, intentionally or not, challenged the duc de Morny and the
Bonapartist party and would pay for it dearly.

Without Missy's knowledge Viterbo, promotion manager for the Moulin Rouge, had printed the Morny coat of arms on the poster. It announced in bold characters "Yssim and Colette Willy in *Un Rêve d'Egypte* (A Dream of Egypt), a pantomime by Madame la Marquise de Morny in 2 acts for 10 performances only," starting January 3.

The scenario was simplistic: a scholar discovers an occult formula that can bring a mummy back to life. By chance, the mummy of a young priestess from the days of the pharaohs lies in a sarcophagus in his study; he pronounces the magic words and the Egyptian mummy comes to life and dances. The scholar falls in love, but his girlfriend tears him away from the mummy in a fit of jealousy. The two rivals try to recapture the scholar's love, but finally the girlfriend expresses such grief, begs the mummy so passionately not to steal her love, that the mummy sacrifices herself and returns to her eternal sleep. The scholar wakes up; it was a dream, *A Dream of Egypt*. The marquise played the scholar, Colette the Egyptian mummy, and Dassan, a dancer, the fiancée.

The pantomime was billed for 11 P.M., at the show's end. The box office was besieged and the price of the seats rocketed. The duc de Morny hired thugs, and all his friends from the Jockey Club came to support him. For once, the royalists joined the Bonapartists to punish the emperor's niece for flaunting her love affair with Colette Willy on stage. Willy and Meg sat in a box overlooking the proscenium.

The curtain rose on an almost empty house. The first sketches, songs, and dances took place while the battalions of the duke's supporters, led by Prince Murat, steadily streamed in and took their seats. The intermission was ominously noisy. At 11 P.M. the master of ceremonies announced, "A pantomime by a marquise whom all will recognize under her stage name of Yssim." Hisses, shrill whistles, and cane-drumming on the floor started immediately. The curtain went up on the scholar's room; the public greeted Missy with a deafening uproar which drowned out the forty musicians. Dassan remembered that the performers went through the whole pantomime without hearing a single note of music. When Colette rose from the sarcophagus and the scholar embraced the mummy, all hell broke loose. Accompanied by screamed epithets, everything that could be thrown onto the stage started to fly: candy boxes, oranges, small footstools, canes, coins, matchboxes and cigarette cases from the smart set, vegetables and garlic bulbs from the hired thugs. Missy and Colette valiantly went on with the pantomime, as if the pandemonium were no affair of theirs; their courage and self-control earned them the applause of their own loyal troops, scattered among the staunch supporters of imperial honor.

The pantomime lasted fifteen minutes. When the curtain fell, the public rose and, in one sweeping movement, turned to the box where Willy sat with Meg, shouting, "Cuckold! Cuckold!" Men flew at him, brandishing their canes, and thrashed him; Willy seized his cane and returned the blows. Assaulted by thugs and enraged gentlemen, Willy was beaten, his monocle broken, his starched white shirt torn. Journalists rushed to Willy's defense; fistfights broke out; the police intervened. The duke's supporters tried to hit Willy even as the police forcefully evacuated the rioting audience, and Meg and Willy retreated to the manager's office.

Meg wrote an account of the scandal to Jacques Gauthier-Villars. "When Papa and I arrived, the whole public turned and stared at us . . . I clapped and applauded, not because I think Colette a clever actress, because she is not and the Marquise is very bad. It amused me to show them I was not afraid. When the curtain went down, the crowd turned on Willy: we fought our way to the door. I hit with my fists like a man. One man I hit went right over. I gave him a swing that caught him on the mouth . . . They are saying I can box like a man all over Paris, and at *Le Gil Blas,* the newspapermen all toasted me." She signed, "Your Sister Meg."[52]

The whole press wrote vitriolic articles. A single newspaper, *Le Courrier Français,* defended Colette in ironic verse:

> *Why should not this exquisite Colette*
> *Play with her divine Marquise?*
> *Why should you give a damn?*

The following day the chief of police, Monsieur Lepine, summoned Mayrargue to let him know that if *A Dream of Egypt* was not canceled immediately, the Moulin Rouge would be closed by his orders. On January 4 *A Dream of Egypt* was replaced by *A Dream of the Orient,* and Georges Wague substituted for Yssim at a fee of three hundred francs per performance for the fifteen-minute part. As soon as Colette rose from her sarcophagus, the public, mistaking Wague for Missy, hissed, whistled, and hurled insults; objects and vegetables flew onto the stage. As he was leaving the theater, Georges Wague heard some spectators say, "It's true, she really looks like a man."[53]

The chief of police was unhappy with the pandemonium. Colette sent a calm note to Georges Wague: "The pantomime is forbidden. I regret it for many reasons."[54] Missy sued the music-hall manager for having printed her coat of arms on the poster. The scandal spread to the provinces. *L'Eclair de Montpellier* denounced Colette with Missy on stage and Willy with his young mistress in a box as the worst possible sign of depravity. Willy replied, asking why he should be held responsible for his estranged wife's actions, specifying that he had attended the show only because he had been challenged to do so.

Because of the enormity of the scandal, Willy was fired from *L'Echo de Paris* and lost the financial security of his annual salary. Meg wrote to Jacques, "Now we are really poor . . . the scandal Colette created made Papa lose his position at *L'Echo* . . ." At a dinner at Missy's, Willy told Colette about *L'Echo de Paris*. "Oh, I am sorry," she said, and went on talking about her own business.[55]

Colette thought she should capitalize on the publicity of the *scandale du Moulin Rouge* and asked Wague if he had any ideas. Meanwhile, she was immersed in a new project; she wanted to found a film company. She had discussed the matter with several businessmen involved in movie production and she was ready to invest ten thousand francs of her own money, since a cinematographer easily earned one hundred thousand francs with one good film. Colette was planning to perform, and the marquise was to run the business for her. Missy would own the film negatives and sell the copies. Colette was eager to act and was negotiating some contracts, including one abroad; she urged Wague to seek even more contracts.

Wague admired Colette for her professional resiliency during the scandal and her cool determination to be a mime as well as a writer. Her success on the stage was a fact; a full-page photograph of Colette Willy was published in *Nos Actrices Contemporaines*. Looking back, Georges Wague wrote:

> Among all my partners, none had Colette's instinctive under-standing for everything related to the theater. No one showed such deep concern, such passionate determination, and I dare barely write the word, such docile humility when it came to the creation of a pantomime. She would disrupt her private life and give the stage absolute priority. Colette wanted to belong to the theater, in spite of all those who have denied her that quality, that faculty. She would carry professional integrity to such a point that I would compare it to a religious commitment.

> She had an extraordinary way of abolishing the old, conventional gestures of pantomime and replacing them with an intense feeling, or a simple glance. She did something I have never seen done, except by her; she could project the strongest feeling, the strongest emotion simply by closing her eyes.[56]

After the scandal, the Parisian press reported that Colette was divorcing Willy. On January 21 Colette sent a short note to *Le Gil Blas* to deny the rumor. "All the papers announce my divorce. I would be grateful if you would print that it is a separation of goods and not a divorce." On January 23 Willy's lawyer presented a plea for legal separation, arguing that Colette had left their domicile and showed no intention of returning. A week later, on January 31, Colette's lawyer, Maître Mignon, counterattacked with another plea, arguing that Henry Gauthier-Villars was living with his mistress. On February 14 the *Tribunal de la Seine* pronounced the legal separation of Monsieur and Madame Gauthier-Villars; the wife "having made permanent a separation which she made public in a way offensive to her husband and on the other hand, the husband was notoriously unfaithful." Willy left for Capri with Meg.

Boulestin gave an account of their parting. "It was disorganized. The Rue de Courcelles apartment was sold, the furniture divided, there were bitter altercations and writs and general aggressiveness, also, more acid quarrels over the royalties of the books Colette had written with Willy, therefore more insinuations in the newspapers — altogether an extremely unpleasant atmosphere."[57]

At stake were not only the royalties of the *Claudine*s and the *Minne*s, but the royalties of Les Ateliers, which in 1906 had produced *Une Plage d'Amour, Jeux de Prince,* and *Le Roman d'un Jeune Homme Beau.* The novel factory had come to a standstill when *La Patronne* went on stage. At stake, too, was the last *Claudine,* entitled *The Vagabond,* which was ready in January for publication under both names — Willy and Colette Willy. Colette was incensed by Willy's move to divorce her and by his article in *L'Eclair de Montpellier* after the Moulin Rouge scandal. Colette went to Ollendorff and demanded the manuscript, leaving an explanatory note to be transmitted to Willy and the director, "You have learned about the request for a legal separation between me and Willy. I must warn you that among the furniture and objects I claim as my own is the part I coauthored in *The Vagabond.* I am taking it to the publisher with whom I am now under contract. I know that Willy owes you a novel. I have no doubt he will give you one sometime later. Mine being written, I take it, this is a race and I arrive first."[58] The title was changed, and *The Vagabond* was published as *Retreat from Love* by *Le Mercure de France* on February 13 with a foreword signed Colette Willy, saying: "For reasons that have nothing to do with literature I have ceased my collaboration with Willy. The same public who liked our six daughters . . . the legitimate ones, the four *Claudines* and the two *Minnes* will enjoy, I hope, *Retreat from Love* and find in it what it liked in them."

Unexpectedly, a few weeks later Colette was again collaborating with Willy. She was "bored"; she found her life with Missy dull. As soon as Willy left for Capri, she missed the buoyancy, fears, euphoria, and crises of her life with him. Her plans for a movie company had gone nowhere and her projects for a foreign tour had not materialized; she felt abandoned by Willy, who was managing Meg's career very well — Meg had just signed a contract with *Parisiana*. Colette was brooding. In a letter she asked him to come back home and to live with her and Meg, a ménage à trois posing as a pseudofamily.

The marquise de Morny wondered what the estranged couple was up to; she wanted to know just what to expect and what, exactly, was her part in the general arrangement. On February 13 the legal separation was completed, but Colette sent Willy a letter calling him "Dear Sweetie" and concluding with kisses "from us both" to share with Meg.

On February 16 Missy wrote to Willy seeking an explanation; she stated frankly that she did not understand the personalities of either Willy or Colette. She did not mince her words. She did not like their compulsion to publicize the situation, and reminded Willy that he was the one who had asked for it — it could have been an agreement made with more discretion. Very bluntly, she told Willy that when he had entrusted his wife to her, she had seen clearly what he expected from her and had accepted taking charge of Colette, although she had foreseen what could happen to the three of them. Now Colette was complaining bitterly, and Missy did not feel she deserved the blame. She described Colette as "a capricious child, not very ethical."[59] She said she did not hold it against her; it was not her fault. Missy understood that Colette was bored with her company because she was old and rather melancholy. She would have liked to be different and blamed herself for Colette's reactions.

This request for a clarification was sensible enough under the circumstances. They were surely all old enough to know what they wanted: Willy was forty-eight, Missy forty-four, and Colette, the "capricious child," was thirty-four years old.

In March Missy and Colette went to Nice for Carnival, where Colette and Wague gave three performances of the notorious *A Dream of Egypt*. Every night the marquise applauded from the wings. Willy was not very far away; he was in Menton with Meg. He wrote to Vuillermoz, "No, I have not seen *A Dream of Egypt,* but I met the young mime at her hotel and she returned my visit by coming to Menton. Keep that to yourself. It is not my fault if I cannot hate her, nor she, me."[60] In a titillating reversal of fortune, Colette and Willy were hiding to meet each other.

Sido kept begging Colette not to abandon her writing career — since she had this real talent, she should rely on nothing else, "for your own position is precarious, you have a lot of enemies, Missy has a family."[61] Colette was indeed writing. On April 27, 1907 she published, in *La Vie Parisienne,* "Toby-Dog Speaks Up" ("Toby-Chien Parle"), an intrepid proclamation of independence and a bold assertion of her right to seek happiness: "I want to do what I want. I want to play in pantomimes and comedies. I want to dance naked if the leotard bothers me and spoils my figure. I want to retire to a desert island if that is my pleasure or enjoy the company of ladies who use their beauty to make a living. I want to write sad and chaste books celebrating landscapes, flowers, sorrow, pride, and the innocence of charming animals who are scared of humans."[62]

Colette declared that she would continue her career on stage, even if people around her spoke of her downfall, her "degradation," her "disgrace." It did not bother her; never had she felt more worthy of self-esteem. She had chosen her new life and she liked show business, the uncouth ballet teacher, the poor little chorus girl, and the rude stagehand. All she needed to be happy when she came home was to hear Missy's sweet voice inquiring, "You are not too tired, are you, my love?"[63] She wanted to love only the one who loved her and give her all that belonged to her in this world: her body, her heart, and her freedom.

"Toby-Dog Speaks Up" expressed the complexities and paradoxes of Colette's life. Freedom had come at a price; she had lost Willy, and the pain and the anger had not faded away. Colette unleashed an attack on

Willy's mistresses, women of all ages who begged him to marry them, who accused Colette of having lovers. They were after him like a pack of hellcats. He was weak, fickle, and in love with the love he inspired. He had released a nasty instinct in all of his mistresses, so that they lied, cheated, and committed adultery out of hatred for Colette as much as out of love for him — she would leave him to this pack, and one day he would see them as she did: "a throng of greedy little pigs." Then he would run from them at last, disgusted by such senseless vice. Colette reached the conclusion that both she and Willy were the victims of his lovers' hysteria. It was no fault of his if women were wild, unethical, ready to do anything to get his attention. Colette was trying to repair some of the damage done to Willy's reputation. During the scandal of the Moulin Rouge angered Bonapartists had shouted, "Cuckold! Cuckold!" at him, turning the most Parisian of *boulevardiers* into a ridiculous character of popular comedy. In "Toby-Dog Speaks Up" and again in an article in *Frou Frou,* Colette denied that she had ever cheated on Willy. He was not a cuckold; this was a rumor spread by women who loathed her. Willy was the victim of his own weaknesses and totally unconscious of the pain he caused her.

This was Colette's illustration of what love is and is not; clumsy "he" did not know how to love, while "she" marveled at the wonders of love and the ever-expanding worlds it created. Love gave her strength, pleasure, and a happiness she found now in the eyes of her trustworthy friend, *ma sûre amie.*

Colette was in a defiant mood. In "Toby-Dog Speaks Up," she declared her right to be different, and in an interview in Nice she spoke of her black ancestors, putting herself at the avant-garde of the new trend. There was a growing enthusiasm for primitive art; Matisse was dazzling the art antiestablishment with wild outbursts of colors; Picasso had revolutionized the vision of the world with *Les Demoiselles d'Avignon.* In her own way, Colette was part of those deep changes in our collective psyche. No one had pushed her into her audacious venture on the stage, but only there could she express her inner struggles and her own ambivalence. She could not express them in words, or, more precisely, she had learned to tone them down. She told Sylvain Bonmariage that literature is the art of suggestion.

The Last Duet

Colette was trying for a reconciliation with Willy; she asked her mother not to write unkindly about him because she felt hurt when she did. Sido was afraid that Colette would be the loser and that she might end up more miserable than herself — to become old and poor was the worst that could happen. Colette replied that Willy had lost all his money but was working hard to rebuild his fortune. Sido answered that she could not believe he had no money when he retained two secretaries, owned a carriage, and kept a mistress. Colette's relationship with Missy raised no questions and no reservations; Sido encouraged her daughter to stay with her wealthy friend, wondering what would become of Colette if she had no one to protect her. Missy's name is in every letter from Sido, and the scandal of the Moulin Rouge is referred to as "a lot of torment that must have depressed Missy."[64] What Sido could not understand was Colette's relationship with Willy. "You say you love him and even very much."[65] She promised to write kindly to him and at the end of a letter in March, she added, "If you still see Willy, kiss him on my behalf."[66]

Jacques Gauthier-Villars, spending Easter vacation with his father, noticed that Colette and Willy lived in separate apartments, but saw each other every day and got along. They discussed and collaborated as in the past. Colette wrote descriptions of Monts-Boucons and a long letter from Claudine to Maugis for Willy's novel, *A Clean Little Old Man* (Un Petit Vieux Bien Propre), for which Willy gave her one thousand francs. In this letter, Colette painted a portrait of Maugis, enamored with the idea of love and losing it in relentless pursuit. In this, their last collaboration, every one of their fictional characters appeared: Toby-Chien, Claudine and Renaud, the beautiful Calliope Van Langendonck. Even Minne returned as a flashback, offering to become the mistress of Maugis, who refused — a reminder of Willy's gentlemanly behavior when Colette begged him to be his mistress. This scene would be repeated as a *lietmotif* in Willy's work. The novel, set in France and London, was replete with attacks against Parisian theater owners and praise for London society, writers, and journalists, from Bernard Shaw and Hall Caine to that dandy of letters, Max Beerbohm, and the caustic Harold Hughes.

Like all of Colette and Willy's novels, *A Clean Little Old Man* was autobiographical to a degree: it was Willy's version of their relationship.

Pimprenette de Folligny (Colette) is trying for a career on stage when she meets Evariste-Anselme Tardot, who lives in retirement at Les Monts. (The everpresent Maugis is introduced in this novel as Tardot's confidant.) Tardot finances Primprenette's career, investing in a theater and financing several music-hall acts. Pimprenette becomes the lover of Lydio, her partner (Georges Wague) because "for us [actors] to go to bed is only to show our friendship." Tardot is promptly ruined by Pimprenette, who becomes the favorite of Mihaïl de Morénie (the marquise de Morny); so as to leave no doubt as to the character's identity, Maugis comments, *"Morny soit qui mal y pense."* But Pimprenette loves Tardot: "I need you to advise me, guide me, scold me and prevent me from doing many stupidities . . . I would prefer to live off our two annuities over there [Les Monts] rather than lose you . . ." Prince de Morénie asks Tardot not to abandon Pimprenette and offers to pay the mortgages on Les Monts and give Pimprenette the estate. Tardot refuses, since Les Monts is the pure image of his own love. Meanwhile, Pimprenette meets some opulent South Americans, has numerous brief affairs with actors, and says to Tardot, who asks how the prince is reacting, "Mihaïl is just like you, as long as he has me, he does not care about the rest."

During a tour in London, Tardot meets a brunette with blue eyes, Lilian Grace (Meg Villars). Pimprenette discovers them and cries, "When I am unfaithful you really do not care, but I do when you are." They decide to remain friends. Tardot auctions off Les Monts, and the prince, Pimprenette and Lydio celebrate the three-hundredth performance of their play, while Maugis toys with the idea of committing suicide. The novel ends on a light touch: Tardot wins the lottery in a Balkan state and is saved from his financial woes.

The novel had been set in Monte Carlo, then at Colette's request at Monts-Boucons and Besançon. While Diard, Willy's secretary, was correcting the proofs, he noticed that the opening sentence read, "From his balcony in Besançon, Monsieur Tardot was amusing himself by spitting into the waves of the deep blue sea." "Can you see the sea from Besançon?" asked Diard. Willy realized the blunder and the novel was revised. But after this slip, Colette's collaboration with Willy's novels ended.

Colette signed a contract with the magazine *La Vie Parisienne,* in which she had published a *Dialogue de Bêtes* in June 1906. From April 27, 1907, to May 1910, she published one feature a month. In October the column, signed "Colette Willy," became "Le Journal de Colette." *La Vie Parisienne* sold wooden puppets of famous people; one of the first was Colette Willy, pen in hand and dressed in Claudine's black smock, with her long panties showing, button boots, books trailing in a leather strap. It was called *Le Journal de Colette.* Her name also appeared in an advertisement for toothpicks.

For Missy she wrote "Sleepless Night" (Nuit Blanche) published by *La Vie Parisienne,* in which she describes herself pretending to be asleep next to her lover, following a stream of consciousness till the break of day; the last line reveals that her lover is a woman. Sido found the prose poem "risqué," but written "in a very beautiful style like everything you write."[67] The text was later reprinted using the masculine form when all traces of Colette's homosexuality were being erased and her affair with Missy — hard to deny — was described as the aberration of an abused, penniless, and abandoned wife. The masculine and feminine forms alternated in subsequent editions, but Colette returned to the feminine form in the definitive edition of her collected works in 1949. In 1907 Colette did not deny her homosexual affairs; on the contrary, when a delivery boy sent by the publisher Charles Saglio failed to find her, she wrote "When I am not at 44 Rue de Villejust, I am at 2 Rue Georges-Ville [Missy's address], a seven-month-old infant knows that."[68]

Colette, Missy, Willy, and Meg spent the summer at Le Crotoy; Colette and Missy in Villa Belle-Plage, Willy and Meg next door in a rented villa. Several photos of Colette and Meg show them in the sand dunes in similar cycling bloomers. Colette called Willy "My best friend." They could not help loving each other: "one thing is certain, the man I married had a talent for relentlessly occupying a woman's thoughts."[69] Willy wrote to Vuillermoz, "She is exquisite, this dear little crazy thing."[70] Some time during that period she sent Willy a letter, saying, "I measure the enormity of my mistake and all alone, I feel I cannot bring myself to live without you, this with the deep down awareness of all you have done for me."[71]

In September Colette entrusted Willy with escorting Renée Vivien to England to help her write her biography of Ann Boleyn. Renée called him "My good uncle." Colette also sent her brother Léo with them. In London, Willy missed her terribly: "I know only too well that she would give up her abnormal relationship to come and live with me somewhere. But how to provide for both of us?"[72] He also wondered how to face the gossip; they would be accused of living together at Missy's expense. A newspaper had already accused him of receiving money from the marquise; he wondered if he should sue for slander. Colette asked Willy to resume married life, "I hear you are well disposed toward me. If I leave Missy, what will you do for me?"[73] She asked him to get rid of Meg Villars. "Am I to throw her into the river?" wrote Willy to Vuillermoz. "Why not keep both women?" "No," replied Willy, "that is the condition set by Colette."[74] He could not get rid of Meg; they had lived on her earnings during those hard times. The problem was money; he wondered how to make enough to keep Colette. And that was not all; the marquise was not to be taken lightly. He thought being free of "the Minotaur" would be nice, but he was certain Colette had not set a penny aside, and she had very expensive tastes.

Colette had such fits of jealousy that she would claw at the windowsill when she hoped to see Willy coming. She was not upset by Meg, who loved her, but Willy was slipping out of her life and she came to realize there was no turning back. She resorted to magic, locking herself in her apartment, staying without food, and for hours repeating Willy's name, hoping he would either return or die. This voodoolike incantation, which she described in "Rain Moon" did not work.

Willy's letters to Curnonsky bordered on despair. Why did he suffer so much? Only because he was far from the only woman he could love; but he could not live with Colette on two francs a day. He thought she was happy with Missy. Willy could not believe that he could feel so much pain. He complained to Vuillermoz that he never thought he would find it impossible to live without her! He did not mean going to bed with her. It was her presence he missed, the ambiguity of her smile, the dazzling speed with which she grasped the meaning of things, the book she would thrust under his eyes, open at the right page, pointing at the right line with her fingertip. He remembered her absurd explosions of joy, her violent and brief explosions of sorrow, her chatter, which was her way of covering up her intense sensitivity, "so selective, so discriminating, always to the point."[75] Most of all, he missed her spells of thoughtful silence, those moments of silence he found so precious. As time went by, the pain grew worse.

With poetic insight and a keen grasp of human nature, Colette had predicted Willy's torments in *Retreat from Love:* "Now whatever he does and whether I remain alive or not, I have taken him over. He came to me steadily, slowly, not without defenses and restrictions, but has entirely surrendered to me."[76]

Colette's legal separation was cause for great anxiety in Châtillon; Sido and Achille were afraid that Colette would not consult them. Sido reminded her that she had five thousand francs written into the marriage contract and that Willy had paid Achille ten thousand francs as a down payment on the house in Saint-Sauveur for Colette. It would be sad if the house she loved "fell into strangers' hands."[77] What was going to happen to Colette's estate, Monts-Boucons? And who was going to own the rare editions of leatherbound books of their library? Sido consulted a lawyer.

Sido had other causes for worry. Juliette had turned into an alcoholic like her father and had become so insanely jealous that she kept inspecting every corner of her husband's room to see if the maids were hidden somewhere. She would not even let her husband glance at a mirror for fear he was secretly looking at a maid. Juliette wanted a divorce, but her husband refused. Sido wrote to Colette that Charles Roché hated his wife and would like to get rid of her quietly. They had "tragic quarrels." Sido found Juliette's situation sad, but not as bewildering as the arrangement between Colette, Missy, Willy, and Meg. Meg had mailed Sido a set of photographs, and Willy sent Achille's young daughters chocolate fish full of candy, a traditional April Fool's Day gift. "Oh, that Willy!" wrote Sido, "How he always remembers to do something kind for people."[78] Willy confided to Sido that, financially, he could not get over the loss of his position at *L'Echo de Paris*. As if Juliette's and Colette's problems were not enough, Léo was living a frivolous life, playing piano in hotels "fit only for La Doce Vita!" With his friend Farroux, who drove a convertible, they raced around at sixty miles an hour, dropped by to see Sido, then showed up at Missy's villa, Belle-Plage. Colette gave the name of Léo's friend to the hedonist husband in the trio of *The Other One*.

Sido's sorrows were not over. The marquis de La Fare, as head of Achille's wife's family, sent a letter to Sido and Achille demanding that Captain Colette's remains be removed from their family vault. The de La Fares were shocked by Colette's notorious way of life and did not want the name "Colette" engraved on their vault. The captain was exhumed and transferred to another graveyard; Colette sent a large sum of money but did not attend the ceremony.

Colette sent *Retreat from Love* to Count Robert de Montesquiou with an appealing letter, saying, "I have so few friends, I am told my way of life is nonconformist, and I am blamed for it."[79] She assured him that there was no low motive in her behavior. The count, who thrived on desperate circumstances, extended a helping hand to Willy, also; he found a buyer for Willy's portrait by Boldini. One by one, Willy was selling his most valuable possessions. Willy's creditors attempted to collect through legal means; he wrote to Vuillermoz that he expected "the seizure of his goods" the following Monday, but "it is of no importance, don't mention it to the Faun."[80] Willy sold a drawing by Ingres and sketches by Toulouse-Lautrec. To pay his debts, he gave up his shares in the Gauthier-Villars Publishing Company. He sold his two remaining horses, but his jockey sued him for his wages amounting to three thousand francs. Colette, who had not paid Redfern, sent Willy the old bills and the judgment assigning her to pay. Hounded by his creditors, Willy resorted to all sorts of schemes.

He sold the rights to *Claudine Married*, now in its one hundred eighteenth edition, to Vallette for twenty-four hundred francs on September 30, 1907; on October 19 he sold the rights to *Claudine at School, Claudine in Paris,* and *Claudine and Annie* to Ollendorff for five thousand francs. The creditors garnering his royalties could no longer make claims against the returns from the *Claudines* or any other novels signed "Willy," which were now the publishers' property. Willy did not inform Colette of this transaction. Unaware of the sale of the rights of the four *Claudines*, Colette asked Willy to put her name as coauthor in the next edition. Willy immediately granted her request, and the next edition was signed "Willy" and "Colette Willy." But Colette wanted her name placed before Willy's, so she wrote a note, which bears corrections in Willy's handwriting, stating that it was only through a typographical error that his name was printed first, when, for literary reasons, hers should have had the honors.

The Flesh

For the opening of the fall season, Colette played the lead in *Le Crin* (The Cantankerous One), a one-act play by Sacha Guitry, in a small theater, the Tréteau de Paris; she intrigued to have the part of Maggie Gauthier, who had created it in June. On November 1 the pantomime *La Chair* (The Flesh) opened at the Apollo, written and directed by Georges Wague. He had written the lead part for Colette, but decided instead to cast la Belle Otéro, who had performed very successfully with him during a tour of the spas. Colette and Missy pressured him to change his plan and prevailed; incensed, Otéro refused to see Colette, and Missy was dispatched to soothe her. Colette sent her "a nice long letter." Still furious, Otéro did not answer, but instructed her maid to tell Colette that nothing had changed between them. Still, she thought "that the part did not fit her. . . ."[81] Rehearsals were turbulent: Colette proved capricious and refused to rehearse in the morning ("you will get nothing good out of me in the morning") or to rehearse at the Apollo at the same time as some funambulist and whirling cylists.

The script of *The Flesh* is violent and sensuous. The action takes place in a hut in the lonely mountains somewhere in the Balkans. Hokartz, a fearless smuggler, is possessed by a devouring passion for Yulka, who shares his dangerous life. But Yulka is unfaithful; while Hokartz is gone on his illegal business, Yulka meets her lover, a young officer. The smuggler finds the lovers together, beats up the young man, and throws him out. He is about to kill Yulka, who is struggling to escape, when her dress tears apart and she appears half-naked. Hokartz stops, thunderstruck by her beauty. *La Chair* (the flesh) is so powerful that he falls to his knees in an act of adoration. She refuses to surrender. Hokartz goes wild with passion and stabs himself, pinning his arm to the wooden floor; Yulka runs to the dying man, who seizes her in his free arm. He dies as she loses her mind in frantic but useless efforts to set herself free. The story unfolds to a musical score by Chantrier.

At the final rehearsal, when the torn dress revealed one leg to the hip and one bare shoulder, the director of the music hall, according to Colette, had a sudden inspiration, stepped back, and shouted, "Let go one breast!"[82] Another version states that Colette suggested it. At any rate, that night Colette's nude breast made its historical appearance on stage.

At the dress rehearsal for the press Colette displayed both her breasts in a grand gesture and vanished into the wings. La Belle Otéro, her friend and rival, chortled and commented loudly on Colette's small breasts; she was proud of her own. (Legend has it that the elongated domes atop the Hôtel Ruhl in Nice were shaped by the architect to imitate Otéro's famous breasts.) Polaire was shocked. The tabloids commented that Colette had vanished too swiftly into the wings after the event, and that "Madame la Marquise did not spare the flowers she had ordered to be brought on stage for her dear Colette."[83]

The nude breast may have created an uproar, but the trade press concurred that Colette displayed authentic talent as the sensuous, wild girl. None was more supportive than *Comoedia,* a new publication on arts, music halls, and theater; Willy had been on its editorial staff since October. Well-financed and publicized, *Comoedia* was soon the leading entertainment magazine, one of the great success stories of French journalism. Colette signed with the Alcazar music hall in Brussels at a fee equal "to what they would pay Polaire," three hundred francs a night — she had made it to the top.

Colette trained with Cernusco and Caryatis, who created a modern ballet based on eurhythmics. She had some of the avant-garde "primitive" aggressiveness that would become familiar with Diaghilev's Russian ballets and their "barbaric" dances. *L'Après-Midi d'un Faune,* danced by Nijinski, would open classic ballet to movements heavily charged with sexuality.

Colette never admitted that nudity was indecent and scoffed at censorship of nudity on the music-hall stage. "Total nudity does not call for frenzy . . . the summit of perfection justifies only seriousness."[84] This parallels Fourier's statement, "Flawless flesh seems to suffice to endow them with a serenity which wards off lewdness." For Fourier, the nudity of beautiful bodies was as chaste as the nudity of statues. In *Harmony* he dreamed of having a living museum offering visual pleasure to promote the development of aesthetic appreciation. He conceded that in our civilization such meetings would be no more than bawdy gatherings "because Taste and Knowledge are not widespread." But the *harmonians* would learn to appreciate physical beauty. Guided by aesthetic motives, "a woman who has only a beautiful bosom leaves the rest covered," while another, perfectly beautiful, "appears completely naked." Men do the same. Fourier believed that if the sight of a statue provokes admiration, "the sight of twenty beautiful nude women should charm us even more."[85] This was Colette's feeling when she enjoyed the sight of a group of nude dancers on the stage of the *Folies-Bergère* or, later, a performance by Josephine Baker. In *"Nudité"* she mocked the censors who condoned the partial striptease of a dancer in skimpy, see-through lingerie with frills and lace, yet demanded the suppression of a motionless nude representing the goddess Diana on a cloud of papier-mâché.

In the "Le Journal de Colette," Colette defended *La Chair* and her right to dance naked on the stage. She dialogued with an imaginary friend, Valentine — a character Colette used to give an antithetical point of view. Valentine asked if it really did not bother her to disrobe on stage. No, was Colette's candid answer. She would never understand why the skin on the hip or on the lower back was more tempting than the skin of her hand or her calf. She rejected the prudish modesty that labeled, inch by inch, virtue and chastity.

La Chair lasted until November 30 at the Apollo, a very successful run. Reutlinger took professional photographs of Colette, some of which can still be found in the booksellers' boxes along *les quais* in Paris. He draped her in six yards of white cloth, half of it soaked in water so that it would cling to her body and emphasize her contours. He took pictures of her undressed and stretched out on a lion's skin, of the "Romanichelle" in rags, and of Colette elegantly dressed by Redfern with her prize bulldog, Poucette. She had bought Poucette in a fit of enthusiasm at a dog show for a whopping nine thousand francs, "while the male of the litter was snatched by some Americans who paid his weight in gold." Colette confessed, "It was beyond my means, so I deprived myself of one tailored suit and one afternoon dress."[86]

The last day of the year dealt a hard blow to Colette. On December 31 she was to be part of a program on the "Love Letters of Famous Women" at the Théâtre des Arts. An actor was to read the text while Colette mimed one of the letters. She had to cancel her appearance at the last minute to go to Besançon to attend the court-ordered sale of the estate she loved so much, Monts-Boucons, which she owned jointly with Willy. He had taken out a twenty-thousand-franc mortgage and could not pay.

In *My Apprenticeships* Colette lamented the loss of Monts-Boucons. "Mr. Willy seemed to give it to me, 'All this is yours.' Three years later he took it back, 'It is not yours any more, nor mine either.'"[87] Willy was in a state of despair that affected his health; he thought he had no more than eighteen months to live. Back in Paris, the Willys suffered another blow; Chez Maxim's had had a wall-sized caricature painted by Sem that depicted the famous Parisians riding in the Bois de Boulogne — Willy was caricatured as driving a carriage in which Colette embraced the marquise de Morny. He sued Sem and Roubille, authors of the infamous mural, for defamation, but to no avail.

VII

THE VAGABOND

"A woman of letters who went wrong"
LA VAGABONDE

LA CHAIR WAS SCHEDULED to play in Monte Carlo and Nice for Mardi Gras. The Préfet des Alpes Maritimes decreed that two bare breasts were a threat to public morality and gave orders that the left breast remain veiled, a compromise accepted by the director of the Théâtre des Capucines, who had focused his publicity on Colette's bare breasts.

Originally the part of Yulka's lover had been played by Marcel Vallée; he was replaced by Christine Kerf, "a beautiful girl and superb dancer."[1] Wague changed the part of the officer to that of a young mountaineer in order to include the folk dances for which Christine Kerf was known. *Paris-Théâtre* commented, "As a young lover, Christine Kerf shows very feminine curves and when one sees pretty Colette kissing this plump peach of a girl and Hokartz, the husband, enraged when he catches them kissing, one fails to understand why he becomes so wildly angry at the sight of this picture straight from the *Songs of Bilitis*."[2]

This time there was no scandal; the scandal of the Moulin-Rouge was due to Missy's aristocratic family. Now the public came to see Colette act out her personal life. ". . . at the Capucines in Nice, I was such a draw — such an unexpected draw . . ."[3] commented Colette. In April, *La Chair* was back at l'Apollo. Critics were more and more favorable to Colette: "This adorable Colette . . . What attitudes! What movements! What an expressive face! And that gesture! The gesture with which she tears off her tunic freeing her beautiful breast!"[4] They wrote that she displayed anxiety, desire, voluptuous teasing, that even her silence was eloquent and she needed no words to express the range of human passion. Louis Delluc, pioneer of the movie industry, wrote, "Colette Willy is the most original of all the mimes, the most true to life. Her attitudes are very *artistique*, very intellectual and yet with nothing strange or far-fetched. She gives the impression of being at once shameless and naive."[5]

Colette was looking for new parts and a more sophisticated repertoire. She thought she could convince Pierre Louÿs to let her perform *Les Chansons de Bilitis,* but he refused. She wrote to Claude Farrère to inquire whether la Belle Otéro was already under contract to play the leading part in a pantomime he had just written; if not, she pleasantly reminded him, she was a very good mime and her goal was to earn her living on the stage as much as with her pen. This, she confessed, took some fortitude. She signed with *Parisiana* to be, at last, Claudine in *Claudine in Paris*. In May she gave Willy an interview for *Comoedia,* which he signed "Nobody." "This unique artist is going to play the part of Claudine in *Claudine in Paris,* which she coauthored some years ago. Tout-Paris knows her well, so lively, with her beautiful eyes which remain strangely serious under the short curls when she smiles. She declared to us, 'Yes, Sir, I am going to play the part after five rehearsals only. Don't congratulate me on such a feat, I know the play so well. . . . The cast is wonderful. There is a young and charming Luce, Miss Mielly, and I don't forget Toby-Chien, my bulldog.'"[6]

"The charming young girl" who was to play Luce was Miss Andrée Mielly, Willy's latest mistress, the daughter of Monsieur Montcharmont, owner and manager of a theatrical touring company, who was pressing Colette to sign up with him. Willy was entangled with Andrée, with Meg, who was becoming suspicious, and with his secretary, Madeleine de Swarte, who had lived in his shadow since 1906. He had not lost his love for Colette, "the only woman I could love totally,"[7] and he asked "Cur" to make sure Colette did not know about his flashes of passion for Andrée. He sent a nostalgic note to Sido to tell her how moved he was by Colette's interpretation of Claudine, "of the character she created and was."[8] Sido was puzzled by this strange behavior. "Do you love each other very much or do you hate each other very much? Everything in your relationship is so abnormal that one is at wit's end."[9]

Colette and Missy spent July and August in Le Crotoy. Colette, who could not find a playwright to write a part she liked, decided to write a play herself, *En Camarades,* a bourgeois comedy. Missy hired Paul Barlet, who for over two decades had been the Willys' secretary and a pillar of the novel factory, to be Colette's secretary.

The last weekend of August Colette left for Geneva to play the lead in *Son Premier Voyage* (His First Trip), a comedy by Xanrof and Guèrin, at the Casino du Parc. Colette needed a comforting presence, so Meg went along with her; Willy poked fun at himself for having given "an English governess" to "his dear child."[10] Colette felt compelled to send Sido a postcard cosigned with Meg. Sido thanked Meg for the loving care she lavished on Colette and sent friendly greetings to Missy and her best to Willy. In Geneva Colette found unexpected success, although "For a very long time Willy and I have been treated as nefarious personalities in Switzerland."[11] The Protestant papers did not mention her show at all, a fact Colette dismissed with a short expletive, happy to have earned 973 francs for two performances.

She had new photographs made by Couture and Walery and wondered if too much nakedness might be counterproductive, "Perhaps one should not overindulge in nudity even in photographs."[12] But Colette in an open, slit tunic left very little to the imagination. She sent a set of her professional photographs to Sido with a basket of fruit and a bunch of flowers. "How dare you pose almost naked?" asked Sido. She had read in *Le Temps* that the police were about to investigate the women who appeared nude in several music halls, including L'Apollo: "Are you going to be one of those naked women? It would be annoying."[13]

Hammerstein was negotiating with Wague to bring *La Chair* to New York and signed a contract in May; *La Chair* was performed at the Manhattan Opera House in December 1908. Christine Kerf was the only member of the original cast to go; Yulka's part was given to Odette Valéry, whom Colette called "that heap." Colette was mad at Wague: "I wanted to become something over there and you turned a potentially good deal into almost nothing."[14] Sido had her reservations about a trip to the New World. The Americans, she said, had hurricanes in their streets because they built houses twenty stories high, "and that will not last long, they will have strange catastrophies, just as they like them."[15]

Since America was not an option for her, Colette pushed Wague to get bookings for *La Chair*. She was contacting several chic little theaters in La Madeleine district and asked him to find a new pantomime and an inexpensive partner. "I underline *cheap* because the deal can only be good for both of us if the third character does not ask for much."[16] Colette was managing her career, and she contacted two theater agencies. She received some offers to play in a comedy tour through the French provinces, but she preferred pantomime. When she acted, she suddenly felt the need to become silent, to express herself by movements only, with body language, and "to dance to the rhythm of my text."

In September Juliette committed suicide. Sido wrote a series of superb, dramatic, suspenseful letters on the death of her daughter. One afternoon Judge Trouillet, Charles Roché's relative, arrived at her door in his automobile, asking her to come immediately to Charny, where Juliette was very ill. "Juliette is dead, I can read it on your face." "No," replied Monsieur Trouillet, "but she may be dead when we get there. Juliette was taking aconite for her heart . . . she must have taken an overdose this morning."[17]

When they arrived, Juliette was dead. Sido asked her son-in-law if his wife took aconite, which he denied, assuring Sido that he always kept his pharmacy locked and showing her the key. But Sido had the nagging suspicion that Roché had given Juliette an overdose.

On September 25 she wrote to Colette, "She committed suicide." Five days later she added that her granddaughter was embarrassed because "she knows her father lied" when he declared officially that Juliette had died from a stroke. The day of the funeral Achille refused to set foot in his sister's house; he drove his mother there and waited outside during the funeral.

Sido chose an unexpected confidant with whom to vent her suspicions and unload her heart; she wrote to Willy that Juliette was desperate because her husband did not love her, that she was jealous of her own daughter, that "there was an abyss" between Roché's caresses for his daughter and his rebuttals of his wife. These caresses made Juliette angry. She did not think they were "criminal," although she had "a tendency not to see or believe any infamy or any rumors." In point of fact, she accused Roché of an incestuous relationship. Then Sido revealed to Willy that Juliette had tried to poison herself two months after her marriage rather than sign the papers that would mean her mother's ruin. Sido felt close to Willy in spite of his separation from Colette. Did she hope that he who had come to the defense of the Colettes against Saint-Sauveur in 1892 would do the same now and paint Roché as a murderer? For Sido literature was the supreme weapon and the ultimate catharsis. Her hatred for her son-in-law brought back many unpleasant memories; he had never compensated his aunt when he took over his uncle's practice, leaving her destitute. Sido remarked that he had had to leave Saint-Sauveur after his father's tragic death, and now "maybe he will have to leave Charny," implying that he had murdered his father, too.

Suffering from backaches, Dr. Roché was dependent on morphine; two years after Juliette's death he sold his practice. He died in 1914. His daughter Yvonne, Colette's niece, married and became an alcoholic like her mother; she cared so little for her two sons that they never attended school. They grew up on the farm inherited from Juliette, La Guillemette. They bought nothing, lived mainly on goat milk and cheese, and kept useless gold coins hidden in a box. They lived in such squalor that a cousin, alerted by some neighbors, tried to convince them to improve their lot, but they showed no interest in bettering their way of life. One brother was found dead in the woods, whether by murder, suicide, or accident is not known; the other died of natural causes. Juliette's story and that of her descendents remains shrouded in oblivion. "My sister with the long hair" is the image left us by Colette of this strange and unfortunate girl, who drifted through a sad childhood and a bad marriage, was shunned by her family, and buried with no regrets.

By mid-September Colette had moved from her apartment on the Rue de Villejust because the building was to be demolished to enlarge the street. She settled in a new street in the seventeenth arrondissement, Rue Torricelli, which became the Rue Saint-Senoch in 1909. It was not the right time for "that damned move." She had several offers, and her first choice was the Olympia with Wague; she wrote to him: "Hurry, Hurry, don't waste a second . . . I hate to be torn between several things."[18]

From September 29 to October 8 Colette, Wague, and Kerf played La Chair in Bordeaux; on October 16 they were in Rouen. From November 16 to the 29 Colette was on tour in Belgium; at the Alcazar in Brussels, she played Claudine fifteen times to a full house. While dining alone in a hurry, she was interviewed at the Taverne Royale and gave her forthcoming schedule:

> "Baret Theatrical Tours are taking me to Lyons in December . . . In March, a grand tour throughout France. Will you come to hear me Wednesday? I will read my *Dialogues de Bêtes*. If you can't come, come to see me in Antwerp tomorrow afternoon."
>
> "In *Claudine?*"
>
> "No, in *Pagan Dances* which I choreographed myself. Monday I go back to Paris."
>
> "To play *Claudine?*"
>
> "But that's an obsession! Not at all, to see to the release of my latest book, *The Vine's Tendrils* and to give the finishing touch to a comedy in two acts which I have written, *En Camarades.*"

Missy was in Brussels with Colette; Willy hopped over from Paris to see the dress rehearsal, leaving by the midnight train. Two days later Colette sent him a telegram, saying she had caught the flu; he rushed back to Brussels, "I don't want to leave her alone there."[19] With Willy and Missy to look after her, Colette felt comforted. She liked the cast, she liked the set, she liked the new publicity — leaflets distributed in the street and her picture on a postcard given to passersby "like the address of a dentist." There was a spate of excellent articles.

Suddenly Colette felt dejected. Willy had left for Ostende and "reassuring Missy" for Paris. Solitude was more than she could bear; she asked Léon Hamel to come, "It would please me so much, I assure you." She missed Paris: "I can't wait to be back! Another ten days here! Hamel! It will never end! I am devastated!"[20] This gloom was on Willy's behalf. He seemed to be on his way back to financial recovery, had regular columns in *Le Rire* and *Comoedia,* and Colette had agreed to write another *Claudine,* "if no one knows about it."[21] But now he was facing a criminal indictment. While in Brussels he learned that he was being sued for two thousand francs for having sold a piano that did not belong to him; Boulestin had trumped up the accusation. He was now living in London where he opened a restaurant in Covent Garden which still exists. He had left Paris after quarreling with Willy over money matters. Willy kept repeating, "I am doomed . . . I tell you I am doomed." To make things worse, Colette was sinking into the state of anguish she always experienced before the publication of a book — "When it comes to literature, I have an inferiority complex."[22]

Early in November Charles Saglio, owner of *La Vie Parisienne* and *Le Sourire,* published *The Vine's Tendrils;* ten of the sixteen stories had already appeared in his daily from May 15, 1905, to September 5, 1906. *The Vine's Tendrils* was promoted in *Le Sourire* with the picture of a woman reading a book. "What is she reading? *The Vine's Tendrils,* the book so prettily perverse just published by Colette Willy, all the women and all the lovers are feasting on this exquisitely sensuous book." "Nonoche" was dedicated to Willy; "Toby-Chien Park" to Meg Villars; three poetic and sensuous tales, "Nuit Blanche," "Jour Gris," and "Le Dernier Feu" were dedicated "to M." In December Colette had a copy printed and bound for Missy with the three stories written for her illustrated with seventeen aquarelles by Gustave Fraipont; Willy received a trade copy inscribed, "To Willy, to my best friend," signed "Colette Willy."

In December Colette played *Claudine* at La Scala in Lyons; the tour was organized by Baret, a theatrical agent who signed on only top performers. Missy, Hamel, and Willy took her to the railroad station. Willy wrote in distress to Curnonsky, "She is off to Lyons. *Merde! Merde! Merde!* I am bored when she is not around. I don't have the money to go with her. Meg is charming . . ."[23]

Colette was not prepared for the demands of a professional tour. "You have to rehearse all day long without respite, morning, afternoon, evening — it is a good school, but it is tough." After the rehearsals of *Claudine,* Colette could rest in the comfort of Le Grand Nouvel Hôtel; while her comrades, "having to perform a new show every four days," had not a moment of their own. In *Music Hall Sidelights* (L'Envers du Music Hall), Colette empathized with the rough stagehands, and struggling actors who did not have even a gleam of a hope of success. She wrote to Charles Saglio that her success in Lyons was "absolutely crazy and out of proportion," complaining that she was not paid enough and counting on the one thousand francs he owed her. She could not wait to get back home. Colette felt in exile whenever she was far from Paris and her friends. In *Provinces,* Colette describes Paris as a puzzle of small provinces, which is what made it so dear to her.

Back in Paris, she gave seven performances of *Claudine.* In the high-powered world of the stars, Colette was elbowing her way up. After having taken on la Belle Otéro's and Maggie Gauthier's parts, she asked Willy for Polaire's part in *Le Friquet.* Curnonsky was entrusted with the delicate mission of prevailing on Baret to sign Colette up instead of

Polaire and he received several letters with detailed instructions. He was to say that Polaire was terribly demanding, her fee "never less than fifteen louis," while Colette would not ask for more than that — "Tell the best you can about the little one."[24]

Colette had agreed to work with Willy again on a sequel of *Claudine,* focused on her present dual fame as a writer and actress — "with a good plan, I can write it in two months."[25] She was adamant on one point: she did not want anyone to know about it. Willy needed an outline for Colette in a hurry and was willing to pay Curnonsky a sizable sum for one. He asked that Curnonsky arrange breaks in the draft for beautiful descriptions of the countryside in order to showcase the best of Colette's talent. Willy read the outline and did not like it; he did not want any love affairs between women, but a struggle "between souls," a tragic struggle, "ending by a pretty murder, yes, a murder."

Then he suggested they bring Willette Collie and Claudine face to face. Willette Collie (Colette Willy) was the mime in *Retreat from Love;* Colette described her as a dancing demon clad in a bathing suit. At the end of the pantomime Willette Collie dragged Annie away, threw her roughly to the ground, stifled her with a kiss, and carried her off under her arm, Annie's long hair and tunic floating behind her. Willy suggested that the opening scene of the new book be the meeting of Willette Collie and Claudine in the wings of a music hall. He wanted a psychological novel based on Colette's two personalities. The title was *The Vagabond.*

He was longing to recapture the best years of their lives. To Paul-Jean Toulet, whose talent he admired, Willy confessed sadly that he had let scandal pile up upon scandal; he had been irresponsible and rash. He had never paid attention to public opinion, and now public opinion had turned against him and crushed him, and he had lost Colette. Toulet understood; addicted to opium, unable to work steadily, he had lost his position at *La Vie Parisienne.* From 1907 to 1916 he contributed to every novel signed "Willy" and was paid a monthly stipend.

Willy was despondent; this separation from Colette was a harrowing experience for him. Their love, which had been battered and stretched to the breaking point, had an incredible resiliency. Paul Léautaud noted in his journal that their behavior showed a persistent feeling for each other. For instance, Willy could not resign himself to depriving Colette of Toby, the dog she had made famous in *Dialogues de Bêtes,* and Colette could not deprive Willy of their pet. So they decided to place Toby-Chien in the care of Willy's secretary, Diard, and agreed to visit him every other day, taking turns.

The year 1909 started on an upbeat note. The writer Paul Reboux gave a lecture on Colette the writer at the Théâtre Michel. On January 9 Colette danced in *La Tour du Silence* (The Tower of Silence), a play by the Swedish playwright G. Coleijn. On January 22, Colette's play *En Camarades* opened at d'Humière's Théâtre des Arts, then moved to La Comédie Royale, one of the most chic of the little theaters, and ran for three weeks. Colette played Fanchette. The critics were divided: the respected Adolphe Brisson wrote in *Le Temps* that Colette was expert as a mime, but lacked professional training as an actress. Her voice was too hoarse, she rolled her r's like the old melodrama actors, he found her tense, and her face expressed nothing. Her play was "the embryo of a comedy, with some subtle ideas, but only sketchy characters." The critic in *Comoedia* liked the dialogue, which he found alert, witty, and natural, but underlined Colette's lack of technique as a playwright. Willy came to the rescue with an article signed "Marc Villars":

> This is the prettiest of comedies, wavering between smiles and tears, we have seen nothing like it in a long time. Madame Colette Willy, excellent actress, is in the mind of snobs, prudish women, and stern protestants the very type of the woman who "is not like everyone else." I wish that more women had the healthy and rustic grace, the adolescentlike strength, the spellbinding candor of the author of *En Camarades* when she appears onstage. The plot is full of *coups de théâtre*. Fanchette and Max, an up-to-date high society couple, advocate total freedom. The curtain rises on Max, openly courting Fanchette's friend Marthe, while Fanchette is busy with *Le Gosse,* the Kid, a handsome young man obviously in love with her. These two charming acts cannot be fairly described, one has to hear the *mots,* the witty lines, all the bubbling champagnelike dialogue. Truly Madame Colette Willy is herself: the tendril of a grapevine on a wreath of laurels.[26]

On February 26 Colette danced *Une Danse Egyptienne* to music for harp and flute by Ingelbrecht at a charity gala at the Théâtre Marigny. Sido congratulated Colette on her play but asked why she was performing again half-undressed in a skimpy exotic costume: "So you are dressed as an Egyptian? As an Egyptian sphinx? You slut, do you think we don't read the papers?"[27]

The wavering relationship between Colette and Willy came to an abrupt end when Colette found out that Willy had sold the rights to the *Claudines*. A letter to Willy dated February 25, 1909, marked the watershed in the couple's relationship. Colette asked in anguish if it were true that those books, so dear to her, were lost to her and to Willy and belonged to the publishers. She could not come to grips with the idea; in a letter to Hamel she wrote that Willy had sold the books, "which were solely mine (morally)," for a pittance. Colette felt that in his secretive way, Willy wished to deprive her of ownership of the *Claudines* even after his death. Legally, the rights belonged to Willy; they had agreed on this point when they separated. "Morally," the books were hers. Colette was desperate. She had every reason to feel betrayed, since for nine years she and Willy had referred to the *Claudines* as "their daughters," "their legitimate daughters." That Willy could sell those books "which meant so much to [her],"[28] without a word was perceived by Colette as a kidnapping. She never forgave him for the secret sale and from that day on her eternal affection for the strange man who had been her husband, friend, and Pygmalion slowly turned into hatred, an unquenchable desire to get even.

Colette acted swiftly. On March 21 she applied for membership in the Société des Gens de Lettres. Her sponsors were Léo Claretie, managing director of the Comédie Française, Léonce de Larmandie, Henri de Régnier, and Paul Margueritte. On March 22 Colette and her lawyer signed an agreement with Willy in which he renounced all claim on *Minne* and *Les Egarements de Minne*. Alfred Vallette and Ollendorff were informed by her lawyer that Colette Willy and Willy had ceased to collaborate and were instructed to print both their names on any future editions of the four *Claudines*. In July Colette signed an agreement with both publishers stating that she would not oppose the sale made by Willy but, in return, negotiated a fixed royalty on each book sold. Contrary to what has been written, Colette went on receiving royalties from the *Claudines*.

On March 24, 1909, Colette forced Willy to acknowledge that she had contributed to a three-act comedy, *La Petite Jasmin*; he wrote that she should inform the Société des Auteurs-Dramatiques of her right to claim half the royalties on that comedy and any translation or adaption and signed, "Your friendly devoted Henry Gauthier-Villars." But he had not agreed to this spontaneously; Colette had refused to return the manuscript unless Willy declared that she would get half the proceeds. The *Claudines'* authorship was to go through more vicissitudes: in 1948 Colette had Willy's name removed. Jacques Gauthier-Villars thought this unfair; his lawyers asked the publisher to reprint his father's name. After 1955 the *Claudines'* editions are signed "Willy and Colette."

The saga of the *Claudines* was about to take another tack. In an interview in *Paris-Journal,* a reporter asked Meg Villars: "There is a rumor that you are about to coauthor a book with Willy on the music hall, which is Claudine's new profession." Colette sent an immediate correction: "Please deny your information. Claudine is a character that I have created, it belongs to me. It can belong to neither Meg Villars nor Mr. Willy."[29]

One Foot in Sea and One on Shore

Paris, blanketed in muddy snow, was in the grip of "sticky cold";[30] Colette, afraid of catching the flu in the drafty wings, welcomed the last performance of *En Camarades.* During the run she and Missy had established their headquarters at Chez Palmyre, Place Blanche, a homosexual gathering place where they dined every night. Colette described the restaurant-bar under the name "Semiramis-Bar" in *Paysages et Portraits.* It was so filled with smoke that even the food had a subtle taste of Maryland tobacco. Palmyre, the owner, was a chain-smoker and ambled between the tables sipping whiskey and soda; she had "the flat snout of a bulldog, a mass of red hair projecting like a cap over the brow and tied in a bun on her nape, and breasts jutting out like a Spanish balcony."[31] Palmyre, a friend of Toulouse-Lautrec's, is Olympe in *The Vagabond.* She cooked enormous meals and fed a crowd of down-and-out young tramps. Colette enjoyed the hearty cooking and "loved to watch girls waltzing with each other . . . young painters' models, young local streetwalkers, dancers without a job . . . two graceful bodies, molded in their thin dresses by the movements of the waltz, two slender adolescent girls who came in their evening shoes through the snow and the slush."[32] Willy described Chez Palmyre as "Le Bar Zénobie" in *Lélie, Fumeuse d'Opium,* "a polyglot restaurant whose eclectic owner and great friend of Vivette Wailly [Colette Willy] encouraged young girls to become courtesans."[33] Colette enjoyed off-beat places. She "would have given her future volumes for one more prank . . . she was bizarre, pretty, impossible, charming, a blend of irony and carelessness, the most unlikely of our Parisian glories . . ." wrote Louis Delluc.[34]

Flattered to host celebrities, Palmyre was full of "maternal attentions" and gave Colette fresh fruit, an expensive luxury in winter. For Missy, who was extremely particular with her diet, she grilled special cuts of steak served with a salad of lettuce stalks — the marquise did not eat the leaves. Chez Palmyre was the place to hear underground news from Lesbos.

To celebrate the end of *En Camarades,* Colette and Missy dined with Véra Sergine, a famous actress from the Comédie Française, and the legendary actor Edouard de Max — both had played in *La Tour du Silence.* Rumanian-born Edouard de Max was addicted to opium and ephebes and had a talent for wild, romantic scenes. Like Sarah Bernhardt, he cultivated his own brand of diction, quivering between speech and song and peppered with Rumanian rolling r's similar to Colette's Burgundian ones. He and Colette shared the adjective "feline" in the Parisian press. A few months earlier Colette and de Max had been at a gala at Robert d'Humières' Théâtre des Arts, located in the working-class Boulevard des Batignolles. De Max arrived in a Beduin costume crowned with a stuffed eagle, attended by three heavily made-up adolescents, two posing as Arcadian shepherds, the third — Jean Cocteau — as Heliogabalus, half-naked under a pearl-encrusted cloak, his hair curled and dyed red. As the new favorite, Cocteau wore de Max's eight expensive rings on his fingers. De Max's flamboyant homosexual camarilla was more than could be tolerated even in decadent Paris; discreet d'Humières, afraid of adverse publicity for his theater, delegated Sarah Bernhardt to tell de Max to have the boys sent to bed.

At a masquerade at the bal Wagram Colette and Missy were dressed as Pierrots. Niçois, Sergine, and de Max were not masked. Colette was struck by the contrast between Véra Sergine, bored and pale, and the festive ambiance. The paradox appealed to Colette; it reflected her own emotions in "Réveil Pon du Nouvel An," in which she is the bored narrator recalling her childhood New Year's Days while a rakish crowd drinks, screams, and celebrates the New Year.

Colette's private life was made up of a string of love affairs, none of which took on paramount importance. She lived in a racy set of actresses, courtesans, celebrities, and journalists who thrived on provocative behavior. One of Colette's *amants en titre* was Willy de Blest-Gana, a wealthy socialite and one of the best swordsmen of Tout-Paris; there was not a single elegant duel over which he did not preside. He was also Polaire's friend.

Colette remained very close to Polaire, and their lesbian relationship was often alluded to in the penny press. Polaire was rich, which meant that a lot of money slipped through her hands; Colette borrowed large sums from her. Among Polaire's lovers was the nineteen-year-old son of a Parisian grocer. She once organized a party *à trois* in her *hôtel particulier* on the Rue Byron; when she left the room, the young man turned his attention to Colette. Polaire returned and pounced on Colette; they fought, and Colette left with a black eye. Two days later they made up. But Colette, as slow to forgive as her brother Achille, plotted to get even. She asked some actresses to send love letters to the young lover, knowing that Polaire would intercept them. To make the revenge even more painful, Colette asked Willy de Blest-Gana to tell his friend Jules Porgès, a millionaire cognac merchant and Polaire's protector, that she used his money to keep gigolos. Blest-Gana refused and this vengeful request turned him away from Colette.

Colette was attracted by younger men. "Wherever man is beautiful and half-naked, women laugh with happiness."[35] She would pick up gigolos at Luna Park, at the Watrin terrace, or, preferably, at the Café of the Sportsmen at Porte-Maillot, patronized mainly by race car owners. There she met the nephew of an influential senator, the twenty-year old millionaire Lucien Fauchon, who was as ill-bred as he was handsome. At the Thé Ceylan in the Rue Caumartin, he welcomed her with friendly slaps on her derrière. When she was asked why she tolerated it, she replied, "The kid adores me and I don't feel his slaps through my skirt."[36] Once at the Carlton bar, where he was "like a sponge dripping with gin," Fauchon confided to Bonmariage that he was fed up with Colette because she was going to bed with "an incredible variety of actors and flashy South Americans." Fauchon explained that Colette never accepted being kept, but in practice, "she is the most expensive mistress."[37] She cost more than if he had paid up front for her apartment, carriage, and expenses, yet despite all he spent on her, he was never master of the house.

Every time he came, the maid happened to appear with bills for the gas, the electricity, the butcher, the cleaner, or the wines. Colette would open her purse and find no money; Fauchon would take care of the bills promptly. In Colette's dressing room at the theater, there was a whole slew of bills for makeup, Caron powder, perfume, and lotions. Then came the unpaid income taxes, the maid's or cook's salary, and, above all, the shopping sprees at the couturiers. "One never pays too much for pleasure," said Colette. "But she never paid for pleasure, she always reaped financial reward and pleasure as well."[38] This was a perfect application of Caroline Otéro's professional advice to Colette that there is always a moment when a man opens his purse if you wring his wrist.

When Lucien Fauchon dropped out of her life, another millionaire playboy stepped in — Auguste Hériot. For four years he had been Polaire's lover, and had given her a famous diamond belt; he had also been a munificent lover of Liane de Pougy's. He was thirty, seven years younger than Colette. Hériot, the model for *Chéri,* was extremely handsome, tall, with dark hair and large green eyes. With the masculine elegance of a cavalry officer and millions backing his spellbinding charm, Hériot was one of the most irresistible Parisian playboys. He practiced boxing and was one of the first men to fly a single-propeller airplane with wings made of wood and cloth. He lived in an imposing town mansion (now the Argentine Republic's legation) with authentic Louis xv antiques and two Gobelins tapestries taken from Fragonard cartons and later sold to Mr. Pierpoint-Morgan for three million francs. In the drawing room, under paintings by Boucher, he set up the first American bar in Paris with the best professional bartender in the city. Like Chéri, Hériot liked money and insisted on receiving a breakup present from a departing lover. From Charlotte Lysès, who left him to marry Missy's "son," Sacha Guitry, he demanded "an ermine blanket like Natalie Barney's" and got it.

Auguste Hériot was overwhelmed by Colette; he stopped seeing his friends and prepared to dedicate his energy and wealth to winning her love, although he tried to hide their relationship from the press. But Colette saw men as a commodity and did not want to be burdened with a serious relationship; she liked her life with Missy. Missy encouraged Hériot, as she would have liked Colette to settle down and write, but "The Vagabond" remained true to herself.

In the spring Colette signed with Baret Theatrical Tours to play *Claudine in Paris* in thirty-two provincial towns in thirty-five days. The tour, which started in her native province, was a personal success for Colette. The *Indépendant Auxerrois* described the packed house, where people came to pay their respects to Madame Colette Willy in a play set in part in neighboring Saint-Sauveur and full of allusions to well-known people. "The evening was pleasant even though it was a little risqué." Another local newspaper wrote a tribute to Willy, credited "with the creation of the typical woman of the century in Claudine, the ultimate modern character." And *Le Petit Bourguignon* declared that "Colette in the part of Claudine is a tremendous attraction; the house will be sold out." From north to south, the reviews concurred. Belfort found Madame Colette Willy's acting outstanding. "She delighted everyone with her spontaneous reactions, her youthful grace, her voice in which one can detect at times, a naive, rustic accent."[39]

The tour turned out to be a vacation, and Colette and Missy went sightseeing. As their chauffered car rode through the countryside, Colette felt energized by the beauty of the landscapes. She wrote to Sido that Missy was a wonderful companion with a sweet temper, always in good spirits. She was aware that she owed her present happiness to her and envisioned a theater tour of Europe in 1910.

The tour was also a journey back to the past. In Toulon, the birthplace of Captain Colette, a full house showered her with bouquets as the curtain fell to a standing ovation, the audience shouting "Vive Colette! Long Live Colette!" She found a postcard with a view of her father's birthplace, le Mourillon, for her mother. Colette was pondering an autobiographical account, which took years to mature and become *My Mother's House* "The Past," which was rushing back to her, was the title of an article she published that month in *Akademos*. On the way to Pau, Colette saw white orchids and pink flowers she would have loved to gather as she did when she was free to flit around in the woods surrounding Saint-Sauveur. She visited her nurse Mélie, with whom she had always kept in touch and who had retired in Pau.

The tour reached Nantes. *Le Populaire de Nantes* called *Claudine* "a play so scandalous that it could make a brazen soldier blush . . . There is no character, no plot, no description of manners capable of interesting the audience. The play is meant for a special public; the debauched, the courtesans, a society that can only be found in Paris."[40] But in Rennes, a university town, Colette was applauded every time she spoke. Raving students shouted her name and wanted her to play the entire second act over again. She enjoyed it so much that she immediately signed with Baret for another tour in October or April.

During the tour Colette wrote "Impressions de Danses" and "Gitanette," the heartwrenching story of a lesbian dancer Colette had met at Palmyre's. Gitanette and Rita, her friend, "tired of women's bars and music-hall lounges," had pooled their resources to pay a *maître de ballet* to choreograph a number for them. Their dances were neither good nor bad, but shielded them "from prostitution and from men, too often nasty." They made it to L'Empyrée. Rita was attracted by the glitter of high life offered by the show's leader, a woman who "poisoned" the drinks by putting drugs in carafes of champagne. Gitanette admitted to Colette that she would have killed her unfaithful friend: "That unassuming girl" knew that killing was the only way to put an end to her grief. "Only death is a choice, for no one chooses his life." Colette was again exploring the theme of betrayal. She concluded in "Gitanette" that there were only two solutions: either nurse your sufferings or commit murder.

During the tour Willy never ceased to send love letters to Colette. He wrote that he could neither eat nor sleep. Paul Barlet, who came to do some editing with her in Toulouse, brought her another version: Willy ate like a hog, saw all his women regularly, was getting fatter, and looked very well. Incensed, Colette wrote to Sido that she would make sure that Willy would pay for all he had done to her. He had become jealous of Missy, and Colette was prepared to fight Willy, "to tear his eyes out"[41] if he attempted to harm Missy in any way.

On May 10 the tour reached Rouen; the next day, in Amiens, was to be Missy's last stop. She was to return to her villa Belle-Plage, traveling with Léon Hamel, who had come to join them. Colette complained to Sido that although it would only be four days of separation, she was losing her bearings; she sent her a postcard of *The Weeping Angel,* a famous sculpture in the Amiens Cathedral. In fact, as soon as Missy left things deteriorated; in Douai, the hotel was awful and the landscape hideous. She sent a telegram to Missy, who rushed to meet her in Lille — hotels became pleasant again. Brussels was fine, Liège was delightful, but in three days Missy would leave again and Colette was feeling a new pang of anticipated loneliness.

During the tour Colette wrote, in chronological order, "Notes de Tournées" for *Akademos,* a plush and short-lived magazine; they were published on August 15 and September 15. Her recollections ended with an ardent prayer to the "Prince of Theatrical Tours," Paul Baret. She begged him to take her again on his eternal merry-go-round. She was ready to rise at 5:00 A.M., eat the bland food and drink the pale coffee of the railroad stations twice a day, and sleep in lumpy beds as long as she could travel every day and discover "the marvelous robe" of Mother Earth. The text was beautifully written although reality was remodeled. Colette wrote as if she had shared the hardships of the poor and unhappy actors — badly paid, badly fed, and badly lodged — and succeeded so well that her readers believed her. In fact, she was the star of *Claudine in Paris* and traveled in style with the marquise de Morny and her own private secretary, Paul Barlet.

Colette was in a period of intense activity. She instructed Georges Wague to refuse a contract with L'Alhambra if they did not pay a "reasonable fee." "When will I raise my fee? . . . at Otéro's age ?" Her fear of growing old was real; she perceived Otéro, four years her senior, as old. Colette had several theatrical agents working for her: Wague, Brouette in Belgium, and Buysens in Paris. In her letters she kept pressuring Wague. Had he sent a letter? Had he finished the script? Had he contacted the theater?

Colette left for Marseilles with Wague and Kerf for six performances of *La Chair* at L'Eldorado. Missy had flowers, fruit, and telegrams delivered to her every day.

Colette did not restrict herself entirely to journalism and theater. She pursued a series of madcap schemes, which she was to continue sporadically all her life. Speculating in real estate seemed a quick way to riches; acting as a go-between, Colette was negotiating the sale of some land in Auteuil, where the large summer estates of the Goncourts, the Prousts, Princesse Mathilde, Natalie Barney, and Jacques-Emile Blanche were being bought up by developers. Colette was in partnership with Missy and wrote to Hamel that he should be proud of "these two capitalists." To Sido she wrote that she had already sent out feelers to René Blum, the future patron of the Ballets Russes and younger brother of the socialist politician Léon Blum, who was to become prime minister in 1936. Colette was also involved in the sale of Missy's house and had retained an interest in her native home in Saint-Sauveur. Yielding to Sido's pressure, she agreed to sell it to her brother for seven thousand francs. On May 30, 1909, she witnessed the sale agreement of the Auteuil lots and promised Hamel that if the sale went through, she would buy him a butterfly from Kirby (a fashionable boutique in London). But there was a damper on Colette's elation; Sido had rekindled her jealousy of the Landoys. On June 22 Eugène Landoy, the editor in chief of *Le Matin d'Anvers,* died. The press ran extensive biographical articles on the Landoys, and Sido basked in the attention given to her nephew. Eugène's widow, Maria, received condolences from state officials and celebrities, "like a princess." *Le Matin* paid for all the expenses of an impressive funeral (five thousand francs, noted Sido), voted a monthly pension of three hundred francs for the widow, and asked Raphaël Landoy to take his brother's position as editor in chief at "a very attractive salary."[42]

Money was a grim obsession with Sido. She was angry because after Juliette's death Dr. Roché had stopped contributing to her pension, and she had complained to her Belgian nephews and sought their advice. Jules Landoy had answered that her granddaughter should go on paying the pension, since she was Juliette's heir. Dr. Roché promptly informed Sido that there was nothing left from Juliette's fortune. Sido, undaunted, decided to sue and consulted a judge, who told her that Roché and Yvonne could be subpoenaed but her other children would have to appear in court as well. She asked Colette to sign an affidavit stating that the furniture in Châtillon belonged to her, in order to lower the value of her own assets. She was told by her lawyer that her monthly pension of six hundred francs was too high to have a hearing in Châtillon. She would have to go to a higher court, without much prospect of winning her case against her granddaughter.

Colette and Missy settled for the summer at Villa Belle-Plage. During the last three days of August, strong tides pushed the waters to the walls of the villa. Colette went into the waves for the excitement of feeling rolled over and almost drowned. She rode her new horse, a present from Missy. Sacha Guitry and Charlotte Lysès spent the summer with them; there was a sense of family life. Colette was putting the final touches to "Notes de Tournée."

These quiet summer days were shattered by the publication of Willy's *Pimprenette.* On the surface *Pimprenette* was a light novel about contemporary mores with a stereotypical trio: a courtesan actress, her rich aristocratic protector, and a writer in love with her who fleeces his rich relations to keep her for himself. The rich protector was Prince Mihaïl de Morénie (Mathilde de Morny), the hero of *Jeux de Prince (Princely Games)*, published in 1906, and the generous prince of *A Clean Little Old Man*. In this sequel a gullible Mihaïl de Morénie is constantly betrayed by his shrewd mistress, Pimprenette de Folligny. The name was an anagram of Folette and Montigny, and allusions to Colette peppered the text. Pimprenette was a nude dancer and an actress "who interprets Claudine naturally"; her maid was called Francine, like Colette's maid; she had a cousin, Mélanie, from "Saint-Sauveur en Puisaye" (Yonne). The portrait of Pimprenette was that of an artful, yet somewhat naive actress who stopped at nothing to get her way. She had a brief affair with a minister who promised to sponsor her debuts at the Comédie Francaise and instead gave her a decoration, the Palmes Académiques. This was an allusion to Colette's affair with Léon Barthou, which the watchful Jules Renard had noted in his 1903 *Journal*. Pimprenette was described as having only a primary education, a talent limited to nude dances, and an insatiable appetite for money. She fell in love with René de Genlys (none other than Willy), who wrote in *Comoedia* and *Le Paillard* and loved Pimprenette. Thanks to her he became the prince's secretary. Since René was an honorable man who could not betray Mihaïl de Morénie while he was his secretary, at first Pimprenette and René worked out a friendship, helping one another and debating their intricate love affairs. But their mutual attraction was irresistible and they became lovers. In order to live with Pimprenette, René, who had spent his inheritance on her, gambled at the racetracks, always living on the thin edge between the legal and illegal. He put all his energies into shady deals and had none left for Pimprenette, who only loved the lover in him. A disgruntled René was left with nothing but the shambles of his dreams. This was Willy's fictionalized version of his downfall.

Missy/Prince de Morénie was told in no uncertain terms that Pimprenette had scores of lovers, including her private secretary. The last pages of the book were set in a courtroom. Henry Maugis, the lawyer-writer, defended Pimprenette, who was accused of indecent exposure on stage "after she had triumphed in a pantomime forty-five times,"[43] a reminder that, thanks to Willy's protection, Colette had never been prosecuted despite repeated attacks by the censors.

On the twenty-eighth of August Colette set to work on "a sort of novel." "I confess it makes me grouchy and edgy."[44] Missy provided her with the latest in office supplies: magnificent ringed binders and an array of fountain pens. Colette's friends were sent hunting for a special brand of paper like airmail paper, only more resistant. She was ready for *The Vagabond*, her answer to *Pimprenette*.

A new clash sprang up between Colette and Willy: Colette wanted Baret to include *En Camarades* in his fall program, while Willy was trying to persuade him to take on one of his own plays. He sent Curnonsky to the tour entrepreneur to find out what Baret's position was concerning "the Willy-Colette disagreement."

The fall tour was postponed, not because of the "Colette-Willy disagreement," but for economic reasons. Clemenceau, forced to resign, was replaced by an independent socialist, Aristide Briand, whose government voted for a pension plan guaranteeing 360 francs to every worker at the age of sixty. To finance this social program, the government was considering an income tax. The stock market reacted negatively, and the summer resorts lost their patrons. Casino directors "were begging to get out of their contracts" with tour directors. "It is terrible," commented Colette, who felt victimized by circumstance and was pushing Georges Wague to finish his new pantomime. It "will be ready when we come back, will it not?" She was negotiating a two-month contract with the Théâtre Réjane with the help of Sacha Guitry, who knew the financier Alfred Edwards. "He only owns the building, but Edwards can always do something somewhere."[45] Colette wanted the reluctant Wague to give her top billing on the poster of *La Chair,* as she was now the true star of the pantomime.

At the end of October Colette went to Lyon for a week of performances of *La Chair* at the Kursaal. She told Missy she felt that Wague had become jealous because she was more successful than he. Colette now perceived Wague as an encumbrance to her own career. She had signed with the Gaîté-Rochechouart to play the lead in Sacha Guitry's *C'te Pucelle d'Adèle* and did not want Wague to know about it. Missy was dispatched to ask the director not to publicize the play until Colette was back in Paris.

In Lyon Colette noticed a newcomer on the stage, the young comedian Maurice Chevalier (Cavaillon in *The Vagabond),* who fell in love with her but kept his feelings to himself. In an interview in 1950 André Parinaud asked Colette what her reaction would have been if Chevalier had confessed that he found her very attractive: "I might not have answered by a 'No.' I had noticed that tall, handsome boy who used to watch me from the wings with expressive eyes during my sketch with

Wague. But I was busy enough doing my best to cool my partner's passion. We were barely dressed and the sketch required Wague to throw himself on me as I lay on the ground. He used to go back to the wings, red in the face and apologizing, 'How can I help it, Colette? It overpowers me!' I must add that Wague was extremely handsome and was the Don Juan of the company."[46]

A few letters from Colette to Missy, scattered over the rare periods when Missy remained in Paris while Colette was on tour, shed some light on Colette's feelings. She wrote that it was a terrible punishment to leave her and she begged for a letter, although she had received several telegrams. In a nightmare she saw Missy going away, frightfully pale, her eyes becoming darker and darker; she woke up with a fever and a migraine headache. Colette wanted to return to Missy, whom she called her true reason to live. But Colette also wrote that there was a rival in the wings; a woman was flooding her with flowers.

In the fall the guerrilla warfare between Colette and Willy escalated. The first shot was fired by *L'Indiscret,* a weekly tabloid that published some innuendos about Colette's greed in her not-too-clear business deals. Colette saw Willy's hand behind these insinuations and vowed that she was ready "to do everything to prevent this from happening again,"[47] threatening Willy with a lawsuit.

On October 16, 1909, Colette's picture was on the cover of *Paris-Théâtre,* which featured a ravie review of her,

> Colette Willy is a mime and actress always acclaimed. Her taste for travel deprives Paris too often of the joy of applauding her, but she is not truly absent: when the actress is gone, we still have the writer. When the sight of her grace is taken away from us, we still enjoy her rare and charming talent in the *Journal de Colette,* which she regularly sends to *La Vie Parisienne,* and in her books.
>
> Before *Retreat from Love* Colette Willy had already published the famous *Claudines,* which sold three hundred thousand copies. (It is true that in those days most of the public did not know that she was the author of the famous novels, today it is fair to give her the credit and the glory since she never reaped the financial reward.) The talent of Colette Willy has triumphed over bourgeois prudishness, her talent is denied by no one. *The Vine's Tendrils* were received last year with enthusiastic acclaim. *The Innocent*

Libertine will meet the same success in a few days, meanwhile Colette Willy, who has no reason to worry about the promotion of her novel, is on a triumphant tour in France and Belgium with her pantomime.

On October 23 a response came, signed "Henry Gauthier-Villars":

In your article devoted to Madame Colette Willy, writer and actress, I read the following: "most of the public did not know that she was the author of the famous novels etc. . . ." No one admires the literary talent of the woman who wrote *Dialogues de Bêtes* "to amuse Willy" more than I do, I have told my admiration in many publications while she was my wife and even after our legal separation. This is why I find inadmissible the perfidious words in your article implying that I hid from the public the participation of Madame Colette Willy in the *Claudines*. I could quote articles in which I proclaimed this precious collaboration, even though Madame Colette Willy did not want to publicize the fact. In an interview she gave in 1904 to La *Dépêche,* she stated clearly: "I have denied for a long time that I collaborated with Willy because I would have preferred that he be known as the only author of those novels. But he says everywhere I participated, so I have to acknowledge it!"

Should I see in your article the first of a series of attacks? I was told that it was the case. I will respond to any attack, but your articles should bear a signature and not some cautious initials. I am not looking for war but I want to be left in peace. Henry Gauthier-Villars.

But war was declared. Colette, invoking Article 3 of the July 29, 1881, law, sent an answer. She stated that since Willy had quoted her interview, she had to say that in 1904, before 1904, and after 1904, she had told lies to protect the reputation and personality of her husband.

I wish Mr. Willy would tell the truth, which is that I did not 'collaborate' in the making of the four *Claudines,* of *Minne* and *Les Egarements de Minne,* but that Willy's part was limited to that of a secretary and a rather careless one, intent on adding lewd or nasty remarks to my text. He should acknowledge that his signature next to mine on the latest edition assigns him an importance he does not deserve. By this supreme concession, I thought I was buying my independence from him and peace.

The war went on, and the press took sides. On October 16, 1909, *Paris-Théâtre* was for Colette: "It is at least fair to give Colette the glory of having written the *Claudines* since she has not reaped the material reward of three hundred thousand published copies." Willy answered that it was an unfair statement, since the royalties of Colette's six novels were only part of the couple's income. The following year, Colette learned that Willy had written a musical comedy called *Claudine*, and she wrote to the president of the Société des Auteurs Dramatiques, requesting that half the royalties go to her, as the creator of *Claudine*. She also demanded half the rights on the songs; Willy agreed, which seems to indicate that Colette did, in fact, write some of the lyrics.

After this exchange of fire, everyone took sides in this very Parisian debate. Colette's supporters and Willy's would assail each other for decades to come. Presently the weekly, *Tout-Paris*, refused to publish any further answers to answers. Having no public forum in which to plead their case, they kept on in private.

Willy's tone was subdued. He needed Colette's testimony in a lawsuit for embezzlement filed against him by his mistress, Madame de Serres. Willy and Colette had known Louis de Serres and his wife Liette since 1898. She was the model for Colette's character, Marthe Payet. Colette had dedicated "Toby-Chien et la Musique" in *The Vine's Tendrils* to Louis de Serres. Willy spoke highly of his music.

Willy told Colette that Liette de Serres had done everything to tear them apart, telling him that Colette had lovers and went shamelessly from one bachelor's apartment to another. She had denounced Colette with such insistence that Willy had come to believe her, and this, he said, caused the breakdown of their marriage. Willy pretended that he had been taken in by this woman until he finally realized what she was up to. He said she should be punished for having wrecked their lives. The best punishment would be to keep all the money she had entrusted to him and to stop paying the fixed return she was entitled to receive. The scheme was risky; Madame de Serres could demand the reimbursement of her investment in the Gauthier-Villars publishing company. There was only one way to make her accept her financial loss without a word: Colette must play the part of the betrayed wife who had found out about her husband's betrayal and was ready to reveal the love affair to Monsieur de Serres, unleashing the worst possible scandal. Colette accepted.

To carry out this Machiavellian plan, Willy gave Colette Madame de Serres' letters, then told Liette de Serres that her letters were in Colette's hands. He thought this alone would be enough to intimidate his mistress. Throughout 1909, Willy worried and schemed. While she was on tour with *Claudine in Paris,* Colette received letters from Willy beseeching her to remain his friend in spite of their separation. In April she received a letter warning her that Liette was bitter and threatening. She had met with Sido — "your mother told her a thousand things so useless that they become damaging, among others the sale of a drawing by Ingres"[48] — and he bemoaned this seepage of confidential material by Sido. He promised never to attack either Colette or Missy, "your friend and my enemy," in any way. But in exchange he entreated Colette to remain his ally in his struggle against Madame de Serres, who, according to him, was bent on destroying him and had the power to do it — he had signed a note promising that the sum Madame de Serres had entrusted to him would be paid back on demand. Willy wrote to Colette that if Liette filed a lawsuit and won, it would mean a jail sentence for him. He seemed so worried that on May 24 Colette sent a short letter to Madame de Serres, begging her to spare the man she had once loved. Willy was in such a state of panic that he convinced Madame de Serres that he was going to commit suicide if she sued him. Liette relented, then decided to go straight to Albert Gauthier-Villars to clarify the matter. Albert, very proper and very cool, had no intention of getting entangled in his brother's deals.

On November 2 after their exchange of articles about the authorship of the *Claudine*s, Willy proposed a meeting. Colette answered that she would meet him only in the presence of Mr. Mounier, her lawyer. The presence of a lawyer was the last thing Willy wanted, since he was planning to offer Colette a payoff for her support in the looming de Serres lawsuit. Cleverly he circumvented the problem by promising to accept her decision. They met and granted each other's requests. Not only did he convince Colette to help, but he promised her a share of the proceeds from a building they could squeeze out of Madame de Serres were she convinced that she was powerless. They agreed to keep up a facade of hostilities, but wept in each other's arms.

In spite of their emotional storms during these years of separation, they were still fascinated by one another and never ceased to be in touch.

Letters from Colette to Willy give an idea of the couple's astonishingly fluctuating feelings. Colette thought her estranged husband was marvelous. She thanked him for his telegrams and warned him that Liette was in Nice — so they should beware — and expressed her admiration for some verse he had written. In the margin of this letter, Willy scribbled that it was sweet to see genius recognizing his merit. By pulling some strings, he obtained the Palmes Académiques for Colette, an honor reserved for writers, artists, and intellectuals. Colette was elated. After the official ceremony, during which a small crown of laurels was pinned on her jacket by the minister of public instruction, she sent a thank-you note to Willy, calling him her true friend. He wrote to beg the marquise to take good care of his Folette.

But soon after the November meeting Willy's book *Le Retour d'Age* was released. He called it an "intimate diary full of vain autopsychology and enough material to turn it into a novel."[49] Willy described in it his long imbroglio with Madame de Serres and disclosed that he had financed her gambling addiction for years. Colette was outraged to learn that he had spent their royalties to pay his mistress's gambling debts. He had also not kept his promise to never attack Missy; there were ironic remarks about her in the book.

Colette started proceedings against Willy for defaulting on the payment of the furniture he was renting from her. This drew an unexpected answer from Willy, who inquired if, despite this legal action, Colette was still willing to back him up against Madame de Serres. Colette put on a show of hostility but wavered between trust and mistrust, for Willy never ceased to astonish her.

In Every Feast of Your Life, Drink the Poison
Poured by Your First, Your Only Love

The legal separation between Colette and Willy was dated February 1907; legally, if no reconciliation took place after three years divorce was automatically granted. As the date approached, there was a flurry of wild speculation and an avalanche of letters. Willy's sister-in-law Valentine came to see Colette. Sido feared that the Gauthier-Villars were conspiring against her daughter, dreading that Colette would reveal what she saw as Willy's "infamies."[50] She advised Colette to accept their money if they offered a settlement, but said that she should demand at least one hundred fifty thousand francs.

Colette told her mother that she was prepared to make some startling revelations, so damaging that the Gauthier-Villars would have to change their name. Sido was quite alarmed. What would Willy say about Colette? Sido was in such turmoil that she begged Colette not to travel alone, to take her brother Léo or Paul Barlet as bodyguards. She also gave Colette some new ammunition with which to defend herself: Achille recalled that when Germaine Villars had been terminally ill, Willy had asked him what amount of morphine could cause death by overdose. After Willy left for Paris, Achille could not find his supply of morphine. He was ready to go to Paris and make a deposition. It would, of course, be necessary to think it over carefully because of the seriousness of the consequences. Sido and Achille were considering charging Willy with murder.

A few days later Sido had to come down off her high horse. Colette told her that Willy had sent her a messenger to let her know that he still loved her, and she believed him. He was about to review her in Sacha Guitry's play! This worried Sido. What was he up to? Willy was to praise Colette's talent in *Comoedia* to counter Sacha Guitry's article denying that she was a good actress. Sacha Guitry preferred the writer to the actress and said so: "Colette's existence, so agitated and so artificial, seems to me exceptionally sad and the dances which she believes sensuous and which she performs before the curious Parisian are sinister and without any grace. Her attempts to dance would have gone unnoticed without the unique wildness of her face. What she lacks for the music hall makes her talent as a writer even more precious." However, he cast her as Adêle in his two-act farce, *C'te Pucelle d'Adèle* (Adele, the Maiden).

From November 19 to December 8 at the Gaîté Rochechouart, Colette performed in *C'te Pucelle d'Adèle*. Guitry inscribed it to Colette with a strong hint: "To Colette Willy, to the author of the *Claudine*s, of *Dialogue de Bêtes* and of *Les Vrille de la Vigne*, I dedicate this trifle as a weak token of my admiration." Adèle, a pretty farmer's daughter abused by her parents, who whip her and beat her, wants to run away but has no money. So she pretends that she is another Joan of Arc, who has to obey heavenly voices commanding her to go to Paris. Her boyfriend, draped in a sheet, provides the heavenly voices with enough talent to convince her parents that saints are calling Adèle. They give her money to fulfill her holy mission and she leaves the farm. The second act is a series of witty dialogues; the plot ends with the return to the farm of a pregnant Adèle.

Willy wrote a glowing if anonymous article in *Paris qui chante*:

> Madame Colette Willy is a delightful Adèle. She brightens up this bizarre part with her youthful and natural mischievousness and manages to give the appearance of truth and reality to Adèle. Her short skirt, her blouse fitting tightly over a round and free bosom, reveal the perfection of her body and this strange beauty which is hers alone.

The actress thus complimented, he paid a tribute to the writer.

> Madame Colette Willy is unique. She is simply one of the greatest writers of our times, either in that famous series of the *Claudines* and the *Minnes* that she does not deny having coauthored with her "widower" who does not deny it either, or in the *Dialogues de Bêtes, La Retraite Sentimentale, Les Vrilles de la Vigne* which have been written by herself alone and could have been written by no one else.
>
> Madame Colette Willy has invented a style and a way of feeling things which make her the equal of the greatest masters of the French language and the French wit. She is one of the women writers whom one can call with absolute certainty a genius.
>
> Well, so it happens that this admirable artist has a taste for the stage and wants to be an actress. This is a great tribute to the profession, even if many think it is a desecration. They cannot fathom that this young woman who writes masterpieces stoops to become the interpreter of plays written by others. She will always remain superior to any text any playwright can give her.
>
> Madame Colette Willy has the right to do whatever she wishes. Molière also was an actor on stage. There remains one question: does she know her trade as an actress? She does, to be convinced of her professional know-how, it is enough to go and see her on the stage.[51]

On December 4 Sacha Guitry asked Colette to be part of a lecture with Sarah Bernhardt and de Max on "Physical Strength, Duels, Courage, and Fear." The subject fitted her well.

Colette achieved indisputable stardom that year; she was quoted as being one of the three most highly paid actresses in France. She had settled down with Missy in a relationship that was proving supportive, comfortable, and secure, and she was finishing her novel. In defiance of Willy, she called it *The Vagabond* — the working title of their last project together, the great aborted psychological novel based on Colette's dual personality and career.

Ollendorff published *The Innocent Libertine* which was *Minne* and *Les Egarements de Minne* fused together. The book was published with a foreword — part of the latest agreement — in which Willy acknowledged that Colette had written *The Innocent Libertine* alone. She signed the novel "Colette Willy."

Yet the belligerence between them gained strength at every turn. Colette sent *The Innocent Libertine* to Curnonsky, inscribing the first page with words meant to create a rift between Willy and his collaborator: "To my old Curnonsky, to the author of *Une Plage d'Amour*, of *Un Petit Vieux Bien Propre*, of *Maugis en Ménage*, etc... from the author of *Les Claudines*."[52] Curnonsky was on Willy's side; he sent her a clipping of Willy's flattering article in *Paris qui chante* and a letter appealing to Colette's literary honesty. He denied that he was the only author of the books she mentioned and urged her to acknowledge that Willy was a good writer and not just a talentless editor of others' work. He told her that those who flattered her ego by demeaning her former husband were wrong. But Colette was preparing an even more crippling attack on Willy in the novel she was writing.

In an interview in January of 1910 Maurice Dekobra asked Colette if she was a feminist. She answered: "Oh, no! I am disgusted with the suffragettes," alluding to their fight in England for the vote for women. "If a few women in France have the gall to imitate them, I hope that they will be told that such behavior is not acceptable in France. Do you know what the suffragettes deserve? The whip and the harem."[53]

Like most Parisians, Colette was in a bad mood. The worst flood since 1658 had changed streets into waterways. "Canals like in Venice," commented the disgruntled Parisians, as they moved about in boats. "It is all due to Halley's comet," groaned the home owners, surveying their wine cellars as the waters of the overflowing Seine lapped at their rows of bottles. In Châtillon the streets turned into rivers. In the hospital of a neighboring town, according to Sido, they had caught fish under a patient's bed.

Colette was struggling with *The Vagabond*. In February she asked Charles Saglio to postpone publication until May 15. She had written an epistolary novel and did not like it. "I realize what is missing, and what has to be reworked."[54] Colette always suffered from a true literary inferiority complex. She had relied on Willy and his team to discuss her previous books, to encourage her, to give her their *imprimatur*. Colette felt compelled to reassure her publisher: "I don't lack self-confidence!"[55] *The Vagabond* was her own creation, and she was not "giving in to the influence . . . shall I say, punctilious, of Paul Barlet."[56]

Her energy and stamina were amazing. She steadily contributed articles to *La Vie Parisienne* and to *Paris-Journal* while she was rehearsing for a new show. The first two weeks in February she was in Belgium to perform *La Chair* at the Folies-Bergère of Brussels. Then she was booked in Grenoble from February 24 to March 2. She appeared in *La Nuit Sicilienne,* a pantomime by Mayargue and Redstone. From March 4 to March 7 she was again Yulka at the Eldorado in Nice. Before leaving for her second theatrical tour she spent March 26 to March 29 with Sido in Châtillon. Sido scolded her for wasting her imagination on articles and short stories instead of concentrating on a major work.

On April 5 Colette left on another theatrical tour. The Tournée Baret was presenting three one-act comedies: *La Bigote* by Jules Renard and *La Cruche* and *La Peur des Coups,* both by Georges Courteline. Colette was Margot in *La Cruche* and the wife in *La Peur des Coups* (The Fear of Blows). She was mad at Baret, who had refused her a part in *En Camarades,* and was glad that his program had not been successful. She had a fixed salary and did not care what Baret made at the box office; she wished him a loss of at least twenty thousand francs and called him "that pig."

The tour lasted from April 5 to May 4 and played in thirty-eight cities. Colette sent postcards to Sido from each of them. Missy and Auguste Hériot, whom Sido called their "patito,"[57] their little duck, escorted Colette. They traveled in style. Missy took care of everything, packed, unpacked, and checked Colette's wardrobe. A photograph shows Missy with a curling iron, doing Colette's hair. Once more she enjoyed personal success on the tour; the public shouted her name and cheered her.

In Brest Colette and Missy took a taxi ride along the seashore. They were looking for an estate on the coast but could not discover the house of their dreams. In May they went back to Brittany and found Rozven, an estate near Saint-Coulomb. It was a manor with acres of land, stables, and a detached keeper's house. The estate ended on a sandy beach in a cove. They made an offer and waited three days for an answer, but the owner would not sell.

Another of Missy's "sons" was getting married. In June Colette and Missy went to the marriage of Prince Ghika and Liane de Pougy, who had amassed quite a fortune and wanted respectability. Liane had counted Hériot among her worshipers and had planned to marry him, but had lost him to Colette. Colette declared that Liane's marriage would not last, that Ghika had married her for her money and was going to ruin and abandon her when she grew old. In 1910 caustic articles appeared in *Le Rire, Le Sourire,* and *Fantasio,* signed by pen names. Liane was upset by these attacks on her young husband. Later, in her diary, she wrote that he was abnormal, hysterical, and degenerate, but in 1910 she resented the attacks because they shed doubt on the credibility of her marriage "for the sake of pure love." Inquiring about the articles' author, she discovered it was Willy. Liane was convinced that he was making fun of her princely spouse just to please and amuse Colette and that Colette herself was the source of the gossip.

On June 21, 1910, the divorce of Colette and Willy became official. Throughout the winter their attorneys had negotiated a settlement in which both parties agreed to share the blame. *Divorces aux torts réciproques* were extremely rare. Colette was in Le Crotoy when the divorce judgment was pronounced, while Missy was making arrangements to rent the Brittany estate she was still trying to buy from its reluctant owner.

From May 21 to October 1 *The Vagabond* was serialized in *La Vie Parisienne.* In *The Vagabond* Wague became Brague; Maurice Chevalier, Cavaillon; Léo Hamel, in part, Hamond; Missy, the main character, Max; and Willy, Adolphe Taillandy, a pseudonym he had used to rent the *pied-à-terre* on Rue Kléber where Colette enjoyed her rendezvous with Georgie Raoul-Duval.

The Vagabond dealt a major blow to Willy's public image. His reprisal came later, but Colette dealt the first serious wound to her former husband by writing a portrait of her marriage. In *The Vagabond,* Renée Néré is very young and very much in love when she marries "that old man," a portrait painter who makes delicate pastels of women. She accuses Adolphe Taillandy of being a master manipulator. He even resorts to violence, but seldom, and only to assert his prestige. She accepts visiting her mother when Taillandy needs to be free to see a mistress. She even accepts taking one of Taillandy's mistresses for a walk to do some shopping while he makes love to another in their apartment. Finally, when Taillandy asks her to stay away for several days, she does not come back. Women cannot escape from Taillandy's spell, and he can assume so many personalities that he is a different man with each one: an experienced lover with the very young, an artist with the refined, a libertine with the blasé, a romantic with the naive. When she divorces, friends, family, and public opinion are all in favor of Taillandy, blaming her for leaving him. Renée is a writer, "a fallen writer" (as one would say a "fallen angel") since she is a mime, a dancer, and an actress. She is also a discredited woman, being a divorcée.

No one could fail to identify Renée with Colette, and every attack on Taillandy was aimed straight at Willy. She tried to destroy his credibility by asserting that Taillandy had no talent. She also pointed out his dishonesty in business. She had been madly in love and had suffered very deeply. "I had been jealous to the point of wanting to kill and die."[58] Renée describes the awe with which she received his first caress, the surprise of her first tears, the first pain caused by love and jealousy. Renée may love again, but her happiness will always be marred by memories. She rejects a new love, marriage, children, and a stable life and chooses to be free and alone. She is now *The Vagabond,* going from town to town, from theater to theater, living a day-by-day adventure without shackles. There are no mentions of her lesbian or extramarital affairs. Colette had turned her experience into a metaphor for liberty in a time when the social status of a woman depended on her husband, and a woman without a husband was automatically *déclassée.*

The Vagabond was a best-seller. Emmanuel Glaser wrote: "Madame Colette Willy is a very strange and very disturbing writer, she is all contrasts, she writes with the most crude realism and also with pure idealism, she is emotional and ironic, tender and cruel, brutal and modest, and her modesty is sometimes more embarrassing than her brutality...."

In *La Nouvelle Revue Française* Jean Schlumberger wrote that the descriptions of music halls and of the life led by Renée on tour were so strong, so moving, that one could not forget it. Maurice Donnay wrote: "You have a great talent, dear colleague, and you write like an angel." Henri Bordeaux said that he felt so much art in this novel that he had to thank the author. In *Excelsior* Ernest Charles declared that Colette was renewing and would go on renewing French literature and the French language. The critic for *Comoedia* estimated the novel "hard to equal." The most surprising comment came from the conservative daily *Le Temps*, whose critic discovered a religious potential in the novel, the possibility of conversion: "The sins of the dancer and mime are a promise of redemption." Rémy de Gourmont praised *The Vagabond* as a treatise on feminine psychology. Out of the ten members of the Académie Goncourt, three voted to give their annual prize to *The Vagabond*. Marcel Ballot commented in *Le Figaro* that she did not receive the prize but "should be one of the famous Ten of the Académie Goncourt."[59]

At the end of 1910 Léon Bailby, a friend of Missy and Colette's and the director of the influential daily *L'Intransigeant,* polled his readers: "If women could be elected to the Académie Française, whom would you vote for? Give three names only." First came Gérard d'Houville, a poetess, with twenty-nine votes. Anna de Noaille, another poetess, came second, with twenty-seven votes. Colette came third, with twenty-two votes. The majority of the readers voted against the admission of women to the three-hundred-year-old institution created by Richelieu. Marguerite Yourcenar would not be admitted to the all-male Académie until 1980.

Colette had several reasons to be happy. She had read Willy's latest novel — *Maugis en Ménage* — and it was a magnificent revenge to read such trash. The novel focused on Maugis' struggle to survive honorably, refusing the help of an American hostess and gallantly declining to marry her wealthy young sister, who was in love with him. The novel did not mention Colette or any of her avatars; she had all but disappeared. In June Colette obtained a court order ordering Willy to pay ten thousand francs in damages for the furniture he had kept and a two-hundred-franc penalty for each day of delay. He was in Monaco gambling when he read the first installments of *The Vagabond* in *La Vie Parisienne*. He wrote to Curnonsky that the Willy-Colette affair was not over with the divorce; it had — in his words — "just begun." He told him to let Colette know that there would be an answer to *The Vagabond*. Willy spread the news that he was about to publish *Sidonie ou la Paysanne Pervertie* (The Perverted Country Girl).

In fact the answer was *Les Imprudences de Peggy* (Peggy's Indiscretions), signed "Meg Villars" and supposedly written by Peggy and translated by Willy. Seventeen-year-old Peggy has an English father, a French mother, and an unpleasant aunt called Sidonie-Gabrielle-Anastasie. Peggy goes to

Robert Parville's (a pseudonym of Willy's) bachelor apartment on Rue Kléber. There she looks at photographs: one of Colette before 1900, several of Georgie Raoul-Duval, and many of Polaire, with tender autographs.

A sad Parville spoke bitterly: "It is not easy to be loved. No woman has ever given me anything without asking for three times the value in exchange. They all extended a begging hand."

"Even that pretty lady?" asked Peggy, showing a picture of Vivette Wailly [Colette Willy].

"Pretty?" answered Parville, "No. That picture was touched up and it was a long time ago. She changed rapidly. Here she is, in 1906, age 33, that bitchy Vivette Wailly."

"My poor friend Taillandy married this country girl, who was clever, shrewd, penniless, and who could not marry in her village because she had left her father's house to go to work for a music teacher in Auxerre, a *fugue* with *divertissement.* "

"She did not love your friend?"

"Neither my friend nor any man. She was tremendously selfish and tolerated his mistresses because she was afraid to have children who could spoil her figure. She also had mistresses. Not always faithful ones, because many of these priestesses of Sappho adopted the religion of Eros thanks to the irrepressible womanizer Taillandy, who made it his duty to convert them to a more normal devotion. This way of life lasted three years, six years, twelve years during which Vivette, scatterbrained and spoiled, ruined her husband to his very last penny. That is when she went completely astray by getting involved openly with an old morphine addict who dressed in men's clothes, the baronne de Louviers. Her husband still had the weakness of feeling some affection for his wife, but since he had always despised Vivette, even in the days of his mad passion for her, it did not make much difference. However, he started to love someone else, an adorable girl who had given herself totally to him, an English girl . . .

"When Vivette understood that she had been jilted for a younger woman whom Taillandy loved more than her, her wounded pride inspired her with the most despicable series of revenges. With the help of Taillandy's ex-secretary [Paul Barlet], a hypocrite to whom she handed down the baronne's old tailored suits, she stole Taillandy's letters and his furniture, accused him of having poisoned one of his mistresses, and managed to hurt his reputation by a scandalous lawsuit, the result of an unfortunate business deal into which she had dragged him and which had been of some profit mainly to herself. At last, triumphant and satisfied, she retired to her manor in Brittany, a gift from the baronne."

Les Imprudences de Peggy was vitriolic in its crude disclosures. No one was spared, nothing was forgotten, not even the furniture. Willy's revenge novel ended with a threat: "Everyone thought that he had accepted the situation with resignation and he thought so himself. But suddenly one morning he walked calmly through the door of the manor where the two women lived and in cold blood shot them both with two bullets each in the head. Then he put the gun to his temple and shot himself, taking care not to drop dead over their two bodies."[60]

Willy had been in a state of rage for months. On November 2, 1909, he had written to Curnonsky that he was destitute: "they are about to cut off the gas in my apartment, it is not as bad as if they were to cut off my balls, but it is bad enough." He hated literature like a woman he could never possess; he had "dreamed of passionate embraces and barely managed to caress her."[61] He tried to make a lot of money, since the literary laurels he longed for were out of his reach. In 1910 his creditors initiated a legal action through the Société des Gens de Lettres, the writers' guild, to garnishee his royalties in the amount of fourteen thousand five hundred francs.

In July Missy and Colette settled the last difficulties concerning Rozven; officially, Colette paid ten thousand francs and Missy paid the balance. Sido, Léo, Léon Hamel, and Paul Barlet were invited; Sido came to stay for two weeks.

From September 21 to 29, Colette was in Dijon to play *La Chair;* in July she had been in Belgium, and on October 4, she played in Marseilles. From the plush Grand Hôtel de Noailles et Métropole she wrote to Missy, longing for her presence; it was two o'clock and no letter from Missy had yet arrived. She had received beautiful carnations, eaten some fresh cherries, lunched alone, and taken a walk. In spite of her relationship with the millionaire Hériot, she was lonely and was counting the days she had to spend away from Missy — two more, plus the day on the train.

On October 9 *La Chair* opened in Paris at the popular Gaité-Montparnasse. In 1910 Montparnasse was still a district outside the limits of Paris proper; it was known for its dancing halls, its country restaurants, and its cheap cafés. Montparnasse did not tax wines and liquor, so people went there to drink. It was not the Montparnasse of the Roaring Twenties, but a quiet, rural neighborhood with trees along the street and bushes around the café terraces. At dusk the greenish lights of the Auer lamps made splashes of color, and on summer nights fireflies glittered in the bushes. Montparnasse had four music halls. Their public was hard to please and had no patience with artists; they would shout, hiss, whistle, and pelt the stage with orange peels or violets.

A reporter wondered how the public not used to Wague's avant-garde pantomime would react. But:

> The public was won over immediately, Chantrier's music was beautifully executed and charmed the audience and when Colette came on stage, a whisper greeted her, "What a beauty!"
>
> The absence of speech in the pantomime surprised at first, but then the spectators said to each other, "It's like the cinema!" The tragic scene at the end unleashed the emotions, the impact of Wague's performance was tremendous when he stabbed his wrist with his dagger; someone exclaimed, "That's real blood!" When the curtain went down, there was thunderous applause with screams and shouts of approval, the kind an artist can only receive in these popular theaters [62]

After her popular success, Colette moved on to Bataclan. November 4 was the opening night of *Aux Bat' d'Af* (At the African Battalion); Wague's pantomime was an adaptation of a popular novel by Bruant. The scenario was a pretext for violence and lust. Colette was a dancer in a sinister bar somewhere in the Sahara, and its customers were the soldiers of the African Penal Battalion. She danced Moorish and Spanish dances, using all her perverse charm to seduce the soldiers. One of them was her lover, but she was coveted by a wealthy farmer. There was a brawl; the farmer called in the patrol; her lover was killed; and, in a fit of despair, she strangled the farmer and went mad.

At the end of the run Colette left for Italy with Auguste Hériot. They traveled to Sorrento and Naples, and he tried to please her by giving her all the luxury she could dream of, hoping she would marry him. She wrote to Léon Hamel that the sightseeing was "worthwhile," but that she was not taken by the beauty of Naples and its surroundings; she remained unmoved by marble and only liked the flower gardens and orange groves. She felt a strange aversion for these southern landscapes and only cool feelings for Hériot. He was a nice "kid" when he was alone with her, but he had too much "built-in sadness"[63] to ever be happy. This journey *en tête-à-tête* had been disappointing — Colette was bored.

In December Colette dealt Willy, still entangled in the Liette de Serres lawsuit, a murderous blow: she gave Madame de Serres' lawyer a folder containing typed copies of Willy's letters addressed to Colette in 1908 and 1909 and a signed deposition in Madame de Serres' favor. It was the bitter end of a long and murky legal struggle. In her deposition signed December 1, Colette stated that she had heard that Madame de Serres had entrusted Willy with a large sum of money from the sale of one of her houses to invest in the Gauthier-Villars press. It was her understanding that Madame de Serres wanted a fixed return on her money; she had made the investment with the provision that any profit above the fixed income would go to Willy as a commission for managing her money.

On December 10, 1910, Willy was called before the judge for a preliminary hearing. Colette was the main witness against him but could not produce any originals of the incriminating documents, only copies and excerpts, probably because she would have incriminated herself in the scheme. She paid for a round-trip ticket so that Marcel Boulestin, who lived in London, where he owned a restaurant, to come and corroborate her story. Willy threatened Boulestin with telling everything he knew about his dealings — Boulestin sailed back to London immediately and did not testify. Due to lack of evidence, the main charge was dropped and Willy was not jailed; he was condemned to pay back his debts, and his royalties were garnisheed in Madame de Serres' favor. When he died in 1931, a balance of five thousand francs was still due.

Journalism Is a Breathtaking Career

The Vagabond opened the doors to high-powered journalism for Colette. She signed a contract for two articles a month with *Le Matin,* a newspaper that had become a giant — with the largest circulation in Europe — when it was bought by Alfred Edwards, a notorious financier. He sold it to Bunau-Varilla, a socialist millionaire who used the daily to promote his political ideas.

From the onset Colette met with strong opposition from some of the editorial staff, especially from Stephane Lauzanne, one of the joint editors in chief, who threatened to resign if "this mountebank" was hired. His objection was easy to understand. Colette published articles in celebrity magazines with gossip columns such as *Gil Blas, Fantasio,* or *La Vie Parisienne,* had blazed a trail of scandals, and was extremely controversial. But she had powerful friends on the editorial staff, among them Léon Blum, whom she had known since the days of *La Cocarde.* Author of *Du Mariage,* a utopian feminist essay, he understood and admired Colette. An agreement was finally reached — she would sign with a graphic, represented by a mask. When Colette's first short story was published on December 2, 1910, a brief introduction gave away her identity: "'La Poison,' the tale published today, is signed with a pseudonym, under which a woman writer, one of the best in our days, hides herself mischievously. Her talent is so personal, so full of exquisite feeling, of such sharp observation, of such youthful fancy! that it has just scored another hit in a sentimental novel which is the latest bestseller."[64] Colette alone could fit that description; when everyone had guessed her identity and the *Le Matin* readership had shown no adverse reaction, she lifted the mask. With her fifth contribution, "The Exiled" (L'Exilé) on January 27, she waved to her readers: "That's me! Colette Willy!"

Colette was finally where she had always wanted to be, on the staff of an important, influential newspaper. Sido could not help making a remark about what it had taken for Colette to become a writer: "I often say to myself what you vaguely say to yourself: if you had not lived several years with that phenomenon, your talent would never have revealed itself."[65]

Yet Colette had no intention of leaving the stage. From January 13 through January 20 Colette, Wague, and Kerf gave alternating performances of *La Chair* at L'Etoile Palace and *Aux Bat' d'Af'* at the Bataclan. Colette wrote to Hamel that the demimonde came eager to see "if they still hold, they do."[66] Her perfect bosom was, she said, the envy of many professional beauties. From Brussels the poet Paul Géraldy's wife asked her Parisian lover, journalist Christian Beck, to let her know the latest gossip about Isadora Duncan and Colette. He replied that he had not seen Isadora, "her thighs being too heavy for my taste," but that he had booked a box on the stage to see "Colette who shows her breast every night, all naked down to the navel." Colette's and Christine Kerf's performances were so sensuous, he would have gone out of his mind if he had any taste for "those ladies."[67]

Colette was slowly coming to grips with the fact that at thirty-eight her music-hall days were numbered. Sido kept reminding her that talent would not make her rich and that her latest suitor, Hériot, was the right one for her. In February Colette, wearing a pearl necklace worthy of Otéro, left with Hériot for the Riviera to dance in Jean Richepin's comedy, *Xantho, chez les Courtisanes*. Sido commented with satisfaction, "So you are leaving with *le petit*. Missy will plant her trees while you are gone, a worthy occupation."[68] Sido was glad to find out how much Colette was spoiled by "this Cherubino."

They stayed in Beaulieu, an exclusive resort, then at the regal Hôtel de Paris in Monte Carlo. Colette joined in a few games of baccarat, but was not interested in gambling; Hériot gambled and lost, but did not mind. He was planning to buy her a villa on Lake Como, in Italy.

Colette's new friend, the actress Lily de Rème, joined them at the Hôtel Majestic in Nice; it was a trio once more. "These two children are strange because they are both in love with me." Colette did not feel comfortable with "little Hériot's" growing love and turned to Hamel for advice; to whom else could she speak with absolute candor about these "two children"? She felt "a maternal satisfaction" on seeing their healthy appetites and their clear complexions and was glad she could make them eat and sleep soundly. She always credited herself with restoring the health of her lovers. She asked Hamel to keep her confidence secret (presumably from Missy) because the "adventure" seemed to affect Hériot very deeply; as for herself, she was "in no moral danger."[69]

In February Missy put Rozven in Colette's name. Colette crossed France by train to sign the sale papers. "Your Rozven! I hope that you will be happy there for a long time,"[70] gloated Sido. After a few days she recrossed France by train and sailed for Tunisia on *Le Carthage,* on tour with *Xantho* and *Claudine in Paris*. Lily de Rème was part of the cast.

Colette left Hériot and did not write to him. Desperate, Hériot rushed for help to Missy, who was in Rozven with the decorators, getting the manor ready for Colette's return. Colette felt that Missy was siding with Hériot. She did not want "a marital arrangement"[71] at Rozven. Lily de Rème, the model for May in *Recaptured,* was also proving herself a burden. Colette found her impossible. "And she proposes a trip with her to India! I would rather die!"[72] Lily was addicted to opium, now weeping, sick, and depressed, then suddenly bubbling with happiness, laughing, dancing, and drinking. Colette liked the giddy girl, but could not stand her lack of culture, her limited vocabulary, or her stupidity. She was interested only in cars, expensive hotels, and dresses. Hériot — Jean in *Recaptured* — was not very different from Lily. In her letters to Hamel, Colette referred to Hériot as "le petit serin" (the little fool).

Colette wrote in *Recaptured* that she had been careless in sharing their lives. Money could not give Hériot or Lily what they did not have — brains and the desire to achieve — they were lazy. Sloth, the only Fourierist sin, was constantly denounced by Colette. She celebrated the hardworking people in show business, humble people with little talent, but earnest and determined to survive. Her idle lovers knew nothing better than spending their money and wasting their lives in opium dens. To replace Hériot with a more kindred spirit, Colette asked Claude Farrère, who lived in Toulon, to come to Tunisia. The author of *Les Fumeurs d'Opium* was tall, handsome, passionate but cool, and tolerated no mediocrity. He could have made her stay in Tunisia more pleasant, but he could not come. North Africa was a paradise for decadent society; opium was easily accessible, as were young boys and girls. Colette loved North Africa. She loved the beautiful eyes of the young North African Jewish girls and was impressed by their pale complexions, so pale that they had a vague green hue. With Lily and the lead actor, Philippe Legrand, they made trips by car through the mountains while in France Hériot was bombarding Sido with desperate telegrams. "But when I say No, it is No,"[73] Colette wrote to her mother.

When the show closed on February 22 she was longing for Missy, and she left Tunisia and her companions behind. "I look at them from far away as if they never existed."[74] Colette was preoccupied with her health, as she had come back from Tunisia with bartholinitis, a venereal disease. She rushed to Rozven and arrived exhausted; Missy was upset to see her so sick. To cure herself Colette plunged into rough physical activity: she cleaned the well and oiled the inlaid floors of the sprawling house. She also made up with Hériot.

Colette hoped that *The Vagabond* would be awarded the Prix Goncourt, the only prize to bring literary recognition as well as financial reward — five thousand francs. Colette turned to Count Louis de Robert, a member of the Académie Goncourt, whom she had known from the early days of her marriage. In her letters she told him that she had taken refuge in Missy's affection and described watching her as she tamed the birds and looked after a bitch about to give birth. Colette was in one of her earthy moods when she invited Count Louis de Robert to Rozven. As Marcel Proust's friend, Count Louis de Robert had been the first to read *Un Amour de Swann* and had found some chapters too daring, singling out the scene between Mademoiselle de Vinteuil and her lesbian friend; but he never critized Colette for the same reason.

Henry de Jouvenel

Early in April Hériot and Colette spent ten days in Compiègne at the countess de Comminges's château; she had invited Hériot because she wanted to meet Colette. The countess was the mistress of Henry de Jouvenel, one of two editors in chief at *Le Matin*. According to Louise Weiss and Sylvain Bonmariage, during the trip the couples swapped partners. Colette and Henry de Jouvenel were very attracted to each other; Colette described their love as a carnal obsession.

Three years younger than Colette, Bertrand Henry Léon Robert, baron de Jouvenel, count des Ursins, was born in Paris on April 5, 1875. He had a younger brother, Robert, and a sister, Edith.

Was Henry de Jouvenel an aristocrat? The "Who's Who" of French politics, *Le Dictionnaire des Parlementaires Français*, states, in a not-too-diplomatic way, "He was one by his style, his manners, he was one by his behavior," and goes on, "his family alleged it came from the illustrious Juvénal des Ursins and flattered itself to be related to the Roman Orsini princes." In fact, his great-grandfather, Bertrand-Joseph Jouvenel, a mathematician specializing in geometry, was knighted on May 16, 1817, by King Louis XVIII during the Restoration. His grandfather, Léon de Jouvenel, was elected senator of the Corrèze, one of the poorest regions in France. In 1844 he bought Castel-Novel, a castle going to ruin near the village of Varetz. Henry's father married the daughter of a senator and was appointed prefect of the Côtes-du-Nord by Napoleon III; he lived above his means and earned a reputation as one of the most lavish prefects of the Second Empire.

Henry was educated at the Collège Stanislas in Paris, run by Jesuit priests. Boys from conservative families with political ambition were sent to this college. Its atmosphere was not austere; the students spent many afternoons in discussion with their teachers and were allowed to go out in the evenings — some haunted the music halls. From the classrooms of the Collège Stanislas came right-wing politicians, as well as leaders of the radical left and social democrats like Henry de Jouvenel.

Henry was a charmer, moody, whimsical, and given to fits of nonchalance. He had a talent that served him well in politics: he could listen to several speakers and then improvise a discourse that synthesized all the disparate views, thus pleasing everybody. He wrote well and was chosen by acclamation in 1895 to represent his school in French composition in the annual national competition between the lycées and colleges. He won second prize (first prize went to the Lycée Condorcet, represented a few years earlier by Marcel Proust). He wrote poetry, but the few verses that remain give more of an insight into his personality than his talent: "I love the name 'geisha'/ These women born to love without ever being loved."[75]

Louis Gillet, one of his schoolmates wrote this profile: "Whoever did not see him at that age has seen nothing. The elegance of his slender person, his bearing, his long and rapid stride, his proud head tossing about a mane of black hair, the dark lock that fell like a feather over his right eye and that he would brush away with an exquisite motion, his charming eyes that held gold and night, fire and caress in them, everything, even that uneasy look of a lanky and slightly savage wolf's cub, were fascinating: he was already *l'irrésistible*."[76] He settled for a career in journalism, but found it difficult to have any of his articles published. Drawing heavily on his family connections, he invited the editor in chief of *Le Matin* to dinner, but to no avail. Penniless, he retired to his crumbling castle in Corrège. Anatole de Monzie urged him to return to Paris, where he had met Joseph Paul-Boncour, a staunch advocate of the National Federation of Trade Unions. Jouvenel joined Paul-Boncour's group, *The Generation*, and they discussed methods to rejuvenate France by syndicalism. A program emerged that gave Henry de Jouvenel a doctrine for the rest of his life.

Anatole de Monzie, then chief of staff to the minister of education, found a position for Henry as private secretary to the minister of justice. There Henry saw an opportunity to launch his own political career as a radical democrat. Barely a few months after joining the minister of justice's staff, Henry was asked to join the editorial staff of the new daily *Le Matin,* founded in 1902 to support the new left. It was rumored that his salary would be an astronomical seventy-five thousand francs. Henry's current salary was nine thousand francs and he had no money of his own. According to Count Bonmariage, the owner-director Bunau-Varilla had set a condition; Henry was to marry his young mistress immediately. Henry wavered. His political career was off to a good start until his boss, the minister of justice, asked him to withdraw his name in favor of his nephew. Henry de Jouvenel had no choice but to oblige. He accepted Bunau-Varilla's offer. In 1902 he married Claire Boas, the daughter of a millionaire industrialist, a radical and freemason. Their son, Bertrand de Jouvenel, was born on October 31, 1903; soon afterward his parents separated and were divorced in 1906. Claire de Jouvenel never remarried, but retained the title of baronne de Jouvenel and had one of the most powerful political salons in Paris. Henry became editor in chief, a position he shared with Stephane Lauzanne on a rotating basis, two weeks each.

Henry led an intense social life. He was a seducer, an insatiable womanizer with no money and luxurious tastes. After his divorce, the aristocratic Countess Pillet-Will, born the comtesse de Comminges and nicknamed "The Panther," became his mistress. Isabelle was one of the most beautiful women in Paris, supremely elegant. She was always surrounded by intimidating pets, Great Danes and Dobermans; at one time she owned a black panther. The Comminges were one of the most ancient families in France. Isabelle was born at the château de Saint-Bertrand de Comminges, a small town with a Roman cathedral and an abbey. Her mother was the Polish princess Lubomirski. Isabelle was married to a millionaire banker, Count Pillet-Will. They had three children.

She had a condescending attitude towards the *nouveaux aristocrats,* including her lover and her husband, who was emotionally unstable and had fits of delusion. At times he thought he was a dog and, totally naked, walked on all fours, barking and relieving himself against the walls. One day he shot his wife's Great Dane dead; Isabelle left. Divorce was out of the question, so she settled in Passy, took back her family name, and became Henry de Jouvenel's mistress. In 1907 they had an illegitimate son, Renaud, who was raised by nannies and governesses. His parents showed only the barest interest in the child, whose first pet was a puma.

At thirty-five, Henry, as described by Louis Gillet, was "one of those men who have only to appear to triumph. He was torn between his taste for pleasure and his taste for love, between caprice and lyricism, adventure and passion; all the women fought for him and he drifted from one to the next. At times he showed the cynicism of a roué of the Regency, at others he was prepared to do penance for his frivolity and devote himself to a single mistress. These successive and fleeting states of heart alternated with fits of disgust and what was left of a Catholic feeling of sin." This man "marvelously intelligent, marvelously amoral,"[77] found in Colette his feminine alter ego. What was to have been a brief libertine interlude unfolded as a passionate affair.

Colette left for Paris for eighteen performances of *La Chair* at the Gaíté Montparnasse, a music hall she particularly liked because Monsieur Dorfeuil, the director, paid her well and treated her like a superstar. Every night flowers from Hériot, Missy, Monsieur Dorfeuil, and larger and larger bouquets from Henry de Jouvenel filled her dressing room. However, it was with Hériot that Colette left Paris for Rozven.

Missy, informed of what had happened with Jouvenel, was angry; Isabelle was a friend of hers. Colette thought that things could be arranged. "Well! My Dear, what a reception!" wrote an astounded Colette. "It is hard — it can be mended — but it is hard."[78]

However, at the end of May Colette wrote to Wague that she had skillfully manipulated her lovers and was grateful that everything had fallen into place, because she just could not bear the stress. Sacha Guitry and his wife were in Rozven and *le petit* Hériot left for a trip to North Africa. He sent two telegrams from Oudja to Colette, asking her to marry him, and several telegrams to Sido, who, unaware of Henry de Jouvenel's existence, imagined that Colette did not want to marry him because of Missy. Sido had a practical suggestion; if Hériot wanted so badly to marry her, he should cajole Missy and obtain Colette from her. Colette was toying with the idea of a marriage with Hériot; she told him to meet her in Switzerland, where she was booked to perform in *La Chair*. Meanwhile, she wanted to meet Jouvenel in Paris and had to find an excuse for Missy. She turned to Georges Wague for help; he was to write her a letter about rehearsals, informing her that he was free to rehearse from May 25 to June 2. As soon as she received the deceitful note, she left for Paris.

She came back to Rozven, where Missy was raising a five-day-old crow and a baby finch on ant eggs. "How pretty Rozven is,"[79] mused Colette, unable to make up her mind.

By the end of June she had left for Geneva and Lausanne, where she received passionate letters from Henry de Jouvenel. On July 1, he turned up in Lausanne fresh from a duel, his arm in a sling, and declared to Colette that he could not and would not live without her. Meanwhile, Hériot was announcing his imminent arrival, and Colette kept him at bay with skillful telegrams.

After passionate lovemaking in Lausanne, the lovers returned to Paris. Jouvenel went straight to Isabelle de Comminges and announced that he loved another woman and that their relationship was over. The Panther declared that if this were so she was going to kill the other woman, whoever she might be. In total panic, Henry rushed to inform Colette of this threat. Colette retorted that she was going to see for herself, and called on Isabelle. She told her that the woman she intended to kill was herself. Isabelle, taken by surprise, collapsed into tears and begged Colette to leave Henry. Two days later she recovered and told Jouvenel that she planned to carry out her threat and murder Colette. Jouvenel completely lost his wits; he assigned Sauerwein, an editor at *Le Matin,* to be Colette's bodyguard, and they drove her back to Rozven.

When the trio reached Rozven, they were greeted by an utterly disgusted Missy. She had been apprised of the events by Isabelle de Comminges, and refused to see Henry. Jouvenel stayed at L'Hôtel du Golfe, waiting for the marquise de Morny to change her mind. Colette was sure she could persuade Missy to accept her new lover. Paul Barlet was armed with a revolver and entrusted with Colette's life. Missy, repulsed by the farcical ambiance, had her chauffeur drive her immediately to Honfleur to spend some days with the Guitrys. Jouvenel went back to Paris. Three days later he called Colette. Sauerwein was to drive her back, because he had found out that the Panther was in Brittany, more determined than ever to murder her. In Paris police headquarters had granted Jouvenel the detachment of an officer to guard Colette night and day at the Hôtel Meurice. The three senior editors of *Le Matin,* Jouvenel, Sauerwein, and Sapène also took turns, never leaving her unprotected.

A disenchanted Missy left Rozven to Colette and bought another house, Villa Princesse, only three kilometers down the road. She did not answer Colette who, pretending that nothing had happened, described her new life in her letters, joking about being a prisoner of love, watched like a monarch by the French police. She kept writing in spite of Missy's silence. She wrote to Hamel that she did not find it necessary to pay for happiness with pain: "Why should I suffer when I see within my reach happiness, even if only the appearance of happiness?"[80] She was doing everything in her power to appease Missy., "I assure you," she told Hamel, "there is no wickedness on my part, I suffer too much."[81]

Colette, who had decided that Missy was overreacting, persuaded herself that Missy was going mad. She consulted Dr. Charles Binet, a neurologist and director of a laboratory of psychology and physiology, who had published two volumes of his controversial study, *The Insanity of Jesus* (in four volumes, 1908–1915). Colette wrote to Christiane Mendelys, "I am worried by Missy's mental state and rightly so." It was blatant self-justification.

The threat of assassination by the Panther ended in pure comedy. Isabelle de Comminges and August Hériot drowned their pain in notorious cocktail parties in Le Havre and suddenly departed together on his yacht *Esmerald* for a six-week cruise. Colette had won, but money was on her mind; she told Hamel that Jouvenel had no fortune, earning only forty thousand francs as editor in chief of *Le Matin*; she earned enough money with the music hall, journalism, and her books, and concluded, "We'll manage,"[82] but she complained that Missy had sequestered things that belonged to her. She added bluntly, "I will be the first to see the marquise asking money from a woman she is leaving."[83]

Missy did not mind Colette's love affairs, but she did not like Jouvenel. Colette did not want to lose her; multiple involvements were her way of life, and she had the deeply rooted Fourierist belief that nature conceived of love in order to infinitely multiply man's social bonds.

In August Jouvenel and Colette drove to Corrèze, to Castel Novel. Back in Paris, Colette settled in the plush Hotel Meurice on Rue de Rivoli, while Jouvenel had work done on a house he had rented at 57 Rue Cortambert. Colette wrote a new series of tales for *Le Matin*. A new character modeled after Auguste Hériot appeared in eight short stories before becoming the stunning *Chéri*.

In October Colette moved to 57 Rue Cortambert. She had no plans to abandon the stage. In September she performed in Le Havre. In November *La Chair* was booked for a week in Paris at L'Etoile-Palace. A new pantomime written by Wague went into rehearsals. It was called *Les*

Vagabonds, but Colette changed it to *L'Oiseau de Nuit* (The Night Bird). As usual, the sketch was violent and sensuous.

Colette's career had reached its peak. Intellectual Tout-Paris came to see her onstage in her "nude dances," and political Tout-Paris joined in, led by the director of the influential newspaper *Le Temps.* She signed with Madame Rasimi, the innovative director of Ba-Ta-Clan, for a show in the Spring.

By fall monogamy had lost its spell. She went back to Rozven to sort out her furniture and decide with Missy what belonged to whom. Colette was unhappy to have lost her. She missed her past; the days at Le Crotoy, the big villa where she lived with Missy, and the villa where her "dear Léon Hamel" resided. "It was sweet to think of the beach, of the terrace, of the tennis court."[84] She decided to take Jouvenel to Le Crotoy. She complained again to Wague that whatever she did, she could not get a sensible word out of Missy; this she could neither understand nor accept.

Late in the fall, Colette took up boxing. Newspapers were quick to report that Colette had been seen in company of Meg Villars, "the bouncing doe," and Christiane Mendelys in a boxing studio just opened by Maitrot, a boxing champion. Music halls had just started to produce sketches in which women boxed. An article in *Fantasio* noted that "the ex-champion gave lessons to one of our most delightful writers, one of our most attractive 'parisiennes' we have named Madame Colette Willy. She is completely thrilled by the latest sport for women, and shows the greatest talent. She is already a boxer to be feared and who has the most vicious punch one can expect."[85]

Willy angrily watched Colette's progress, informed by the publicity around her every move. He launched another scathing novel with a catchy title: *Lélie Fumeuse d'Opium* (Lélie, the Opium Smoker). Curnonsky and Toulet were instructed on how to write it. With *Lélie,* Willy wanted to deal the final blow to Colette. "I want the baronne Bastienne de Bize to be the carbon copy of Colette Willy; she should have the same appearance, the same behavior, except that Colette, this depraved country girl, has never found a woman who had physical charm as well as brains."[86] This was an allusion to Andrée Mielly, Willy's mulatto mistress, presented as the charming and clever Lélie, whom the baronne tries to seduce in vain. Willy wanted the portrait of Colette to be immediately identifiable, except for her literary talent. (Willy never ceased to affirm that Colette was one of the greatest of literary geniuses.) He directed Curnonsky to add expressions from Colette's native Saint-Sauveur to the baroness's speech and allusions to her accent with its rolling r's. He told him that she used to keep a notebook with dialectal expressions, reviewing them in her bathtub before going to a party. The portrait of Colette was ruthless: "Madame de Bize was no longer in the prime of life, she was in her forties." Colette was exactly thirty-eight, and it was of vital importance for her to keep her youthful image as long as she was a music-hall star. In his lust for revenge, Willy drew readers' attention to her physical flaws.

"A bitter wrinkle cut across her cheek, a wrinkle caused by her perpetual and contrived smile. Her derrière, which had been praised by her friends of both sexes for its shapely curve, was growing unbecomingly heavy. Her waist was thick and rolled over hips which reminded one of a pumpkin rather than of a Greek urn. Crow's-feet marked her eyes over high mongol-like cheekbones. Her eyelids were covered with kohl, those eyes with the cunning glance of a peasant which made an amusing contrast with the mouth half-open in a childish way, carefully studied in front of her mirror."

The character's name was chosen to ridicule Colette: "Bize" means "kiss" in child talk — Colette was baroness of kisses — but it also means the dry northerly wind, "the black wind." Baroness de Bize wants to seduce Lélie by taking her to an opium den owned by Rapalin (Paul Masson), implying that Colette had smoked opium early in life. Rapalin greets his guests with a lecture on opium; the baroness interrupts him "with a serpentine movement of her arm which she had learned from the mime Paul Frank and asked, would you be kind enough to tell your boy to prepare me my first pipe of *touffiane*, I believe that is the right word. For if she did not smoke on a regular basis, the baronness was not having her first experience with the drug."

Willy drew the dagger right through her heart: "For one moment she forgot her usual fears, always carefully masked by her boisterous good humour. The fear that old age was almost upon her pushed her toward younger and younger prey, Lélie almost a child, and gigolos who could have been her sons."

At the story's end, Bastienne is smoking opium in the company of her lover Maduré while her husband, the baron de Bize, watches, hidden behind a screen; they discuss money. Bastienne is rich, for "she had kept the mansion in Brittany for herself. Yet she had so many debts that she did not dare confess them to her husband. She was dreaming of a donation, a procuration or a will in her favor; her lover wondered if Bastienne was Eve before the sin, did she know the difference between right and wrong?"

Lélie was his answer to *The Vagabond;* "this is how two old horses, who have a little blood left in their veins, tired of pulling together the same cart, exchange for the fun of it a few vicious kicks."[87] He had not forgotten that in *The Vagabond,* Taillandy was presented as an unscrupulous businessman; in turn he showed Bastienne de Bize unscrupulously retaining the manor in Brittany and engaging in crooked real-estate deals for a commission. Willy asked Curnonsky to let Colette know that all the nasty descriptions and damaging accusations were responses to the attacks she had made against him; he also instructed him to write to Colette that to hate her so passionately meant that she had been loved with an equal fury.

There was a growing rumour in the Parisian press, spread by Colette's friends, that Willy was not the author of the books he signed. Paul-Jean Toulet, his loyal coauthor, spoke up to defend Willy's reputation at a dinner party given by the Guitrys and attended by several journalists; Willy sent him a long telegram to thank him for having come to his defense "alone against all the others."[88] He still commanded some fierce loyalties. In November the magazine *Les Guêpes* (The Wasps) devoted a whole issue to Willy. The director, Jean-Marc Bernard, wrote: "It is outrageous that a writer would suddenly be abandoned, vilified and hated by scoundrels or imbeciles." Several scholarly publications such as *Le Feu, Le Divan,* and *L'Occident* celebrated Willy's talent, wit, and culture. A selection of Willy's texts was released with comments by well-known writers. The opening piece was a *Chant royal pour consoler Willy de la mort de Maugis* (Royal song to console Willy on the death of Maugis). Fagus, a well-known critic, wrote that "Willy represented the epitome of French culture." Henri Martineau struck a dissenting note: according to him, Willy had sacrificed his talent for quick rewards. "He would rather live well than write. I have the feeling that it is the case of a marvelous talent wasted."[89]

Willy was staying away from Paris, living in Monaco or Brussels, where he contributed articles to several newspapers. On April 24, 1911, in *Comoedia,* he said farewell to the readers of "La Lettre de l'Ouvreuse," which had launched his fame as a music critic; after twenty years of unequaled success, the "Usherette" was gone. He had married Meg Villars. According to Jacques Gauthier-Villars, Willy was not very eager to re-marry, but Meg had threatened suicide. By 1913 the marriage was on the rocks; Meg left for the United States with a wealthy lover, with whom she lived throughout World War I. She remained on intimate terms with Colette and seemed to share with her more than lovers or boxing lessons; in a letter from Meg to Colette, she told her that she was sending her some hashish from England.

On February 16 Colette's play *En Camarades* reopened at the Theâtre Michel in Paris, then moved to Monte Carlo; Colette and Jouvenel traveled in a convertible, the status symbol of daring sportsmen. They criss-crossed the Riviera. Colette was recognized and greeted everywhere. She told Sido that she would be astonished if she saw all the *brouillades* (scrambled eggs) with fresh truffles, the crayfish and thrush they devoured. Gourmet food was Jouvenel's weakness; he spent his money on it as if he had inexhaustible funds at his disposal. Colette called him "Pasha," or "Sidi" (a North African word meaning chief or prince). Jouvenel's son, Renaud, would describe him as a man who wished to emulate the princes of the Italian Renaissance and lived magnificently. Jouvenel scheduled their trips around lunches and dinners at famous inns; "We eat a lot and well" is a *leitmotif* in Colette's letters. Sido, who at seventy-five was still proud of her slim silhouette and dancing gait, made some humorous remarks about her plump daughter, who "had so much to sit upon."[90]

Back in Paris, Colette was the star of a lavish show at the Ba-Ta-Clan, *Ça grise* (It Makes Me Tipsy). Ba-Ta-Clan was the largest French music hall, with two thousand seats; it was on the brink of bankruptcy when Madame Rasimi rescued it with extravagant shows and sumptuously undressed girls, soon known as the "Rasimi girls." It was on the stage of the Ba-Ta-Clan that Buffalo Bill ended his tour of France — during his performance as a sharpshooter there, he badly wounded his wife, and was unable to convince the police it was an accident.

The publicity for *Ça Grise* was centered around Colette Willy. She was cast in *La Chatte Amoureuse* (The Cat in Love), directed and choreographed by Georges Wague. The program explained the pantomime in detail: In the days of Pericles, the sculptor Pygmalion falls in love with his statue, Galatea. His mischievous slave Ganymede steals the maid's beloved cat and hides it in the statue's pedestal, planning to make cat stew for his dinner. The maid, Madame Mycles, looks everywhere for Myrrha, her cat; Pygmalion finds her intruding in his studio. In order to be forgiven, Madame Mycles reveals to the sculptor that Doctor Pulsocon, a famous American scientist, has just invented an electrical machine that brings marble to life. Pygmalion buys the machine and turns the statue into a woman. Irradiated, the cat in the pedestal is now of human size and falls instantly in love with the first man she sees — Ganymede, who loves Galatea. Myrrha the cat pounces around the couple of lovers. Meowing, she manages to arouse Pygmalion's suspicions. He implores the gods for their help; thunder strikes Galatea, who reverts to her marble state; and the cat shrinks back to her normal size and is taken home by a delighted Madame Mycles.

A note at the end of the program informed the public that Jules Clarétie, director of the Comédie Française, was planning to add Jean-Jacques Rousseau's *Pygmalion* to the repertoire of the National Theater and hinted that *La Chatte Amoureuse* was its preview. Was the Comédie Française the next step in Colette's career? For some time, critics had been toying with the idea that pantomimes should be included in the national repertoire. Georges Wague was campaigning to have a mime section included in the curriculum of the Conservatoire National d'Art Dramatique. Rousseau's *Pygmalion* was "an operetta without singers," the actors miming and dancing to a musical background. The play, which had been produced once at the Opéra in 1775, had fallen into oblivion. Before the opening of *Ça Grise,* Colette had given a lecture on mimodrama on February 8 at the exclusive Cercle de l'Union des Artistes, illustrated by an Assyrian and a Montmartre dance. *Comoedia* praised Colette in *La Chatte Amoureuse* and "the lithe, lascivous and exciting originality of her talent."[91] But the scheme to crack the Comédie Française did not go further; Wague was viciously attacked in *Les Guêpes* in an article titled "A Woman of Letters: Colette Willy."

> How could this little bourgeoise, charming, well read and so delicate, fall as low as the *Caf' Conc'* in company of a ruffian, who treats her like a whore. "Move your buttocks," says this horrid rogue to his partner before going on stage to mime with frightful contortions more or less lewd scenes.
>
> The author of *Claudine at School* has come down to this. In a poignantly sad book, she has told us some of her adventures on

tour. The miserable buffoon, who travels with her and imposes on her his shameful presence, has been the target of damaging remarks from this woman, who is witty, kind and bears the pain and bitterness of this infamous life.

But can he understand anything, this sinister *Pierrot* with his murderer's face, his rages, his vulgar feelings as the exquisite *Vagabonde* drags him along, desperate to be involved with a character who could not be more repugnant.[92]

This anonymous article bore Willy's imprint.

Colette, too, had a loyal following, and the April edition of *Femmes d'Aujourd'hui* was devoted to Colette Willy, "writer and dramatic artist." It opened with a sarcastic poem directed against Willy by Martini, a humorist who depicted him as an old satyr lusting for teenage girls. The brunt of his attack fell on Willy's lack of talent, which had become Colette's vengeful *leitmotif*. Willy answered with an article against "that Martini who invented neither the cocktail nor the cheese-wire." On April 17 Willy and Martini met on the grounds of the Parc des Princes stadium and fought a duel in front of the press and the cameras.

At a dinner party Colette described how unhappy her life with Willy had been. The hostess, Madme Langlé de Bellème remarked: "It was very easy not to get married if Willy did not appeal to you." "I was sixteen and I was marrying an old man," replied Colette. Count Bonmariage corrected her unpleasantly: "Willy was only thirteen years older than you ... You were past twenty and remember how you wept, begging everyone around you to reunite you with your husband."[93]

Paul-Jean Toulet, whose admiration for Willy never wavered, quipped, "She makes me think of those fanatic Spanish women who, after having prayed to a saint, slap the statue when they do not get what they want."[94]

At the close of *Ça Grise,* Jouvenel and Colette left for Trouville to spend a few days at La Roseraie, the estate of Jean Sapène. He was with his mistress, the singer Jane Pierly, and Valentine Boyer, who entertained them with anecdotes about her husband, Lucien, the composer of *La Violetera* and *Ramona*. Colette took long walks in the woods and felt nostalgic once more for Le Crotoy. She complained to Hamel that she was putting on weight, but could not resist bread crusts rubbed with garlic.

Colette was not satisfied with a bimonthly byline at *Le Matin;* her goal was to become a reporter. Reporting was a male preserve, better paid and better recognized. Only Louise Weiss had made a name for herself as a journalist, but Colette was determined to enter the field. The day after the closing of *Ça Grise* she covered the capture of the Bonnot gang, a group of anarchists who had terrorized Paris for months, specializing in bank robberies and killing several employees and passersby. Bonnot and his accomplice Dubois had taken refuge at Choisy-le-Roi. The police had been tipped off and were about to launch their final assault on the house in front of the media.

Colette had come with a press pass, only to be told by a gendarme that she could not join the other reporters, since "everyone in a skirt must stay here, quietly."[95] Unable to cover the action, Colette turned to the excited crowd and described its emotions. Her article "In the Crowd" was not published until May 2; there was a strong inside opposition to Colette. The article was published in the literary section, under the caption *One Thousand and One Mornings,* with a foreword: "Last Sunday our brilliant collaborator, Mme Colette Willy followed the events of the bandits' last fight . . ." That was a gesture of appeasement, but it was not to Colette's liking; no one was going to prevent her from becoming a reporter. In 1953 *Combat,* Albert Camus's newspaper, paid homage to the quality of Colette's work as a journalist. "Her prose is directly in touch with the event . . . she has the talent of recreating the picture, she has the self-restraint and the daring, the art of the right expression which is typical of any page written by Colette."[96]

Buneau-Varilla had instructed *Le Matin* to support aviation. Colette saw her chance, and to show her commitment to the politics of *Le Matin,* on January 26 she boarded the *Caudron* Airbus. On June 13 the indomitable Colette was aboard the dirigible *Clément-Bayard,* reporting on its maiden flight over Paris. Three days later she was named special correspondent for *Le Matin* to cover the Grand Prix of the French Aeroclub. The aces of French aviation were to fly from Angers to Châlet-Saumur. Airstrips were opening everywhere; Colette felt that the thundering sounds of the flight schools poisoned the countryside. Near Paris the Issy and Le Buc airstrips attracted not only the daredevils and sports enthusiasts, but Sunday strollers and idle playboys, what Prince Paléologue called "the dissolute mob of the airports" — Marcel Proust, shivering in his furs, Jean Cocteau, de Max, and Maurice Rostand, heavily made-up.

The following week she was on assignment in Tours to cover the murder trial of Houssard, accused of killing his lover's husband. Colette was interested in psychopaths and murderers. She felt that a man who kept repeating, "she is innocent, I loved her . . . she refused to belong to me . . . I killed him because I loved her," deserved some leniency. Colette's articles were now on the front page of *Le Matin*.

Insecure in her private life, Colette was planning to part with Jouvenel. She told Hamel, "I do not despair to treat him as lightly as Hériot, you know." She informed Jouvenel that if she took a fancy to someone she found "beddable," she would let him know. Her fury against Jouvenel was growing, "yes, a frightening resentment against that bitch of a man, who does not know how to feed a woman or fight for her." But she missed "his warmth, the sound of his voice, his lies, his childish behavior and his ridiculous ways."[97] For the first time in her life, Colette's financial security was really threatened; Jouvenel had an aristocratic disdain for money. When it flew his way, he financed his friends, air shows, or the budget of his village, Varetz. When he had none, he used *Le Matin* as a lending institution, borrowing more than nine hundred thousand francs. Colette confided to Hamel on black-edged notepaper, which reflected her mood, that she had only 1,500 francs left, "not enough to move and settle down, nor to travel."[98] She remarked bitterly that Jouvenel, who was to have given her one thousand francs in August, had not done it yet. She wanted a place of her own and made vague plans to move in the fall, when she would perform at the Ba-Ta-Clan. In the meantime she was working on a novel, *Le Raisin Volé* (*Stolen Grapes*, the original title for *Recaptured*), turning Auguste Hériot's, Lily de Rèmes's, and her own stories into fiction. She was also selecting twelve short stories about animals, previously published in *Le Matin* or *Paris-Journal*, for Paul Barlet, who was opening a publishing house, *La Librairie des Lettres*. *Prou, Poucette et Quelques Autres* was a deluxe print run of three hundred. Colette had a volume specially printed for Léon Hamel, who had financed the venture.

In times of personal turmoil, Colette took refuge in music; she was now working on several pieces by Schumann on her new grand piano. Jouvenel had no intention of ending their affair and Colette marveled at "Jouvenel's carnal tenacity"; since she experienced the same sensual attraction, "it made for good moments."

Meanwhile, she plotted "a sexual escape"[99] and went to London with an escort. She had not given up the idea of an international theatrical tour and wrote to Robert Sherard, editor of the *Saturday Review* and Oscar Wilde's biographer. Like Frank Harris and Max Beerbohm, he had visited her salon at the Rue de Courcelles. Sherard pretended he could not meet Colette, because he did not want to introduce his wife to "the heroine of a scandal."[100] London society, whose private life was less than saintly, had been shocked by Colette's open relationship with the marquise de Morny. Diplomatically, Robert Sherard sent a letter saying that he was sick and included a recommendation for Sir Rivers Boddily, president of the corporation that had financed the Coliseum theater. She went to see him, but nothing came of the meeting.

In August Colette was making new plans to leave Jouvenel and asked Auguste Hériot, "the only person who could give me discreetly a sizable sum,"[101] to lend her money. She gave him her pearls as collateral. They drew up a legal document, and a friend, Monsieur Von Emden, signed for Hériot, since Colette did not want Jouvenel to know she was seeing him. Now she was free "to leave within two hours." She opted for a wait-and-see attitude and decided to write to "the baron who was over there swaggering about and getting into debts." She tried to reassure Léon Hamel that she would not "offer him money."[102] But if we are to trust Colette's *Julie de Carneilhan,* that is precisely what she did. In the novel, the baron d'Espivant mentions a note for a loan of one million francs from Julie, who had given up her pearl necklace as collateral. Jouvenel came back, Colette let herself yield "to an ephemeral, brutish happiness." She was wallowing in "the presence of the necessary being," wondering if all this would last. Never one to admit defeat, even a hypothetical one, she concluded: "At least, I reap the reward of my stupid obstinacy, of a perseverance that everybody reproved except . . . Bunau-Varilla whom I do not know."[103] The whole staff of *Le Matin* was following the ups and downs of Henry de Jouvenel's tumultuous affair with Colette Willy.

September went by like a dream. She worked on a new novel, *Stolen Grapes* and rehearsed *L'Oiseau de Nuit.* They were at the opening night of Sacha Guitry's play *Pas Complet,* at the inauguration of the renovated Ba-Ta-Clan. In mid-September, Colette performed *L'Oiseau de Nuit* eight times with more diligence than enthusiasm. For the first time her love for the stage was waning: "I'll have no merit when I leave the *Caf'* *Conc.*"[104] Yet she had no immediate plans to put an end to her career. Dining at Marguerite Moreno's, she was asked by the actor Daragon:

"Are you going to play or to write?" She replied, "my intention is to go on doing both. It's like having a right hand and a left hand." [105]

Wague was negotiating a twenty-one day tour in Rumania and Russia for January of 1913. Colette haggled about her salary: "They say that in Russia everything is out of reach, dreadfully expensive." [106] She would not go to Russia; her life was going to take an unexpected turn.

APPENDIX

REGARDING COLETTE'S BLACK ANCESTRY

$\mathcal{I}$N 1787 Robert Landois, a wealthy young mulatto, arrived in Charleville, a smuggling center for colonial goods between
France and the Netherlands. He opened a grocery on the main street,
rue Saint Charles. An article published in 1936 by René Robinet, an
archivist of Charleville-Mézière, concerning Colette's maternal line has
been the basis for all of Colette's biographies up to this point. According to Robinet, Robert Landois was the descendant of generations of
field hands and was born at La Neuville near Cormicy, but the dates of
his birth certificate and of his death certificate do not match and
Neuville is not mentioned as his birthplace. By accepting the archivist's
findings it became difficult to explain Colette's Caribbean origins.
Robinet states that "the family tree of the Landois has no African
ancestor" and that "the earthbound" destiny of Robert changed when
he married: "The Mathis family, as opposed to the Landois, is of a traveling mood, when one is a boatman . . . one moves about . . ."[1] But the
traveling mood of bargemen on the River Meuse does not explain
Colette's "harvesters of cocoa." Inland water transport is not sailing the
seas. Defining the Landois as "field hands" is to disregard the historical

fact that field hands were often bonded to the land. The king abolished serfdom in his domains in 1779, but the practice was not put to an end until the night of August 4, 1789, when the aristocracy and the church renounced their privileges. How could a field hand's son of barely twenty have the means and the connections to establish himself as a trader? However, as the son of a wealthy planter, Robert Landois would have had the training and the means.

To be an *épicier* at the end of the eighteenth century was to be a trader, a member of the powerful spicer's guild, which enjoyed the exclusive right to sell paint, cork, citrus fruit, coffee, and chocolate. At the end of the century the guild was the most powerful commercial establishment in France, with close links to the colonies. It had agents in every port and in every frontier town. To be an *épicier* required three years of apprenticeship, followed by three years as a journeyman; only then was the apprentice admitted as a guild member.

Robert Landois had to pay nine-hundred pounds for his title, a sizeable sum. Three years later, in 1790, he married Marie Mathis, born in Grand-Pré, the daughter of a bargeman from the Ardennes region.

He came from a line of Huguenots who had taken refuge in Martinique in the seventeenth century. The island was at that time divided into nine districts called *compagnies,* each subdivided into small self-sufficient *cazes,* which were military outposts as well as fledgling farms. One was known as the Compagnie de Monsieur Le Vassor de la Touche, the acknowledged leader of the French Protestants in the West Indies. At a time when Protestants in France were subjected to constant abuse and forced to convert to Catholicism, King Louis XIV, in a political gesture, had commissioned Captain Le Vassor to settle the islands, for most of the buccaneers who sailed the Caribbean sea were Protestants, and many were refugees from France. They were more likely to be persuaded by a Huguenot to declare the numerous islands of the West Indies, their ports of call, as French possessions. These were coveted by Protestant England and Holland.

In the first census taken in Martinique in 1664 one of Le Vassor's *cazes* is headed by François Landois, age thirty-two. Under his command he has Jean La Treuille, age fifty-four, Jean Musgnier, twenty-eight, and Pierre Lesné, twenty-eight, a carpenter; they had sailed together from Le Havre. Later the census shows in his *caze* two black women and two black children, six and thirteen years old. Seven years later in 1671, as the persecution of the Protestants intensified, Colette's direct ancestor, Pierre Landois from the Champagne region, appears on the roll call of the Compagnie Le Vassor. He has one negro servant. He comes from La Neuville, a hamlet where he has left his wife, Barbe Guyard, and his son, Guillaume, born in 1664. Guillaume is the first Landois to figure in the parish registry. It was a prudent move, for Catholic priests refused to register the birth, marriage, and death of Protestants, thus denying them legal status. Pierre Landois made sure that his son, baptized as a Catholic, would be safe until he could find a way to smuggle him out of France. But the repression became more fierce; anyone caught trying to leave the territory was chained as a galley slave on the ships of the royal navy. Guillaume Landois remained in Champagne and worked as a field hand. Three generations of Landois grew up as field hands. However, while laborers were illiterate, all the Landois — Henri, Jean-Louis, and Robert — have left in the parish register firm and even elegant signatures. Protestants practiced their religion secretly; in the most humble family children learned to read the Bible and to write.

Pierre Landois settled in Martinique. In the census of 1678, the Compagnie Le Vassor has 82 men, 55 women, one named "femme Landois," 43 boys, 44 girls, 46 indentured servants, 123 black men, 118 black women, and 77 black children.

In France, in a supreme attempt to quash the heresy, the dragoons of the royal cavalry received the order to convert the Huguenots by terror. Burgundy and Champagne were among the hardest hit provinces. A third Landois, age forty, managed to flee with his wife Madeleine, forty-two, and his sons François, ten, Christophe, eight, and Pierre, five — to the haven of Monsieur Le Vassor in Martinique. In 1680 he is a prosperous planter. In his *caze* he has nine black men, eleven black women, six black children, and one indentured servant, Jean Mabeil. Colette's distant ancestors prospered in Martinique.

In the paternalistic order of the plantation, legitimate and illegitimate children were both baptized and given their father's name. *Le Code Noir,* which ruled the lives of the black population on the island as well as in France, mandated that any male black slave who visited France with his master be taught a trade by a guildmaster. This policy was implemented with economic goals in mind, for in the eighteenth century it became clear that there were not enough indentured servants to match the needs of an expanding economy. Mulatto sons usually passed their apprenticeship specially in the *Guilde des Epiciers.* Some stayed in France as trading agents. 158 negroes and mulattos resided in Bordeaux, 65 in La Rochelle, about the same number in Le Havre, 3 in Dieppe, and 5 in Calais. Their number increased throughout the turbulent eighteenth century.

The English launched three attacks against Martinique. The Dutch buccaneers raided the islands, and a series of natural disasters disrupted the economy. Several planters sailed back to France. Pierre Landois, the great-great-grandson of Pierre Landois *le Champenois* settled as a trader in colonial goods at Le Havre in 1780. Three generations of Landois would live in Le Havre. Colette's grandfather, known as "the gorilla," would carry on Pierre's business. His daughter Irma, Colette's aunt, a milliner of easy virtue, was born there.

The French government, worried by the growing numbers of blacks and mulattoes residing in France, ordered them to register and carry *cartouches*, police certificates established for identification purposes. Those undeclared would be deported. This policy was a failure almost from the onset. War broke out with Britain, and the government granted an extension for the repatriation of the slaves. In 1782 a police report estimated the number of both freed men and slaves at four to five thousand. But the 1777–1778 *Table Alphabétique des Nègres et des Mulâtres* lists only 777 names. This large discrepancy was due in part to the constant arrivals and departures of a floating population and in part to the fact that blacks and mulattoes born in France were excluded from the list. For example, François Fournier de Pescaye, born in Bordeaux, who founded a school of medicine in Brussels and was the private surgeon of Ferdinand VII of Spain, is not listed.

Mulattoes produced family papers proving that they were born in France and were therefore free to remain undisturbed. A forged or borrowed identity could serve the purpose; evidently this is what Colette's ancestors did. Like many, they obtained certificates proving that they were registered in a parish. A borrowed identity, preferably from some relative, was the simplest way to dodge the law. The Protestant diaspora and other less respectable sources could provide fake genealogies.

Pierre Landois established his two sons in the grocer's trade, Pierre *fils* in Paris on the Rue des Fossés Saint-Jacques, and Robert, Colette's great-grandfather on the Rue Saint Charles in Charleville, a thriving center of contraband goods from the West Indies to Holland. In return came a flow of manufactured goods such as cigarettes and chocolate that were heavily taxed in France. It explains why this young mulatto settled in Charleville and married the daughter of a boatman.

ABBREVIATIONS

Works frequently cited are referred to by author or abbreviated title after the full citation.

Colette. 3 vols. Paris: Robert Laffont, 1989.
— EACH VOLUME IS REFERRED TO BY ★, ★★, ★★★ FOLLOWED BY THE PAGE NUMBER.

Colette. NRF La Pléiade. 3 vols. Paris: Gallimard, 1984–91.
— EACH VOLUME IS REFERRED TO BY PLI, PLII, PLIII FOLLOWED BY THE PAGE NUMBER.

LM : ———. *Lettres à Marguerite Moréno.* Paris: Flammarion, 1959.

LP : ———. *Lettres à ses pairs.* Paris: Flammarion, 1973.

LV : ———. *Lettres de la Vagabonde.* Paris: Flammarion, 1961.

LS : *Lettres de Sido à sa fille, précédées de Lettres inédites de Colette.* Paris: des Femmes, 1984.

Note: Whenever there are several quotes from the same work, the note is indicated at the last quote with all the relevant pages.

NOTES

PROLOGUE

1. Letter of 12 October 1905, *Une amitié inattendue: Correspondance de Colette et de Fancis Jammes* Paris: Emile Paul Frères, 1945.
2. *Vins,* ★★★, 986.
3. *L'Eclaireur de Nice,* 14 December 1910.
4. PL, XLIII.

I — COLETTE'S FAMILY

Sido: the leading character in my life
Journal à Rebours, ★★★, 51.

1. LS, 357.
2. LS, 12 June 1907.

Sido's father: a mulatto with pale eyes

3. *La fille de mon père,* ★★, 237.
4. *L'Etoile Vesper,* ★★★, 631.
5. Robinet, *Etudes ardennaises* 9 (April 1957).
6. Archives de la Chambre des notaires, Minutier central 1905: 563.
7. Landoy, Eugène. "L'Illustration," *Journal Universel,* (19 June 1852): 407.
8. On the reverse side of Sophie's miniature Henri wrote: "My children never forget your noble and virtuous mother" and signed "Eugène Landois." His great-granddaughter, Jenny Landoy, a Belgian novelist, wrote, "I have under my eyes that famous tree (the genealogical tree of the Landoy) and at the top, the ancestor, Eugène Landois, who had two sons, Paul and Eugène, and a daughter, Sidonie." She omitted her Aunt Irma, who died in an asylum. *L'Etoile Vesper,* ★★★, 631.
9. Minutier central, Etude Edmé Foucher, inventaire des biens Landois, 1835.
10. For clarity's sake, we will refer to the eldest Landoy Henri, and the younger Eugène.

11. Une Guêpe exilée, Salon 1842, Bruxelles, préface 1 ère livraison.

12. *La fille de mon père,* ★★, 237.

13. Une Guêpe exilée, Salon 1842, Bruxelles, préface 1 ère livraison.

14. *LS,* 115.

15. *LS,* 337.

16. *Journal à Rebours,* ★★★, 51.

17. Fourier, Charles. *Oeuvres complètes* (Paris: Editions Anthropos, 1966), 1: 92.

18. Ibid., 6: 390.

19. *La Naissance du Jour,* ★★, 590.

20. *LS,* 288.

21. Hugo, Victor. *Correspondance,* 2: 31.

22. *LS,* 115.

23. *LS,* 86.

24. *Claudine à Paris,* ★, 198.

25. *LS,* 56.

26. *Bulletin de l'Académie Royale de Langue et Lettres françaises de Belgique,* April 1936, 37.

He was ugly . . . more or less retarded but he was rich
   Rapport du juge Crançon au procureur impérial, 15 November 1865.
   Fonds Colette de Saint-Sauveur.

27. *La Maison de Claudine,* ★★, 210.

28. *Sido,* ★★, 770.

29. Ibid., 773.

30. *La Maison de Claudine,* ★★, 265.

31. *La Cire verte,* ★★★, 1343.

32. *Le Sauvage,* ★★, 211.

33. Pierre François Pietresson de Saint-Aubin to his son Napoléon, quoted in La Société des Amis de Colette, *Cahiers Colette* (Paris: Flammarion, 1977), 8.

34. Rapport du juge Crançon.

35. Compte-rendu du jugement du procès de Mme Givry contre Robineau-Duclos, Tribunal d'Auxerre, 1856.

36. *La Maison de Claudine,* ★★, 210–11.

Marriage brings no happiness . . . except if one aquires a great fortune
   Fourier, *O.C.,* 1, 204.

37. *Claudine à l'Ecole,* ★, 9.

38. Robineau-Desvoidy, *Essai statistique sur le canton de Saint-Sauveur en Puisaye* (Brussels: Imprimerie d'Amédée Gratiot et Cie., 1838), 47.

39. *Claudine à l'Ecole,* ★, 9.

40. *La Maison de Claudine,* ★★, 211.

41. *LS,* 166.

42. *Sido,* ★★, 760.

43. Rapport du juge Crançon.

44. Boivin, interview by author.

45. He died in 1879 at fifty-one, having led a life of leisure and pleasure. He never

forgave the people of Saint-Sauveur for his political defeat and loss of face. He left ten million gold francs and his château to the Gandrille Foundation, stipulating that it become a nursing home for the poor living in the seven townships in which he owned land. He specifically excluded the eighth one, Saint-Sauveur, stating that none of its inhabitants could ever be admitted to the château nursing home. From beyond the grave Marien-Victor Gandrille created an administrative quagmire. In 1982, after years of litigation, Saint-Sauveur bought the château, very much in need of repairs, to house a Colette museum, but the grounds and the parks remain the property of the Gandrille Foundation.

46. Rapport du juge Crançon.

Born to seduce and to fight . . . he was a poet and a man of the world.
  La Maison de Claudine, **, 226, 779.

47. *LS,* 28 June 1911.
48. Sartre, Jean-Paul, *Lettres au Castor* (Paris: Gallimard, 1983), 1: 227.
49. Amblard, E. *Bulletin de la Société des Sciences historiques et naturelles de l'Yonne,* 97 (1957–1958).
50. *Le Zouave,* ***, 1238.
51. Dinesen, Wilhelm. *Boganis* (New York: Striar and Myles Striar, 1987).
52. *Les Heures longues,* p. 1239.
53. Godchot. *Le Premier Régiment des Zouaves, 1852–1895,* (Paris: Librairie Centrale des Beaux-Arts, 1898), 2.
54. *Le Zouave,* ***, 1239.
55. Rapport du juge Crançon.

II — GABRIELLE

1. *Le Fanal bleu,* ᴬᴬᴬ, 757–58.
2. *Claudine à l'Ecole,* *, 11.
3. *Cahiers Colette,* 7: 12.
4. *Le Voyage égoïste,* **, 149–50.
5. *Prisons et Paradis,* **, 986.
6. *LS,* 4 July 1912.
7. *Autres bêtes,* ***, 816.
8. Mme de Saint-Aubin, 18 December 1880, quoted in *Cahiers Colette* 9: 5–6.
9. Landoy, Jenny. *Rhamsès II* (Paris: Simonis-Empis, 1894), 14–15.
10. *La Naissance du Jour,* **, 650.

I never had friends of my kind
  Claudine à l'Ecole, *, 11–12.

11. *Claudine à l'Ecole,* *, 12.
12. *Aventures quotidiennes,* **, 484–85.
13. *Journal à Rebours,* ***, 60.
14. *Claudine à l'Ecole,* *, 11.

15. *Journal à Rebours,* ★★★, 48.

16. *La Maison de Claudine,* ★★, 224.

17. Colette interviewed by Alain Parinaud, 1949. Archives Sonores, Institut national de l'audiovisuel, 1991.

18. Colette, Sidonie-Gabrielle. *Oeuvres complètes,* Edition du Fleuron, (Paris: Flammarion, 1948), 15: 344.

19. *La Maison de Claudine,* ★★, 225.

20. *Flore et Pomone,* ★★, 450.

21. *En Pays connu,* ★★★, 1008.

A Fourierist education

22. *En Pays connu,* ★★★, 957.

23. *La Naissance du Jour,* ★★, 589.

24. *Sido,* ★★, 768.

25. *Des mères et des enfants,* ★★★, 955.

26. Ibid.

27. Fourier, *O.C.,* 6: 335–37.

28. *En Pays connu,* ★★★, 867.

29. Ibid., 955.

30. *La Fleur de l'âge,* ★★, 966–67.

31. *LS,* 335.

32. *LP,* 242.

33. *La Maison de Claudine,* ★★, 226–27.

34. Ibid., 293.

35. Ibid., 226.

36. *En Pays connu,* ★★★, 860.

The lore of a village

37. *La Maison de Claudine,* ★★, 293.

38. *Claudine à Paris,* ★, 179.

39. "Claudine au concert," *Gil Blas,* June 1903.

40. *Journal à Rebours,* ★★★, 60.

41. *En Pays connu,* ★★★, 963–64.

42. *Rêverie de Nouvel An,* ★, 620–21.

43. *Claudine à Paris,* ★, 272.

44. Ibid.

45. Ibid., 240.

She banished all human religions
Sido, ★★, 770.

46. *Ma mère et le curé,* ★★, 266.

47. *Noëls anciens,* ★★★, 965.

48. *Ma mère et le curé,* ★★, 264.

49. *Sido,* ★★, 790.

50. *La Maison de Claudine,* ★★, 265.

Savages, savages . . . What to do with such savages
    Sido, **, 787.

51. *Sido,* **, 788.
52. Ibid., **, 800.
53. *La Naissance du Jour,* **, 589.
54. *La Maison de Claudine,* **, 273.
55. *Autres bêtes,* ***, 816–18.
56. *La Maison de Claudine,* **, 234–35.
57. Ibid., 237.
58. *Sido,* **, 794.
59. *Pour un herbier,* ***, 714.
60. *Claudine s'en va,* *, 507.
61. *Journal à Rebours,* ***, 59.
62. Robineau-Desvoidy, preface.
63. *Chambre d'hôtel,* **, 1511.
64. *Pour un herbier,* ***, 717.
65. "Lune de pluie," **, 1511.
66. *Le Pur et l'Impur,* **, 947.
67. *Fièvres,* ***, 34–35.
68. *La Femme cachée,* **, 428.
69. LM, 264.
70. *En Pays connu,* ***, 860.
71. *Le Miroir,* *, 663–65.
72. *Sido,* **, 774.

My mysterious half sister
    Sido, **, 177.

73. *Sido,* **, 798.
74. *Cahiers Colette,* 10: 39.
75. *Ma soeur aux longs cheveux,* **, 443.
76. *Belles Saisons,* ***, 554.
77. *La Maison de Claudine,* **, 246.
78. Ibid., 244–46.
79. LS, April 1907, September 1907.
80. *Sido,* **, 789.
81. Ibid.
82. Ibid., 799.
83. PL I, cxxvii.
84. Saint-Aubin, quoted in *Cahiers Colette,* 5: 31.
85. *Ma soeur aux longs cheveux,* **, 246.
86. Saint-Aubin, quoted in *Cahiers Colette,* 5: 31.
87. *La Maison de Claudine,* **, 246–47.
88. *Maternités,* **, 247.
89. Lettres de Mlle Terrain, Austin, Texas Humanities Research Library.
90. *La Maison de Claudine,* **, 239.
91. Ibid.

92. *Sido,* ★★, 780.

93. *Le Képi,* ★★★, 336.

94. Colette, "Contreé offensive pour l'orthographe," *Le Figaro Littéraire,* August 2, 1952.

95. *Sido,* ★★, 775–76

96. *Le Fanal bleu,* ★★★, 804.

97. *L'Etoile Vesper,* ★★★, 666.

She reshaped for us the whole chart of human feelings
   En Pays connu, ★★★, 957.

98. *La Maison de Claudine,* ★★, 224.

99. Ibid., 242.

100. Ibid., 257.

101. Ibid., 224.

102. *LS,* 57.

103. *Sido,* 776.

104. *La Naissance du Jour,* ★★, 590.

105. Fourier, *O.C.,* 1: 130.

106. *Journal à Rebours,* ★★★, 57.

107. Ibid., 211.

108. *En Pays connu,* ★★★, 955.

109. *La Naissance du Jour,* ★★, 590–91.

110. *Bella Vista,* ★★, 1372.

111. *La Maison de Claudine,* 227.

112. *Le Miroir,* ★, 664–65.

113. *Sido,* ★★, 772.

114. Ibid., 773.

115. Ibid., 774.

116. *La Naissance du Jour,* ★★, 610.

It is the story of this man that should be told
   Mes Apprentissages, ★★, 1209.

117. *L'Ami,* ★★, 259.

118. de la Hire, Jean de. "Willy et Colette," in *Ménages d'Artistes* (Paris: Adolphe d'Espie, 1905).

119. *L'Ami,* ★★, 260.

120. Ibid., 261.

121. Ibid.

122. Ibid., 262.

123. Ibid., 260.

124. *Mes Apprentissages,* ★★, 1209 and *La Vagabonde,* ★, 827.

125. Caradec, François. *Feu Willy* (Paris: Carrère-Pauvert, 1984), 28–29.

126. Ibid., 29

127. Richard, Noël. *Le Mouvement décadent* (Paris: Nizet, 1968).

128. Caradec, 30.

She was a terrible tomboy

    Mlle Terrain, quoted in *Cahiers Colette,* 7.

129. Larnac, Jean. *Colette, sa vie, son oeuvre* (Paris: Krâ, 1927), 41.

130. "Sources de Colette. Souvenirs inédits de deux condisciples de Claudine," *La Grive,* July–September 1960.

131. *Claudine à l'Ecole,* ★.

132. Colette interview with Parinaud, 1949.

133. *En Pays connu,* ★★★, 865

134. *L'Almanach de Paris an 2000,* (Paris: Gescofi), 1949.

III — MADAME GAUTHIER-VILLARS

1. *La Maison de Claudine,* ★★, p. 275.

2. Caradec, 58.

3. Rousseau Raaphorst, Madeleine. Colette et sa mère Sido, Lettres inédites concernant le premier mariage de Colette, Rice University Studies, 59(3, Summer 1973): 61–69.

4. *Le Fanal bleu,* ★★★, 791, and Lettres de Sido à Juliette, May 12, 1892.

5. Willy, *Indiscrétions et Commentaires sur les Claudine* (Monte Carlo: Pro Amici, 1962), 22–23.

6. Ibid.

7. Ibid.

8. Lecomte, Georges. *Willy, Les Hommes d'aujourd'hui* (Paris: Vanier).

9. Ibid.

10. Rosny, J.H. *Portraits et Souvenirs* (Paris: Compagnie française des Arts graphiques, 1945), 83.

11. Lecomte.

12. *Noces,* ★★★, 444.

13. Rousseau Raaphorst.

14. Willy, préface to *L'Année fantaisiste,* (Paris: Delagrave, 1890).

15. Sido to Juliette, 28 November 1892.

16. Pl, Introduction LIX.

17. Sido to Juliette, n.d. 1892.

18. Caradec, 63.

19. Ibid., 64.

20. Ibid., 65.

20. Ibid., 65–66.

21. Ibid., 64–65

22. Sido to Juliette, 5 May 1893.

23. Ibid.

24. *Noces,* ★★★, 440 and Caradec, 70.

25. *Noces,* ★★★, 442–44.

26. *La Vagabonde,* ★, 827.

27. *La Naissance du Jour,* ★★, 592.

28. *Claudine en Ménage,* ★, 305.

29. Ibid.
30. Ibid., 306.
31. Ibid., 308.
32. Ibid.
33. *Le Pur et l'Impur,* **, 905.
34. *La Maison de Claudine,* **, 265.
35. *Mes Apprentissages,* **, 1229.
36. Ibid.
37. Ibid., 1230.

When I was very young, I hoped that I would become somebody
   Mes Apprentissages, **, 1204.

38. Blanche, Jacques-Emile, quoted in Rudorff, Raymond, *La Belle Epoque: Paris in the Nineties* (New York: Saturday Review Press, 1972), 156–58.
39. Ibid., 139.
40. Blanche, Jacques-Emile, *La Pêche aux Souvenirs,* (Paris: Flammarion, 1949).
41. Ibid.
42. Caradec, 75.
43. PL I, p. 229.
44. Ibid.
45. B**, p. 1211 and Trois-Six-Neuf, ***, p. 371.
46. Willy to Apollinaire, 1914, quoted in Caradec, 74.
47. Lettres à Mlle Terrain, PL I, preface xv.
48. *Mes Apprentissages,* **, 1204.
49. Rudorff, 61.
50. de Tinan, Jean. *Aimienne.* Dossier Tinan, 27, Bibliothèque Nationale, Paris.
51. Rudorff, 281.
52. *Mes Apprentissages,* **, 1267.
53. Ibid.
54. Ibid.
55. *Journal à Rebours,* ***, 53.
56. PL III, 1800.
57. Goudeket, Maurice, Close to Colette, p. 78.
58. *Mes Apprentissages,* **, 1267.
59. Gavoty, Bernard. *Reynaldo Hahn, le musicien de la Belle-Epoque* (Paris: Buchet-Chastel, 1976).
60. *En Pays connu,* ***, 869.
61. Notes et Variantes, PL III, 1800.
62. Gavoty, 28.
63. Cocteau, Jean. *Oeuvres complètes,* (Paris: Marquerat, 1951), II: 101.
64. *Paysages et Portraits,* 391.
65. *En Pays connu,* ***, 874.
66. *Mes Apprentissages,* **, 1008.

The midnight Angel
  Nickname given to Colette by Forain. *De ma fenêtre,* ★★★, 224

67. *Mes Apprentissages,* ★★, 1212.
68. Bonmariage, Sylvain. *Willy, Colette et moi* (Paris: Charles Frémanger, 1954), 35–36; *Mes Apprentissages,* PL III, 1012.
69. Viel, Marie-Jeanne. *Colette aux temps des Claudine* (Paris: Essentielles, 1978), 116.
70. Rudorff, 156–85.
71. Baudelaire. *Oeuvres complètes* (Paris: Gallimard, 1951), 1213.
72. Rachilde. *Mémoires* (Paris: Mornay).
73. Rachilde. *Portraits d'homme* (Paris: Ed. Mornay, 1929).
74. Willy, "Lettres à Rachilde," *Bulletin Coulet-Faure,* 112–13.
75. *Le Pur et l'Impur,* ★★, p. 949.
76. Art et Critique, August 23, 1890.
77. Florian-Parmentier. *Histoire de la Littérature de 1885 à nos jours,* (Paris: P.E. Figuières et Co., n.d.).
78. *Paysages et Portraits,* ★★★, 112–13.
79. *LP,* 26.
80. *L'Envers du Music-Hall,* ★★, 1016.
81. Ellman, Richard. *Oscar Wilde* (London: Penguin Books, 1987), 333.
82. Lettre à Saint-John Perse, *LP,* 398.
83. Clive, H.P. *Pierre Louÿs: A Biography* (Oxford: Clarendon Press, 1978), 224–25.
84. *Le Pur et l'Impur,* ★★, 903.
85. *Correspondance Mallarmé-Whistler,* (Paris: Barbier, 1962), 68–69.
86. *LP,* 390–91.
87. PL I, lxii.
88. Caradec, 105.
89. *Sido,* 759.
90. PL III, 179.

Private Life

91. Gauthier-Villars, Jacques, "Willy et Colette, un couple de la Belle Epoque", *Les Oeuvres libres,* Nouvelle Série, No. 161, 1959, 175–76.
92. Viel, 57.
93. Letter to Curnonsky, Caradec, 91.
94. Curnonsky. *Souvenirs littéraires et gastronomiques* (Paris: Albin Michel, 1958), 296.

IV — FROM COLETTE TO CLAUDINE

1. *LP,* 11–12.
2. *Mes Apprentissages,* ★★, 1212.
3. Willy. *Souvenirs littéraires* (Paris: Editions Montaigne, 1925).
4. *Mes Apprentissages,* ★★, 1212–13.
5. *Mes Apprentissages,* ★★, 1218.
6. Ibid.
7. *L'Entrave,* ★, 1075.

8. *Mes Apprentissages,* ★★, 1214–15.

9. Ibid.

10. Ibid., 1220.

11. In *Claudine à Paris,* Colette described her mysterious illness as "something like a cerebral fever with symptoms like typhoid fever." We believe that Colette had syphilis, a belief that stems from a statement by Doctor Marthe Lamy, who took care of Colette at the end of her life. She said that Colette had never forgiven Willy for having infected her with a venereal disease. In *Mes Apprentissages* Colette discreetly wrote that Willy was *endommagé* (damaged), a euphemism used to refer to the unmentionable disease, and Willy, in *Un Petit Vieux Bien Propre,* made several mentions of Doctor Jullien and his book on syphilis. Given the aura of shame surrounding the illness there are few facts available, but they are fairly decisive. Her attending physician was the leading specialist in venereal diseases, the authority on syphillis, and her symptoms were common to tertiary syphilis — severe headaches, upper respiratory infections, and pains in the eyes due to progressive atrophy of the optic nerve. If treated, the symptoms disappear after two or three years. But all her life Colette suffered from the aftereffects of syphilis. Back from her first trip to North Africa in 1911, Colette wrote to Sido that she suffered from bronchitis, but to her friend Hamel she wrote that she had a bout of venereal disease. Her robust constitution helped her overcome it; Willy was not so lucky. He had severe fits of depression and by 1906 had become impotent and incapable of sustained intellectual concentration, which explains his growing reliance on ghostwriters. Impotence is central to *Maugis Amoureux* and *Maugis en Ménage;* in his correspondence, Willy complained of his incapacity to write and several times contemplated the idea of suicide. There was another side to syphilis; doctors prescribed celibacy for two years to anyone who had contracted it. This would explain Willy's reputation as a voyeur and why he encouraged Colette to have lesbian affairs. They gave the impression of a couple with a great affection for one another; it had been an unusual union from the beginning, and they subsequently gave each other a surprising amount of latitude.

12. *Mes Apprentissages,* ★★, 1219; *Claudine à Paris,* ★, 231.

13. *Mes Apprentissages,* ★★, 1220.

13. de Goncourt, Edmond. *Mémoires de la vie littéraire 1894–1995* (Paris: Fasquelle-Flammarion, 1957), 17.

15. Schwob, Marcel. *Le roi au masque d'or* (Paris: Crès, 1917), 13.

16. Champion, Pierre. *Marcel Schwob et son temps* (Paris: Bernard Grasset, 1927), 130.

17. *LP,* 24.

18. *LP,* 18–19

19. *Mes Apprentissages,* ★★, 1220.

20. Ellman, 236–37.

21. de Goncourt, 3 April 1893.

22. Ellman, 335.

23. *L'Entrave,* ★, 1047; *De ma fenêtre,* ★★★, 224.

24. *De ma fenêtre,* ★★★, 224.

25. Willy. *La Revue encyclopédique* (Paris: Librairie Larousse, 1894).
26. PL I: 1736.
27. PL I: 1735.
28. *Le Képi,* **, 279.
29. *L'Entrave,* *, 1034–35.
30. *LP,* 25.
31. Ibid., 15.
32. Ibid.
33. Ibid., 15–17.

My exquisite, loving, depraved kid
    Willy to Curnonsky, Caradec, 223.
34. Chastenet, Jacques. *Histoire de la III République,* 3: 29–30.
35. *Claudine à l'Ecole,* *, 9.
36. Colette, Letter to Rachilde, *Bulletin Coulet-Faure,* no. 6 et 24, (Paris: Hachette), sd,
    111–14.
37. Ibid.
38. Willy, *Indiscrétions,* 25–28.
39. PL I, lxv.
40. Cocteau, Jean. *Portraits-Souvenirs* (Paris: Marquerat, 1951), II: 101.
41. *LM,* preface, 9–10.
42. Caradec, 89.
43. *Claudine en Ménage,* *, 410.
44. Caradec, 223.
45. *LP,* 25.
46. *L'Echo de Paris,* 1 December 1889.
47. Castle, Charles. *La Belle Otéro,* (London: Michael Joseph, 1981), 71; Lewis, Arthur.
    La Belle Otéro (New York: Trident Press, 1967).

Jean Lorrain
48. Schwob, *Journal,* 18 September 1892.
49. Rachilde, Portraits d'homme, p. 49–59; Merviel, Jean, "Colette et Judith
    Gauthier", Les Lettres Françaises, May 5, 1945.
50. Ellman, 178.
51. de Pougy, Liane. *Mes Cahiers bleus,* (Paris: Plon, 1977), P.
52. Francis, C. and F. Gontier, eds. *Poèmes de Proust,* in *Cahier Proust* (Paris: Gallimard,
    1982), 10: 7–8.
53. Kolb, Philippe. *Correspondance de Marcel Proust* (Paris: Plon, 1980), 1: 385.
54. Ibid., note on page 386.
55. Ibid., 385.
56. Dossiers Colette, Bibliothèque Nationale, Paris.
57. "Max Reinhardt et la mise-en-scène," *La République,* 10 December 1933.
58. Clive, 108.
59. Ibid., 108, 110.

Colette's Salon

60. Kolb, 13: 353–54.
61. *Mes Apprentissages,* ★★, 1258.
62. *LP,* 27.
63. *Mes Apprentissages,* ★★, 1218.
64. Caradec, 84.
65. *Mes Apprentissages,* ★★, 1223.
66. Willy, *Souvenirs littéraire.*
67. Caradec, 50–53.
68. Ibid., 53.
69. *De ma fenêtre,* ★★, 293.
70. Caradec, 294.
71. de Tinan, *Aimienne,* Dossier Tinan 27, Bibliothèque Nationale, Paris.
72. Gauthier-Villars, Jacques.
73. Cocteau, *Portraits-Souvenirs,* 203.

V — CLAUDINE

1. PL III, 1056.
2. Armory, *Cinquante ans de vie parisienne* (Paris: Renard, 1943), 36–37.
3. PL III, 1030.
4. Lyonne de Lespinasse, "La Peur de l'être," *Frou-Frou,* 1907.
5. Dossiers Willy, Bibliothèque Nationale, Paris.
6. PL I, lxxi.
7. Ibid., lxii.
8. Renard, Jules. *Journal,* ibid, year 1900.
9. Rachilde, *Mercure de France,* 4(1901): 188–89.
10. PL I, lxvii, *L'Intransigeant,* 6 March 1957.
11. Colette interview with Parinaud, 1949.
12. Larnac, 41.
13. *Flore et Pomone,* 449–51.
14. Rachilde, *Mercure de France,* 1901: 188–89.
15. Baunier, *La Revue Bleue,* 6 April 1902.
16. *LP,* 47.

Georgie Raoul-Duval

17. Lettre de Claudine à Renaud, *Le Damier,* April 1903.
18. Willy, *Indiscrétions,* 20.
19. Ibid., 28
20. *Claudine s'en va,* ★, 497.
21. *Claudine en Ménage,* ★, 328
22. Ibid.
23. *L'Etoile Vesper,* ★★★, 670.
24. Dossier Willy, Bibliothèque Nationale, Paris.
25. *LP,* 47.

26. *LP,* 46.
27. Caradec, 151.
28. Rachilde, *Mercure de France,* April–May 1902.
29. Boulenger, *La Renaissance latine,* 15 June 1902.

Polaire

30. Caradec, 131, 136.
31. *LP,* 49.
32. Charles, Jacques. *Cent ans de Music-Hall* (Paris, 1936), 119.
33. Polaire, *Mémoires* (Paris: Figuière, 1933), 126–27.
34. Ibid., 129.
35. Lettre de Claudine à Renaud, *Le Damier,* April 1905.
36. de la Hire, Jean. "Willy et Colette" in *Ménages d'artistes* (Paris: Adolphe d'Espie, 1905).
37. *Claudine en Ménage,* ★, 328.
38. PL III, 1062–63.
39. Polaire, 126–27; *Mes Apprentissages,* ★★, 1261–62.

Paris-Lesbos

40. Cocteau, Jean. *Portraits-Souvenirs 1900–1914,* (Paris: Grasset, 1935), 57–58.
41. Caradec, 136.
42. Barney, Natalie. *Souvenirs indiscrets,* 96–98.
43. *Gil Blas,* 15 December 1901.
44. Barney, 187–89.
45. Casella, Georges, and Ernest Gaubert. *La Nouvelle Littérature 1895–1905* (Paris: Sansot, 1906), 123.
46. Ibid.
47. Ibid.
48. Rudorff, 63.
49. *Gil Blas,* January 1903 to June 1903.
50. Ibid.
51. Ibid.

The crazy tandem never hesitates to cross the limits beyond which no limits are to be found
    Willy, *Maugis,* 335.
52. de Solenière, Eugène. *Willy* (Paris: Librairie Sevin et E. Rey, 1903).
53. Charles-Roux, Edmonde. *Chanel,* (New York: Knopf, 1975), 189.
54. Willy, *Maugis,* 235.
55. Boulestin, *Myself, my two countries,* (London: Cassel, 1937), 82–85, and *Maugis amoureux,* 23–25.
56. Delarue-Mardrus, Lucie. *Mes Mémoires,* NRF Gallimard, (1938), 141.
57. Boulestin, 53.
58. *Claudine en Ménage,* ★, 343.
59. *Maugis amoureux,* 23.
60. Gold, Arthur, and Robert Fizdale. *Misia* (New York: Knopf, 1980), 126.

61. Tual, Denise. *Le Temps dévoré* (Paris: Fayard, 1980), 112–13.
62. Bonmariage, 32–33.
63. Ibid.
64. Boulestin, 52–54.
65. Delarue-Mardrus, 124.
66. Ibid., 141.
67. PL I, 1028.
68. *Claudine s'en va,* ★, 508.
69. PL III, 1028.
70. Willy, *Indiscrétions,* 28.
71. *Claudine s'en va,* ★, 426.
72. Ibid.
73. de Miomandre, F. *Figures d'aujourd'hui et d'hier,* (Paris, Dorbon Aîné, s.d.).
74. Fonds Gauthier-Villars, Bibliothèque de l'Arsenal, letter no. 26.
75. Caradec, 160–61.
76. *LP,* Letter to Jammes, 1903.
77. *LM,* to Moréno, September, 1903.
78. Colette interviewed by Parinaud, 1949.
79. Caradec, 166.
80. Solenière, 259.
81. Ibid., 260.

The Novel Factory

82. *Mes Apprentissages,* ★★★, 1236.
83. Caradec, 169
84. *Maugis amoureux,* 29–30.
85. Ibid., 75.
86. Ibid., 21–22.
87. *La Revue Illustrée,* July 1905, 125.
88. PL I, lxix.
89. Rachilde, *Mercure de France,* April 1904.
90. *Une amitié inattendue,* 30.
91. *LP,* 16 October 1904, 129.
92. *Une amitié inattendue,* 30.
93. Ibid., 37.
94. PL II, 1285.
95. Preface de Jammes, ★★, 807.
96. *Une amitié inattendue,* 51.
97. *Les Tablettes,* 30 May 1911.
98. *La Revue Illustrée,* July 1905.
99. *La Vie Parisienne,* August 1905.
100. Willy, letters to Rachilde, *Bulletin Coulet-Faure.*
101. Fourier, *O.C.,* 7: 390–92.
102. Minne, ★, 700.
103, Ibid., 701.
104. Ibid., 699.

105. Ibid., 694.

106. Ibid., 739.

107. Ibid., 767.

108. Ibid., 795.

109. Ibid., 806.

End of an Era

110. *Mes Apprentissages,* PL, ★★, 1052.

111. Ibid., 1065.

112. Ibid., 1066.

113. PL I, lxxxvi.

114. PL I, 1531.

115. *Mes Apprentissages,* PL, ★★, p. 1071.

116. Franc-Nohain, "La Nouvelle Etoile," *Fantasio,* 1 November 1900.

117. Caradec, 169.

118. *Mes Apprentissages,* ★★, 1232.

119. Ibid., 1257.

120. *Le Képi,* ★★★, 298.

VI — THEATER AND MUSIC-HALL

1. *La Vie Parisienne,* June 1905.

2. Malige, Jeanine. *Colette, qui êtes-vous?* (Lyon: La Manufacture, 1987).

3. *Mausolées,* ★★, 478.

4. *Le Pur et l'Impur,* ★★, 918.

I Belong to Missy

5. Boulestin, 55.

6. *LS,* 39.

7. *LS,* 26 September 1905.

8. Ibid.

9. *LS,* 21 November 1905.

10. *LS,* 38.

11. Antée, Bruxelles, No. 7, 1 December 1905.

12. Boulestin, 84.

13. Text of the program, Dossier Colette Willy, Bibliothèque de l'Arsenal, Paris.

14. Boulestin, 90, 165.

15. "Un printemps de la Riviera," PL I, 1060.

16. Boulestin, 85–90.

17. Ibid., 52, 91

18. Newton, Joy, and Jean-Pierre Bruel. "Colette et Robert de Montesquiou d'après leur correspondance inédite," *Kentucky Romance Quarterly,* 25(2): 216.

20. Ibid., 216; Exposition Colette Catalogue, Bibliothèque Nationale, Paris.

A new star
   Fantasio, November 1906.
21.   *Paris qui chante,* 14 October 1906.
22.   *LV,* 32–33; *Les Albums du Crapouillot,* December 1972; *Fantasio,* 15 February 1910.
23.   *Le Journal,* 17 November 1906.
24.   *Le Cri de Paris,* 28 October 1906.
25.   Boulestin, 92.
26.   *Le Cri de Paris,* no. 513, November 1906.
27.   *Le Cri de Paris,* no. 514, 2 December 1906.
28.   Manuscripts Colette, Bibliothèque Nationale, Paris.
29.   *La Retraite Sentimentale,* *, 597–98.
30.   Ibid., 572.

Paniska
31.   Dossiers Music-Hall, D. 894, Bibliothèque de l'Arsenal, Paris.
32.   *Le Rire,* 15 December 1906.
33.   *Le Siècle,* 10 December 1906; *Le Verveins,* 9 December 1906.
34.   Bonmariage, 16–17.
35.   Ibid., 19–21.
36.   Ibid., 22.
37.   Caradec, 90.
38.   Ibid., 188.
39.   Colette to Francis Jammes, 25 April 1906, 57.
40.   Ibid., 59.
41.   Ibid., 60.
42.   Ibid., 60–61.
43.   "Une Nouvelle Étoile," *Fantasio,* 1 November 1906, .
44.   *LS,* 56–57, 3 October 1906.
45.   *LS,* 20 March 1907; 29 March 1907.
46.   *LS,* 9 March 1908, 7 April 1908.
47.   *LS,* 3 October 1906.
48.   Ibid, 15.

I want to dance naked, . . . I want to write chaste books
   Toby-Chien parle, PL I, 994.
49.   *Fantasio,* 15 December 1906.
50.   *Le Rire,* 29 December 1906.
51.   Boulestin, 93.
52.   Caradec, 199.
53.   Tristan, Rémy. *Georges Wague, un mime de la Belle Epoque,* (Paris: Georges Girard, 1964).
54.   *LV,* 15
55.   Boulestin, 92.
56.   Tristan, 73.
57.   Boulestin, 93.
58.   PL I, cxiv.

59.   Caradec, 201–2.
60.   Ibid., 206.
61.   *LS,* 28 January 1907; 27 April 1907.
62.   PL I, 933, 1537.
63.   Ibid.

The Last Duet

64.   *LS,* 18 January 1907, 8.
65.   *LS,* 20 January 1907.
66.   *LS,* 83.
67.   *LS,* 20 June 1907, 107.
68.   *LV,* 16.
69.   *Mes Apprentissages,* ★★, 1266.
70.   Caradec, 205–6.
71.   Bonmariage, 19–21.
72.   Willy to Vuillermoz, quoted in Caradec, 206–7
73.   Bonmariage, 211–12.
74.   Willy to Vuillermoz, Caradec, 207
75.   Letter to Curnonsky, 14 September 1907 quoted in Caradec.
76.   *La Retraite Sentimentale,* ★, 567.
77.   *LS,* March–April 1907.
78.   *LS,* April 1907.
79.   Letters from Colette to Montesquiou, ibid.
80.   Caradec, 180.

The Flesh

81.   *LV,* 18.
82.   Wague, 73.
83.   "NOUS," *La Presse,* 1907.
84.   Colette, Editions Le Fleuron, I, 431.
85.   Fourier, *O.C.,* 8: 331.
86.   *Le Fanal Bleu,* ★★★, 792.
87.   *Mes Apprentissages,* ★★, 1244.

VII — THE VAGABOND

1.   Wague, 82–83.
2.   *Paris Théâtre,* 25 April 1908.
3.   *LP,* 145.
4.   *Le Messager de Bruxelles,* Dossier Colette Willy, Bibliothèque Royale de Belgique.
5.   *Comoedia Illustré,* 5 January 1913.
6.   *Comoedia,* 9 May 1908.
7.   Caradec, 242–43.
8.   *LS,* 14 May 1908.
9.   *LS,* 29 April 1908.

10. Caradec, 216.
11. *LV,* 21.
12. *LV,* 21.
13. *LS,* 7 April 1908.
14. *LV,* 22–23.
15. *LS,* 24 August 1908.
16. *LV,* 23.
17. *LS,* 204–7.
18. *LV,* 24.
19. Caradec, 217.
20. *LV,* 26.
21. Caradec, 217.
22. Colette interviewed by Parinaud, 1949.
23. Caradec, 218.
24. Ibid.
25. Letter to Curnonsky, November 3, 1908, 217.
26. *Akademos,* No. 2, February 15, 1909.
27. *LS,* 258.
28. Letter to Hamel, *LV,* 28 February 1909.
29. *Paris Journal,* 30 October 1909.

   One foot in sea and one on shore
      Much Ado About Nothing, Shakespeare.
30. *LV,* 30.
31. *Paysages et Portraits,* 48, 54.
32. Ibid., 54.
33. Willy, *Lélie Fumeuse d'Opium* (Paris: Albin Michel), 54.
34. Deluc, Louis. *Chez de Max* (Paris, 1918), 229–30.
35. *Automne,* ★★★, 49.
36. Bonmariage, 144, 217.
37. Ibid., 144–45.
38. Ibid., 215–18.
39. *L'Indépendant Auxerrois,* April 1909, *Colette En Tournée, cartes postales à Sido,* (Paris: Persona, 1984), 19 April 1909; *Le Petit Bourguignon,* PL I, 1333
40. *Le Populaire de Nantes,* 5 May 1909.
41. *LS,* 22 June 1910.
42. *LS,* 24 July 1909.
43. Willy, *Pimprenette de Foligny,* (Bibliothèque des Auteurs Modernes, 1908), 120, 192.
44. LV, 38.
45. LV, 37.
46. *L'Ecoute,* April 1950.
47. *LV,* 38.
48. Dossiers Gauthier-Villars, Bibliothèque Nationale, Paris.
49. Willy, preface to *Le Retour d'Age,* (Paris: Albin Michel, 1909).

In every feast of your life, drink the poison poured by your first, your only love
La Vagabonde, *, 888.

50. *LS,* 11 April 1909.
51. *Paris qui chante,* 5 December 1909.
52. Caradec, 226.
53. PL II, ix–x.
54. *LV,* 39.
55. Ibid.
56. *LS,* 321.
57. *LS,* 356.
58. *La Vagabonde,* *, 827.
59. *Le Figaro,* 10 December 1910.
60. Villars, Meg. *Les Imprudences de Peggy, traduit par Willy* (Société d'Edition et de Publications parisiennes), 236.
61. Letter to Curnonsky, Caradec, 232.
62. Dossier Colette Willy, Roll 642, Bibliothèque de l'Arsenal, Paris.
63. LV, 45.

Journalism is a breathtaking career
L'Etoile Vesper, ***, 606.

64. *Le Matin,* 2 December 1910.
65. *LS,* 4 February 1910.
66. *LV,* 62.
67. Dossier Christian Beck, Bibliothèque Royale de Belgique.
68. *LS,* 4 February 1910.
69. *LV,* 14 February 1911.
70. *LS,* 419.
71. *LV,* 57.
72. *LV,* 31 May 1910.
73. *En Tournée,* 94
74. *LV,* 21 March 1912.

Henry de Jouvenel

75. Binion, Rudolf. *Defeated Leaders: Caillaux, Jouvenel, Tardieu* (New York: University Press, 1966), 122.
76. Ibid., and Weiss, Louise. *Mémoires d'une Européenne* (Paris: Payot, 1968) 1.
77. Binion, 123, and Bonmariage, 226.
78. *LV,* 53–55, 58.
79. *LV,* 54.
80. *LV,* 55.
81. *LV,* 58.
82. *LV,* 59.
83. *LV,* 60.
84. *LV,* 20 September 1911.
85. *Fantasio,* 15 February 1911.
86. Caradec, 241.

87. Willy, *Lélie Fumeuse d'Opium,* 63–64, 313.

88. Caradec, 252.

89. Caradec, 252ff.

90. *LS,* 497.

91. LV, note 4, 64.

92. *Les Guêpes,* 25 April 1912.

93. Bonmariage, 158.

94. Ibid., 136.

95. *Dans la Foule,* ★, 1305.

96. "Hommage à Colette," *Combat,* 1953.

97. *LV,* 69.

98. Ibid., 72.

99. Ibid., 73.

100. Bonmariage, 183

101. *LV,* 74.

102. *LV,* 75.

103. Ibid.

104. *LV,* 79.

105. Bonmariage, 160.

106. *LV,* 78.

APPENDIX

1. Robinet, *Etudes ardennaises* 9(April 1957).

SELECT BIBLIOGRAPHY

Bonmariage, Sylvain. *Willy, Colette et moi*. Paris: Charles Frémanger, 1954.

Boulestin, FIRST NAME?? *Myself, My Two Countries*. London: Cassel, 1937.

Caradec, François. *Feu Willy*. Paris: Carrère-Pauvert, 1984.

Colette En Tournée, cartes postales à Sido. Paris: Persona, 1984.

Colette, "Contreé offensive pour l'orthographe," *Le Figaro Littéraire*, August 2, 1952.

Colette, Sidonie-Gabrielle. *Cahier de Colette*. Paris: les Amis de Colette, Premier,
Deuxième, Troisième, 1935 — Quatrième, 1936

——. *Lettres à Annie de Pène et Germaine Beaumont*. Paris: Flammarion, 1995.

——. *Lettres à Hélène Picard*. Paris: Flammarion, 1958.

——. *Lettres à Moune et au Toutounet*. Paris: des Femmes, 1985.

——. *Lettres au Petit Corsaire*. Paris: Flammarion, 1963.

——. *Mes Cahiers*. Paris: Aux armes de France, 1941.

——. *Oeuvres complètes*. Edition du Centenaire, 16 vols. Paris: Flammarion, 1973–76.

——. *Oeuvres complètes*. Edition du Fleuron. 15 vols. Paris: Flammarion, 1948–50.

Colette, Sidonie-Gabrielle interviewed by Alain Parinaud, 1949. Archives Sonores,
Institut national de l'audiovisuel, 1991.

Dossier Colette Willy, Bibliothèque de l'Arsenal, Paris.

Dossier Willy, Bibliothèque Nationale, Paris.

Dossiers Colette, Bibliothèque Nationale, Paris.

Dossiers Gauthier-Villars, Bibliothèque Nationale, Paris.

Exposition Colette Catalogue, Bibliothèque Nationale, Paris.

Fonds Gauthier-Villars, Bibliothèque de l'Arsenal, Paris.

Fourier, Charles. *Oeuvres complètes*. X Vols. Paris: Editions Anthropos, 1966.

Gauthier-Villars, Jacques. "Willy et Colette, un couple de la Belle Epoque," *Les Oeuvres
libres*, Nouvelle Série, 161(1959).

Goudeket, Maurice. *La Douceur de vieillir*. Paris: Flammarion, 1955.

Goudeket, Maurice. *Près de Colette*. Paris: Flammarion, 1955.

de la Hire, Jean. "Willy et Colette" in *Ménages d'artistes*. Paris: Adolphe d'Espie, 1905.

Landoy, Eugène. "L'Illustration," *Journal Universel*, June 19, 1852.

Landoy, Jenny. *Rhamsès II*. Paris: Simonis-Empis, 1894.

Larnac, Jean. *Colette, sa vie, son oeuvre*. Paris: Krâ, 1927.

Lecomte, Georges. *Willy, Les Hommes d'aujourd'hui*. Paris.

Malige, Jeanine. *Colette, qui êtes-vous ?* Lyon: La Manufacture, 1987.

Rachilde. *Portraits d'homme*. Paris: Mornay, 1929.

Rapport du juge Crançon au procureur impérial, November 15, 1865. Fonds Colette de
Saint-Sauveur.

Rousseau Raaphorst, Madeleine. Colette et sa mère Sido, Lettres inédites concernant le premier mariage de Colette, Rice University Studies, 59(3).

Rudorff, Raymond. *La Belle Epoque: Paris in the Nineties*. New York: Saturday Review Press, 1972.

La Société des Amis de Colette, *Cahiers Colette*. Paris: Flammarion, 1977.

Une amitié inattendue. Correspondance de Colette et de Francis Jammes. Paris: Emile Paul Frères, 1945.

Viel, Marie-Jeanne. *Colette aux temps des Claudine*. Paris: Ed. Essentielles, 1978.

Villars, Meg. *Les Imprudences de Peggy, traduit par Willy,* (Société d'Edition et de Publications parisiennes.

Willy. *L'Année fantaisiste*. Paris: Delagrave, 1892.

Willy, "Lettres à Rachilde," *Bulletin Coulet-Faure,* 112–113.

Willy. *Indiscrétions et Commentaires sur les Claudine*. Monte Carlo: Pro Amici, 1962.

Willy. *Lélie Fumeuse d'Opium*. Paris: Albin Michel.

Willy. *Le Retour d'Age*. Paris: Albin Michel, 1909.

Willy. *La Revue encyclopédique*. Paris: Librairie Larousse, 1894.

Willy. *Maugis*.

Willy. *Maugis amoureux*.

Willy. *Pimprenette de Foligny*. Bibliothèque des Auteurs Modernes, 1908.

Willy. *Souvenirs littéraires*. Paris: Editions Montaigne, 1925.

ACKNOWLEDGEMENTS

*W*E ARE ESPECIALLY grateful to the archivists and librarians without whose full cooperation this book could not have been written. We have received valuable assistance as we consulted in France: les Archives de la Ville de Paris, les Archives de la Ville du Havre, le Minutier central des notaires de Paris, les Archives nationales: Etats généraux des Fonds: Marine et Outre-Mer, les Archives des ports: état civil des gens de couleur, les Archives juridiques de la Ville de Versailles, les Archives du Rectorat de Paris, les Archives de la Gironde, les Archives départementales de l'Yonne, la bibliothèque de l'Arsenal, la bibliothèque de l'Opéra, le musée de la Légion d'Honneur.

IN BELGIUM:
les Archives de la Ville de Bruxelles, les Archives notariales de la province de Brabant, la Bibliothèque royale de Belgique, les services démographiques.

IN THE UNITED STATES:
The libraries of the universities of California at Los Angeles, the University of Texas-Austin, the University of Princeton.

We most gratefully acknowledge the assistance of Claude Giraud, la Société des manuscrits et autographes français; Frans de Haes and Madame Grunhard, Musée de la Littérature, Brussels; Hubert Collin, Archives départementales et communales de Charleville; Michèle Le Pavec, curator of the département des manuscrits de la Bibliothèque Nationale; Marguerite Boivin, secretary of the Bibliothèque des Amis de Colette à Saint-Sauveur and Agnès Marcetteau, archivist-paleologist of the Médiathèque de la Ville de Nantes.

Several private collections were consulted for this biography. To safeguard anonimity we have omitted their names but not our warmest thanks.

We wish to thank Gladys Fowler-Dixon and Roger Fowler-Dixon for their unstinting help over the past years.

INDEX